Consuming Citizens

SUNY series, Genders in the Global South

Debra A. Castillo and Debarati Sen, editors

Consuming Citizens

Countercultural Bodies in Twentieth-Century Mexico

Iván Eusebio Aguirre Darancou

SUNY
PRESS

Published by State University of New York Press, Albany
© 2025 State University of New York
All rights reserved
Printed in the United States of America

EU GPSR Authorised Representative:
Logos Europe, 9 rue Nicolas Poussin, 17000, La Rochelle, France
contact@logoseurope.eu

For information, contact State University of New York Press, Albany, NY
www.sunypress.edu

Library of Congress Cataloging-in-Publication Data

Names: Aguirre Darancou, Iván Eusebio, 1987– author.
Title: Consuming citizens : countercultural bodies in twentieth-century
    Mexico / Iván Eusebio Aguirre Darancou.
Description: Albany : State University of New York Press, [2025] | Series:
    SUNY series, genders in the global south | Includes bibliographical
    references and index.
Identifiers: LCCN 2024042805 | ISBN 9798855802306 (hardcover) | ISBN
    9798855802313 (ebook) | ISBN 9798855802290 (paperback)
Subjects: LCSH: Counterculture—Mexico. | Mexico—Economic conditions—20th
    century.
Classification: LCC HM647 .A36 2025 | DDC 306/.10972—dc23/eng/20250129
LC record available at https://lccn.loc.gov/2024042805

To Ramón Martínez, for your laughs and your joy and your sharp wit that continue to guide me.

To my ancestors and those who came before me, who paved the way for me to be here and write.

To all the dissidents of sexuality, pleasure, and music in Mexico and beyond. To the jotos and lenchas and putos and putxs. May we continue to find spaces in the undergrounds to meet and gather; may we continue to share our pleasures and make worlds.

Contents

Acknowledgments

Writing a book is always a collective endeavor, and the thoughts in these pages have come about after years of shared discussions with colleagues and friends. Archival work is but the beginning of a long and shared process, and I can only hope to give back to the many minds and bodies who shared with me as I wrote and put our thoughts on paper. There are many folx to whom I remain in gratitude and debt beyond these few acknowledgments. I am grateful to my parents for their support in my childhood as I sought out quiet corners to shut up and read, and I am in gratitude to my ancestors who have led me to this day. To all of you, thank you deeply for breathing life into me and guiding my paths.

And now, specific thanks for this project. First of all, thanks to *Romance Notes* for allowing the republication of an article that was the seed of chapter 3 and first thoughts on rock journalism. Thanks to my editors Brian Price and Olivia Cosentino and the editorial crew of the University Press of Florida for the republication of a chapter from *Lost Cinema of Mexico: Reading 1960s–1980s Cinema Against the Grain*. Thanks to my editor Frederick Luis Aldama at Routledge for the republication of a chapter from *Routledge Companion to Gender, Sex and Pop Culture in Latin America*, in which I first started exploring some thoughts on super 8mm film and received wonderful editing and feedback from readers. An earlier version of chapter 4 first appeared in these two texts. And thanks to my editor Ignacio Sánchez-Prado and the folx at Bloomsbury Academic Press, an imprint of Bloomsbury Publishing Plc., for allowing the republication of a chapter from *Mexican Literature as World Literature*, published in 2023, in which I explored the frameworks of psychedelic studies as analytical modes for cultural studies. An earlier version of chapter 4 also appeared in this chapter. I am very grateful for these permissions, but especially for the opportunities to publish when I did, which motivated me and gave me opportunities to polish my own writing and expression of my ideas. Deep gratitude.

I want to thank the Latin American Studies Department at Washington University in St. Louis for providing the support for research. The summer grants with which I visited archives proved invaluable and I would not have expanded this project in the direction it took without them. Special thanks to Mabel Moraña for having guided my research in those early stages and questioning it thoroughly, showing me a path to critical analysis.

Thanks to my wonderful dissertation committee, who guided this book in its early stages with deep curiosity and support. Thanks to Ignacio Infante, who pushed me to consider a more global approach to thinking of theater, poetry, and homoeroticism. Thanks to Stephanie Kirk, who taught me to look closely at the silences and the gaps in the text to trace pleasure and resilience. Thanks to Vincent Sherry, who stoked my passion for Leopold Bloom and taught me how to listen to pleasure in the text. And especially a huge shoutout and many thanks to Ignacio Sánchez-Prado, who led me through this project from the first day when I sat down with him, worried about writing about drugs and literature; he guided my worries by reminding me to focus on academic rigor and theoretical solidity. His support in classes and project was invaluable, but especially I am grateful for his modeling of how to work with reciprocity in our field and livelihood. Nacho, you continue to support me and so many others in our field, and for that I and we are so grateful. Gracias.

Special thanks go out to Olivia Cosentino, for our adventures in Ciudad de México and for our continuing conversations about Gloria Trevi, Lucerito, *los Caifanes*, and especially Angelica María. I will never forget that concert we went to together, and all the little archival findings we share with each other. Shoutout to Carolyn Fornoff, who dialogued with me for so many years as I developed this project and who supported my writing. Thanks to Mónica García Blizzard, Julia Brown, and Francesca Dennstedt for all our shared conferences where we listened to each other and gave feedback and discussed. All of you make belonging to our field so enriching, and I am grateful for all the opportunities I have to listen to and learn from you. You make my thinking deeper and more complex.

Extra-special shoutout to UC-Mexicanistas for listening, discussing, and always giving feedback to our writings and thoughts. Y'all make spaces for us strange thinkers to share our wild ideas and always dialogue with us intergenerationally, and this is so valuable in our field and world. The work you have done to sustain, nurture, and grow our field of Mexican studies is amazing, and I am honored to be a part of this group. Special thanks to Viviane Mahieux, Brian Price, and Xiomara Cervantes-Gomez and Fran for your generous support and fellow mischief-making as we explore and share together.

Deep gratitude to my colleagues at UCR starting in the Department of Hispanic Studies. To the Latin American Studies Research Center and our writing group, for making space for us to sit down and write every week. Colegas who I write with, I see you! Deep gratitude as well to my colegas in the Mexican studies faculty working group: Adrian, Xochitl, Claudia, Jorge, José, and others. Our community is rich and deep, and I am extremely grateful to be a part of it and to have you as colleagues. May we continue to collaborate and support across the disciplines.

And finally, but most importantly, deep gratitude to G and Z for being there for me whenever I sat down to write or left home for a coffee shop or my office. You give me life, and I would not be who I am without you. And a special thanks to Puddles for sleeping by me when I wrote and edited and wrote.

Introduction

What Are Countercultural Bodies and Why Do They/We Matter?

Opening

As I write these words, the nations that cut the planet's geography through borders and fences are still recovering from the COVID-19 pandemic and the multiple socioeconomic inequalities of oppression it has exacerbated, highlighted, and ultimately de-ideologized to reveal them as the systems of oppression they are. The migration patterns that have characterized life in this world, from birds to butterflies to humans, are facing ever-more militarized borders, sometimes shut down completely; in some areas of the world, these borders have become death zones where violence is unleashed to protect or further control a peoples' movement. From the southern and eastern reaches of what is known as Europe to the northern and southern borders of the territories called Mexico, peoples are facing the violent exclusionary tactics of the nation as it has been defined and built during what we now refer to as Modernity-Coloniality, the period over the last 500+ years.[1] For the past six years, Mexico has been experiencing the self-proclaimed Cuarta Transformación (Fourth Transformation), a political-social national project molded under the leadership of Andrés Manuel López Obrador (2018–2024) and his cabinet, which ultimately rests upon the recovering of the public sphere as it was defined by the ideologies of nation and nationhood during the Institutional Revolutionary Party (PRI) regime, albeit while distancing itself from the corruption of that same government. At the same time, the media scandals of "whitexicans" focusing now on politicians, on social media influencers, and on socialites bring forth this dynamic of redefining/policing the nation through what is "really Mexican" by conjuring the unspoken pigmentocratic and racist social structures that underpin modernity. In a similar way, Europe has been experiencing these political dynamics for decades, as well as the rise in popularity of extreme right-wing politicians in the Netherlands, France, Spain, or Hungary, to name a few. In Mexico and across the globe, these sociopolitical dynamics coalescing around national identities are increasingly common as mediatic strategies and ways of representing citizenship, society and nation that ultimately end up shaping policy and social interaction. This continuous feedback loop between political and medial representation sometimes culminates in the use of violence to exclude bodies that don't fit within the narrative of the nation; the most extreme cases of ethnic hate

1

crimes, LGBT+ and particularly trans* hate crimes, and migrant hate crimes are but a few salient examples.

In the third decade of the 2000s, forty years after the end of the political triumph of neoliberalism (after several decades of economic hegemony), the nations of the globe are facing the environmental, political, and gender-violence crises produced by our own histories of colonization-modernization. We are experiencing the urgent need to resolve the (perhaps fundamental) paradox imposed by the modern-colonial world system: the transformation of relationality as ontology-economy-politic into the exclusionary binary of self/other.[2] Modernity-coloniality has and continues to impose a binary structure that justifies exclusion (from family, the nation, and the world), and it eventually motivates violence in order to maintain the binary order. The environmental, social, political, gendered, and racial crises that neoliberalism is exacerbating to a breaking point increasingly push us, in so many ways, to question the implications of this paradox. How can we reshape the nation to include nonhuman citizens to protect and nurture our geographies and ecosystems? What needs to be revisited in the assemblage of nation-state we have normalized? What nonbinary structures can be used to come together as peoples in political/economic relations? What histories of relationality, porosity, and becoming-nations have been silenced by the hegemony of the colonial order that continuously reimposes a white, male, heterosexual, and able-bodied history as supreme, unquestionable, and exclusive? These are some of the questions that have guided the writing of these pages. And as our planetary sociopolitical structures (that is, nations) seek to explicitly address the effects of the capitalist-colonial system upon the populations they manage, it is my hope that these and similar questions can bring forth relationality, reciprocity, and regeneration into our many broken histories, systems, and bodies.

Introduction

This book engages the construction of Mexico as a nation — economic, political, social, cultural — under the influence of a strong state during the twentieth century, opening with the postrevolutionary period of the 1920s and ending in the late 1980s as neoliberalism solidified into policy and "common sense."[3] During the transitionary period between the murder of presidential candidate Luis Donaldo Colosio in 1994 and the return of the Partido Revolucionario Institucional (Institutional Revolutionary Party, PRI) in 2012, Mexico experienced the acceleration of extreme violence characteristic of gore capitalism as the economic regime increasingly depended on the commodification of death and violence, as well as on the progressively tight networks between bureaucratic and political members of the state, international military, and intelligence agencies and drug cartels. The devastating toll of this so-called War Against Drugs, coupled with the rise of gender-based violence, has led the country to a political and social reckoning that is being experienced under the political regime of President Andrés Manuel López Obrador (2018–2024), once the mayor of Mexico City (2000–2005) and the Cuarta Transformación (4T) he leads.[4] While the last two years have been marked by the political scandals, right-wing resistance, and reorganization of the public and cultural spheres that are typical of a change in partisan politics, social and economic change seems to be on the horizon, with COVID-19 throwing a fog between us and the potential results of these policy changes against neoliberalism. The reason I bring this current moment in Mexico to the forefront is because in the social, economic, and political projects driven by the 4T — particularly in its visual iconography and cultural vocabulary — there is a strong reformulation and reification of the notions of a *mestizo* Mexico: one where Día de los Muertos rules supreme, where Emiliano Zapata is the paragon of national masculinity, and where the serpent and the eagle are redrawn into the logo of the new National Guard. And this mestizo nationalism — which builds itself on the symbolic capturing of Indigenous historical past while expanding the processes of dispossession and extractivism that Indigenous people across the continent have faced and continued to resist — is where this book seeks to intervene and unsettle.[5]

In the contemporary discussions around the historical and current dynamics of Mexican nationalism, Pedro Angel Palou's (2015) *Mestizo Failures* emphasizes how the nation-building project of modern Mexico was a century-long enterprise that rescued the figure of the mestizo from nineteenth-century liberal circles and remobilized it into a master signifier, particularly with the work of intellectuals such as public educator/politician José Vasconcelos and anthropologist Manuel Gamio (Palou, 2015). Palou's study builds on anthropology's thorough critiques of mestizaje, such as the works of Roger Bartra or Claudio Lomnitz, both of whom are critical of Octavio Paz's paradigmatic *Labyrinth of Solitude* (1950), which updated Samuel Ramos's popular psychology treatise *Profile of Man and Culture in Mexico* (1934) with the effect of centralizing an inferiority complex as a result of the (racial, ethnic, cultural, economic) miscegenation processes dictated by *mestizaje*. Currently, *Labyrinth of Solitude* is not read mainly as an illuminating text of Mexican identity, but rather as a text that reveals the racist, sexist, and ultimately hyperviolent social imperatives that structure contemporary nationalism as an iteration of coloniality. As Mexico's state institutions developed during the modernization of the twentieth century alongside (and sometimes sponsoring) the cultural spheres of muralism, the Golden Age of cinema, and the literary field, the *mestizo* identity functioned more and more as the master signifier of the nation and its own imagining, always providing an ideological counterpoint to the visual, cinematic, artistic, and social representations of imagined and real citizens as they engaged their country.

In this milieu, this book traces the underside of this national project through the assemblages of countercultural bodies. This approach highlights and foregrounds the bodies of Mexican citizens who have not or do not fit within the ideal model of the mestizo. While this concept will be fleshed out fully in the coming pages, I anticipate now that counterculture functions throughout the book as both a descriptive concept allowing the understanding of particular social subgroups in the specific temporal contextualization, and as an ethical-political positioning that gestures toward anti-colonial, anti-patriarchal, and anti-capitalist subjectivities, sociabilities, and economies contained in the notion of culture. The assemblages of counterculture and body thus allow for a history of Mexican bodies generating alternative forms of consumer socialization, citizenship, nationalism, and political action that ran and continue to run against/outside state-controlled platforms and cultural spheres. In this way, tracing the Mexican countercultural bodies of the twentieth-century works toward another cultural history of the nation, one that may allow for refracted and more nuanced understandings of civil society and personal politics in the later 1980s and 1990s. I argue that countercultural bodies demonstrate the existence of alternate nations, economies, and sociabilities, and that their engagements with both state and market not only challenge both but ultimately become moments of decolonial praxis carried out in the territories of the body and its desires, consumption praxis, and ethics.

The bodies that occupy the popular songs, paintings, poems, newspaper articles, short stories, theater plays, novels, magazine articles, and super 8mm movies and horror films in the coming pages become countercultural as they move to generate affective politics, grounded in the assembling of their corporality as *the* site where politics become policies, where law is made tangible. Countercultural bodies want to *feel* culture by materially and ideologically disengaging from the disembodied culture of modernity/coloniality saturated with whiteness constantly seeking to abstract and extract itself out of the violent history of colonization through claims of universalization.[6] Countercultural bodies are those who will use the *potentia* generated by both state and market developments to dissent with both, initiating a process of becoming bodies of culture as they assemble with other marginalized and silenced populations. The spaces occupied by these bodies become countercultural in that they provide avenues of affective political redemption built upon radical inclusion that explicitly recognize the bodies and beings (plant, animal, machine, or otherwise) and their participation in the creation of a nation. In this way, countercultural bodies enact and embody ethics of radical empathy toward themselves and other bodies around them, making explicit the structures of oppression that surround them all and how the other bodies around them can be and already are, in some way, countercultural. I use the term "radical empathy" here to underline the differences between these countercultural and non-countercultural bodies (for example, women underscoring how men are also caught in gender normativities, homosexual men making explicit how heterosexual men are also alienated from their desire, substance users signaling how "straight-edge" citizens are also consuming ideologies and products that change them) and how these countercultural citizens are choosing to engage in an ethics of empathy, a politics of care that centers their shared embodied existences rather than their differences. By understanding these bodies as part of greater a regional/global phenomenon, as Christopher Dunn signals in his work on Brazilian *tropicalia*, *desbunde*, and other countercultural movements in the country, I believe we can approach understandings of nation (as a political form of the collective) while explicitly rejecting and discarding exclusionary state-nationalism. Ultimately, these artists and cultural producers are pushing to reactivate the nation's foundational debates on citizenship, political subjectivity, and nonheteronormative sociability projects. This book thus seeks not only to contribute to a deeper comprehension of cultural phenomenon across Latin America, relating these studies to the more canonical analysis of the English-speaking world, but also to problematize and expand current approaches to issues of nationalism and nation-building, which so often take for granted the centrality of the anthropocentric, male-identified, and white political subject. Countercultural bodies, in their actions, writings, and histories, make visible the multiple dissenting strategies mobilized by citizens as their capitalist societies are structured around nationalist ideologies developed in tandem with other postcolonial economies around the globe. It is through these strategies of desubjectivation of citizens from the mestizo racial and sexual complex that calls itself nationalism, as well as the strategies of resubjectivation of bodies into inclusive and anti-capitalist sociabilities, that the bodies populating these pages provide an alternate history of Mexico, one that existed and exists outside the paradigms of exclusionary identities and authoritarian cultural spheres.

Counterculture and Countercultural Bodies

First, a note on terminology. Counterculture has been a cultural phenomenon usually approached through sociological and historical approaches, particularly as a global singularity tied to the late 1960s to the mid-1970s. While these global and national/regional studies have proved many times over the central importance of this moment in contemporary global history, their temporal limitations oftentimes limit the scope of counterculture as an ethos, a politics, and a worldview. Aside from this, intersectional approaches considering race, gender, and sexuality have only recently become more common, sidelining the white cis-hetero middle-class male subject so often conjured when hippies are mentioned.[7] Building on these studies, this book uses a critical cultural approach to step outside these temporal limitations to theoretically describe counterculture vis-á-vis our current sociopolitical and cultural situations. In order words, the "culture" in counterculture is usually taken to define the "mainstream" everyday culture of the moment; following Theodore Roszak, this book mobilizes a definition of counterculture that understands "culture" to be the complex inherited set of social, philosophical, artistic, and political structures that centralize colonial, capitalist, and liberal (in general, "Western") culture as the operative and defining components of it.[8]

I understand counterculture, then, first as the material and embodied existence of dissenting citizens in space and time; second as a cultural representation directly related to and responding to the histories of (internal) colonization, capitalism, and Western expansion; and third as an intersectional node in a series of relational assemblages that come together through nonnormative acts of consumption (of music, fashion, gender/sexual roles, and plant and chemical substances). By exploring *why* and *how* the acts of consuming a psychedelic/ entheogen, or listening to rock music, or engaging in nonheteronormative sexual practices become countercultural acts, and registering their connections to global phenomenon while remaining in the specific cultural milieu in which they exist, this book will be closely engaged with the nation of Mexico as a cultural construction. In these dynamics, countercultural acts become moments of constructing nation/society outside of the colonial-capitalist complex dressed in ideologies of nation; in Mexico specifically, counterculture moves outside of the mestizo complex while playing with it. Underneath the understanding of counterculture is the act of consuming something foreign/prohibited/abject, and this book traces the ways certain habits and practices of consumption generate spaces of community where citizens marginalized and at times outright rejected from the mestizo nation come together to form alternative sociabilities, sometimes explicitly proposing alternate nations. In the specific case of Mexico, these consumption practices — carried out under capitalist structuring of economic/social relations and mediated by the hyper-present nationalist discourses promoted by state/cultural institutions — become lines of flight that citizens follow to escape from the limiting gender, sexual, ethnic, linguistic, racial, and other norms inherent in the mestizo subject.

These consumption practices and acts become inscribed onto the countercultural body, and these inscriptions necessarily must pass through the intersectional power dynamics that order society. Countercultural bodies thus take many forms, but they do so in a relational manner to the discourses of race, gender, sexuality, ethnicity, ability, and morality, particularly those that shape the bodies the forces of (state)nationalism are constructing at that sociocultural moment. Countercultural bodies are also in direct relation to the variants of those discourses that capitalism is mobilizing according to its impulse to subjectify bodies into producers and consumers.[9] In specifically theoretical terminology, a countercultural body is a molecular subjectivity that responds with productive dissent to the specific singularities assembled by the forces of nationalist socialization and capitalist economic subjectification.[10] This double dynamic of nation/market is a defining factor in countercultural bodies, as they are sometimes generated in explicit political positions but they can also sometimes be assembled in the mere existence of bodies as popular citizens belonging to a specific polis no matter their legal existence as legitimate citizens. What matters is that they are generated by the cultural flows that reach most bodies inside the nation as well as without (what does it "mean" to be Mexican/American/British/Brazilian . . .) *and* by the capitalist drives of consumption and production of new and novel substances, cultural products, and forms of sociosexual economic organization.

Historically speaking, countercultural bodies appear on the (global and national) stage when cultural spheres and their flows are strong enough to gather sufficient variety for citizens to pull and reassemble their geographically situated and embodied subjectivities from. They require economic markets strong enough and, most importantly, accessible enough so that individuals are not isolated bourgeois consumers who circulate in private and policed spaces (since colonization, privileged bodies have been able to consume and have consumed "exotic" global goods); countercultural bodies require being able to come together physically and symbolically in diverse communities. Their consumption habits and practices, defined by their countercultural tastes running against the habitus of the nationalist state, generate spaces for molecular embodiments to come together, to assemble their existence into a series of already-existing and ever-expanding rhizomes of other bodies and forms of culture that connect in underground, sometimes illegal, or prohibited networks. In a sense, the countercultural bodies of the twentieth century (flappers, hippies, jazz cats, disco queens, gays and homosexuals, substance users, certain internet communities) are directly related to the *flâneurs* of the nineteenth. Their sensibilities are informed by cultures far beyond the national borders and subjective boundaries imposed by their normative culture; at the same time, their consumption is *not* unique or fortuitous, but rather the logical consequence of an expansion and diversification of markets, as well as the consequential exploration of ideas that any form of social/cultural repression inevitably leads to.

Countercultural bodies are a response to politics of exclusion because they intrinsically embody an immanent politics of inclusion that is continuously actualized through acts of radical empathy. They come into existence through an ethical engagement with another body that settles (sometimes uncomfortably) in the in-between of their shared consumption practices, what Marlene Wayar has described in philosophical terms as the *nostredad/togetherness* that defines a relational ontology. This engagement with other bodies is carried out through their embodied differences whose cultural signification depends on gender, racial, ethnic, linguistic, or other forms of social marginalization. Countercultural bodies embody intersectionality in that their bodies as national citizens are assembled through a recognition of the multiple identities that cross their existence and their active refusal to silence one over the other. The hegemonic processes of nationalization view these bodies as faulty, with an inability to delineate and define one of those identities as exclusionary, fixed, unmovable, and essentially contained in the individual, denying relational construction with other bodies and discourses. For the countercultural bodies, these in-between moments where their intersectional and relational existences are made visible, tangible, and embodied become molecular opportunities to escape the confines of exclusion and to establish alliances with others. They are historically contingent but chronologically related since their existence can be mapped in time and space by tracing the flows of culture and economy connecting marginalized individuals. In their multiplicity and diversity, countercultural bodies tend to freely (sometimes chaotically) combine ideologies with strong anti-dogmatic ethics while centering equality, justice, and peace. They usually present heavy critiques of the notion of identity precisely due to their experienced marginalized positions in the social hierarchies organized around whiteness and identity politics.

It is important to note that counterculture understood in this way is an oppositional concept defined against the histories of modernity-coloniality. These oppositions are productively used by individuals and collectives to generate alternative sociabilities and relational subjectivities — oppositions not only with each other but directly speaking to the histories of violence they want to distance themselves from. This structural definition based in opposition separates counterculture from other liberatory movements that are less reactionary, in some ways less youthful in their reaction to mainstream or normative culture. However, following Marlene Wayar's political injunctive to recognize the power of negative/oppositional definitions, I underline the potential of counterculture to initiate processes of becoming.[11] In this sense, a countercultural body is intrinsically nonhuman in the sense of "human" being an identitarian category of anthropocentric modernity; they anticipate the post-anthropocentric bodies Rosi Braidotti describes as nomadic subjects whose "consciousness is an unfolding of the self onto the world and an enfolding within the self of the world" ("Animals, anomalies and inorganic others" 530). Countercultural bodies emerge from the cultural, economic, and political centers of nations and global capitalism and, as such, bodies marked by whiteness and capitalism; though all bodies (human and nonhuman) are subjected to systems of oppression in this space, countercultural bodies begin with a degree of privilege (class, racial, gendered, ethnic) that allows for their inclusion and mobility through the cities and other spaces they inhabit. However, these bodies choose to disengage from whiteness and capitalism in ways that change their body, and, to use Resmaa Menakem's term, they begin to move individually and collectively toward becoming bodies of culture that recover, rebuild, and reshape culture collectively. In this sense, the consumption potentialized by global capitalism as it expands and brings cultures together, albeit in the form of commodities in the marketplaces, allows for these bodies to increasingly recognize their own individual and collective histories of culture built through experiences termed as illegal/illegitimate/forbidden/transgressive, and they increasingly become bodies of culture.[12]

A core component of countercultural consumption — explored in depth in later chapters — is the use of substances such as cannabis, lysergic acid, psilocybin (mushrooms), or mescaline (peyote). Psychedelic research has recently seen a surge across fields and disciplines, and as such I want to be explicit about some core approaches this book rests upon. First, these substances have existed and have been used for ritual purposes throughout centuries in many societies in the geographic and cultural milieu of what is now known as "the West," not to mention the cultures native to what is now known as "the Americas."[13] Second, it is imperative to understand these substances in the roles they have played in the development of philosophy and other sciences, one whose roots go back to Plato's dissertations on the pharmakon, and most importantly, to establish inter- and transdisciplinary ties in order to approach these substances as the biochemical agents of individual and collective change that they are.[14] As catalyzers for "alternate states of consciousness," psychedelics and other drugs have been serious objects of study in anthropology (Peter T. Furst), psychiatry (Charles T. Tart and Joel Elkes), evolutionary biology (Ronald Siegel), chemistry (John Mann), religious studies (Walter Pahnke and William Richards), and, of course, philosophy (Walter Benjamin, Gilles Deleuze, and Michel Foucault).[15] Following the imperative of "set and setting," first popularized by the early psychedelic pioneer Timothy Leary, this book will approach the textualization of these substances in close consideration of the settings they appear in, the mindset and cultural composition of the characters/consumers, and a careful attention to the processes of integration that current psychedelic research emphasizes.[16]

Considering these characteristics, countercultural bodies can be observed to appear in a variety of locations and times across the planet. What matters is that their corporeal assemblages are directly relational to the possibilities of multiple and diverse consumption that increases as global capitalism reaches the farthest corners of the metropolis. Their existence can also be seen before and after the chronological limitations of the global 1960s, adapting to the social and political conditions of the moment while always remaining critically anchored in a cultural heritage, usually refracted through the lens of the national. Theirs are not projects of starting society anew, founding utopias, and escaping reality (or if they do establish these projects, these are not isolated or disengaged); they tend to explore projects that dissent with the normativity of their moment and engage the public sphere through shared visual/symbolic vocabulary. For instance, rather than a bourgeois consumer singing a popular song in a foreign language, a countercultural body gravitates toward rewriting the song in their own language and adapting their own linguistic and cultural vocabulary to the strange sounds. Less than a matter of dressing like an exotic otherized person, for a countercultural body the radical change rests in modifying their behavior, particularly along the sociosexual hierarchies that dressing has codified in Western culture. In short, countercultural bodies can be seen when citizens refuse the national subject (defined through gender, racial, sexual, and moral normativity) by using the commodities global markets provide to reshape and reinscribe their own bodies through dress, consumption of substances, music, and more.

I use the term and theoretical framework of counterculture even though most of the bodies studied in this book fall in their late teens to early thirties to distinguish this approach from what is commonly referred to as youth studies. While I agree that youth is a socially constructed category that serves to define the experiences of semi-independence between childhood and adulthood, and that most of the bodies approached here can be described as falling within these categories, it is the ethics and behavior that I understand as counterculture (that does emerge typically within these age ranges) that I find compelling and provocative, rather than an age limitation. Thus, while youth studies are a useful framework to understand generational differentiation and can illustrate processes of social and economic change, counterculture — and, in particular, countercultural bodies — serve to better understand the particular positionings and embodied strategies that individuals use to distance themselves critically from colonial, state, and capitalist formations that reproduce Western epistemologies. While the idea of a developmental stage between childhood and adulthood is a defining characteristic of postindustrial modernity, I believe counterculture is useful to understand ethics and behaviors that predate modernity and that exist outside of specific temporal ranges. I also avoid the category of youth general because of its vagueness, particularly when considering how the key actors of much of twentieth-century history have been technically youth, from the soldiers of the World Wars and the revolutions to the waves of migrants who traverse the globe and cross borders, to the most active members of social movements and revolutions from the 1960s to this day. Furthermore, there is often a close link between consumerism/advertising industries and youth cultures, and while I acknowledge that there are similar links particularly when considering the hippie cultures of the global 1960s, counterculture reaches outside of advertising mechanism and allows for more nuanced understandings of consumer culture that emphasize the agency, positioning, and ethics of the consumer, particularly those who chose to consume prohibited, illegal, or forbidden products or fashions. Thus, youth studies may serve as another way of understanding counterculture, and yet countercultural bodies remain the analytical framework I will mobilize throughout this book to approach these dissident citizens who choose to go against their cultural, gender, sexual, and political norms as they construct another Mexico.

Mestizo Mexico

Counterculture never exists disconnected from a concrete political landscape and moment. This book will centralize the moment in Mexican history where mestizo nationalism solidified as a political and cultural project that shaped the country and society as we know it today; a very brief history of this concept can provide a cursory roadmap. Though cultural producers and intellectuals had mobilized the notion of mestizaje or racial miscegenation as the positive defining mark of what would come to be known as Mexico (Sor Juana Inés de la Cruz wrote tocotines to be sung in Nahuatl, Carlos de Sigüenza y Góngora created picaresque heroes, Fray Servando Teresa de Mier wrote treatises connecting Saint Thomas to Quetzalcoatl and Tonantzin to the Virgin of Guadalupe), it was the official caste system imposed by the colonial order that stratified society in clear racialized roles where racial mixture was a mark that placed bodies in lower positions.[17] It wasn't until the nineteenth century when the Bourbon Reforms had impacted colonial society deep enough to catalyze the various independence movements — most of them led by either New Spain born "Spaniards" (criollos) or racially mixed priests and generals — when mestizo as an identity started gaining valence once again. Intellectuals like Ignacio Altamirano in his novel *El Zarco* (written in 1884–1886 and published in 1900) sought to create representations of liberal political subjects where the Indigenous and colonial histories of Mexico could be fused together. Painters like José Obregón in his grand canvas *El descubrimiento del pulque* (*The Discovery of Pulque*, 1869) idealized the Aztec past imperial grandeur by representing their bodies in a classical Greek-inspired pose and style; the visual fusion in miscegenated bodies that bore the color of the earth but moved like European Christians. Meanwhile, the Porfiriato regime — which lasted from 1876 to 1911 and "paused" sixty years of civil war — implemented a capitalist modernization economic model that hurtled toward greater class division in the country through the hacienda system of private land ownership pressing down on the campesinos and the industrialization of railroads, textile factories, and mines built on the backs of workers. The irony of dictator Porfirio Díaz whitening his face with flour and makeup for the newly introduced modern photography camera while the country strained under the pressure of exploitative labor underscores the illusory yet compulsive power of the mestizo complex even when it remains ideologically unnamed.

Then came the Mexican Revolution. Between 1910 and 1920 (1927 by some counts who consider the Cristero War as the final stage), Mexico was caught in the first of the great political, military, and social upheavals that shaped the global 1900s. After the initial middle-class-led uprising through the overthrown electoral process of Francisco I. Madero in 1910, peasant armies led by Emiliano Zapata and Francisco Villa — whose ranks often included female soldaderas and other insurgent groups hailing from marginalized populations — held the country in a game of cat and mouse with various military generals until the Constitution of 1917. In that second half of the armed struggle, military leaders Alvaro Obregón and Venustiano Carranza solidified the armed forces that backed a strong capitalist state protecting the interests of foreign capital (US and British oil and mining investments). By the end of the intense years of armed struggle in 1920, and not counting the death of the Cristero conflicts or later labor struggles, between two and three million Mexicans had died in the greatest demographic catastrophe of the twentieth century for the whole of the Americas.[18] With military peace and political stability came increasingly modernized state institutions, chiefly among these the Department of Health (to combat the diseases brought on by unchecked urbanization), the Ministry of Communications and Public Works (to connect the country and meet the demands of an increasingly global market), and the Ministry of Public Education (to combat illiteracy and modernize the labor force).

It was the last of these ministries that transformed the cultural composition of the country to the nation recognizable today, whether through the globally circulating lens of US cartoonists in the stereotyped images of Speedy Gonzalez or through Alfonso Cuaron's *Y tu mama también* (2001). In the aftermath of José Vasconcelos, the secretary of Public Education from 1921 to 1924, and his grand educational project of cultural missions anchored in his philosophy of the cosmic race — a utopic blueprint of at times symbolic, at times literal miscegenation bordering on eugenics — postrevolutionary Mexico experienced the hegemonic solidification of the mestizo body as the ideal citizen.[19] Visually depicted in the murals of Diego Rivera and other muralists as well as the new-fangled photograph prints, and literarily represented in the pages of *novela de la revolución* epitomized and canonized in Mariano Azuela's *Los de abajo* (*The underdogs*, 1915/1920), the mestizo was the synthesizing character serving to coalesce the ideal of a masculinist, capitalist, and white-supremacist nation. He would reappear in the foundational Golden Age films of Emilio "El Indio" Fernández and Fernando de Fuentes, slowly but surely becoming the essential paragon of Mexicanness that philosopher Samuel Ramos studies in his 1934 *Profile of Man and Culture in Mexico*, later retaken and expanded by Nobel Prize–winner Octavio Paz in his 1950 *Labyrinth of Solitude*, arguably his most published and recognized text.[20] The circulation of these texts and films outside of the country itself only strengthened this essentialized identity of conflicting racial syncretism as it coalesced on the global stage, with the latest iteration of Mexican cuisine (from street vendors to high-end restaurants) as a most recent example.

While the city was urbanizing and modernizing from the 1920s onward, the institutions of the state were focused on defining and promoting what has been referred to as mestizo nationalism. José Vasconcelos's treatise *La raza cósmica* — first published in 1925 but whose ideas date back to his tours of Latin America as an invited philosopher to the bourgeoning universities of the region years before the essay's appearance — became the cultural text that finally cemented the mestizo body into the growing national edifice.[21] The idea of a mestizo nation was not necessarily novel, dating back to the nineteenth-century independent movements, whose historical reinterpretation after the erosion of the aristocratic and French-inspired Porfirian dictatorship would refocus on the mestizo body as one able to "symbolize the resolution of the central political problem of the time, the negotiation of sovereignty and hegemony, the formation of a state that would not only represent but also somehow reflect its nation" (Lund xvii). The recent popular and peasant revolutions made it difficult to visualize a national subject as white, European, academically educated, and urbanized, particularly if that subject was to be seen as the leader of the people. The mestizo, a body produced by the genetic mixture imposed through the force and violence of colonization, became ideologized into a cultural miscegenation where European superiority is (apparently) equalized.

Countering the hegemonic process of the mestizo as the ultimate signifier, this book will recover a history of othered countercultural bodies. I focus on the period between the 1920s — once the dust of the revolution was settling in the soon-to-be global metropolis of Mexico City — and the 1990s when the mestizo nation was shaken to its core by the economic crises of 1994 and the eruption of Indigenous national subjects (long thought relegated to a mythical past) into the public sphere embodied in the Zapatista Army of National Liberation (EZLN). While the book moves in a chronologically linear fashion, it must be stressed early that this decision is not meant to underscore a teleological development, but rather to underline the diversification of countercultural bodies as markets and institutions grow in material terms. For this reason, this book will be divided into two sections, the first focused on the body as a site of struggle and a territory of resistance through the political use of sexuality and sexual practices, and the second focused on the body as the territory of political resignification through the consumption of substances and objects that become inscribed/embedded on the body itself. In this way, the two sections explore the double nature of bodies as both biological *and* cultural, personal *and* collective, fixed *and* malleable/shifting, gendered *and* always already queer . . .

Within the two sections, each chapter engages with a particular moment in the cultural and material development of Mexico, and specifically Mexico City, to provide a structural understanding relatable to metropolitan experiences across the globe. Each chapter is also structured around a thematic approach that focuses on a precise countercultural embodied assemblage: female sexual desire and pleasure, homosexual desire and particularly anal pleasure, the consumption and culture of entheogens/psychedelics, and the aesthetics of excess and world symbols. The dual topical/temporal nature of each section is approached through a case-study methodology that reveals the ways in which countercultural bodies come together always against the backdrop of hegemonic biopolitical subjectification in key moments of postrevolutionary history. The 1920s were a decade of industrial modernization that emphasized the use of radically new technologies such as cameras, typewriters, automobiles, and concrete to literally reshape and reimagine the nation.[22] The 1930s to the 1950s saw the explosion of visual culture in Golden Age cinema as well as popular print media in calendars, postcards, and comic books, the perfect stage for the solidification of the heteronormative mestizo male body in visual terms, directly connected to the economic boom that the Mexican Miracle of the mid-1940s represented. On the heels of mass university student organizing in the 1950s, the 1960s was the decade when youth culture coalesced globally, relationally defined through the figure of the student but well outside the university walls onto the streets as youth became consumers in ever more globalized music, fashion, and illegal-substance markets. And finally, the long 1970s ended with the devastating earthquake of 1985 and the electoral scandal of 1988 as the first wave of neoliberalization of public life and the increasing commodification of counterculture, as much as culture itself. These four key moments (industrial modernization, visual representations, corporeal consumption, and cultural commodification) serve as organizing principles not only due to their specificity to the Mexican cultural context, but mostly because they are comparable moments in the development and expansion of global capitalism and can serve to help us better understand how counterculture provides alternative histories wherever Western culture colonizes and changes societies and cultures.

Mexican mestizo nationalism has shaped the subjective existence and political relationality of its citizens based on a series of exclusionary definitions (informed by coloniality) through official cultural apparatus and intellectual working within and broadcasting structures of feeling and citizenship. The rural and urban visual variations of the macho in the films starring Pedro Infante or Jorge Negrete are complimented by the submissive mother/teacher that Diego Rivera memorialized in his murals and that Emilio Fernández continued to shape in the female characters of *Maclovia* (1948)*, María Candelaria* (1943), and *Río Escondido* (1948). The countryside that began to be idealized in the photographic images of Hugo Brehme during the 1920s and the sweeping muralist movement was only surpassed by the lens of Gabriel Figueroa, ultimately constructing a hyper-ideologized and depoliticized representation of rural Mexico as an idyllic *camposcape* that contained the true essence of the nation, an idea that continues to reverberate today in mainstream cinema and cultural representations (see Alfonso Cuaron's 1999 film *Y tu mamá también*).[23] Even political action, which in the early years after the revolution included union organizing led by sex workers and domestic employees, was progressively policed until there was only the "correct" form of being political by organizing in syndical politics held under the iron grip of the Partido Revolucionario Institucional; the hegemonic structures of citizenship have centralized taking the streets as the *only* legitimate model of political engagement (the histories of both the public marches led by AMLO in 2006 and the right-wing resistance marches of FRENA in 2020 are vivid examples of this dynamic). In mestizo Mexico, the personal is rarely the political. In countercultural Mexico, the personal is the only way to hope to be political.

Chapter Overview

Nationalism, and particularly state nationalism, is a political organizing force that has become successful in reproducing itself and establishing a certain degree of hegemony through the erection of ideological and geopolitical borders, whose role is to draw geographical and political/ethical/philosophical limits and generate spaces of exclusion. On the other hand, capitalism functions by smoothing spaces and expanding markets, establishing free-trade zones, and breaking down the limits on physical and ideological movements/*potentia* in order to better establish increasingly connected networks of consumption for the increase of profit. In their entwined histories with roots in conquest and colonization, these two socioeconomic superstructures have sometimes been at friendly odds with each other, sometimes in direct conflict and sometimes in intimate collaboration. Ultimately, both forces generate citizens who must consume, whether it be a particular form of the narrative of nation or a particular consumer product. Bodies become subjects/citizens through consumption, and those who resist consumption will be dealt with. The increasing criminalization (with a long colonial history) and "popular"/anonymous violence against ecological activists, gender-violence activists, trans*, sex workers, anti-capitalist activists, and labor organizers is our current moment in that history, in Mexico, and in the world. Bodies who do not consume the norms of the "nation" (no matter the laws) are not seen as legitimate citizens, and the violence against them will remain impugn until the normative order is questioned in its patriarchal and capitalist structure.

Despite their seemingly antithetical stance — nationalism centrifugal in gathering bodies around a master signifier and symbolic vocabulary that encapsulates a gendered, racialized, classed, and anthropocentric order, while capitalism centripetal in ever-expanding networks of production-consumption — these two forces shaped twentieth-century Mexico as an economy and a population, updating its coloniality embedded in cultural and social structures. Inscribing, digesting, fashioning, sexualizing, and painting themselves onto bodies, they mold citizens in ways that reflect/refract/reify the consumption of nationalist ideological structures (in state ceremonies or co-opted popular rituals) as much as their tacit acceptance of capitalist economies as hegemonic.[24] This book argues that countercultural citizens are made up of bodies whose existence (sometimes always already, sometimes with time) does not fit within the ideological limits of the nation, and yet they nevertheless exist within its very real borders as documented citizens who may even serve in public offices at times. Who they are, in their embodiment so poorly described by the processes of racialization, sexualization, linguistic othering, and yet so politically relevant, matters. These citizens use their positions to critically/dissentingly/parodically consume in both systems, undermining nationalist structures *and* capitalist markets/economic networks in the process, and sometimes utopically creating alternate nations and economies. This book shows how a flapper writing about radio and sex, a poet who found sexual pleasure with other men setting up plays where macho revolutionaries are queered to the point of camp, a young hippie woman writing about acid and revolutions while forming communes, and a film director who narrates the nation exclusively through the sounds of rock are all part of horizontal genealogies, parallel to and dissenting with the state formations and their capture of events and bodies into symbols. In response to these subjectification processes, the locally contingent and political forces of radically sexual and sexualized men and women, rural queer men, rock bands, and psychedelic-substance users first pushed back in their bodily territories, then looked around to create symbolic communities. In the short-lived and often-silenced state-oppressed or marginal countercultural spheres that cropped up throughout the decades, these countercultural bodies assembled in rhizomatic lineages that refused the cultural genealogies imposed by coloniality while simultaneously demanding their legitimate recognition as political subjects. Through these countercultural acts, practices, and texts, these men and women situated themselves in explicitly politicized positions, attempting to construct alternative social, gendered, and ethnic relations in the face of the violent mestizo social order.

Readers familiar with Mexican cultural politics may quickly notice that the countercultural bodies gathered here come from very different social and cultural scenes. While the geographical locus of this book is mostly Mexico City during the twentieth century, within this space there existed and still exists a wide diversity of cultural spheres that at times coexist in a shaky balance and at times enter direct conflict. Places like the offices of the newspaper *El Universal Ilustrado* in the 1920s become loci that gathered these countercultural bodies through labor, and yet they did not bring them together in any other way; here, both Salvador Novo and Cube Bonifant wrote and published, and yet their writings can be seen as directly at odds and sometimes outrightly against each other, as Novo wrote vitriolic content against women cutting their hair short and Bonifant continuously poked at the "educated" men of her time. In later decades, the *ondero* movement and the global countercultural moment of the 1960s brought together literary figures such as Parménides García Saldaña, Fernando del Paso. and Alejandro Jodorowsky, and yet these figures did not necessarily become friends, produce in tandem, or even move in the same circuits regularly. So, I want to underline how the unlikely bedfellows are gathered in these pages not because they all belong to the same movement or produce within the politics, but rather to underscore how countercultural bodies are such because they share an ethics and a way of moving through the world. The tensions among them remain as tensions that illustrate the diversity and conflict within counterculture itself as a phenomenon that is characterized by difference and dissidence, and which cannot be neatly defined or described by partisan politics.

The book is broken into two sections: *Desiring Bodies* and *Consuming Bodies*, maintaining the double direction of desire and consumption. Each section in turn contains two chapters that explore various case studies as countercultural bodies take clearer and more defined shapes. This constant and apparent dichotomy echoes the double bind of economic and political forces I am considering, but the reader will (hopefully) see that the pairs are less binaries than they are close readings of different relations established between bodies and their external contexts. The first two chapters explore the ways in which desire (for touch, movement, expression, et cetera) experienced throughout time but expressed according to contextual social norms, pushes citizens to challenge the sociosexual order imposed by mestizo gender politics. The last two chapters present a constellation of bodies moving through space and time mobilized by their desire to consume, whether it be ingesting lysergic acid, drinking Coca-Cola, listening to English-language rock bands, or more; similar to the *anthropophagic* cultural theorizations being revived in Brazil midcentury, these Mexicans wanted to "eat" both the national subjects they saw on screen and on paper and the global citizens beginning to circulate freely in the aftermath of World War II. Consume and become both, and neither. Again, the intention is not to clearly delineate differences and separate historical moments and bodies, but rather to explore some of the various strategies and assemblages that countercultural bodies make up in their relationality. This book is an opening and a first approach.

Desiring Bodies

Chapter 1 focuses on female citizens writing themselves into the nation. During the decade of the revolution (1910–1920), Mexico City maintained a 500,000 population as armies and diseases came and went; by 1930, however, it had grown to over 1 million residents. These new citizens inserted themselves onto the cityscape itself through their labor and their movements in space, sometimes sexualizing on their own terms their already sexualized bodies, and regularly engaging with technology as they embodied the city in its growth and development.[25] As government buildings, factories, and urban housing went up, the city witnessed an explosion of technological modernity. Cameras, sound recorders, printing presses, electric cables and lighting, automobiles, concrete . . . Rubén Gallo has documented this history in close detail, emphasizing the new configurations of the city that generated a dynamic utopia by continuing the affective event of the violent revolution into everyday revolutions, breaking the refrains of liberal nation-building that spilled over into the Porfiriato.[26] This first chapter brings emphases to women participating in the public and cultural spheres, centering on textualizations of female bodies visualized in their own experiences.

It opens with a close reading of a popular *corrido*, "Ya no lloverán pelonas" ("It's not going to rain flappers anymore") before focusing on journalist/radio producer/film critic Cube Bonifant and socialite/muse/painter/poet Nahui Olin. In the context of women joining the professional, domestic, manual, and sexual workforce in great numbers, Cube Bonifant uses the space of the public press to assemble a sexual femininity as a legitimate citizen of this new nation. She writes as a "fashionable" reporter, a *literata* (the authorized public female who consumed fashionable feminine literature), but she also writes as a self-fashioned citizen, a "poser" who consciously manipulated her image by engaging her readers and critiquing the common spaces they inhabited, as citizens in a gendered society with all-female and all-male salons and cafés. The author establishes herself as a double woman, experiencing and inscribed with the codes of normative femininity, but also experiencing sexual desire and a desire to move through the city as a collective urban space; these experiences coexist and relationally construct collective gendered and sexual citizenship. Moved by desire and surrounded by machines (typewriters, radio studios and antennas, cameras), Bonifant uses fiction to explore what Elizabeth Grosz terms "bodies-cities," a model of relations between bodies and urban ecosystems where neither exist as total entities, but as assemblages and microgroupings.

The second important female cultural producer this chapter presents is Nahui Olin, born Carmen Mondragón into an elite Porfirian family in 1893. She changed her name in 1921 after meeting Gerardo Murillo (Dr. Atl) who would become her lover and she his muse. The name comes from Nahuatl, meaning fourth movement of the sun, the renewing force of the universe. Though a recent museum exhibition has brought attention to Nahui Olin's presence and production, she has been a figure rarely studied, particularly in relation to the grand narrative of Mexican muralism depicting the fiction of a postrevolutionary mestizo brotherhood.[27] This is particularly striking since Nahui Olin is embedded in the visual construction of this nation, pictorially in many of Rivera's murals as his muse and model, as well as in photographs and portraits that circulated in these years.[28] In the face of this visual and cultural capturing, the artist herself has carried out a series of performances, photographic exhibits, and writing ventures where she takes control of her body as a physical and social construct to be wielded against patriarchal/heteronormative impositions, and in her embodiment assembling alternative models of citizenship. In 1922, she published *Óptica cerebral. Poemas dinámicos* (*Cerebral optics. Dynamic poems*), a daring exploration of modern subjectivity close in style to the Stridentist use of technological and scientific vocabulary to describe urban experiences. Thus, the female figures covered in these chapters are not female bodies seen as depositories for the mestizo nation's Indigenous roots (that is, Diego Rivera and José Vasconcelos's nationalism), nor are they female bodies as symbols of technological modernity (that is, Arqueles Vela's short novels and the use of the deco body in publicity, art, and early pornography). Rather, they are representations as assemblages that result in "affectively troubling — generating affective confusion and interdeterminacy — in terms of ontology, tactility, and the combination of organic and nonorganic matter" (Puar xxvii).[29] By textualizing and drawing their sexual agency, these two artists assemble countercultural bodies grounded in the characteristics of the new mestizo citizen (consumption practices and refashioning Indigenous past) while extending their futurity well beyond the domestic limits of heteronormative nationalism.

Chapter 2 engages with a brief homosexual history of countercultural bodies in Mexico, focusing on the writings of Salvador Novo and Abigael Bohórquez, both northerners who moved to Mexico City as the metropoli expanded; the former migrated to escape revolutionary violence in his homestate of Coahuila to eventually become the official chronicler of the city, while the second migrated to pursue education and escape the *machista* heteronormative physical and symbolic violence of the Sonoran Desert, only to be marginalized by the literary and cultural sphere due to his outspoken political and sexual views. This chapter approaches these queer countercultural bodies by analyzing their relation to the hegemonic male mestizo bodies, both urban and rural. These images of virile, violent, revolutionary men were being imposed on the citizenry through the institutional representations of the *novela de la Revolución* and the films of the Golden Age, as well as the market forces exploring the early years of print and media advertising. It is through these images that desire is increasingly structured into strict exclusionary bodies that must repress any transgressive desire and actions or face the consequences of normative violence. This chapter explores the countercultural homosexual production of another Mexico through a focus on anal pleasure, eliding identities in favor of acts. In the face of the symbolization of sexuality into top/bottom, man/woman, *chingón/chingada*, the pleasurable sexual act of anal penetration is unable to be narrativized neatly and proposes a new refrain that reverberates across bodies as they experience this pleasure in the face of a masculinity that represses, denies, and ultimately enforces violence upon those who express it.

In his prose writings, Salvador Novo exercises a constant contemplation on the changes happening in the modernization of Mexico City and the impact these changes are having on him, how they shape his body and his sociosexual subjectivity, and how in turn he can shape the cultural reality around him. Novo's is a countercultural homosexual body because — especially in *Pillar of Salt*, an autobiographical text from 1945 first published in 1998 — he constantly places emphasis on acts over identities, working to resist the imposition of a single identity over a multiplicity of bodies and experiences. I also analyze Novo's writings in the popular bus-driver journal *El Chafirete* where he published under the pseudonym Radiador, a name self-given by the writer in a section titled "Decálogo de camión" (Bus decalogue), where the writer enlists the ten essential parts of these new machines hurtling through the streets with a cargo of workers. But what is more important, Radiador (as a constructed sociosexual subjectivity) sees himself at the vanguard of everyone, including the Contemporáneos and other cultural agents, textually constructed as an explorative and machinic assemblage fully up to date on what every other *camión* is saying. Recognizing but not centralizing the performativity of gender through transformation and clothing, Novo constructs in his texts a homosexual body assembled through interclass engagement and alliances. His movements through performativity signal a voluntary playfulness and an unwillingness to remain on a single position on the gender spectrum, exploding the various urban spaces where classes mingle as spaces of resistance to the gender norms of mestizo Mexico. In doing so, Novo's text allows for an intersectional understanding of sexuality by foregrounding class, ethnicity, and racialization.

Complimentary to these novel urban sexual experiences Novo is textualiz-ing, Abigael Bohórquez (1936–1995) staged queer nationalism in his theatrical and poetic oeuvre of neobaroque utopias where being modern and queer was always rooted in the experiences and the history of rural Mexico. He assembles the geographies and cultures of the deserts into the Mexican nationscape — a region historically constructed as the space of barbarians, from the Chichimeca of the colonial chronicles to the Villista and Yaqui armies of the North. For Bohórquez, the deserts populate the national space with queer bodies artic-ulated through neobaroque aesthetics (poetic style, images, references) that help situate Mexico in a colonial history. These queer bodies thus appear in/on the poetic space/stage as utopic agents pointing toward a queer horizon of the nation, in the sense José Esteban Muñoz gives utopia.[30] The representa-tion of homosexuality through sexual acts and desire becomes the foundational moment of other nations, now inclusionary through a series of intersectional feminist alliances with other marginalized bodies. His plays generate a queer erotics of politics anchored in the social-political present and with roots in a colonial past; the future is foreclosed to signal an urgent need to construct uto-pia in the here-and-now, as opposed to the there-and-then.[31] His texts generate countercultural bodies driven by homosexual desires who not only defy the active-passive dichotomy usually conjured to "understand" homosexual behav-ior, but moreover resists being genealogically related exclusively to the dandies, *fifíes*, the 41, the Contemporáneos, and other elitist representations of homosex-uality.[32] In the one-act play *La madrugada del centauro* (1964), Bohórquez tells the story of Sagitario, the youngest son of Floriano, who embodies the violent postrevolutionary mestizo patriarch. The short play proves symbolically dense: Sagitario's queer desire is staged as a radical sexual attraction to Galana, the mare he has taken care of since birth. This humanimal intersubjectivity, an assemblage linked by desire, becomes a way to distance understandings of the homosexual desiring body from the urban tradition of homosexuality and its biopolitical and criminological capturing. In this and other plays, Bohórquez continually constructs desiring bodies whose actions disrupt the seamless vio-lence of the mestizo nation, particularly as the continuation of a colonial order signaled in the neobaroque style.

Consuming Bodies

The previous two chapters focus on citizens and characters experiencing desire and redefining themselves as they move through the national and urban space as desiring bodies. The chapters in this section will cover citizens and char-acters experiencing the expansion of markets and consuming plants, chemi-cals, music, and films that radically reshape their own embodied subjectivities. In approaching particularly the first of these consumption practices, I want to emphasize that while psychedelic studies thrived in the 1950s and 1960s before being rapidly shut down with the enforcement of the Controlled Substances Act in 1971 and are only recently experiencing a resurgence in therapeutic and medicinal research, the approach I am taking considers the pharmacological, psychological, neurological, philosophical, and cultural effects, histories, and uses in light of this contemporary therapeutic and scientific research. This section delves into the implications of these findings in relation to a sociocultural reading of the use of psychedelics as tools for individual and social change in the history of Mexican counterculture. Following the general guidelines of the therapeutic protocols being established (with roots in the experiments and therapeutic experiments of the 1950s and 1960s), these chapters focus on a specific modality of recreational substance use, one that not only changes the characters but most importantly provides a space, time, and state of being to engage in some form of self-knowledge as well as societal/social transformational knowledge. In the current therapeutic context, the temporary diminution of the DMN (Default Mode Network) and subsequent activity increase in other neural networks that happens during consumption of a psychedelic substance is carefully functionalized, particularly through a watchful control of external stimuli during the therapy sessions when the substance is consumed.[33] The core structure used today is grounded in the principles of set (the mindset under which the psychedelic is consumed) and setting (the physical environment where the psychedelic is consumed) developed in the 1960s. Using the tenets and structure of psychedelic-assisted psychotherapy (PAP) as analytical guidelines, these chapters understand the consumption of substances as acts of liberation and transformation and emphasize how this modality of consumption can also be seen reflected/refracted in the countercultural spheres of rock music and liberated sexuality.

Chapter 3 engages with Mexico during the 1960s when the effects of the postwar economic boom of the Milagro Mexicano had trickled down to the first generations of student activists from the Universidad Nacional Autónoma de México (UNAM, founded in 1910 but massively expanded in the 1950s) and the Instituto Politécnico Nacional (IPN, founded in 1936). Youth culture was being established in the crossings of university-supported student groups, an increasing presence of global advertising (rock and roll, fashion, music) and the history of state-supported youth activities (sports, arts).[34] In this charged decade of student activism, the journalistic texts of rock novelist Parménides García Saldaña (1944–1982) and the novels of writer-cum-anthropologist Margarita Dalton (1943–) tackle the social and political struggles being experienced by youth from a very different angle than the classical *Onderos* usually taken as representative of 1960s Mexican counterculture, using literature and journalism as creative, public, and politically productive spaces.[35] Their texts construct youthful bodies beyond their resistance to their parental/societal norms, generating novel assemblages engaged in practices of community and nation-building through their consumption practices. Here, they strive to generate alternative sociabilities informed by their own experiences in these youth spaces and culture, as well as explicitly address the shortcomings of the mestizo sociability that depends on patriarchal and heteronormative gender performances and interpersonal relations. Global counterculture (that is, rock concerts, communes, acid trips, music records, pop art, fashionable continental philosophy, and other texts breaking their academic boundaries) becomes a visual and embodied language they fuse with national issues and contemporary problematics (that is, student activism, how to engage with an increasingly violent state). In doing so, they generate a multiplicity of lines of flight for the growing urban population. Mobilizing the body as a platform of biochemical change (Dalton) and as positioned entities in a male-dominated cultural sphere (García Saldaña), both authors propose alternative definitions of explicitly male/female contemporary counterculture through embodied experiences of modernized urbanity, national cultures, and alternate states of being.

Margarita Dalton published *Larga sinfonía en d y había una vez . . . (Long symphony in D and once upon a time . . .*) in 1968, telling the story of Roberto (Mexican), Ana (unknown origin), and Martin (Australian), a trio of youth who come together in London in the summer of 1968 and drop acid one afternoon. By presenting multiple views of/from three very different countercultural bodies (the artist, the revolutionary, the sexually liberated woman), Dalton constructs a countercultural sphere as multiple, diverse, sexual, and inclusive, as Bohórquez and Bonifant have done before. In moving to London, a central space in the global countercultural stage (the departure point for the infamous Hippie Trail), Dalton enacts a decolonial gesture by asking (and answering): What does the global Southerner have to say about global counterculture and youth/student activism, especially in the face of violent authoritarianism from those in power (France, Mexico City, Kent State . . .)? The body becomes the crucible for knowledge construction *and* the site where the capitalist processes of subjectification become inscribed; an exemplary scene is when the advertising billboard literally injures the trio's bodies as they walk past it. To counter this, the psychedelic experience provides the youths with an opportunity to generate embodied knowledge from their relationships with each other and the environments around them, both the "natural" world of plants and objects and the "human" world of politics and society. This aspect of understanding is reinforced throughout the text, experienced by the characters until the end of the novel when their narratives mesh and fast-forward in time. This premature aging — contextualized within the famous countercultural catchphrase "never trust anyone over the age of thirty" — takes on a meaning of revolutionary happenings already in place within the three characters, metonymically inside the *onderos* who were choosing to take this avenue of personal growth. Read through the lens of PAP and critical mystical experiences, this chapter analyzes how the novel explores the possibilities of countercultural bodies as they engage with psychedelic substance use as tools of liberation and consciousness construction.

The chapter then turns to Parménides García Saldaña in his journalistic work to focus on his embodied approach and textualization of the musical and literary countercultural movement, often referred to as *Onda/Onderos* but with a much greater variety than the categorization implies. In journals such as *Piedra Rodante* (the unauthorized Mexican version of *Rolling Stone*), he writes from an embodied position as a cultural translator/guru who navigates multiple music/literary scenes, languages, and linguistic codes; this in-betweenness pushes him to assemble substances and music with direct politicization, an urge shared by his student-activist peers and grounded in his years as an economy student in the UNAM and the Universidad Iberoamericana. His texts construct this critical consumption (not a rejection, and not a celebration) as an option of resistance, capable of subverting the national hegemonic subjectification of the youthful and joyful citizens.[36] García Saldaña exemplifies his countercultural ethics (of consumption, gender relations, political action) through a series of positionings in various cultural and countercultural spheres where he carries out historical and contemporary rereadings of sociocultural events by invoking a fluid dynamic of potential transculturation. He uses his knowledge of economy to explain cultural developments as effects of these changes, and thus to critically approach the various options for politicizations that have changed for youth culture (direct action, theater/arts as activism, the capturing of syndicates and unions into partisan politics), all of this grounded in the cultural expressions of rock as an alternative sphere. García Saldaña establishes for his readers embodied cultural ties between different (and oftentimes excluded) members of the nation, presenting them with the effects of a transnational space where bodies are coming together in revolutionary potential. In these spaces, as well as in the concerts that García Saldaña covers, collective consumption becomes countercultural by escaping the commercialized sphere of rock in depoliticized films, rehashed *refritos*, and private consumption.[37] While Dalton embodies the consumption of psychedelics (lysergic acid but also *ololiuhqui* and mushrooms) as political actions in the constructions of alternative nations, García Saldaña writes about the musical/cultural phenomenon of rock in concrete collective spaces as countercultural moments in the construction of alternative national identities and social movements. Together, their writings exemplify the urgency of the construction of cultural spheres that defy the logics of literary/cultural autonomy as structures of capitalism/coloniality. During the 1970s and 1980s, these spaces would be silenced or captures by the forces of the state and the market, resignifying the nascent counterculture as commodities to be consumed on screens, records, and airwaves in an uncritical manner. In the communes and acid trips, the *hoyos funkis*, and the outdoor concert fields, Dalton and García Saldaña, alongside rockers such as Javier Bátiz and Alex Lora and actresses like Meche Carreño and Julissa and many others, shaped counterculture as a sphere of national renegotiation and a pivotal moment in the formation of sociabilities that defied mestizo subjectivity, if only for a few brief years.

Chapter 4 approaches the phenomenon of counterculture commodified as an aesthetic to be marketed from two distinctly separate and contextualized positions: world literature and experimental film. While these processes of commodification began with the introduction of rock and roll in the late 1950s and the remaking of teenage bop movies into Mexican stories, they gathered steam and accelerated in the 1970s, aided by the increased state violence directed toward youthful bodies. In this decade, Mexico began to experience neoliberal reforms set in motion by one of its most authoritarian presidents, Luis Echeverría (1970–1976); overt and covert state violence across the country was matched by the symbolic violence of advertising and heteronormative consumer subjectification as markets expanded. In this context, Fernando del Paso (1935–2018) published his second novel, *Palinuro de Mexico* (1977), in Spain, although he already enjoyed certain prestige as a young writer in Mexico; the fact that the novel parodically re-creates the violent events against students between 1968 and 1971 was most likely a decisive factor in its publication out of the country. The novel would be translated to English in 1989 and gain great literary prestige due to its complex literary style drawing on James Joyce, Lawrence Sterne, Jonathan Swift, and Rabelais as much as on a thorough knowledge of nineteenth to twentieth-century Mexican history. In the same period, director Sergio García Michel (1945–2010) was producing the bulk of his super 8mm film production, beginning with short films in 1968 and culminating with the rock operas of 1988. From distinctly different cultural and material positionings, they both respond to the dynamics of commodification and the need to expand counterculture from an aesthetics into an ethics. In films and novels, countercultural bodies respond to the neoliberalization of Mexican nationalism by foregrounding how advertising shapes/constructs the normative body and reproduces violent gender norms, and by choosing cultural expressions that impede a rapid commodification of their work in the Mexican cultural sphere: a long and difficult novel form and a super 8mm film career.

Writing with feet firmly planted in the national literary sphere, Fernando del Paso's novel is global in style, structure, and production. He began developing the novel while living first in Iowa as a member of the International Writers Program, and then in London with the Guggenheim Fellowship where he worked as radio producer, writer, and host for the BBC. The novel is a Joycean epic that tells the story of student Palinuro as he moves through medical school, works at advertising agencies, and revisits his revolutionary family through memory and anecdote. The narration unfolds into two great threads: Palinuro and Estefanía in their apartment in the Plaza de Santo Domingo, and Palinuro's adventures with his friends Molkas and Fabricio, with interspersed chapters on their families. As the novel progresses, the two protagonists consume LSD and cannabis in various moments, and it is through these moments this chapter centers its analysis, since the imaginary, geographic, political reflections/explorations become key in constructing intercorporeal subjectivities assembled into global cultural flows. In this way and from a geopolitical and generational distance, Del Paso addresses the issues negatively affecting/marking the Mexican countercultural youth in the 1970s as both singularly national and intrinsically global. While textualizing an example of the therapeutic modality of substance consumption and maintaining a critical consumption of drugs as liberatory practices in the novel's characters, the novel nevertheless cautions of the "anti-riot drugs that will be used against revolutionaries of the future" (441). In the novel, as the protagonist Palinuro unfolds into the various other characters, becoming is the central process that defines this countercultural body in opposition to a specific being. The body becomes an assemblage where a variety of sociocultural dynamics intersect: discourses of nationalism embodied in a cemetery or in statue-filled streets, discourses of capitalism embodied in the advertising agencies Palinuro must work in, dissident gender discourses embodied in Palinuro-Estefanía's sexual and erotic relations and the varying degrees of nonnormative activities therein, and finally liberatory linguistic discourses in the varying acts of renaming they carry out through the novel. Using a critical psychedelic studies approach and a critical world literature framework, this chapter resituates *Palinuro de México* as a countercultural intervention on the cultural and literary sphere that reenacts a series of national therapeutic sessions to assemble alternative national psycho-subjectivities embodied in Palinuro, Estefanía, and other characters in such a way that resist their acritical commodification as youth.

Sergio García Michel, on the other hand, basically taught himself film during the mid-1960s while working in advertising agencies to buy his first camera. He chose super 8mm as his medium and established a filmic sphere that flourished in the years between 1968 and 1975, before the rest of the directors moved to larger film formats or the commercial film industry. García Michel continued producing and screening in the Foro Tlalpan cultural center he founded in 1980, which became a parallel to the legendary Tianguis del Chopo where Mexican rockers continue to come together to trade and sell rock merchandise. In the aftermath of the 1960s, García Michel would become a central figure in the development of a countercultural cinema, due not only to his prolific super 8mm production but also to his continuous collaboration and support of other filmmakers. As film technology became more accessible in Mexico, his film grew from short, quirky, politically incisive stories soundtracked exclusively with rock during the 1970s to long documentaries and rock operas in the 1980s. Instead of trying to use cinema in a simple and direct engagement with an established language of representative political action — the same one that the state legitimizes and recognizes — García Michel and other countercultural *superocheros* sought to generate a "cinema that raises consciousness, but does not form it" (171). Three of his films will be analyzed in this chapter through an affective reading focusing on how characters are embodied on-screen and the affective engagements the films construct as catalyzers for social and political action. In the aftermath of the violent and disruptive event that was the massacre at Tlatelolco, García Michel strategically uses rock music throughout his films to deterritorialize affects relatable to the youth audience, following what film critic Anna Powell has underlined about the deterritorializing force of music on-screen, particularly when sound is not emanating from the representations in the image (45). He uses camera and sound to showcase representations of dissident, politicized, and liberated female sexuality existing (and sometimes thriving) in the face of the violently heteropatriarchal social order that on-screen Mexico was rearticulating in the 1970s and 1980s, particularly through the increasingly explicit sexualization and objectification of women in commercial and b-rated film (the infamous *sexycomedias* and other exploitation genres), as well as the pop music industry through stars like Angélica María. While underlining in the films how advertising, consumerism, and exclusionary/hierarchical mestizo gender roles are actively shaping the population into compliant citizens, García Michel's films re-create communal social structures that provide refuge for female and other marginalized bodies. These social structures extend countercultural ethics well beyond the use of substances or listening to rock music, as García Michel emphasizes collective social action in the wake of the 1985 earthquake, for example. Finally, in choosing a small format that sidestepped the major film industry (he is the only director of his generation who did not move to industry films), García Michel also counterculturally constructed other networks of cultural circulation that actively resisted the commodification of rock and *jipismo*, providing representations dissenting with the portrayal of these in state-controlled media and creating spaces that, albeit briefly, brought countercultural citizens together.

This book concludes with a coda that looks at Chilean-Mexican director Alejandro Jodorowsky's last Mexican film, *Santa Sangre* (*Holy Blood*), released in 1991. I do so partly because of his particularly global history — born in Chile to first-generation immigrants, trained in France under Marcel Marceau, directing/writing theater and film in Mexico until his global fame with *El Topo* (1970) and *La Montaña Sagrada* (*Holy Mountain,* 1973) — and partly because *Santa Sangre* illustrates many of the cultural and economic dynamics that the book has covered, from strict gender roles embedded in state-constructed national identities and their close relation to extreme forms of violence, to the ways in which capitalist expansion through advertising, consumerism, and increasingly accessible markets make possible moments of cultural, social, and political dissent. Ultimately, however, it is *Santa Sangre*'s fusion of historical facts (the 1940s serial killer Gregorio "Goyo" Cárdenas, who became a national sensation) with Jodorowsky's countercultural aesthetics and liberatory ethics that I find most enriching, and which is the main reason it closes the book. Whereas his earlier films focused on individual psychological development isolated from specific social contexts, and as such were quickly celebrated by global countercultural icons such as John Lennon who introduced them into the midnight cult circuit, *Santa Sangre* re-creates a classically Freudian family drama by contextualizing it within an explicit, historicized, and culturally nuanced Mexican context. The film depends on the filmic conventions of horror and uses them to present to the viewer alternative social assemblages vis-à-vis the self-destructive and hegemonic family unit.

Santa Sangre is also characteristic of the market dynamics in which counter-culture thrives and expands. The film operates in the marketable horror genre, had an Italo-Mexican production led by horror grandmaster Claudio Argento, and was distributed widely across the globe thanks in great part to it being released in English, reaching a much wider audience than Jodorowsky's previous cult films. However, the specific Mexicanness of the film works toward an undoing of the *mestizo* master signifier that underlies normative nationalism. Incidental music ranging from bolero to rancheras generate an audiotopia that compliments the visual representation of downtown Mexico City and nearby areas, narratively assembling communities of marginalized social subjectivities (orphans, neurodiverse citizens, crossdressers, nonnormative cis-men, children) that come together to collectively resist the violence of the mestizo heteronormative familial structures: a macho father who uses the phallus in all its manifestation to enforce violence, and a mother characterized by abnegated suffering of sexual and physical violence. By retelling the story of serial killer Gregorio Cárdenas through the protagonist Fénix (played by Axel Jodorowsky, the director's son), *Santa Sangre* presents an embodied archetype of Mexican mestizo heteronormativity, now psychomagically reassembled through music, genre conventions, gory aesthetics, and geopolitical contextualization in Mexico. Fénix becomes a countercultural citizen increasingly aware of and resisting the destructive behavior possession/ownership, violence, and domination inherent in the mestizo sociosexual normativity, and one who speaks from and to the nation as part of a greater cultural globality, appealing to both national and international audiences. As we continue to experience the real-world consequences (environmental, racial, political, and economic) of the failing liberal notions of anthropocentric political subjectivity, it is my hope that these academic representations and theorizations of a series of embodied cultural practices serve to question the hegemony of national identitarian constructions and their effects, as well as to question our academic approaches to debates on nationalism and national culture outside the domain of the state, critically considering how people make nations in their daily and personal lives.

A Geopolitical Side Note

While the following pages engage with the ideological, cultural constructions of Mexico as a nation vis-à-vis capitalism, I consciously restrain my analysis to the locality of metropolitan Mexico City, not to generalize from that experience but rather to recognize and engage with the considerable symbolic, political, and economic importance of that region. First, as a nexus of origin in the nodal network that will become the country from where material institutions (state and cultural) broadcast norms. Second, as the political center of the country, debated for decades during the nineteenth century until centralization was established, and perhaps undermined by the Fourth Transformation's intention of the distributing of the ministries main offices across the country (the effects of which remain to be seen). Third, and perhaps most importantly to think of Mexico as part of a community of nations, because of the city's model history of extremely rapid urbanization, industrialization, and mass migration that is currently also being experienced in many other urban regions of the country, as well as around the globe. Mexican cultural history is rich with instances of politicians, economists, intellectuals, and artists questioning the centrality of Mexico City in relation to the nation. By focusing on cultural producers within this space and time who are actively engaged with expanding the ideological limits imposed onto their (and all) national bodies, I want to underscore the political alternatives that appear when processes of urbanization, capitalist modernization, and nationalization engage each other, particularly in spaces occupied by a diverse (albeit oppressed) classed population. As the twentieth century developed, geopolitically and economically strategic cities grew into massive metropolises, many of them important nodes in colonial economies during European expansion through colonialism and slavery (Mexico City, Rio de Janeiro, Mumbai, Lagos, Tokyo, Singapore). This book presents a countercultural history of one of them in the hopes of providing models to think of how these and other cities serve not only as nexuses of state-sanctioned capitalism, but also as places where dissent gathers and citizens reimagine nation, reshape bodies, and restate social contracts.

Chapter 1

Pelonas, pintoras y periodistas

México as a Metropolis of Women

Si Adelita estuviera Pelona,
una peluca le había de comprar,
sus enaguas a la Tut-ank-amen,
pa' llevarla a Chicago a bailar
[If Adelita was a flapper and had short hair,
I'd buy her a wig,
her petticoats in the style of Tut-ank-amen,
to take her dancing to Chicago.]

— *Ya no lloverá Pelonas*[1] [It will not rain flappers anymore]

Walking along the crowded and bustling downtown streets of the hustling capital (soon-to-be global metropolis) of Mexico City in 1928 was already a sensory-charged and socially overloading experience, as someone who traverses these streets today could describe this somatic experience of human relation. On the corner of the Alameda, a street band distributing leaflets of illustrated lyrics could have been performing their take on the new song *Ya no lloverá pelonas*, the passersby laughing as they heard the *corrido* structure in several rhythms and the short-haired women rolling their eyes at the stereotypes as they bustled along to their secretary, typist, telegrapher, and domestic-service jobs. Following these women as they paid the *cobrador* (fare collector) holding the door of the Ford bus that would take them to their workplaces, one might have sat down between a lawyer's clerk and a construction worker heading to the same street, albeit on different sides, the older institutions being renewed as much by young trained professionals as by the new cement and steel buildings that would soon house government offices and updated downtown housing complexes. The young man might have had under his arm this week's copy of *El Universal Ilustrado* and opened it to read Cube Bonifant's column, captivated by the dissident femininity the author constructed into her writings in a publication surrounded by men who saw women only as symbols. The clerk, riding a bus and wearing modern-cut pants, could have identified similar markings of modernization in Bonifant's writings and looked up to smile at the *pelona* sitting across from him, humming the latest *corrido*. As the bus went down Calle República de Argentina, someone might have looked out the window and seen the small crowd gathering around Diego Rivera as he made his way into the building along with Nahui Olin, who was posing for some of the feminine figures in the mural at the Secretaría de Educación (Secretariat of Education). Tina Modotti might have taken a break from the photographic documenting of the mural with this new public attention and strolled down the street to Julio Antonio Mella's makeshift office to photograph his typewriter. The clerk might have remembered the night a year before when he was invited to an exhibition of photographic prints of Nahui Olin, artistic nudes shot under her direction by Antonio Garduño, blown up in print and superimposed onto the night skyline of the nascent metropolis downtown. As the streetcar came to a halt at one of the newly created stops — so new there was nothing on the street itself to mark it — someone stepping off might have walked into the bookstore and picked up the latest of the Estridentista novels Xavier Icaza's *Panchito Chapopote*. Later that night, the clerk and the *pelona* could have come across this same citizen as they met up with friends on one of the many *carpas*, circus-like tarps set up in the downtown area where performers entertained audiences with comedy, vaudeville, and political satire. Or they might have splurged their *aguinaldo* (Christmas bonus) and headed to the more established theaters to enjoy a performance of French or Brazilian revues with foreign dance companies. In either of these spaces, they might have danced to the popular *Vacilópolis,* a foxtrot that talked about the *vacilón* or playfully irreverent behavior that was allowed at night in the growing city.[2] The constant soundtrack for the whole day in these comings and goings would have been the noises of building, metal clanging, and the yells of *albañiles* (construction workers) tempered by automobile and streetcar honkings as they sped down the streets; Mexico City was modernizing, and the machines were making it move!

In the verses of the popular songs, the *crónicas* (chronicles) and short stories by Cube Bonifant in *El Universal Ilustrado*, the poems and photographic happenings of Nahui Olin, and the general participation of women in the newly defined country, different national bodies were becoming new citizens as they were populating the streets and workplaces. This chapter argues that these feminine, avant-garde, and worker bodies visualized, wrote, and positioned themselves in relation to the debates of what Mexico was going be now that the core-shaking revolution was settling down. In these positionings and self-definitions, women as both objectified (muses, models, dancers, and sex workers) and subjectified (consumers and much-needed workers) sought to portray, describe, and build Mexico as a nation where, despite their exclusion from political participation (women's suffrage was only until 1953), women were the bases of this new society. While (male) authors were consumed with the anxiety best expressed by Julio Jimenez Rueda's 1924 article "El afeminamiento de la literatura Mexicana [The effeminacy of Mexican literature]" published in *El Universal Ilustrado* — prompting them to write think pieces, parodies, illustrated satire, and literary analyses that recentralized a more "virile" and "masculine" literature represented by Mariano Azuela's *Los de abajo* (1915/1920) — these women sidestepped political rights as the *only* way to form a body into a national subject and worked instead toward tracing and assembling a gendered citizenship.[3] These public debates not only ended in the canonization of Azuela's novel as *the* representation of Mexicanness post-Porfiriato, particularly proper and improper masculinities, but, more importantly, they impacted the construction of commercial consumption (of literature, as well as arts, music, journalism) as explicitly feminine, something a "proper" heterosexual man should not engage in (Mahieux, "The Chronicler as Streetwalker" 173). Further, these debates contributed directly to the silencing of homoerotic and homosocial dynamics in the construction of these early nationalist cultural and public spheres, where masculinity was something to be represented but not critically acknowledged as it ordered the social relations around normativity (Irwin, *Mexican Masculinities* 123).

Producing from an embodied national subjectivity, these women insert their own bodies into the cityscape itself, self-sexualizing their bodies and the city with them by using technology, from an automobile to a photographic camera. In doing so, they dissent with the processes of objectification shaping them into docile women and question the social normativity where women cannot participate in certain activities. It is no wonder that the Estridentista (Stridentist) movement arose in this context, celebrating the virility of the urban workers erecting the city and pushing for faster and faster speeds in their automobiles in the throes of embodied modernity. However, in contrast to this as well as the much more visible ideal of a virile revolution led by the great men of military and cultural power being painted on mural walls and textualized in the nascent *novela de la revolución* (*novel of the revolution*), the streets of Mexico City were increasingly populated by national and international migrants, especially women fleeing from the violence and unrest still impacting the countryside. This chapter goes from popular song lyrics, *crónicas*, short stories, poems, photographs, vaudeville performances, and news reports with the threading argument that these eclectic products trace an alternate nation. These marginalized citizens (in their gendered, racialized, and classed embodiments) critically voiced their concerns on the debates of this early postrevolutionary Mexico and generate what can be seen as a proto-civil society, a social formation grounded in the use of communication technologies (newspaper, photographs, radio) worried about the nation's development as a collective.

Ignacio Sánchez-Prado has proposed the idea of intellectual nations as counternarratives to official state ideologies that produce political and social imaginaries expressed through literature to mark the ideological limits of that national hegemonic culture and generate alternative national projects (*Naciones intelecuales* 1, 102). In a similar gesture, this chapter presents alternate nations (which I resist naming as feminine nations for several reasons) explicitly centered around the embodied experiences of women. These conditions emerged from the economic development promoted by the surge in capitalism as the world entered a decade of relative peace, coupled with the nationalist ideologies of the state. Countercultural citizens — here women singing, dancing, writing, painting, *feeling* — were engaging with both economic markets and nationalist ideologies through consumption, not only being consumed in their writings, paintings, and sexual engagements but also consuming the new sounds, styles, and political ideologies that flappers around the world were constructing.

As general Álvaro Obregón took the presidency (1920–1924), the nation began to be defined through state ritual, institutional development, and capitalist market growth; ultimately it was the coalition of these distinct spheres where *mestizaje* was forged to become the hegemony of *mexicanidad* (Mexicanness). The 1921 Centennial of Independence festivities can be considered among the first of these moments and a blueprint for this cultural-economic imbrication up until now; the latest civic festivities commonly involve hiring global neoliberal production companies to present alongside military parades (Martinez 145). Although these are never planned strategies as such, they result in cultural-political networks where market opportunities, governmentality and biopolitics, entertainment and cultural industries, artists, academia and intellectuals, and the public come together in a space produced by and for the nation. On the private economic sphere, one can point to 1921 when Félix Palavicini — the owner of newspaper *El Universal* and the city's major theater entrepreneur — came together with the government of Álvaro Obregón seeking to legitimate itself after years of civil in-fighting between the revolutionary *caudillos* to produce the yearlong celebrations, which included military parades, hero commemoration, theater plays, operas, ballets, and parades with "populist orientation and ethnicized interpretation of the nation" (López, *Ethnicizing the nation* 50). Perhaps the best example of this is the *India Bonita* contest, thoroughly reviewed by Rick López and Apen Ruiz, which reveals how both the state and the market mobilized artistic and cultural institutions.[4] Aside from focusing on publicly (and in appearance collaboratively, through the false participation dynamic structured in beauty pageants) constructing definitions of "proper" national femininity rooted in the racist associations with Indigenous women (subservience, domesticity, unspoken), these celebrations served to model behavior for nationalist women as well. López calls attention to the photographs where María Conesa — a *tiple* (star) in the theater and carpa night world — stands next to contest winner María Bibiana, both wearing Indigenous-marked skirts and braids, with the difference that Maria Bibiana's appears homespun and unfitting, while María Conesa's is stylish and form-fitting and she sports modern makeup. We (and the public who saw these images in the newspapers) see that "Bibiana represents the 'authentic' India Bonita, whose authenticity resided in her supposedly unselfconscious Indianness, and Conesa stood as the self-created and more readily consumed simulacra — María Bibiana as the raw material, and María Conesa as the manufactured *nationalized* type" (54). This policing of both Indigenous and *mestiza* femininity forming the development of nationalist femininities continue to shape the nation today.

And it was not all parades and festivities. The Secretariat of Education led by José Vasconcelos (1921–1924) was key in setting the paradigms for the *mestizo* nation through state-sponsored cultural projects, from the infamous cultural missions distributing ancient Greek philosophy to illiterate and isolated communities to the muralist contracts and the musical compositions of Carlos Chávez and Manuel M. Ponce. The thread running through these enterprises was the multiplicity of bodies populating the country increasingly becoming the single national identity of the *mestizo* body. Anthropologists such as Claudio Lomnitz, Roger Bartra, or Guillermo Bonfil-Batalla, among others, call attention to the close relationship between public intellectuals and the postrevolutionary state institutions in the historical construction of this identity. Keeping this in mind, the following marginalized bodies of women are placed within the greater context of the construction of *mexicanida*, particularly refracted through the *mestizo* signifier. Since their participation in the nation has been included under the rubric of nonideal citizens, this critical nationalist approach is necessary to avoid the pitfalls of categorizing their actions as personal choices marked by cosmopolitanism; while it is true that Tina Modotti, Anita Bremmer, and Chavela Vargas (to name a few) were foreign women working in and shaping the national-cultural context of the moment, Mexican women also intervened as legitimate national-builders in their labor, education, and artistic practices.[5]

As the metropolis grew with the influx of (inter)national migrants, the state developed the normative *mestizo* identity to absorb and subjectify these bodies into a modernizing capitalist economy. Porfirian intellectual Federico Gamboa's bestselling novel *Santa* provides a hyper-crystallized literary representation of the anxieties produced when the state is unable to properly transform these bodies into workers: the plot revolves around a young woman from outside the metropolis who breaks sexual norms, migrates to downtown Mexico City to become a sex worker, and joins a multitude of other migrants who, time and again, are punished either by law or health for their inability to become proper modern workers. For male citizens, ascribing to this identity meant reworking the rural images of the *charro* (associated originally with the feared *rurales*, Porfirian rural police known for their extreme violence) into a modern aestheticized version through the accessories of hegemonic masculinity (mustaches, gruff voices, charro clothes).[6] For female citizens, the models of femininity were firmly anchored in the reproductive discourses of colonial patriarchy, with motherhood (*madres de la nación* [mothers of the nation]) and teacher as two representations common in the *mestizo*-refracted nation in construction.[7] However, in this first long decade before the full institutionalization of the revolution after Presidents Lázaro Cárdenas (1934–1940) and Miguel Ávila Camacho (1940–1946), women who began repopulating the metropolis were able to explore, negotiate, and redefine other embodied subject positions that engaged critically with the ideologies of modernity (fashion, sexuality, communism) and coloniality (racial miscegenation) while strongly resisting the exclusionary limitations on gender and indigeneity the *mestizo* body imposes.

This chapter navigates these (self)representations of female citizens in popular songs ("*Ya no lloverá pelonas*" and "*Vacilópolis*"), journalistic spaces (Cube Bonifant's writings), poetic texts, and photographic performances (Nahui Olin's artistic work). In doing so, I underscore the hyper-productive cultural milieu of the long 1920s, since these women were producing alongside the avant-garde Estridentistas and Contemporáneos, painting and photographing alongside the muralists and Edward Weston and Tina Modotti, and working in the government and business offices next to the men who shaped the country. My argument lies less in providing a single narrative of alternative national projects and more in approaching and analyzing various ways through which countercultural bodies categorized as female have been constructed. In their engagements with urban development, sexuality, and the erotic (pleasure), citizenship and racial diversity happened alongside the becoming-*mestizo* that was shaping the national project, much the same way global cosmopolitanism and nationalism intersect with global capitalism today. In covering these decades, historians Ageeth Sluis and Anne Rubinstein have demonstrated how the expansion of markets allows for female mobility through class and social structures, while simultaneously capturing female bodies into biopolitical discourses of health, fashion, and sport that are able to synthetize modernity and tradition into the *mestizo* complex. Aware of these dynamics, Bonifant works in the well-distributed journal *El Universal Ilustrado* and carves out a space for female participation in the public sphere. I argue that through these various cultural texts, countercultural bodies are constructed in their representation circulation as bodies repositioning themselves outside the dynamics of exploitation/ extractivism that coloniality-capitalism imposes on female bodies, and they do so particularly by demanding a citizenship that is based on participation and legitimacy in the public sphere, alongside but not limited to state recognition through suffrage.

Si Adelita estuviera pelona: Mestizo Nationalism Containing Urban Women in Song and Stage

Between 1910 and 1920, Mexico City steadily held a population of fewer than 500,000 as upper classes left, diseases struck, and revolutionary armies invaded time and again. By 1930 the city had reached one million residents, and most of these newcomers were migrant women and men from within the nation fleeing the devastation of years of civil violence. By 1920, the revolutionary armies were increasingly co-opted by the Sonoran elite of generals Álvaro Obregón,

Adolfo de la Huerta, and Plutarco Elías Calles, and the fighting was contained to rural areas. These generals and their military cohorts were collecting the broken-down national institutions and placing them in the hands of humanist intellectuals such as José Vasconcelos, Antonio Caso, Martin Luis Guzmán, or Manuel Gamio, many of them members of the Ateneo de la Juventud, which sought to distance intellectual thinking from the positivism associated with the Porfiriato. Their efforts guided a cultural production focused on directing the diverse bodies walking the streets toward one progressively unified and racially harmonized patriotic ideal — an ideological framework subjectifying bodies into workers, soldiers, and consumers — that conflated the heroes and leaders of the revolution into one harmonious narrative of redemption, where the state and modern institutions of public health and education appear as the pillars of modernity.[8] Historian Ilene O'Malley, working with the structures proposed by Roland Barthes in *Mythologies*, signals how, particularly during this turbulent post-conflict decade, the state apparatus (as well as the "popular" memory circulating in private newspapers and theaters) mobilized mythology as a way of making sense of the world. In the social, political, and economic aftermath of the *fiesta de la Revolución* (party of the revolution), a mythology anchored in patriarchal and extremely virile mystification was central "to the official ideology of the Mexican regime as well as to the political culture which supports and is supported by it" (5).[9] The ideal revolutionary men — both military officers and peasant soldiers — were elevated as true citizens of this newly founded nation, giving male citizens a mythical ideal to aspire to.

In contrast to this ideal of a virile revolution led by the great men of military and cultural power — a stark disconnect from the reality of peasant-armed struggles fought alongside women standing against trained military armies protecting private interests — the actual streets of Mexico City were increasingly populated by women seeking professional training or jobs in nursing, stenography, typography, secretary or, domestic labor, as well as by working men and peasants who lost their lands or factories. This disconnect commonly erupted in the cultural spheres of the decade through a harsh gendering of society in every activity imaginable. Viviane Mahieux has pointed out how the act of open consumption was feminized, specifically the consumption of literature marking it as feminized (30). This feminization was then further sexualized, in particular because migrant women inhabited the metropolis in the most precarious of social positions, abject not only due to their lower-class position but most of all their "public" status as women who offered services on the street.[10] This hypersexualization of domestic labor (and women workers in general) can be seen in the cultural history of the pejorative term *gata/gatita* (kitten/kitty), used to conjure a "vulgar" domestic worker who might also "ask for it" in the logic of violent and predatory masculinity.[11] Cultural institutions responded to this wave of much-needed female laborers in the modernization of Mexico by providing female symbols of modernity through the figures of the flappers, modern girls, and pelonas, clearly delimited in racial, ethnic, and class formation.[12] As historian Anne Rubinstein has reconstructed, these chicas modernas (modern girls) embodied the peculiar (and at times contradictory) sexual politics of the postrevolutionary period, caught between tradition and modernity: chaste, yet simultaneously blunt in their interactions with men, they "obeyed nobody — except, perhaps, an employer" (Bad language 46). The forces of capital — bringing job opportunities as well as the commodities to consume with this income, and the education of taste and sensibility to access them — assemble these women as exemplary consumers of worldly products and ideologies. In embodying this novel citizenship, however, these modern girls brushed against the patriarchal and virile values that were being attached to the mestizo revolutionary project, whose male affiliates extended the ontological violence onto the streets occasionally by ganging up on short-haired women and shearing their heads.[13]

Elizabeth Grosz asks us to think of the body as a site of inscription, a threshold of some sort between the interiority of psychic subjectivity and the exteriority of sociopolitical and economic systems (*Space, Time and Perversion* 33). The inscriptions function in both directions, from the outside in and from the inside out. Even more, the inscriptions from the outside are not unilateral, just the desires that inscribe from the inside are shaped in some way by the experiences the body receives from the outside. Staying on the outside for a moment, the body is marked on the one hand by the demands of national institutions and social orders, and on the other by the demands of the market; the result is a social behavior, a pattern of consumption, and social behaviors that can satisfy both.[14] Understanding desire — that most intimate of forces, the conatus that mobilizes bodies of all kinds — as social is key in this juncture to better grasp the feedback loops that are created between the environment/exteriority and the individual/interiority. French economist Frédéric Lordon writes about desire and work conditions under neoliberalism — an exacerbation of management processes that can be traced to the urban industrialization moments of the early twentieth century — emphasizing:

> Very often, however, the combined effect of human ambition and the depth of the division of labor is that desires for material production have to be pursued collectively, thus in a strict etymological sense, *collaboratively* [. . .] however, since it is a desire, an enterprise — both in general and specifically the productive, capitalist enterprise — can only arise, and can only be assumed, in the first person. The entrepreneur's exclamation is thus essentially reducible to an "I feel like doing something." Well then, great! Do it! But do it on your own — if you can. If that is not possible, the problem changes completely. The legitimacy of wanting to do something does not extend to wanting to make other people do it. Hence the ambitious development of an enterprise to the point that it necessitates *collaboration* requires a fully independent answer to the question of the forms that these collaborations should take. The issue here is that of

the political participation of individuals in the organization of the collective processes and the appropriation of the products of their common activity; in other words, it is the issue of capture by the subject of the master-desire (3).[15]

The material production Lordon references (in his study, the neoliberal work conditions that require willing collaboration from employees even when not "working") can be understood also as a template for the industrial modernization and nationalist processes that shaped the twentieth century in Mexico, as it was usually through a discourse of improving the nation that these megaprojects were built (highways, roads, hospitals, government offices, irrigation, sewage, et cetera.). In Mexico's case, modernization was accompanied by a strong desire for peace after over a decade of bloody civil conflict. In these conditions, capturing the bodies of citizens was key — particularly the bodies of these new workers entering the (un)official workplaces of factories, kitchens, and offices. And when the two master desires of the nascent nation-state and the expanding capitalist market don't exactly agree on how to best capture these bodies and what roles or limits to assign them, other more interesting and dissenting bodies begin to populate the city.

The song "*Ya no lloverá pelonas*" ["It won't rain pelonas anymore"] (figure 1.1) — attributed to tenor and songwriter José Moriche, a Spanish-born artist working in Southern California, Mexico City, and New York — is one example of this double injunction and the ways in which citizens respond *in their bodies*.[16] I cannot stress enough the fact that the song is meant to be heard and danced, made flesh through movement as much as in the physical and geographical references it makes. In it, the Mexican embodiment of the *modern girl* or flapper is rewoven into the nation both as a symbol of modernity in the progressive female sexuality to be imitated (the dance movements and style) as well as being placed squarely within the control of a humorous but male voice who knows enough to tell their story, flirts with them, fight for them, seduces them with technology, disparages them, laughs at them, and threatens them. As in the US Hispanic context of those decades in Los Angeles and other Latinx-populated spaces, Brown flappers were seen as the "fun-seeking icons of a burgeoning consumer society" (Feu Lopez 193). The key difference is that in the nascent *mestizo*-nationalist Mexico, these consumption practices and habits — focused on foreign products associated with modern fashion trends — also marked them as "victims" of cultural assimilation.[17] This dynamic was coupled with the "defense" of virility across various cultural media (literature, mural art, poetry), resulting in casting these particular women who danced, smoked cigarettes, enjoyed music, and socialized openly as foreigners in their own country and, as such, subject to the occasional yet structural violence of heteropatriarchal nationalism to "correct" their behavior.

Figure 1.1. Leaflet for the song "Ya no lloverá pelonas" ("It won't rain pelonas anymore").

Ya no LLOVERA PELONAS

Estribillo
La Moda de las Pelonas
yo se las voy á cantar,
pues todas se ven muy monas
cuando salen á pasear.
 Ando en busca de una novia
pues mi pecho está vacante,
pero quiero sea pelona
porque es muy interesante.

Jarabe.
 Muy alegres bailemos jarabe,
un jarabe muy bien zapateado,
que se luzca tu cuerpo gracioso,
chaparrita de mi corazón.
 Cuando mueves tu linda figura
se me llena el alma de embeleso
y quisiera de amor darte un beso,
chaparrita de mi corazón.

Coplas.
 No pienses que yo te quiero
porque te miro la cara,
que muchos van á una Feria,
ven, y nunca compran nada.
 Me mandastes á decir
por carta, que me olvidabas,
cuando aquella me llegó
ya de tí no me acordaba.

Jesucita en Chihuahua
Por tus amores
no llores, Peloncita,
porque puedes tu cara de rosa
tan preciosa, despintar,
y me dá mucha pena,
dulce Nena,
que parezcas azucena
revolcada en muladar.

Coplas.
Peloncitas guapetonas,
aquí traigo mi camión,
pa llevarlas y pasearlas
de purito vacilón.
 Bailaremos las Pelonas
agarraditos los dos,
y si tú me das un beso
¡sea por el amor de Dios!

Huapango.
Cuando veo que se baila
mi dulce morena,
un alegre Huapango,
 Tarango,
Siento que yo me muero,
 Salero,
porque mucho la quiero y venero
 Y el Huapango es un baile
de lo más gracioso,
y más zandunguero,
 Salero,
y al bailar con tu amada
 no hay nada
que nos haga feliz.

Coplas.
Las mujeres desdeñosas
son como las aceitunas,
que la que parece verde
suele ser la más madura.
 Los enemigos del alma
todos dicen que son tres,
y yo digo que son cinco,
con mi suegra y mi mujer.

Adelita.
 Si Adelita estuviera Pelona,
una peluca le había de comprar,
sus enaguas a la Tut-ank-amen,
pa llevarla á Chicago á bailar.

Coplas.
 Dicen que el Baile, el Cariño
y el Amor de una Mujer,
lo inventó una noche el Diablo
cuando no tenía quehacer.
 Si se te apaga el cigarro
no lo vuelvas á encender,
si te despide la novia
no la vuelvas a querer.

El Perico.
 Ay! Señora, su periquito
me dijo: Vieja Pelona
y corrí frente á un espejo
y me ví que estoy muy mona.
Pica, pica, pica, perico,
pica, pica, pica la rosa,
pica, pica, que aunque no quieras
pica, pica, yo estoy preciosa.

Coplas.
Un amante es como un niño
que se enoja y tira el pan;
y en haciéndole un cariño
se lo come y pide más
 El demonio son los hombres
cuando empieza á querer
y el diablo son las Pelonas
si empieza á aborrecer.

Me voy para San Luis
Yo ya me voy para San Luis,
donde hay Pelonas de carquís;
yo ya me voy, no volveré,
me voy y ahi me casaré.

Coplas.
Aquí se acaban cantando
los versos de las Pelonas,
que hoy la moda están usando
hasta las viejas jamonas.
 Y se acaban ya las coplas
terminando la canción;
con un beso á las Pelonas
y que siga la función.

REGISTRADO POR E. GUERRERO

Dated between 1922 (the year in which Tutankhamun's tomb was uncovered, a reference in the lyrics) and 1923 (the earliest it appears pressed on a record), "*Ya no lloverá pelonas*" is a hodgepodge of genres where each stanza is sung/performed in a different popular genres such as huapango, jarabe, adelite, or corrido. This ends up establishing and reinforcing an affectual relationship, not only between the male voice and the *pelona* he talks about, but also among the listeners/dancers and the musicians themselves; the musical and historical references reinforce a sense of shared experiences that appeal to national circumstances as much as international events and fashions. The song opens with "la moda de las pelonas // yo se las voy a cantar // pues todas se ven muy monas // cuando salen a pasear [the fashion of the short-hair girls // I will sing for you // since they all look so cute // when they go out to walk]," instantly capturing the female body in a fluid and changing circuit of fashion that the singer has access to.[18] The stanza opens up a space to approach the *pelonas* as interesting and worthy citizens, yet lacking in something to be considered a national body attached to a location. In this decade, Mexican modernity was commonly imagined by representing female bodies with short hair and tight-fitting clothes who carried a much more relaxed moral behavior than their elders; the short novels by Estridentista writer Arqueles Vela are exemplary avant-garde representations where the female protagonists are literal embodiments of the desire to be modern, and yet disembodied representations that do not exist outside the page and the fantasy, at least in the patriarchal imaginary.[19] In more concrete terms and describing the reality for women at the time, historian Ageeth Sluis has signaled how "in her search for social and physical mobility, the chica moderna clashed with the mainstay of revolutionary programs for women that allowed women a measure of power only as mothers. And a traditional, abnegating mother, the chica moderna certainly was not" ("BATACLANISMO!" 492). These *chicas modernas* did not have to be active members in the nightlife, as Anne Rubinstein has documented in her writings on the *pelonas* and the attacks they faced by radicalized *mestizo* youth policing their bodies; nursing students, telegraph students, and other professional women were often the target of policing focused on their short hair and modern dresses that clashed with the gender norms of this nascent nationalism (Rubinstein, "War on 'Las Pelonas'" 66–69).

This policing of women's choices, particularly when revolving around their bodies, reveals how consumption is always already gendered, differentiating "proper" (ideologically sanctioned) male consumption patterns from female consumption patterns that cross the ideological limits of the nation and, in doing so, construct other bodies. In these particular cases, consumption (of short haircuts, dresses, makeup, specific dances) transforms the female body into a woman able to control access to her own body, particularly by using the structures of power and capital (money) that embody the hierarchy hidden in the trapping of the *mestizo* society.[20] It is this particular threat that the song documents in the opening stanza, placing the female body of the *pelonas* under authorial, epistemological, and social control of the male voice. Characterized by the modern rhythms of the foxtrot that appear in the *coplas* (chorus), the *pelonas* must be contained within the popular genres being woven into nationalist music: the *corrido*, the jarabe, the huapango, and the *adelita*. This attempt at capturing echoes the India Bonita contest — which synthetized modernity, tradition, and the Vasconcelian dream of a cosmic race in her dark skin and feminine value — since the *pelona* then becomes the representation of a proper *mestizo* woman, consuming yet contained within the proper limits of domesticity and male control.[21]

Nevertheless, this changed body of the *pelona* the singer identifies and names is too powerful to contain. In self-constructing himself, the speaker of the *corrido* marks this tension by explicitly following the *pelona* (and the population as a whole) in her modernization. He states, "aquí traigo mi camión, // pa' llevarlas y pasearlas, // de purito vacilón [here I bring my truck // to take you out for a ride // in pure party and fun]," and presents himself as a figure authorized to approach the *pelonas* due to his modern technological profession of urban bus driver that can promote a night of fun, and not the foundational sexual union that the *adelita* or the *china poblana* will increasingly offer as the female revolutionary fighters are ideologized into submissive cooks and women readily available for reproduction or sexual gratification. Their consumption of global market goods and ideas is transformative and anchored in their urban positioning, reflecting the migration patterns of these women: "si Adelita estuviera pelona, // una peluca le había de comprar, // sus enaguas de Tut-ank-amen, // pa' llevarla a Chicago a bailar [If Adelita was a flapper and had short hair, // I'd buy her a wig, // her petticoats in the style of Tut-ank-amen, // to take her dancing to Chicago]." Though the singer mockingly condemns the revolutionary woman for cutting her hair, he cannot stop himself from attaching other global commodities to her body, from the foxtrot they will dance in Chicago (a nod to the international migration patterns) to the skirts of King Tut. Mary Kay Vaughn has described how the *adelita* — feminist revolutionary in her rejection of sexual, moral, and national mores of conduct — transforms her body to modernity through consumption to become an urban citizen (24). While it is important to keep in mind how the patterns of consumption also always subjectify into a capitalist consumer position, in these early instances these fashions (which can only happen due to a specific socioeconomic position that gives access to the commodities *and* with a sentimental education that allows for an understanding of the commodity) flood urban markets and become the avenues through which these women use their bodies to become modern, and to resist traditional roles in the process.[22]

Distributed in leaflets, "*Ya no lloverá pelonas*" is reminiscent of another popular *corrido* of the times that celebrated marginal and yet paradoxically hyper-national figures. *El corrido de los 41* tells the story of an underground and illegal transvestite dance party (a Mexican variation of a queer ball) that was held in 1901 and ended only when the police raided the place and imprisoned forty-one men. In the context of the marginal sexualities silenced by the hypermasculinity of the revolutionary *mestizo* history, Robert McKee Irwin's anthology studies the way in which the event, its novelization, and its cultural repercussions (songs, newspaper comics, journalistic covering) were shaped by class conflict, misogyny, and racism; the fact that the partygoers belonged to the upper echelons of Porfirian society highlights effeminacy as proof of the bourgeois decadency the revolution would eliminate and exemplifies the weaponization of dissident and queer sexualities as tools of class warfare and resistance. Ultimately, the *Corrido de los 41* and engravings by José Guadalupe Posada were distributed in printed leaflets that ridiculed the figure of the homosexual, but they did so in an affectionate, sympathetic, and ethically engaging manner (Irwin, *Mexican Masculinities* 80). In spite of the highly problematic (classism, racism, sexism) nature of the event and its resolution in imprisonment and torture for some with unpunished freedom for others, forty-one has become a number synonymous with male-male sexual desire and is slowly being reformulated into a cornerstone of homosexual culture in Mexico. The *corrido* and the newspaper comic parodies while celebrating the existence of homosexual desire through popular formats, albeit to ridicule the upper classes, generating different alternative accounts of being Mexican. They do not call to violence or suppression of these subjectivities, but to recognize their presence in the national stage.

In the same way, "*Ya no lloverá pelonas*" recognizes the legitimate existence of these other different bodies — women expressing and constructing themselves through music, dance, and fashion — even if it seeks to contain their subversive potential within the folds of the *mestizo* nation through popular rhythms and the voice of the male singer. This recognition comes also without a totalizing tolerance that reaffirms the other person as Other, nor a deep change of the self in the face of this other person; in the words of Slavoj Žižek, this moment of recognition where the song testifies between the male voice singing popular culture and the female *pelona* adapting to the city becomes "a space of sociability that is the solidarity of the vulnerable" (139). In this sense, the musical and performative space is ephemerally captured in the print space of the leaflet, hinting at a national space where the citizens of popular Mexico City engage with *pelonas* through the discourse of nationalism, but now embodied in the sounds and dances of the population. Instead of being represented through the national imagery of murals and textbooks, a national community begins to solidify in the song through the establishment of a relationship between bodies (male singers and female dancers) in a continuum that consumed both national sounds and foreign images and fashion.[23] While it is crucial to recognize the power dynamic established by the male singer, the song nevertheless describes female bodies in motion, consuming foreign objects and fashion, and thus expanding the limits of the narrow *mestiza* identity grounded in domesticity and reproductive labor. In the song, a collective popular and national identity emerges into a public space where countercultural bodies can move in, while simultaneously being subjected to a series of "tests" to prove their national belonging. These *pelonas* are not seen as sexual deviants nor even sexually charged bodies, but simply seeking the "purito vacilón [pure party and fun]" that "*Vacilópolis*," another popular song of the moment, constructs.

The control over the newly national (female) bodies that coalesced around the virility debates of 1925 was not a phenomenon emerging only from the elite intellectual spaces. Rather, it was a specific response to the more general social anxiety that was produced as technological and economic development increased the work opportunities for women (and other marginalized citizens), while major cities and Mexico City in particular were growing with this particular migration. Seen from this history, the control over Indigenous bodies that defined (and continues to do so) *mestizaje* as a social process of incorporation — with the consequential loss of language and culture — can be seen not just as a continuation of the histories of colonialism, but also as a response to the social anxieties these citizens whose bodies are marked as "different" are producing (and continue to produce) in their greater participation in the cultural and economic markets of the nation. Complimenting the discourse of institutional *mestizaje* emerging from the state and its allied intellectuals, "purito vacilón" can be seen as a strategy to striate and place order on an urban space overflowing with desire; *vacilópolis* as the Mexico City experiencing and responding to the modernization of its sociosexual and cultural norms.[24] In turn, these responses can reimpose order on the apparent chaos of desire in all its manifestations, on all of the bodies populating these newly urban spaces. To approach these dynamics with a more complexifying gaze, I want to keep the sexualized, racialized, and gendered strategies of control in mind always, intersectionally understanding their impact on the bodies of these newly formed citizens, particularly vis-à-vis the masculinities that were gathering strength and would eventually become hegemonic in *mestizo* nationalism.

The *novela de la revolución* that emerged out of this anxiety, later defined as *the* textualization of the virile *mestizo* male citizen, was also in part a response to the "feminization" of literature during the late Porfiriato and early postrevolutionary periods.[25] Accelerating as more and more people had access to the markets of global commodities, this "feminization" rested fundamentally on the understanding that the act of consumption was a properly female act; this trend would continue and reach a high point in the 1980s, when "light literature" appears as a way to discredit the literary production of authors such as Guadalupe Loaeza or Ángeles Mastretta. In the literary field, the professionalization of the figure of the writer that began in the late *modernismo* increasingly allowed for a questioning of male control over publication spaces. This control and its enforcement were made further visible by the growing numbers of female typists, stenographers, and secretaries in the previously male-exclusive offices and other spaces. Even when this economic relation does subjugate women as manual laborers working under order from creative male employers, it also permissible for women to follow the same path of professional writers and become themselves producers of cultural knowledge, as the latter case of Cube Bonifant explores. Nevertheless, the polemics of virility along with *Ya no lloverá pelonas* and other cultural manifestations signal the centrality of gender vis-à-vis citizenship, and more importantly how the nation can become modern in moments of transformation of a market of masculinities.[26] The *mestizo* masculinity that coalesced out of this market structured around order and competition excluded any kind of feminine-marked behavior, silenced any kinds of homosexual/homoerotic actions, and, above all, established a class-marked relation of property ownership that began with one's own body and its ownership (or lack thereof) reproduced in the later writings of Samuel Ramos, Octavio Paz, and Carlos Fuentes, as well as in the films of Alejandro Galindo or Fernando de Fuentes. McKee Irwin notes that (heterosexual) desire in *mestizaje* must be contained within the heteronormative structures of marriage, further defined in turn by the parameters of class and property relation, and then placed as the exclusive model of interpersonal sociosexual relations.[27] While the implications of these gender/class structuring forces must not be lost, I want to point out the limitations of this *mestizo* nationalism, particularly in the years in which it coalesces and begins to be firmly institutionalized. The multiplicity of other forms of sociosexual behavior, identities, and actions that emerge in these moments of modernization defy the rules of engagement that *mestizo* nationalism is imposing, particularly when the class positioning is made explicit and used to thwart/subvert instances of bodily control.

Ya no lloverá evidences the difficulty of approaching gender without a firm and contextualized class analysis. The song, and the leaflet it was printed on, points at a class dynamic that seeks to contain lower-class working women into models of global modernity *and* nationalist types; whereas upper-class citizens had access to these global citizenship models, it is when lower-class and Indigenous bodies mobilize them that symbolic violence is exercised to contain them within these categorizing models. In the heteronormative *mestizo* nation, dissident sexualities, whether homosexual or sexually empowered women, are a moral *and* national issue that require the intervention of a male authority to reimpose order, as the nameless singer of *Ya no lloverá* does.[28] In contrast to the lettered archive, countercultural production functions closer to the ephemera than the written word. José Esteban Muñoz approaches the ephemera as the "traces of lived experiences and performances of lived experiences, maintaining experiential politics and urgencies long after these structures of feeling have been lived" ("Ephemera as Evidence" 10). The song thus becomes an ephemeral trace — albeit contained within the *mestizo* gaze — of uncontrollable bodies surging with desire, dancing across the space as they embody a global and national modernity. *Tiples* (night-life theater revue stars) and *pelonas* populated the *carpas* and *tandas* (circus-like entertainment tents) to perform a female sexuality that was both homoerotic in engaging with each other and troubling for the male control that was being reimposed on the chaotic social order of Mexico City in the 1920s and 1930s. These emerging sociabilities paralleled what would also happen in the cabarets of the Weimar Republic and the jazz era of New York, Chicago, and New Orleans, where women and queer citizens were occupying the public gaze as entertainers and workers in increasingly urbanized city life. Thus, rather than reading the songs and photographs as foundational texts, their ephemeral traces signal alternative structures of feeling-being assembled and enacted by these dissident citizens in their attempts to expand the limits of the *mestizo* bodies.

Heteronormativity worked to co-opt these female citizens as they migrated into the urban centers and encountered the images of foreign femininities that began to populate the nightlife of *carpas* and other popular and elite theater, and traces of these dissident bodies remain in the spaces between normativities. Esther Gabara documents how their hybrid female bodies crossed popular sectors and neighborhoods, nascent consumer cultures and mass media, and even some avant-garde groups (151). Darker-skinned and more Indigenous-marked bodies were captured into the folds of the state through the implementation of public performances such as the India Bonita beauty pageants, where anthropology (as academic discipline *and* tool of the state) allied itself with private commercial interests to generate official "authentic" representations of female indigeneity. Organized under the celebrations of the Centennial of Independence (1921), *La India Bonita* was both a beauty pageant and a theatrical performance planned by private newspapers *El Universal Ilustrado* and *Revista de Revistas* in collaboration with government agencies.[29] Rick López has documented how *El Universal Ilustrado* actively participated in the definition of what Indigenous beauty meant through the self-publication of selected photographs of urban domestic workers in "traditional" clothing, as well as informative articles by leading anthropologist Manuel Gamio.[30] In this way, the public space of the newspaper was motivated by the capitalist injunction, educating their urban readers in how to commodify the Indigenous bodies surrounding them by maintaining clear boundaries between modernity/indigeneity. This visual and marketing strategy functioned alongside the photographs of *charros* and *chinas poblanas* by Hugo Brehme and the later anthologizing work by Anita Bremer, creating aesthetic representations of a past and rural Mexico accessible to the consuming citizen. In the contest in particular, this aestheticization of an Indigenous past served to generate a domesticated and docile female body, a stand-in for the new Mexican citizens who were pushed by the cosmic race of Vasconcelos and the *mestizo* society it birthed to embrace their past while projecting themselves onto the modern future through the incorporation of these bodies into the urban space (López, "The India Bonita Contest" 259). María Bibiana Uribe, the sixteen-year-old winner of this first contest, was paraded in elite social and political events during the centennial celebration of that year, "portrayed as a rural *mestiza* woman newly arrived in the modern cosmopolis of Mexico City and as a woman who maintained her ancient and enduring 'Indianness' while simultaneously demonstrating her capacity to become modern enough by virtue of her participation in a beauty contest" (Ruiz, "La india bonita" 284). What is most important here is that the domestication of María Bibiana Uribe was carried out by commercial agents who mobilized intellectual discourses in the public sphere of the newspaper journals and government parades in major streets. The capturing of Uribe's body — which she actively resisted by laughing when agents would misname her ethnicity or her precedence — was embodied in a cultural constructed and controlled female body that depended on and reinforced the stereotypes of *mestizo* femininity and female indigeneity. Ultimately, the effect of the newspapers and pageant organizers was to generate educated consumer citizens who chose to and could access the "authentic" nation; that year, readers would buy the sandals that María Bibiana Uribe advertised in *El Universal Ilustrado*, in performative nationalism in their own bodies as well as to dress the other citizens around them.

This was one of the ways in which Indigenous and racialized female bodies now populating the streets of Mexico City were recast into the camposcape of an idealized past and distant geography, in spite of their living in the city and navigating the nuances of modernity with ease.[31] Historian Ageeth Sluis describes the camposcape as constructed upon the images of Indigenous bodies appearing in paintings of Diego Rivera and other muralists, as well as in photographs by Manuel Álvarez Bravo and Hugo Brehme — a visual imaginary that gave form to the nativist roots of Mexico as a construct, in the sense that they anchor the imaginary nation to an ideologically purified past, following the Vasconcelian example. As Irene O'Malley has demonstrated in studying the mystification of the male pantheon of revolutionary heroes Francisco Villa, Emiliano Zapata, or Venustiano Carranza, these attempts by state-market assemblage to mystify female bodies into consumable images contain/thwart the dangerous potential of *adelitas* and Indigenous women coexisting with middle-class women in their work and urban environments. As the *India Bonita* contest recognized the existence of ethnic and racialized bodies in the nation while constructing and disseminating an apolitical and mythically mediatized engagement, so the song *Ya no lloverá pelonas* takes the problematic *pelona* body and recasts it into the nation by firmly placing it *only* in relation to the musical rhythms and images of the *mestizo* imaginary. As Lopez underscores, the *India Bonita* contest "extended the nationalist project into the realm of aesthetics and the pricing of the female indigenous body, which would come to shape narrations of ethnicity, class and collective identity" (*Crafting Mexico* 53). Similarly, *Ya no lloverá pelonas* and other representations of women in the public sphere, such as advertising campaigns that constructed the Deco Body, shaped the representations of ethnicity that became central to the *mestizo* national project, as in later images by hyper popular painter Saturnino Herrán circulated in calendars and postcards. What is more important in all these instances is that these cultural agents (newspapers, contest judges, critics, songwriters) were not exactly tools of the state, but rather were cultural producers working within a greater ideological framework.

Mestizo culture served in this way to make visible and incorporate previously excluded citizens into the social space, and women such as Tina Modotti, the Campobello sisters, Antonieta Rivas Mercado, Lola Álvarez Bravo, Cube Bonifant, Nahui Olin, and countless factory workers, sex workers, secretaries, and nurses used this political opening to participate in the formation of a modern nation. On the cultural side, however, women who decided to participate in the modern spaces of fashion, dance, and other more "frivolous" and less "serious" activities were continuously recast into the narrow limits imposed by a sexualized heteronormative *mestizo* identity. In *Ya no lloverá pelonas*, it is interesting to note that even though the structure is a hodge-podge/mélange where the lyrics speak of dancing in Chicago, the foxtrot mentioned, or any other foreign dance rhythm, was not added onto the song with lyrics, even though it is well documented that Mexican bands were producing these kinds of rhythms and the song features snippets of it.

In contrast, one could listen to another popular song, *Vacilópolis*, written by Emilio de Urania in 1925 in the wake of the extreme success of the visiting *Voilá Paris: La ba-ta-clán* show, a touring French grand variety spectacle that premiered in the Teatro Iris in Mexico City that same year (Sluis, *Deco Bodies* 61). This song title may reference Estrindentópolis — another version of urban modernity pushed forward by the Estridentista collective during their time in Veracruz — and what's most striking is the weaving of the foxtrot rhythm into a Mexican-specific milieu: *vacilar* is a slang term that refers to a playful social engagement with the undertones of romantic or sexual play, while *vacilón* may refer to a joker/trickster person, as well as to the space where *vacilar* is a normalized and encouraged behavior. Close to the more recognized *relajo/echar relajo*, *vacilar* is a sensual activity that engages the full body through all the senses used in order to generate play among the speakers and that embeds playfulness onto social dynamics.[32] Though the lyrics are short in comparison to the music itself (it is music meant to be danced to, after all), they generate a collective and inclusive space structured around *vacilar*, educating the dancers in distancing themselves from moral codes and rejecting a domination dynamic as their bodies move across the dance floor: "Con las caras muy juntitas // Y los cuerpos muy pegados // Corazón con corazón, // Y los cuerpos muy pegados // ¡Ay, caray! ¡Qué vacilón! // Las mejillas muy juntitas // Corta la respiración // Me besaba y me dejaba //¡Ay, caray! ¡Qué vacilón! [With their faces close together // and their bodies very tight // heart to heart // and their bodies very tight // oh, my dear! What a fun time // The cheeks close together // the breath cut short // she kissed me and I let her // oh, my dear! What a fun time!]"

In the camposcape of *mestizaje*, bodies are firmly gendered in exclusionary binaries as they are culturally constructed in an idyllic setting where sexuality only exists within heteronormative reproductivity.[33] *Vacilópolis* rejects this setting and uses urban rhythms to anchor itself in a cityscape where the sexuality of women is not subject to nationalist reproductivity in the form of marriage or sexual union, but as a body that moves as a counterpart for the modern male citizen. While the song describes a moment of dancing, the term refers to a whole form of ethical engagements in the entertainment nightlife, a refusal to reproduce *mestizo* heteronormativity:

> El reino de Vacilópolis es decididamente moderno . . . tam-bién existen escuelas que enseñan el arte de besar -por el puro sonido se sabe el grado al que pertenece la ejecutante-, mujeres que demandan su divorcio por motivos que tienen que ver con longitudes y tamaños, rancheros que viajan en zepelines y aterrizan en tierras donde escasean los hom-bres. Vacilópolis, tierra de tentaciones dónde a los inte-grantes de la mexicana alegría se les reconoce porque les gusta el pozole con trompita . . . lugar de reunión de todos aquellos que no se sienten satisfechos con los espectáculos que la tranquilidad hogareña proporciona . . . y prefieren ser cómplices del ritual de la provocación, del bailoteo deslenguado de unos cuerpos sin ataduras, el simulacro de la voluptuosidad . . . Vacilópolis no es solamente una vitrina donde los machos contemplativos echan tacos de ojo, *es también un territorio ganado para los desplazamientos femeninos*, una nueva presencia social de la mujer
> [The kingdom of Vacilópolis is decidedly modern . . . there also exist schools that teach the art of kissing — just by the sound alone one can tell the degree to which the executioner belongs to — women that demand divorce due to reasons that have to do with length and sizes, ranchers that travel in zeppelins and land in places where men are scarce. Vacilópolis, land of temptations where the members of the Mexican joy are recognized because they like pozole with snout . . . land of reunion where all those that are not satisfied with the spectacles of homely tranquility come together . . . and they prefer to be accomplices to the rituals of provocation, the foul-spoken dancing about of bodies with no ties, a simulacrum of voluptuousness. . . . Vacilópolis is not only a glass storefront where contemplative *machos* get some eye candy, *it is also a territory won by the feminine move-ments,* a new social presence of women]. (Morales 64–66)[34]

It is in this empowered social space where the female body in the song is one capable of cutting short the breath of the male singer, affecting the body rather than controlling it. These are bodies sensually, erotically engaged with each other, dancing in a routine where the woman initiates the action in a show of will and potentiality. Elizabeth Grosz speaks of how bodies experiencing and expressing disturb the supposed passivity of the body inscribed by normative orders, and ultimately of how, in the activity of desiring, bodies inscribe each other as they express these desires (*Space, Time and Perversion* 36). Desire, especially when experienced and expressed by bodies inscribed as passive, generates instances of pushing back against normative ideologies. Ageeth Sluis thoroughly accounts for how the *revista* [revue] theater, in both the high-class establishments and circles that brought revues from France and overseas as well as the more popular makeshift *carpas* in the Zocalo and other downtown areas, became spaces of ideological exploration "as both a space of sociability and a challenge to normative discourses" (*Deco Body* 297). These spaces allowed for women and other citizens to generate alternative bodies — the Deco body among them — that provoked desire in their male spectators. Most importantly, these bodies also promoted desire in themselves, thus "educating" these female citizens in the experiences of their own desire; in those instances, there emerged possibilities of resisting heteronormative domination of bodies in their labor, desire, or pleasure.

Cube Bonifant: Writing Female Bodies onto the Cityscape

While cultural journals were being led by male writers debating the feminization of national literature, women who wielded the pen and typewriter (and cameras, in the case of Tina Modotti) appear more preoccupied with exploring the possibilities of desiring (female) bodies moving about in these new modernized urban environments than with the debates. Cube Bonifant was perhaps *the* women to publish in the pages of *El Universal Ilustrado*, the first professional female writer that jumped out of the strict limitations for publishing women relegated to domestic journals, advice articles, or "feminine" columns. Extremely multifaceted in her career, the chronicles, short stories, radio scripts, film reviews, and advice columns provide a sharp and incisive counterpoint to both the heteronormative fears of her male peers as they navigated the new city *and* to the supposed consumerist habit of her female peers, both of which appeared next to her writing in the articles and advertisements of *El Universal Ilustrado* and other journals. Born in 1904 in El Rosario, Sinaloa, and christened Antonia Bonifant López, Cube migrated to Mexico City in 1920 after living briefly in Guadalajara as she and her family fled the revolutionary violence that destabilized the country. She was hired by editor Carlos Noriega Hope as a chronicler for *El Universal Ilustrado* and it became "un ingreso estable para ayudar a mantener a su madre y sus hermanas, ya que el padre de Bonifant, ingeniero de minas de origen francés, no llegó a la capital y no se sabe si pudo apoyar económicamente a su familia [a stable income to help support her mother and sisters, since Bonifant's father, a mine engineer from French origin, did not arrive at the capital and it is unknown whether he was able to economically support his family]" (Mahieux, *Una pequeña marquesa* 15).

Founded in 1917 and owned by Félix Palavicini — the entrepreneur who also sponsored the *India Bonita* contest — *El Universal Ilustrado* was a weekly illustrated literary magazine that accompanied the broadsheet *El Universal*, founded in 1916 and still active, though commonly discredited as one of the unofficial voices of the government in power due to funding and censorship. *El Universal Ilustrado* became one of the central and most public journals where Mexico's nascent literary sphere consolidated as writing (and other arts) became more professionalized and globalized. As the cultural part of a newspaper that heralded the assemblages of late capitalism between news conglomerates, global corporations, and a close relationship to state officials, *El Universal Ilustrado* was the ideal public space where gender roles, expectations, and limitations could be tested within the safety of the parameters that professionalization builds (in contrast to the always-latent exploitative violence of the entertainment industry).[35] As such, it helps understand the alignment of the state subjectification processes with the profit-driven market structurings of desire; *El Universal Ilustrado* was the place where the polemic around virility began in 1925. Furthermore, the publication served as the crossroads between the "masculinity" of intellectual pursuits embodied in the avant-garde writers in its cadre and the impulse to "feminize" the consumer-readers through advertising agencies and consumer education. Its editor Carlos Noriega Hope was the sponsor of both the Estridentistas (the futurist avant-garde) and the Contemporáneos (the aesthetic modernists) while also being a promoter of film and radio as modern technologies, building radio stations, and supporting theaters. Very active during the 1920s, the journal was important in establishing an institutional anchor for the cultural sphere, as well as in promoting a mode of advertisement and consumer engagement that some termed "frivolous"; *estridentismo*, Contemporáneos, and the *novela de la revolución* all emerged from the journal, whether in their publication or in the collaborative work environment the journal helped created. With over 50,000 issues in circulation, the journal functioned as a successful cultural enterprise of the Compañía Periodística Nacional [National Journalistic Company] that professionalized journalistic writing, set a baseline for frivolous reportage of urban and political events, and increased the connections between readers and writers (Hadatty Mora 174).

In line with the increasing female readership of this nascent consumer culture developing in the advertising sections of the journal, Cube was hired and backed by the editor Carlos Noriega Hope. However, *pelonas* and other modern women were a touchy subject for the journal's male writers. In the October 5, 1925, section "Nuevos conceptos sobre el ultrapelonismo [New concepts on ultrashorthair]," members of the Contemporáneos group — who went on to become central figures in the institutional development of the nation's cultural sphere — responded to this fashion trend with an aggressive reimposition of male dominance over female bodies. Salvador Novo, in the face of his openly known desire for other men, ridicules women's decision to cut their hair as it will force them to undertake weekly visits to the barber shops where "tendrán, por fuerza, que leer los periódicos del día [they will by force have to read the newspapers of the day]" (34). Though he hints at women becoming more informed citizens, the satire in his words underlines the power dynamic of his masculinity in his perception of women as uninformed. More explicit in his dismissal of the *pelonas* is Jaime Torres Bodet, who later will serve as Secretary of Education (1943-46) and sees short hair as the undressing of the female body, where "lo que sucede es que el vestido corto no basta ya al afán que nuestras mujeres tienen por desnudarse y el cabello era todavía — por lo menos en los sonetos de los poetas románticos — una túnica, la más atrevida de las túnicas [what happens is that the short dress is not enough anymore with the desire that these women have to undress themselves and the hair was — at least in the sonnets of the romantic poets — a tunic, the most daring of tunics]" (35). Not only is body-shaming mobilized as a way to control women's bodies, but this control is also constructed as part of a greater Western tradition that includes romantic poets; this position was echoed in the violence of the student groups that shaved *pelonas* on the street (Rubinstein, "War on las pelonas" 68). In another section of the same issue titled "Ultrapelonicemos la vida," an anonymous author uses satire and wit to ridicule *ultra pelonas* as a social issue of "paz para la inteligencia y el corazón. Mientras aquella tenga menos en qué pensar y éste menos en qué enredarse, el mundo caminará mejor [peace for the intelligence and the heart. As long as that one has less to think about and this one less to get wrapped up in, the world will walk better]" (36). According to this anonymous critic then, women's bodies are not meant to think and are especially dangerous since they hinder the freedom of men's bodies; the article continues to describe a woman with short hair as a seductress with "la sonrisa más definitivamente ponzoñosa [the definitely most poisonous smile]" (37). For the male writers in the journal, women are not intelligent readers nor critical fashion consumers, only stereotypical seductresses authorized to wear their hair short only because it makes them a better, more modern commodity to be consumed by the male gaze. I reference this journalistic context not to signal it as extraordinary, but rather to underline some ways in which gendered ideologies of nation were reproduced in the cultural sphere. It is from here that Bonifant writes and denounces the captured yet modern female bodies, able to exist as Deco and *pelonas* due to their modernity while still being vilified and rejected from the greater social body due to their constructed lack. Bonifant pushes back by mobilizing desire as a way of breaking from the control over her own and other women's bodies: sexual and erotic desire is what can erode these gendered ideologies of nation — and not simply intelligence, which in the normative gaze is equated with hair length and, even when present, is contained to the domestic space inhabited by the *literata*.

Without forgetting the capitalist economic relation to which she was subjected as a worker for this journal, Cube's weekly chronicles and writings carved out a space for female participation in the public sphere. Going beyond fashion reporting and even the limited space of the *literata* (an authorized public woman who consumes fashionable literature), her writings construct self-fashioned citizens, her own persona an explicit poser who consciously manipulated her image by engaging her readers and critiquing the common spaces they inhabited, from the symbolic nation as female citizens with labor rights if not voting rights to the real spaces such as salons, theaters, and streets.[36] Her writings focus on how women are being subjectified by the state and the market as docile consumers reproducing heteronormative futurity, and she signals this for the female readers in their complicity as much as for the male readers in their action. She raises alarm at the mobilization of the Deco body as a new corset, forcing women to reshape their bodies to conform to the (male) definitions of modernity; in the same breath, her chronicles look harshly at the *literatas* and other high-class women who gather to read and be modern while lacking a voting-rights consciousness. In the chronicles and short stories, Bonifant develops the female body in relation to the city itself, territories that permeate the spaces through which bodies move as much as the bodies themselves. Following Elizabeth Grosz in this regard and Rosi Bradiotti in her approach to body machines, I approach Bonifant's texts as ephemeral traces signaling ways in which some women were dissenting from both the modern *mestizo* nation and the market subjectification forces through their bodies, eroticizing their movement through the city and eroticizing the city itself in the face of a normative gaze that centers visuality as a strategy of control.

Rosi Braidotti describes the paradoxical and violent dichotomy of heteronormativity that generates an image of women "as a disempowered reflection of a dominant subject who casts his masculinity in a universalistic posture" (*Metamorphoses* 12). Thinking especially of the increasing participation of women in work environments and the changes (or not) that happen as more women work alongside men, Bonifant's texts focus a particular critique of female consumers who embody this patriarchal femininity as they move through the city, calling out their reinforcement of feminine stereotypes while simultaneously using her own *pelona* and flapper self to model alternative female bodies.[37] In "Psicologías en la alfombra," published on October 13, 1921, in the midst of centennial celebrations and the early definitions of what it meant to be a modern *mestiza*, Bonifant unfolds herself into Antonieta, a girl-child character, and Cube, the first-person narrator. In doing so, the author establishes herself as a double woman experiencing and being inscribed with the codes of normative femininity, as well as experiencing sexual desire and an urge to explore the city as a different and allowable urban space, the codes and the city coexisting and informing her actions as a whole political subject. Antonieta is described as having "calcetines y moño en el pelo recortado . . . parecía un muchacho que para evadirse del colegio se hubiera puesto cosas de mujer . . . pensaba que le sentaban bien los zapatos de bebé y los calcetines [stockings and a bow in her short hair . . . she looked like a boy who escaped boarding school by putting on women's clothes . . . I thought that the child's shoes and stockings fit her well]" (81). Cube, on the other hand, wears "medias" and a "traje" (socks and suit). Antonieta is a product of the changing times in fashion, and when Cube finds her, she is writing a short love story about a woman and her lover in *frac*, which Cube finds detestable because of the story's feminine sentimentality. Antonieta embodies a private and spiritual femininity, contained within the household and surrounding herself with books, papers, and imaginations, while Cube takes that critique and places it in the context of public engagements (the chronicle itself as a textual space), alerting readers to the constructed nature of emotions and the class relations that may lay underneath them.

In the short dialogue between the boyish yet sensitive Antonieta and the sporty Cube crossdressing in a suit, Bonifant appears critically aware of how the Deco body could be used as a way of subjecting women into controlled social positions. Sluis calls attention to how "if Deco bodies facilitated women's entry into male practices such as sports, they remained deployed as female sexed and sexual bodies so as not to upstage the gender binary" (*Deco Body* 80). The chronicle presents these two models of femininity, a young Deco body and an adult *flapper* crossdressing, and mobilizes their engagement to signal the limitations that patriarchy is imposing on the greater social body. Antonieta's love story between a beautiful and serious young woman and a worldly young man full of frivolities is destined to fail according to her, since the man is too frivolous for the young woman and Antonieta can't kill the character for fear of breaking the woman's heart. Cube then realizes the "poca importancia de las rodillas y las piernas sin medias, ante las pequeñas truculencias del drama de *mi amiga espíritu* [little matter of the knees and legs without stockings, faced by the small gruesomeness of my spirit friend's drama]" (Bonifant 85).[38] Contrasting the physical body of Cube with the spiritual body of Antonieta, Bonifant signals how modern haircuts, clothes, and bodily behaviors are not indicative of critical or feminist positions. Antonieta is "stuck" in the paradox of a patriarchal society that valorizes virile masculinity and apparently dissenting femininities only to ultimately produce women as objects to be consumed by the male gaze; her lover is too frivolous (code: not virile) to be her lover, and yet she the writer is unable to remove him. That Antonieta is called her "spirit friend" signals as well the double bind that codes of behavior and body manipulation are imposing on women in that time, pointing at more inclusion/movement in the social spaces while simultaneously imposing a "muscular corset, women's own means of restraining themselves" (Sluis, *Deco body* 81). Bonifant uses this psychological theater to present to the readers a glimpse at the inner psychological landscape of a Mexican flapper using her body to break the corset of patriarchal society even as she wears it.

On December 8, 1921, Cube published the chronicle "Cabellos largos e ideas cortas," a title playing on the stereotypes of patriarchal femininity; she tells the story of her visit to a gathering of *escritoras* and *literatas*, presenting the readers with an intimate insider view of a female-centered space. After lighting a cigarette "con la misma poca elegancia con que los encienden los hombres . . . (Siempre me ha gustado extraordinariamente las actitudes masculines: creo que nací mujer por equivocación) [with the same small elegance with which men light them . . . . (I have always extraordinarily enjoyed masculine attitudes: I believe I was born a woman by mistake)]" (98), Cube is politely requested not to smoke by the ladies and complies with, "tengo que ser caballero con estas damas [I must be a gentleman with these dames]" (98). As the ladies discuss literature and entertain each other with song, Bonifant observes; the chronicle emphasizes throughout the performativity of gender as Cube moves from masculine-associated behavior (smoking, talking about politics, social activism) to feminine-associated behavior (gossiping, popular songs, emotional journaling). She gravitates toward a gentlemanly attitude of politeness and winks at her unspoken desire to start a voting-rights discussion and organize the ladies against bull-fighting. After noticing these things won't happen and the ladies prefer to continue discussing their travel diaries focused on the Madre Patria Spain, Cube leaves with a "huida silenciosa y felina [silenced and feline flight]" (100). For Rosi Braidotti, women "can be revolutionary subjects only to the extent that they develop a consciousness that is not specifically feminine, dissolving 'woman' into the forces which structure her" (*Metamorphoses* 81). Cube's fluidity serves to question these forces, her gender-bending carried out with a political intentionality; in a way, she is signaling her own actions as disruptions while marking the depolitical power of normative gender and the ways in which the ladies are reproducing it, and she does so from an inside position of solidarity and recognition without creating an either/other–self/other dynamic.

While surrounded in a social space created by women for women, Bonifant uses her own body to reshape her political subjectivity, the short hair and cigarettes serving as markers of masculinity woven into her body through her own will and able to be negotiated precisely because of that. The chronicle ends with her leaving the gathering with "la complacencia egoista y risueña de mis cabellos cortos de mi poca feminidad [egoistic and cheerful complacency of my short hair and small femininity]" (100). To be egoistic here is less a question of morality and more a question of political praxis springing from the educated will of the individual. She is educated in the fashion and trends circulating across the increasingly globalized world, and willful in that she chooses to disengage with the ways in which the modern nation is constructing/socializing women as simply objects to be consumed by the male national/modern gaze. Her laughter as she exits is not only a way of countering the "seriousness" imposed on her behavior by the morally upright women, but most of all, it is an assemblage of her own body, an activation of the political consciousness through laughter and joy (in contrast with rage or anger). This laughter and joy allow for her body/self to navigate the somber tones of the manly business world she is laboring in and writing from, *and* the serious flirtation of the female dancer who is pushed to act out the object role created by patriarchy. Thus, Cube's chronicle showcases a woman who exemplifies the attitudes of *pelonas* and *bataclanas* that walk with her in this new nation, now unfolding in a professional space. Her willful refusal of "proper" behavior, with the ladies and *literatas* as well as with the male writers and artists she engages with, transform her political subjectivity/consciousness by first transforming her own body and reshaping it according to her desires, informed by global fashion as much as by the discourse of revolution.

The chronicle, a genre that emerges from the public sphere of the newspaper (with roots in the colonial *crónicas de Indias*) as *the* narrative territory of modernity, was a space where Cube's position as a female writer stepping out of symbolic and real domestic spaces was precarious at best, and directly attacked at worst; her continuous posing was a strategy to provoke conversation and debate, explicitly critiquing and joking with her female audience while pushing feminist causes (Mahieux, *Urban Chroniclers* 139). The most visceral of the social critiques were focused on women, and most particularly on the uncritical consumption of books, haircuts, clothes, and fashionable acts (*Una pequeña marquesa* 31). Whereas the chronicle's limitations as a public sphere shape Bonifant's posing, in her fiction she can explore the potentially liberating aspects of urban technological femininity in productive terms. The story serves to explore, trace, and embody what Elizabeth Grosz defines as body-cities, the model of relations between bodies and urban environments where the material makeup of space (streets, automobiles, traffic laws, and stores and shops) defines bodies themselves by becoming specific points of assemblage (*Space, Time and Perversion* 108).

In textualizing a changing reality and appealing to collective experiences, the chronicle of the early 1900s is more suited to signal the limitations of current normativities than to explore alternative realities being created in the shared spaces; chronicling about marginalized, censored, or dissident subjectivities erodes the still-precarious legitimacy of the journalist. Fiction loosens the restriction by allowing the representation of realities whose public recognition pushes against normativity; as the city was growing with women working and moving, their bodies were repositioning in such a way where "the city provides the order and organization that automatically links otherwise unrelated bodies: it is in the condition and milieu in which corporeality is socially, sexually, and discursively produced" (Grosz, *Space* 104). As a woman living through these technological changes in the city — from her typewriter to the automobiles she drove and the radio she helped found — and being able to move through the cultural and entertainment spheres, Bonifant experienced firsthand how the city reshaped her own body. While the architectural and urban changes of Mexico City were consciously carried out to generate consciousness subjectivation as *modern* citizens, aiming to "physically build a new Mexico, and to both construct and communicate a new identity for itself and its people . . . an identity linked to the rejection of the imperial past and the embracing of modernity" (Winfield 7), women were time and again excluded as political subjects. And that did not stop Bonifant and other flappers from transforming the objects around them, such as a streetcar or an automobile, to redefine them: first, in terms of their technological use and symbols of progress, as the Estridentistas and other avant-garde groups were doing, aestheticizing technology; and, most importantly, by transforming these technologies and tools into embodied components of a female and nonheteronormative sexuality and, by extension, pushing back against the limits of mestizo nationalism.

For Grosz, the material makeup of the city (streets, automobiles, traffic laws, stores, shops, office buildings) assembles bodies as much as it is assembled by the bodies that connect and link the space (*Space, Time and Perversion*, 108). Bonifant's short story "El amor en automóvil" ("Automobile love"), published in *El Universal Ilustrado* on November 19, 1926, is a tale of a man and a woman who traverse the city in the back of a vehicle presumably driven by a chauffeur; with the bumps and swerves of the street, and a little motivation on the part of the girl, the couple end up in each other's arms.[39] Together, the couple and the automobile become a machine-body, to use Rosi Braidotti's terminology, an assemblage that expresses and embodies sexuality, here subverting the norms of both *mestizo* masculinity and femininity in the most quotidian and modern act of moving through the city in a motorized vehicle. Desire is the structuring element of individual and collective change; Bonifant takes the sexual desire felt by the woman and eroticizes it, embodying it "con los brazos y las piernas al aire y una piel chiquita alrededor del cuello [with her arms and legs exposed to air and a small fur around her neck]" (337), and ultimately assembling it with the automobile itself as an urban technology. The automobile here is not a fetishistic metonymy of modernity in the more typical avant-garde approach of futurism, but instead becomes one more mode in the expanding networks of market and desire: "la marca del automóvil no importa, pero si usted insiste, le diremos que es la marca que este semanario anuncia más [the brand of the automobile doesn't matter, but if you insist I will tell you that it is the brand announced more by this weekly]" (337). What matters is not the technology itself so much as its functioning as a consumer object in an urban network, allowing for its drivers and users to engage the city in a particular manner. In the same way, the two bodies don't have anything particular about them in terms of class, ethnicity, race, et cetera, except for the fact they are both inhabiting the vehicle: "sin que ello tenga de extraordinario, van una mujer, como muchas otras, y un hombre, como tantos otros [without it being something extraordinary, there goes a woman as many others, and a man as many others]" (337). The couple become Everyman and Everywoman, whose only characterizing trait is their relation to technology and an urbanized Mexico City as a space connected by streets and wheels, and bodies. What matters in the story is the use of desire and technology.

As Everyman, the male protagonist is characterized as timid, speaking in a low voice and complying with the norms of a proper middle-class moderate masculinity, far from the idealized and violent variations of mestizo masculinity. Visually assembled on the walls of muralism painting "the masses as symbol into the new nationalist rhetoric while at the same time undermining their real political effectiveness and subordinating them to the centralized state" (Adéle Greeley 18), this masculinity anchored in an idealization of labor, violence, and virility was embraced by the revolutionary state apparatus as the epitome of manhood, further textualized in the fighters that appear in the *novelas de la revolución*, the novelistic genre that ended up becoming the national paradigm. Mariano Azuel's *Los de abajo* (*The Underdogs*) is perhaps the most salient example, but the Estridentista narratives also fit within this paradigm as their public persona was grounded in their ability to penetrate the city and perform public acts of disruption, while their male protagonists did the same with women's bodies. In the same way, the creative representations in muralism where revolutionary peasants populate the walls of institutional buildings are reflected in the painters' public personas, from Diego Rivera to David Alfaro Siquieros and Dr. Atls, whose fame for carrying their revolvers and shooting at each other in political/artistic debates was legendary. Contrary to this virile and violent masculinity, Bonifant's man "mira a hurtadillas y se asusta cada vez que los movimientos del coche lo hacen tocar con su brazo el de la mujer [looks stealthily and gets frightened every time the car's movements make him touch the woman's arm]" (338). However, this man is not exactly a *fifí* or a *pollo* (an effeminate middle-/upper-class man, seen as weak and/ or homosexual); rather, he's simply an alternative model for the male citizen also learning to navigate and inhabit this urban modernity, and he does so by taking advantage of the technology available to him. The man and the automobile become one and change each other in doing so. For Rosi Braidotti, the machine-body is "yet another figuration for the non-unitary nature of the subject. The 'machine-like' part merely refers to the subject's capacity for multiple, outward-bound interrelation with a number of external forces or others" (*Metamorphoses* 254). Thus, this man engages the machine, and the machine engages back in its movements, and so the couple in the speeding of the vehicle and each other cease to be isolated man/woman, as well as the triumphant and reproductive couple that will populate the nation by navigating *vacilópolis*. They become with the vehicle itself, participating in a sensual erotic encounter and assembling as a union between human and technology, contained within the closed "womb" of the vehicle itself.

Just as technology reshapes and transforms the bodies that engage it, technology is itself transformed by these interactions with (non)human bodies, its existence taking on other meanings, uses and circulations (Grosz, *Space, Time and Perversion* 92). Thus, the automobile — which Estridentista artists had already used in avant-garde stunts in the port city of Veracruz during their inhabiting and assembling of *Estridentopolis*, appearing in their texts and poems as symbols of modernity, speed, and a new appreciation for masculinized urban space — becomes a medium/space in which to perform alternative sexual behaviors, constructing dissenting *mestizo* bodies. It is important to underscore here how this sexual automobile is not driven by the man in the dynamic; the dominance over the machine thatwould exemplify his own prowess and virility (as in the automobile culture of the United States) is discarded as the vehicle is driven by an anonymous chauffeur. For Bonifant, what matters is *how* the technology potentializes specific actions and agency, particularly in relation to female bodies; it's less about who is using the technology and more about other bodies emerging.

The woman in the vehicle is aware of her own erotic desire pushing her body — shaped by fashion and style — more toward autonomy, and she thus uses the automobile in a symbiotic alliance where both end up resignified, breaking the sociosexual codes of conduct and taking her male companion with her. As Esther Gabara signals in relation to Tina Modotti, Nahui Olin, and other women who drove vehicles in these years, "the threat of women taking control of the vehicle that represents their sexuality is that they might be able to *manejar* (drive) their own desires in the open streets" (177). Even though she is not driving, the female protagonist shows more ease in the bumps and swerves of the vehicle, already assembling with the machine and using its physical movements in order to culturally produce a model of a female body that a reader can consume, understand, and emulate; without anthropomorphizing the artifact or technologizing the body in a cyborg metaphor, Bonifant presents sexual urban and national bodies as sites of "political, cultural and geographical inscriptions, productions, or constitutions" (Grosz, *Volatile Bodies* 23). As the afternoon continues in the car, where they spend more than four hours, the couple becomes more and more engrossed in each other's bodies, until the end when another car cuts in front of theirs and provokes them into an embrace with the moral of "todos los hombres tímidos deberían hacer el amor en automóvil [all timid men should make love inside an automobile]" (340). The automobile, that "vehicle of choice to map women's physical and social mobility onto an increasingly sexualized urban landscape" (Sluis, *Deco Body* 167), becomes the disruptive force and space where these timid citizens of a novel urban nation can construct subjectivity.[40]

After 1927, Cube Bonifant took up the pseudonym Luz Alba and dedicated herself mostly to chronicling and reviewing Mexico's nascent film industry as a professional film critic, a job she held for several decades. As Viviane Mahieux has documented in her archival recovery, Bonifant's acrid critiques of gender roles became precise critical accounts of cinema as an art, a profession, and an industry, strengthening what would become the greatest entertainment industry of Latin America for some time. However, Bonifant's early texts written in the context of a barely institutionalized Mexico reveal a critical engagement with technology as a fact/tool of modern life and not as a symbol. Akin to Tina Modotti's photographs, who uses the camera and the physical advantages of the device in order to generate a new way to look at the world, Bonifant seeks to show how much technology — especially that associated with (male) revolutionary modernity, such as the automobile that politicians and generals drove — is shaping, determining, and defining the possibilities of alternative behavior for male and female citizens.[41] Alongside the earlier chronicles, she constructs female bodies that are more than *flappers* or *pelonas*, for their sexual potential is underscored alongside their agency and will to mobilize this potential: bodies reshaped in fashion and form as well as in desire, intelligence, and will.

Nahui Olin: A Poetic Erotics of Female Desire

In these same early decades, other female cultural producers were exploring in more direct terms and depth the political power of female sexual desire in the economy of gender, particularly in the visual expressions where state nationalism was institutionally developing. Nahui Olin, photographer Tina Modotti, patronness Antonieta Rivas Mercado, painter Frida Kahlo, dancer/writer Nellie Campobello, and many others were integral components of the male-dominated artistic sphere of muralists, poets, and playwrights. In documenting and reconfiguring these women as important female producers in the early cultural mapping of modern Mexico, Tatiana Flores signals how "their strategies included critiquing dominant avant-garde models, experimenting with diverse media that challenged the parameters of high art, employing pedagogy and activism as a means to effect social and cultural changes, and asserting the relevance of art that engaged personal experience" (12). Complimenting the approach developed by Jean Franco in her foundational *Plotting Women* where (self)destruction is the most accessible route for women when engaging the dominant order, I want to follow Flores in approaching these women as they portray a fluid femininity that resists the processes of *mestizo* nationalism in dissenting and productive terms. For example, the images of corn, sombreros, *carabineras* [bullet belts], rifles, and (female) peasants in Modotti's photographs become ways to counter the institutional visual narratives placing women in subordinate positions, while the short stories of Campobello counter the revolutionary culture emerging from the normative male-centered literary spheres, particularly in the essentialist equation between virility, violence, and masculinity. What is shared in these artists is an enriching approach to *mestizo* nationalism that embraces some elements of modernity and rejects others, incorporating citizens through their desire-driven bodies.

Carmen Mondragón was born in 1893 to a prominent military family of the Porfiriato, her father General Manuel Mondragón was the inventor of the Mondragón rifle used by German armed forces in World War I and the Mexican military during the revolution.[42] Nahui Olin was reborn in 1922 under her chosen Nahuatl name roughly meaning "fourth movement of the sun" or "four movements," the renewing force of the universe.[43] Back in Mexico City in 1921 after a period of exile in Spain, she met Gerardo Murillo, aka Dr. Atl (1875–1964), an older member of the muralist generation specializing in volcanoes and other imposing elements of the Mexican *camposcape*. Their infamous and torrid love affair, which ended in 1925, allowed for Nahui Olin's direct engagement and participation with the greater cultural sphere of the decade, particularly the visual arts. On the negative side, for many decades it caused her own creative work to be read mostly — if not exclusively — in light of her relationship with this muralist and volcanologist.[44] From 1923 onward, she worked as a teacher of drawing and manual arts in the Department of Fine Arts of the Secretariat of Public Education, a job title she held until her death in

1978. Though she published five books and showed her work in Barcelona and several locations in Mexico City such as the Palacio de Bellas Artes in Mexico City and the Galería del Bosque de Chapultepec, for decades her work was considered a footnote under the entry of her romantic and sexual relationship with Dr. Atl and other muralists. Recently, scholarship has shifted to approach Nahui Olin as a central female cultural producer in the midst of a whole collection of male artists, some of whom saw her exclusively as a model (Diego Rivera, Jean Charlot, Edward Weston), and others who saw her as a savior (David Alfaro Siqueiros).[45] Following the monographs by Patricia Rosas Lopátegui, Adriana Malvido, and Felipe Sánchez Reyes, a recent museum exhibition curated by Tomás Zurián Ugarte was held in Mexico City's Museo Nacional de Arte (July to September 2018), where Olin's visual oeuvre was displayed and reconstructed as a central character in the construction of Mexico during the 1920s as well as a woman who challenged the many normativities experienced by women in Mexico.

While I understand that by introducing her in relation to the muralists and other *mestizo* intellectuals I am reiterating her position as relational in a network of male figures, I want to underscore what will become visible in the textual analysis as Nahui Olin mobilizes these connections between her body and men in order to make visible a series of instances of control over her own body and female bodies by extension. At the same time, in her poems and paintings. Nahui generates strategies of disruption and resistance anchored in her embodied subjectivity as expressed in her liberated sexuality. The grand narrative of Mexican muralism demanded that she remain anonymous while being literally painted onto the nation in many of Rivera's murals as a muse and model.[46] Though cultural history has taken this image of Nahui Olin as silent subject and compliant female citizen of the new nation, the artist herself carried out a series of performances, photographic exhibits, and writing ventures where she takes control of her own body as a material and social construct to be wielded against patriarchal/heteronormative structures, as well as intercorporeally assembles alternative models of modern Mexican citizenship for women and men. As art historian María Cecilia Rosales points out, Nahui disrobed her body and seeks to divest her subjectivity from class and gender prejudices to gain access to sexual pleasure and, most importantly, to the erotic pleasure of self-representation (4). In her artistic career, Nahui appears as an erotic agent intervening on the nation, her painting and photographs and texts subjectivizing herself onto the Mexican city/nationscape and generating figures of erotic *mestizas*.

Nahui Olin self-constructs herself as a woman in charge of her own destiny, but most importantly as a citizen who responds to the challenges of urban life without appealing to male protection. Elena Poniatowska has referred to her as the first woman in postrevolutionary modernity to see herself as "mujer-cuerpo, mujer-cántaro, mujer-ánfora [woman-body, woman-pitcher, woman-amphora]" (63). Like Tina Modotti in her rejection of being categorized as a female artist, Nahui Olin sees herself foremost as a body with the right to occupy the nation, and from that point she begins to explore her gender and map the contours of her subjectivity. Perhaps the most poignant example of this self-construction process is the photo exhibition Olin organized from September 20 to 30, 1927, on the rooftop of her apartment at 5 de Febrero No.18. in downtown Mexico City. Hiring her photographer and collaborator Antonio Garduño to take a series of nudes in studio and location, Olin exhibits the prints on the rooftop itself, overlaying her body onto the city as it is being built and modernized. In the invitation to the opening, Nahui self-fashions herself as a seemingly stereotypical *pelona* of the times while showing a critical awareness of how this Deco body was circulated as a commodity to be consumed by the male gaze. Besides the information of place and time, the small piece of paper has an illustration of Nahui with short hair and her characteristic eyes staring back at the reader. In this way, she anticipates the showcasing of her body on the rooftop, overlayed onto the city itself; rather than being a commodity to be consumed by the gaze and guests, she engages with this consumer by generating a fluid Deco body in invitation, photographic print, and her own embodied presence, a sexual agent of a body that troubles the norms of patriarchy.[47] Similar to Bonifant's self-construction through her short chronicles, Nahui uses the textual-social space of the invitation to assemble her persona, "oscillating between the femme fatale and the misunderstood, alienated woman" (Flores 20) in an act of transgression of both bourgeois and nationalist moral codes; she is self-exhibiting herself as a social and sexual subject in the face of the object of contemplation of the male gaze she is subjected to. She is also mobilizing technology as a feminist tool, hiring and ordering a male figure to use the camera and subverting the male gaze that normatively seeks to place her onto the cityscape as an object of consumption; by ordering Garduño how to take her pictures, and how to compose them onto the cityscape, she is providing a template for social cocreation of alternative modes of viewing, literally exhibiting her image on the rooftops.

Carmen Mondragón became Nahui Olin in 1922 when she lived with Dr. Atl in the old Convento de la Merced. Although the name referenced Nahua language in the same way that *mestizaje* discourse celebrated the ancient and glorious Aztec past, Nahui Olin mobilized the political and gendered significance of her name many times throughout her career, while at the same time distancing herself from a visual or aesthetic *mestizaje*. In her 1927 essay titled "Nahui Olin," she describes herself as a self-generative entity, a body refusing to respond to "las leyes gubernamentales establecidas por estafadores despreciables que a sabiendas que son mentiras las hacen regir con el vulgo al cual todavía le hacen pagar un nombre, un número en el archivo de sus imposiciones criminales [government laws established by despicable swindlers that knowing they are lies enforce them onto the people whom they still force to pay for a name, a number in the archives of their criminal impositions]" (182). Most importantly, the essay refuses the name as a tool for state subjectivation, the way in which a population is transformed from generative bodies into productive subjects through criminalization and inscription in the state's archives.[48] Countering this capture of the body undertaken by the federal register, as well as the symbolic capturing through the discourse of *mestizaje*, Nahui Olin resignifies her name as "la voz de mi fuerza mental y que tiene un sonido que no se puede nombrar sólo gustar profundamente y lo más cercano en palabras a él es NAHUI-OLIN, que es la significación de una rebeldía y superioridad [the voice of my mental strentch and that has a sound that cannot be named only deeply enjoyed and the closest thing in words to it is NAHUI-OLIN, which is the meaning of a rebelliousness and a superiority]" (183). While Nahui Olin emerges from the mediation provided by the *mestizaje* discourse and its early intellectuals idealizing the Aztec past and weaving it into the modern nation, she uses this same name to break with her aristocratic past as well the heteropatriarchal order the modern state is constructing, simultaneously claiming her citizenship in cultural and legal terms in the public registry. More than a catchy nativist claim, Nahui Olin becomes an instance of personal ownership over her own body, assembled now with the potential and force evoked by the philosophical concept without exoticizing her body into a *camposcape* aesthetics.

In the essay, as in her photographic nudes where she uses the artistic medium to push back against the normative male gaze, she underlines the social mechanisms — particularly the name, the signature that generate a subject — that subjectify bodies into citizens, underscoring her own attempts to mobilize the body itself as a productive and assembled entity, choosing rather to embark on a process of becoming, fusing the Indigenous past her name references with a body self-shaped by fashion choices of modernity. In doing so, she generates models of national subjectivity that circulate as examples to other women around her.[49] She recovers the Indigenous past to signal and shape a feminist future, where she becomes "la hacedora de su propia historia, la mujer inteligente y culta que no se somete a los preceptos de los demás, la que hereda el poder de la creación [the maker of her own history, the learned and intelligent woman who does not bow to others' precepts, who inherits the power of creation]" (Rosas Lopátegui 36). Nahui Olin references an earthquake, a seismic movement that signals her body once more as a territory empowered to resist patriarchal structures imposed upon it. Rather than fetishize Indigenous bodies (as Rivera in the mural) or idealize a mythos (as Vasconcelos), Nahui Olin presents an alternative to *mestizo* nationalism based on the idea of revolution, resisting all structures of oppression. In this sense, this places her more in line with Tina Modotti and her own revolutionary use of photography as a medium of representation to counter the strategies of othering and exoticizing in the normative culture being shaped in the Mexican Curios movement, muralism, or the images of Hugo Brehme.

In 1922, Nahui Olin published *Óptica Cerebral. Poemas Dinámicos,* a collection of poetic prose with illustration by Dr. Atl. The initial reception of the book categorized it (and by extension her, as a female artist) as mysterious, exotic, otherworldly, French, and feminine.[50] Read outside of this male-centered dynamic that placed her in the shadow of Dr Atl, the collection stands as a daring textual exploration closer to the Estridentista use of technological and scientific vocabulary to describe the urban female experience. As Mariano Meza Marroquin has pointed out, Nahui Olin's intimate knowledge of scientific vocabulary dates to her time in Spain and her contact with the writings of French astronomer Camille Flammarion, whose texts sparked the early science-fiction writings of the likes of H. G. Wells (41). Her style visually constructs the poem as a journey across the page, the words tracing a path while the use of vocabulary, including words such as *logaritmo, átomo, fibras miscroscópicas, vibración eléctrica, matemáticas, elecromagnetismo, inercia, astros que gravitan en el espacio, galaxias* [logarithm, atom, microscopic fibers, electric vibrations, mathematics, electromagnetism, inertia, stars that gravitate in space, galaxies] and more inscribes her writings, especially when focused on her and other female bodies, as countercultural texts. While the Estridentistas used the vocabulary of technological modernity to characterize their experiences in the urban environments without placing their body onto the technologized landscape itself, Olin goes a step further in describing her own body, its exploration, and its assemblages with other bodies and technologies. In this way, she rejects the construction of a female body as representative/embodiment of "natural" forces that disassociate the female body from the greater social body. Instead, by describing her bodily existence with scientific and technological images that assemble her body coursed with electromagnetic forces and shaped by them, she uses the technologies associated with this urban modernity to reshape herself in processes of becoming, of continuously and constantly reshaping her body and subjectivity as it is transformed in these engagements with technology and other bodies around her.

Rosi Braidotti describes the mixing of linguistic registers and vocabularies as a "process of undoing the illusory stability of fixed identities, bursting open the bubble of ontological security that comes from familiarity with one linguistic site" (*Nomadic Subjects* 43). In the same manner, Olin's texts sever the female body from its normative position as Other, serving to identify and give the illusion of fixed identity to the *mestizo* citizens around her. Counter to the other technologically avant-garde texts of the period where the Estridentistas construct exotic and mysterious female bodies that at the same time represent modernity and the Other —particularly in the short novels of Arqueles Vela — Olin's poems and prose undo these fixed illusions by recognizing and constructing an organic *and* technological body. They undo the illusion of fixedness by describing the body with scientific language that does not gender it, nevertheless herself remaining a female body in her embrace of fashion, haircuts, and "feminine" products of the time. This apparent paradox is signaled by Estridentista scholar Elissa Rashkin, who emphasizes how the Señorita Etc, a central character in Vela's novels, becomes the epitome of modern femininity by being "inseparable from the beauty parlor, the cinema, the hotel, and the café, public spaces that challenge patriarchy's traditional confinement of women to the domestic sphere" (*The Stridentist Movement* 138).[51] Similarly and beyond, as a citizen and not a character, Olin recognizes this consumption as a feminist praxis in moving the body into public spaces and goes beyond it by mobilizing her body in a nude and unclothed manner. Thus, while adopting fashion to modernize herself and reject her aristocratic background as well as the nativist fashion pushed by the immediate cultural milieu, her texts assemble a body that maps her existence onto the city and the universe. As the poems showcase, Olin uses her body to construct models of femininity as representations of techno-citizens in postrevolutionary modernity.

The poem "Ojo-elemento humano" opens with a visual zoom-in that reflects the camera's workings, describing the eye as "agua, elemento — mar, esmeralda abismática, ojos immensos de segundo elemento [water, elements — sea, abysmatic emerald, immense eyes of the second element]" before continuing to "en tu absorvente [*sic*] materia todo lo que abismas lo *intensificas* en densidades verdes y eres el verde ojo desmesuradamente abierto de la tierra, y en tu fuerza asombrosa eres débil [in your absorbing matter everything you abysm you intensify in green densities and you are the green eye disproportionately open to earth, and in your astonishing strength you are weak]" (69). [52] The green eyes that characterize Nahui Olin and reappear in her own paintings as well as in depictions by others now become the depository of intensifying cosmic powers, a body (part) at once liquid and earthy. This human element becomes "potencia, luz, *penetración* más rápida de la distancia, *perforación* de rayos luminosos en todas las cosas; *emanación* de colores intensificados en lo que somos [potency, light, most speedy penetration of distance, perforation of luminous rays in every thing; emanation of intensified colors in what we are]" (69). A metonym for the entire body, the eye can penetrate and pierce the world around it at the same time it is penetrated by light itself. An eye that is at once receptive and expansive becomes a way to understand the body, particularly the sexualized and sexual body that can be penetrated as much as it can penetrate the city and move through streets, stores, and plazas. It is a body that can thus be shaped by ideology as much as it can become an artistic creator that challenges and reshapes societal norms.

Ultimately, the poem anchors this cosmic green eye that is Nahui and embodies it in bodies in plural, now charged with the potentiality of light and color, "infinito que buscamos — estás en nosotros mismos [infinity that we search — you are in our selves]" (70). While springing from a personal and individual body, this poem and the collection present bodies as continuums, collectively embodying cosmic and social life even if it is still an individual body. As Rosales signals when studying Olin's pictorial works, the eye is emblematic of the creative power of the cosmos (the individual who orders the world through sight) and as a vehicle for (self)knowledge (88). A known metaphor for the growing technological presence of the camera, the eye as defined by Olin is different in its hinged nature, both looking at and creating with, penetrated by light and emanating colors (and the social order that categorizes color and other natural differences). For Grosz the body is the hinge between the inside and outside of human experience; similarly, for Olin the eye is an active agent shaping the world while being a spectacle to be consumed by the male gaze. Deco bodies were being increasingly commodified as sexual objects as the decade advanced with market and institutional solidification, criminalizing and creating underground sex markets while negating and silencing the history of sexual liberation and civic engagements that sprung out of this female-dominated labor and cultural milieu. Dialoguing with this process, Olin presents her own green eyes, as powerful as "el sol de todos los sistemas solares [the sun of every solar system]" (69), shining across time and space in a way that marks them as subjects impacting the world around her, as much as the world is constructing her as an object.

In another poem, titled "La eternidad creada por la magnitud del espíritu," Olin approaches the esoteric concepts of eternity and spiritual existence and reassembled them with scientific categorizations: "choques cerebrales cargados unos de electricidad positiva y otros de negativa, que intensificados en nuestro espíritu son aumentados cada vez que reproducimos la vibración y sensación transmitida a la materia en luz refleja [cerebral shocks charged some with positive electricity and some with negative, that are intensified in our spirit and augmented every time we reproduce the vibration and sensations transmitted to matter reflected in light]" (95). Bodies cease to be either a collection of fleshy substance or the repository for spiritual essence and rather become "motores agotados . . . aparato transmisor de telegráficas y completas vibraciones [tired motors . . . transmitter apparatuses of telegraphic and complete vibrations]" (96). The poems trace a map of spiritual, biological, and technological existence onto bodies themselves; a machine-body that emerges as the skin is laid naked onto the cosmos itself, reconceptualizing it as the body breaks from social structures of gender, sexuality, political ideology, and more. In this way, Olin's poetry explores the implications of technological modernity on the individual and social self, as Manuel Maples Arce had done before in his poetry *Andamios interiors* (1922) and *Vrbe. Super-poema bolchevique en 5 cantos* (1924). However, Olin directs the critical attentions toward a specifically female body, and more specifically the urban female bodies she saw and embodied herself. For Maples Arce, the image of construction scaffoldings becomes a metaphor to understand the interiority of the avant-garde subject as a work in progress needing support from machinic structures. For Nahui Olin, scientific vocabulary is subverted, particularly as a key discourse of a male-centered modernity and used to promote a machinic Deco body composed of motors, transmission, green eyes, short hair, and painted lips. Relationally assembled with technological objects and discourses around her, Olin's poems emphasize distinct and unique body parts and redefines them as *also* motors and transmitters of electrical currents. The fertility that *mestizo* nationalism imposes through the association of the female body with the idyllic *campo* is transformed into a productivity that marks this machinic body as it interacts with the space around it.

This relational subjectivity emerges as an answer to the harsh critique of essentialist approaches to gender and sexuality that coalesces particularly in the poem "El cáncer que nos roba vida [The cancer that steals life from us]," which opens with "el cáncer de nuestra carne que oprime nuestro espíritu sin restarle fuerza, es el cancer famoso con que nacemos — estigma de mujer [the cancer of our flesh that oppresses our spirit without dimishing strength, is the famous cancer with which we are born — stigma of woman]" (103). Using medical vocabulary, particularly the language of pathology and infectious diseases that was circulating more in the wake of the 1918 influenza pandemic, Nahui Olin signals the embodied oppression that women experience. The subject of the stigma becomes thus women in plural, oppressed and yet not powerless, only held down by the "microbio que nos roba vida [que] proviene de leyes prostituidas de poderes legislativos, de poderes religiosos, de poderes paternos [microbe that steals life from us that comes from prostituted laws of legislative powers, religious powers, paternal powers]" (103). Institutional heteronormativity and patriarchy are clearly linked in a chain of sexualization/prostitution that ties state, church, and family under the powerful yet contagious phallus. The female body subjected to this order is equated to "flores de belleza frágil, sin savia, cultivadas en cuidados prados para ser transplantadas en macetas inverosímiles [flowers of fragile beauty, without sap, cultivated in manicured prairies to be transplanted into implausible pots]" (103), flowers shaped by political, social, and religious constraints — above all, flowers *contained* in a certain space (the flowerpot, the home, the position of the female citizen disempowered from the state through rights). This containment is key in Olin's poem, since it underlines how "el problema de la educación se yergue para crear la fuerza que ha de sostener a seres enfermos del cáncer que roba vida [the problem of education rises to create a force that must support beings sick from the cancer that steals life]" (105), where the female body holds potentiality unable to be seen within the pot.

This poem serves to understand the paradox that critics have signaled in Nahui Olin's reproduction of normative discourse of female sexual expression and a gendered society. While the image of women as flowers borders on being stereotypical and cliché, the poem takes care to place these flowers in pots, emphasizing their trapped existence and pointing at women caught within the ideals of femininity as isolated from a greater ecology. Thus, the poem collectivizes her own personal experience as plural and shared by other women. This collectivity of female bodies allows for a break from the normative representation made by art critics of Nahui herself, isolating her and attaching her only to Dr. Atl, and reestablishes her in a continuum with other women who "luchan y lucharán con la sola omnipotencia de su espíritu que se impondrá por la sola conciencia de su libertad [fight and will fight with the sole omnipotence of their spirit that will impose itself by the mere conscience of its freedom]"

(105). The flower, a symbol of purity and innocence tied to patriarchal power stuctures as in the term "to deflower/*desflorar*," becomes a vegetable body as an image that describes contemporary urban female bodies, transforming society into a complex ecology ripe with potentiality; on the one hand, social structures become government institutions dictating positions and possibilities of (female) bodies, while on the other hand, the erotic female body can counter this sexualization/objectification by connecting with other bodies. This collectivization of the female experience is also a hinge, hinting at the outer experiences shared by bodies marked as female as much as by the inner experiences of their shared embodied existence.

Closing Thoughts

While the roaring twenties reshaped gender politics across the Western world — from Magnus Hirschfield's Weimar Republic sexual and gender paradise, to the *flappers* of the US, to the female workers of the Soviet Union — Mexico's *pelonas* and *flappers* transformed the urban nightlife and the city's public spaces with their daring challenges of normative femininity and cheeky reworking of *mestizo* nationalist ideology and visuality. Although quickly commodified by a nascent entertainment industry that captured their potentially transgressive Deco bodies as cyborgian assemblages of flesh, machine, and energies and redefined them as objects to be consumed by the male gaze, the traces of popular culture that remain signal the ever-present and ephemeral dislocations where alternative social orders emerge, mediated by pleasure, joy, and mischief. Countercultural bodies come together in these spaces of entertainment (culture mediated by market) populated by the urban intellectuals, *Vacilópolis*, that urban nightlife exploding after the violence of the revolution and the expanding global markets, briefly existing before the institutionalization of the *camposcape* and other *mestizo* imagery that solidified gendered social roles in film, literature, and popular culture. The eruption of *pelonas* and *bataclaneras* provided alternative modes of femininity, and their rapid sexualization captured these countercultural bodies into strictly objectified positions; in a similar way, normative national culture equated consumption with femininity, thus establishing a measure to police both male and female behavior vis-à-vis the nation.

Countering this cultural ordering, Cube Bonifant and Nahui Olin's texts present and construct female bodies visualized not as depositories for Indigenous roots (that is, Rivera and Vasconcelos's *mestizo* nationalism), nor as simply symbols of technological modernity (that is, Arqueles Vela's short novels and the use of the Deco body in art and advertising), but as assemblages that are "affectively troubling — generating affective confusion and interdeterminancy — in terms of ontology, tactility and the combination of organic and nonorganic matter" (Puar xxvii).[53] By textualizing, drawing, and photographing their social and sexual agency, these two artists assemble countercultural bodies grounded in the social milieu of the new *mestizo* citizens (the modern habits of consumption for Cube Bonifant and the link to an Indigenous past for Nahui Olin) while extending their futurity as women beyond the limits of heteronormative capitalism/nationalism.[54] Countering and complimenting the Vasconcelian notion of cosmic race grounded in the reproductive function of femininity as the biological carrier of the mixed-race *mestizo* body, these two women present sexual bodies who recognize *and* reject their reproductive function as the *sole* function they place in the creation of a new nation, refusing to be mothers while remaining connected to the women around them. They demand to be counted as citizens fully authorized to participate in the definition of the new nation, especially if this means breaking the limits of the ideal *mestizo* national subjects established by state and market institutions.[55] I use citizens here to underline how the use of national subjects, visually constructed in the murals and other cultural manifestations, may reproduce the ethnic, sexual, racial, gendered, linguistic, et cetera, limits intrinsic to the very process of subjectivity in the history of modernity/coloniality. It is my hope that by understanding the cultural agency and representation of these women in the 1920s through the ideas of the citizenship they claim and mobilize and the bodies they weave into the nascent nation, we can better comprehend and grapple with the multiple and multifaceted understandings of national identities that today push the limits of Mexicanness/*mexicanidad*.

Chapter 2

Neobaroque Bodies and Same-Sex Desires

Anal Politics of Salvador Novo and Abigael Bohórquez

"the bottom—who comes to stand in as
the embodiment of anal penetration—
becomes the object onto which national
and collective anxieties are projected and performed."

— (Xiomara Verenice Cervantes-Gómez 337)

Mexico City, 1930s: Parque La Alameda

The sun is setting on the horizon and the last rays shine on the people walking on the paths of the central city park. Secretaries and typists swish their skirts and click their heels as they head home, while bankers and bureaucrats take a shortcut to their favorite *carpa* to revel in the nightly entertainment. Soon, the park will be dark and lit only by the faint glow of the lamps, shadows falling on the bushes and hedges around the trees. Men will start walking the park then, slowly strolling on the paths and keeping a watchful eye for each other. The buses on the busy streets finish their daily rounds and the mechanics, *chafiretes* (bus drivers), and errand boys have started to head home, though a few of them amble toward the park, perhaps for a shortcut or for another kind of stroll. As the night progresses, the shadows in the park begin to take on shapes in the darkness, vaguely human forms disappearing and melding into the bushes. If one were to walk into the Alameda paths (or the paths of many urban parks then and now) and listen attentively, one might hear the quiet moans and rustle of leaves as men masturbate together or perhaps engage in other more explicit sexual activities, such as oral sex or even penetration. For those men who knew about these pathways and these circuits of pleasure, the Alameda was an ideal and central spot to find other men looking for pleasure. Parks, public restrooms, quiet alleys, and public plazas have served as these cruising territories for centuries, spaces where men have engaged each other in sexual activities right under the nose of the violently homophobic social order that would punish them, sometimes severely.[1] Pleasure is a great motivator for political resistance.

Somewhere in rural Mexico, 1940s. A moonlit *campo*.

The two men first saw each other a few days ago when the newcomer landed the caretaking job to watch over the cattle after some recent attacks; no one could figure out if it was a stray wolf or mountain lion or by a band of highwaymen. Tonight, he was to post guard over the herd in case anything happened. He had been quietly smoking and reminiscing about his hometown, remembering his teenage escapades, when he was suddenly startled by the quiet footsteps of the other young man, another farmworker from town. He greeted the first man and approached softly in the moonlit darkness. The two men sat side by side on the rock outcropping overlooking the herd after a quiet greeting, the first one offering a cigarette to the second as they sat and smoked; their hands resting on the rock slowly inched closer to each other until they touched, suddenly dropping their inhibitions to kiss each other, caressing their bodies as they engage in passionate and consensual sexual activities. Their moans and grunts mark their mutual pleasure as they switch roles throughout the encounter. When they finish and recover their breath, they both look over into each other's eyes and reiterate how this will remain *acá entre nos* (just between us), a moment of *cotorreo* and *vaquetonadas* (mischief) that will remain unspoken in the greater world and celebrated in each other's memories and bodies as they go on with their daily activities and wait for another night to find each other in the quiet *campo*, away from the watchful eyes of the other men in town.[2]

Although based on oral histories and material archives that document the various sexual practices of men within Mexican history, both of these vignettes are completely fabricated by me and based as well on my own personal experience navigating contemporary sexualscapes in Mexico. I bring them forward now as fictional though not fully untrue accounts of what may been a moment, a practice, and a culture that existed alongside *machista* normativity to better understand how sexual practices have shaped spaces and bodies. With the full political and economic installment of the postrevolutionary state apparatus and the promotion of mestizo racial ideologies as defining the newly nationalized and increasingly urbanized population, male bodies that had previously been excluded, ridiculed, or downtrodden in the earlier socioeconomic and political regimes had a chance to gain a foothold in the new nation. Their entrance into the nation marked a bodily passage into the nationalist discourses and images promoted by the state and allied institutions. Modernity manifested itself in the assemblages between bodies and machines in service of the nation's development; chauffeurs, mechanics, bus drivers, urban workers, savvy hacienda managers, and engineers all labored in developing the urban and rural land-scape. In the same breath, these (male) bodies had to negotiate their entry into the nation by denouncing, denying, and rejecting sexual acts that were increas-ingly tied to the construction of sociosexual identities; as sodomy (an act) gave way to homosexuality (an identity), male-identified bodies navigated an urban landscape where their actions were scrutinized, symbolized, and ultimately tex-tualized in the efforts of marking (and breaking) the limits of the mestizo nation. In the aftermath of the debates on virility and nation that buzzed in the cultural spheres of the 1920s and 1930s, homosexuality gradually became a solidified social identity as the term circulated more and more in medical and crimino-logical discourse. Although it was the publication of Luis Zapata's novel *El vampiro de la colonia Roma* (*The vampire of the colonia Roma*) in 1979 that completely broke the cultural silence and fully placed homosexual Mexican men in the cultural landscape after their eruption onto the public stage with the marches of that same year, the close relationship between homosexual desire and nationalism is deeply embedded in the mestizo complex, albeit repressed.

In this chapter, I focus on the autobiographical writings of Salvador Novo and a theatrical work by Abigael Bohórquez, both informed by their poetical writings and their biographies as openly homosexual northerners who moved to Mexico City early in their lives, one to escape the revolutionary violence in the state of Coahuila and the other to escape the heteronormative physical and symbolic violence coalescing in the wake of the revolution in the state of Sonora. In approaching their textual and theatrical representations of male and masculine bodies, both their own and others, I propose a re-understanding of their work as countercultural and not simply homosexual: first, because their representations counter the dominant cultural and sexual political nature of the emerging *mestizo* nation that promotes a single and normative understanding of male bodies; and second and most importantly, because their representa-tions are characterized by movement and action (in the sense that they depend either on specific actions remembered and written or specific actions meant to be staged and embodied), and it is through their actions that a homosexual poli-tics and ethics emerges in solidarity with other bodies rejected from the *mestizo* nation: lower-class Brown bodies, Indigenous peoples, women and feminized citizens, and foreigners. The explicit and dissident sexual acts of the queer bodies analyzed below — autobiographical, theatrical, and poetic — directly answer to the hegemonic urban and rural *mestizo* bodies being assembled under masculinity in *the novelas de la Revolución*; the films of the Golden Age with stars like Pedro Infante, Jorge Negrete, Pedro Armendáriz, and even Cantinflas; and the growing market increasingly subjectifying male citizens into proper consumers.

The sexual bodies of men in Novo's autobiography, *La estatua de sal* (*The pillar of salt*) (written in 1945, published first in 1998), and Bohórquez's *La madrugada del centauro* (*The centaur's dawn*) (1964) reimagine how national bodies take shape, generating their own assemblages of national masculinity that erode, redefine, and expand the constraints of the *mestizo* state. These countercultural bodies re-create masculinity by inflecting its assemblages with sexuality, race, ethnicity, class, religion, cultural, and linguistic backgrounds, historicizing their flesh and shaping the (homo)sexualized histories of the nation.[3] In this way, homosexual citizens are woven into the fabric of the nation through their bodies, their work/labor/livelihood, their language (particularly spoken word), their clothing, and their bodies as interrelational entities. Rather than adjusting their bodies to the hegemonic norms of biopolitical behavior and control — visually depicted in mural and film, literarily described in novels and architecturally defined in new public baths and hygiene campaigns — these countercultural citizens mobilize their dissident sexuality in the face of criminalizing and medicalizing discourses, particularly in the consumption nexus where nationalist normativity and capitalist subjectification came together (the streetcar, theater as genre and stage, popular music). In chapter one, the women of Cube Bonifant's characters, the *carpas* and cabarets, and Nahui Olin all mobilized their sexual bodies in the face of the sexualized objects that *mestizo* normativity was enforcing on female normativity through the virgin-whore dichotomy. Here, homosexual men use their corporal existence and their dissident desires to defy the active-passive binary used to reiterate patriarchal normativity as well as to defy the macho-sissy binary used to categorize homosexual identity and contain sociopolitical dissidence.

Since it is crucial to recognize the pitfalls of homosexuality understood as an identity, particularly while focusing on male-male (and other dissident) desire as integral to countercultural bodies, it is helpful to remember the close relationship between biopolitical, criminological, and homophobic discourses in the construction of homosexual identities, as Siobhan McManus has signaled in her critically important historical work. Homosexual desire is to be understood as different from homosexuality understood as identity. Building on the work of Robert Mckee Irwin and Robert Buffington, particularly their readings of the 1901 scandal of the 41 and the concurrent class conflict mediatized in homosexual bodies, this chapter approaches homosexual desire by focusing on the textualized acts themselves and how they function in relation to nationalist discourse.[4] Focusing on an embodied sexual desire, particularly anal pleasure, allows for a respite from both identitarian approaches and more troublesome criminological/biopolitical discourses that so easily capture bodies into neat categories and identities.[5] Furthermore, this approach opens up understandings of sexuality and sexual acts that do not fall within an exclusively symbolic reading, as in the passive-active dichotomy that structures the so-called Mediterranean complex in the general Hispanic world, or in Octavio Paz's theorization of sex as violent rape in the concrete case of Mexico.[6] When anal pleasure is foregrounded, the sexual act becomes a corporeally productive moment where the relations between bodies generate assemblages that remain beyond the act, constantly resisting the oppression of the normative sex-gender system.

Thus, I approach homosexuality here by focusing on the textualized and re-presented (homo)sexual acts themselves, informed by the writings of Félix Guattari and Guy Hocquenghem, particularly their collaborations in the journal *Trois milliards de pervers: Grande enciclopédie des homosexualities* (1973).[7] This will allow me first to bring forward the bodily manifestations of an expressed sexuality assembled through moments of pleasure, as opposed to the moments of danger that mark criminal or prohibited acts. Approaching these moments of pleasure creatively counterpoints the violently limiting power of identity, particularly in the service of medical and criminal discourses mobilized in this time period to identify, categorize, and institutionalize (sexual) bodies. Second and most importantly, these textual, poetic, and theatrical sexual acts tend to be messy, overflowing with bodily fluids as much as with desire and pleasure, unable to be contained in discrete bodies neatly separated into symbolic categories. Pleasure, and particularly the anal pleasure of penetration, resists the exclusively symbolic understanding of sexuality that popular culture as well as academia use in their approach to Mexican homosexuality have historically constructed and reified; that is, the passive-active dichotomy present in the Mediterranean scheme of sexuality or in Octavio Paz's theorization of sex as violent rape.

In the wake of the global sexual liberation movements that solidified in the 1960s and 1970s, Guattari and Hocquenhem turn their attention to the relations between sexuality and capitalism. Their writings illuminate the (homo)sexual nuances of the countercultural bodies as I have been tracing them previously, as they are motivated by an urgent revolutionary desire toward action, since "we can no longer sit idly by as others steal our mouths, our anuses, our genitals, our nerves, our guts, our arteries, in order to fashion parts and works in an ignoble mechanism of production which links capital, exploitation, and the family" (Guattari, "To have done away with the massacre of the body" 209). Countercultural bodies assemble their corporeal liberations through sex and pleasure with psychic, embodied, and ideological liberations. In the current (homo)normative realities lived by Mexican cultures on both sides of the border where the capturing of desire emerges from the political-economic-symbolic structure of the binary (civilization/barbarie, macho/chingada, top/bottom, *activo/pasivo*), tracing homosexual desires through sexual acts and anal pleasure offers different approaches to the polymorphous diversity of bodies. Defying the binary structuring of their bodies, the histories of homosexual acts in Mexico offer a way to rethink (homosexual) desire in relation to the psychic, economic, and political structures of hetero-capitalism. In critical recognition of the bodies I am writing about and my own corporeality both relationally assembled to flows of capital, nation, and civilization, I am constraining myself to cis-male bodies when approaching (homosexual) desire in this way.[8] This constraint is a political decision to exemplify a particular variant of countercultural bodies through the singularized corporealities in the histories of Mexican homosexual pleasure (full of mayates, chichifos, jotas, jotos, and plenty of *putería*). I do not wish to speak for the realities of trans*, femme, or radically queer Mexican histories, and I can only hope to share with feminist theory a desire to undermine and dismantle patriarchy and its all-too-present structures. I am acutely aware of the ethical implications and consequences when discussing homosexuality *only* through the writings and lives of cis-male citizens, silencing the rich history of two-spirit, trans*, femme, female, and other sexual citizens. Thus, I emphasize that I do not wish to speak for or about all bodies in the LGBTTTQQIAA+ community, but rather reflect on and theorize from my own positionality and a specifically cis-male homosexual homoerotic national history.

This chapter opens with a brief critical historical overview of homosexuality as a criminal and medical category used to describe sexual acts between male-identified bodies to underscore the biopolitical implications of visibility and representation. Following the work of scholars like Héctor Domínguez-Ruvalcaba, Robert McKee Irwin, Robert Buffington, and others, I signal the problematic uses of homosexuality as a social category and bring forward a focus on sexual acts, particularly dissident sexual acts whose representation serves to delineate the limits of normative masculine identities. I then focus on the autobiographical and public writings of Salvador Novo, briefly in his travel journals *Ensayos* and *Continente Vacío* and in the bus drivers and mechanic's newsletter *El Chafirete*, tracing the explicitly described and implicitly alluded sexual trysts as assemblages of pleasure, body, and machines. Finally, I close with an approach to the humanimal intersubjectivities that Abigael Bohórquez stages in *Madrugada del centauro* where homosexuality is theatrically re-presented through an exploration of dissident desires and gender solidarity; this analysis builds on scholarship focused on his poetic oeuvre to explore the queer bodies that Bohórquez stages in dialogue with the intersectional and open homosexual desires his poetry often presents. By approaching homosexuality grounded in this historical, criminological, and medical history, I bring forward an understanding of dissident desires as deeply political engagements that challenge *mestizo* normativity while constructing brief and illusory utopias marked by sexual pleasure, and particularly anal pleasure.

A Brief and Critical Approach to Modern Mexican Homosexualities

While there are records of masculine homosexual acts scattered throughout Mexican history, from the scandalous mentions by the Franciscan monks composing the *codices* in the conquest years to the colonial criminal documents evidencing the persecution of sodomy, homosexuality as an identitarian category was not mobilized until the criminal campaigns of the later Porfirian dictatorship.[9] Sodomy itself as an act of anal penetration was decriminalized in Mexico with the installation of the French penal code during the brief reign of Maximilian I (1864–1867); however, this did not mean that homosexual acts (kissing, groping, penetration, and more) could not be legally and socially punished under the categories of *ataques a la moral y las buenas costumbres* (an attack on morals and good traditions), which the new penal code of 1871 introduced as a measure meant to control foreign and deviant citizens. The historical reappearance of the *ataques a la moral* time and again illustrates the deep connections between sociosexual behavior and national identity; while the French penal code decriminalized a specific sexual act (where the specific bodies at play did not matter as much as what they were doing), the new penal code criminalized social behavior, thus working to transform a sexual act into a body marked as a sociosexual Other. This process reveals one of the often-silenced underpinnings of modernity/coloniality and nation-states in their biopolitical organization: the centrality of the marginal. The deviant citizen, the *invertido* (literally "inverted man," a term used to describe men engaging in homosexual acts or homosocial behavior) is a constitutive part of the modern nation in the sense that the hetero-hegemonic national subject *cannot* be defined except insofar as the "proper" citizen in relation to these margins.[10] This marginality at the constitutive center of *mestizo* modernity is analogous and runs parallel to the processes of sexualization that female bodies experience in the virgin-whore binary; as seen in chapter 1, in order to be considered legitimate citizens, female bodies *must* comply with the hetero norms of the *mestizo* nation and state or be punished. Sexual bodies (male, female, and nonbinary) that mobilize their sexuality outside the strict norms of hetero reproduction are rejected from the nation and thus generate alternative territories as they map their bodies onto the geopolitical landscapes. From this vantage point, the fiction of the *mestizo* citizen demands the textual and cultural existence of these deviant bodies, the *invertidos* who constitute the real material bodies populating the streets that ultimately serve to define the boundaries of the normative structures of the *mestizo* state.[11]

Homosexuals thus existed for decades in the pages of the *nota roja*, the various sensationalist journals and newspapers that focus mostly on physical violence and bloody murder, as well as freak accidents and general natural disasters especially with deadly consequences. Here, "homosexuals" would generally be men having sex with other men and would appear as murderers or victims, sometimes of each other and sometimes of police raids and criminal crackdowns, their life tied to a greater social order united by pleasure and yet marked by violence. The Frente de Liberación Homosexual was established in 1971 and united artists, intellectuals, and students; they published manifestos and public statements about homosexual and lesbian existence. In 1973, the American Psychiatric Association eliminated homosexuality as a disorder in the Diagnostic and Statistical Manual of Mental Disorders, and this major paradigm shift trickled down across medical institutions across the world, including Mexico. In 1979, the first Marcha del Orgullo (Pride Rally or March) happened with around 100 citizens, but by next year that number grew to 5,000, and by 2023 it included over 250,000 people from all over the city, country, and beyond. However, it wasn't until 2007 that the national Codigo Penal punishing "ultrajes a la moral pública y las buenas costumbres [affronts to public morality and good traditions]" was changed to "delitos contra el libre desarrollo de la personalidad [crimes against the free development of personality]," thus impeding the use of legal language to criminalize and punish social identities. In 2006, the Distrito Federal (Mexico City) code changed to tacitly recognize same-sex marriage through an acknowledgment of the Ley de Sociedad de Convivencia, where making a home no matter the gender was enough to merit legal protection as household. In 2009, same-sex marriage itself was explicitly recognized as a right in Mexico City and has since been extended by decree from the Supreme Court to the rest of the country. These and other social changes have not happened in a vacuum, however, and are credited to a long history of academic and public activism, beginning with the Frente de Liberación Homosexual but including many more organizations and individuals. This rich history of activism today includes a series of public government officers from senators, magistrates, and other public representatives, as well as a myriad of organizations that speak to a defiance from society at large to accept the limited and limiting criminalization and pathologization onto their bodies, the diversity of the LGBTTTQQIAA+ is beginning to be truly seen and felt in the modern social fabric.

I want to emphasize in this history how homosexual social identity is thus deeply linked to criminological categorizations of biopolitical control. After the sexual acts themselves were decriminalized in the nineteenth century, sociosexual identities were increasingly assembled with gender performance; while the cross-dressing scandal of the 41 served to make a boundary hyper-explicit, the *paseos* of the *fifís* and dandies (men who took extra care with their physical appearance and clothing usually following the styles emerging from Paris and London in the nineteenth-century tradition of decadent masculinity) served as public performances that skirted around the limits of normative masculinity. With the installment of the postrevolutionary state influence by eugenics and the racial theories circulating globally in the 1920s, homosexuality solidified as a social identity anchored in pathologized bodies in need of medical or criminal attention, as can be seen through the influence of Italian criminologist Cesare Lombroso in the writings of Mexican criminologist Carlos Rougmanac.[12] In the wake of these scandals, effeminacy was assembled with these deviant sexual practices, paradoxically bringing marginal social subjectivities to the forefront of public discourses while erasing other embodied assemblages emerging from sexual acts more than gender performance.[13]

As historians and cultural critics have pointed out, the postrevolutionary state established in the 1920s was founded on the military culture that ended up winning the armed conflict, thus further establishing a strong national homosociality rife with misogyny and homophobia (Domínguez Ruvalcaba 4). While *adelitas* were celebrated as female revolutionaries and memorialized in song and dance, their existence remained tied to the popular armies of Francisco Villa and Emiliano Zapata, not the militaristic armies of Álvaro Obregón or Plutarco Elías Calles that established political, social, and economic order. By the mid-1920s, the cultural discourses around gender and sexuality debating the virility of Mexican literature demonstrated how homophobia and misogyny organized hegemonic male bodies into those authorized to speak *for* the nation and signaling the other bodies that needed to be silenced by any means necessary lest they irrevocably injure the nation. Jean Franco has already signaled how "the problem of national identity was thus presented primarily as a problem of *male* identity, and it was male authors who debated its defects and psychoanalyzed the nation" (131). It is also not simply male authors but rather exclusively heterosexually identified and masculine-performing male bodies who were the writers (and painters and directors) of the nation, particularly by being legitimized as cultural producers authorized to represent this new *mestizo* Mexico. Researchers Siobhan Guerrero McManus and Claudia Schaefer push to historicize this deep intertwining of homophobia as a major force in both the construction of hetero- and homosexual identities in Mexico, examining its transformations and placing cultural texts in this very conflicting context where sexuality, gender, and citizenship must be performed in specific ways.[14] Following Domínguez Ruvalcaba, I understand these representations of homosexual acts historically alongside the male citizens who performed them by placing them in their social, political, religious, and nation-building contexts, since it is these that enable the perception of homosexual bodies as such within the nation as well as the particular meaning of these acts in a great context.

Homosexuality's grand entrance on the national stage began with the infamous scandal of 1941, when police forces raided a private all-men party where half the gatherers were dressed and acting as women while the other half performed their masculine roles. Most of the men were from elite political and economic origins, the most famous of them Ignacio de la Torre, then dictator Porfirio Díaz's son-in-law. Since the official count had the men at 42 but only 41 were sent to the penal colonies of the Yucatán peninsula as punishment, popular culture has ascribed the number 41 as synonymous with homosociosexual deviance. However, given the strong class component of this scandal in the ball as well as its latter commentary in newspapers, engravings, and *corridos*, I want to underline how this public appearance of homosexuality into Mexico's modernity is marked by a silenced intersectionality that conflates this nascent homosexual identity with aspects of class (middle-upper), race (white over Brown), gender performance (man-woman), and sexual positionings (penetrator-penetrated). As McKee Irwin and others (2003) have demonstrated, more than providing a "birth" of homosexuality in the public sphere, this "entrance" serves as proof of the constant negotiations of power that manifest themselves in the public discourses of sexuality and gender: in this particular case, an association of a virile masculinity with lower-working class and Brown bodies and an effeminate masculinity with upper-class and whiter bodies.[15]

Taken as a starting point to begin to understand Mexico's recent history with queerness, the scandal of the 41 is a core moment in the genealogy of homosexuality in Mexico that underscores urbanity as its central component (never mind the thousands of men engaging sexually with other men across the national territory). After the 41 prisoners are shipped off, the next homosexual men to take the cultural and public state are the Contemporáneos, the loose group of writers, painters, and theater producers that included Salvador Novo, Xavier Villaurrutia, Elías Nandino, José Gorostiza, Jorge Cuesta, and others. Pedro Ángel Palou and others have written on how these men founded the literary institutions that ended up generating the autonomous cultural sphere in the new country; nevertheless, their (sometimes not so) private lives served to reinforce the images of homosexual men as urban, cosmopolitan, and, aside from Novo, free from scandal. Homosexuality will then become a social weapon to be wielded against deviants, and it is with the activism of the 1970s that Miguel Capistrán and Luis González de Alba begin their careers as public-facing homosexual activists, alongside writers such as Luis Zapata and José Joaquín Blanco. However, as historian of science Siobhan Guerrero McManus cautions, emphasizing the 41 as the founding moment of this homosexual genealogy is controversial at the least; not only is upper-class cross-dressing woven into the center of a cultural homosexual identity, but there is also a depoliticization that erases *how* the 41 came into the spotlight precisely in order to critique the Porfirian elite's "incompetence to rule life and labor" (247). Silenced are the manifestations of lower-class homosexualities, both rural and urban, and particularly those that defy the binaries of patriarchal modernity. McManus proposes an approach that engages with the nonnormative, lower-class, and rural sexual acts at face value, reactivating their political significance and social positioning in the cultural and national public sphere even when we have only traces and hints of their existence; this approach becomes even more paramount when we consider how the criminalizing discourses were so frequently mobilized against dissident citizens, particularly of the lower and working classes. The archive of the Fototeca Nacional del INAH (National Institute of Anthropology and History) holds a series of photographs, some candid shots and some mugshots, of young men arrested and imprisoned for attacks on morals and good traditions (see figure 2.1). Beyond the criminalization of their existence, we can see in the images a dissident and defiant pose, attitude and clothing that pushes against the *mestizo* heteronorm surrounding them with bricks and bodies, evidencing a communal resilience that looks back into the camera's eye.

Figure 2.1. Homosexual men arrested and detained in a police station. Published with permission from Instituto Nacional de Antropología e Historia.

The criminalization of sociosexual behavior became a stand-in for any deviancy from heteronormative gender and sexual performance; it would legally legitimize multiple *razzias* (police raids) during and after the infamous Mexico City mayor Ernesto Uruchurtu's tenure (better known as the Iron Regent during his time in office from 1952 to 1966). In 1947, homosexuality was a main theme at criminological conferences held at the Supreme Court, where the Cuban criminologist José Agustín Martínez was invited by the former ambassador to Cuba, José Ángel Ceniceros, to lecture on how homosexuality profiled a criminal citizen.[16] Though not directly criminalizing sexual acts themselves, this discourse legitimized treating bodies as hormonally imbalanced and unhealthy, making them prone to criminal behavior and thus promoting their persecution and specific targeting by public authorities as well as the public at large.[17] It is no surprise, then, that homosexual identities take the public sphere on their own terms in the first LGBTTTQQIA+ demonstration and parade in 1978 during a ten-year commemoration of the bloody student massacre at Tlatelolco. After this appearance of organized citizens under the very wide umbrella of lesbian, gay, bisexual, transexual, transvestite, transgender, intersexual, queer, and more identities, their history was marked by a direct opposition to institutions of both law and medicine, demanding (and achieving) legal equality and medical acceptance over the social or familial rights that have come to characterize the pink market of neoliberal culture in the 2000s. Following McManus's call, I want to end this history by underlining how my approach to both Salvador Novo and Abigael Bohórquez seeks to follow the traces of lower-, working-, and middle-class homosexuality in its resilience and defiance; rather than essentializing these two writers as exemplary, I want to highlight their engagements with other men — in pleasure and in dissident desires — as ways of constructing countercultural sexualities that continue to circulate in Mexico's overlooked populations.

In this (too brief) history of Mexican homosexualities, I want to further delineate the distance between homosexual acts and identities by thinking a bit more about the machine of *cruising* (the hookup, *el ligue*, the sexual encounter) as a contemporary machine produced in part by the machinery of capitalism and to underline the importance of its politicization in order to cut the flows and avoid reproducing the sexual politics of hetero-patriarchal capitalism. Thinking from the homosexual politics of the 1970s, Guy Hocquenghem describes how the homosexual encounter (cruising) — particularly when homosexuality was increasingly "tolerated" and sexual activity was moving from being defined as promiscuous toward being seen under the logic of the corporeal consumption of the other, as bell hooks and others have signaled — is a machine that assembles the body into the greater machinery of capitalist accumulation.[18] Nevertheless, homosexual encounters and the Mexican variation of *el ligue* maintain a political potential in their construction of sociosexual relations that move toward an equality and reciprocity founded on mutual pleasure. Luis Felipe Fabre describes Salvador Novo's poetry as part of a radical tradition "that not only originates in the anus and declares as much, but that also *writes with the anus* and resists its sublimation . . . brutal and menacing poetry not sublimated before reaching the mouth, and if it reaches the mouth, the poetry turns it into an anus" (*Writing with Caca* 21).[19] These particular representations of anal pleasure and the pleasures associated with the anus reveal a poetic function pushing back against a normativity that rests on silencing and sublimation. This public reve(a)ling of anal pleasure not as a void, an absence, a hole, or even a grave assembles it as an immensely productive site from which polymorphous desires emerge, prodigal and excessive: desires to desire and desires to be desired.[20]

These desiring bodies are thus characterized by their acts and not mainly their identities, as these are a construction from legal and health institutions that punished their bodies for enacting their desires. The ephemeral nature of these desires interests me, as their enactments become moments of pleasure whose mere existence is already a defiance of the punishment enforced on the body, by being ephemerally traced in neobaroque poetry and oral traditions that hide while revealing a body in pleasure and joy that does not conform to hegemonic codes of masculinity. Thus, I focus on the sensual embodiments of pleasure as acts of countercultural world reconstructions whose ephemeral nature solidifies in the homosexual bodies themselves as they make up city and society. I see them less symbolic than literal textualizations of pleasure and enjoyment that were shared across a homo-nation, at least those who enacted their desire. In this social context, a text like Luis Zapata's *El vampiro de la colonia Roma* (1979) comes to light as a picaresque novel of sociosexual defiance that central-izes homosexual desire and pleasure as a way to understand the main character, a sex worker living in the central colonial Roma. In the face of the criminal and pathological traces of ephemeral homosexual life, fictional accounts such as this and the ones analyzed below serve to glimpse the ways in which (homo) sexual desire was and still is mobilized as a dissident force, a way of resistance, and a way of creative alternative worlds grounded in pleasure.

Consent, Mutual Pleasure, and the (Homo)Sexualization of the Modern City in Salvador Novo

Salvador Novo (1904–1974) was the son of a Galician-Spanish immigrant father and a Zacatecas-born mother. He lived his first years in Mexico City with maternal family, moving to the northern city of Torreon, Coahuila, in 1910 when the revolution hit the capital and social unrest was inevitable; Novo spent his childhood and early teenage years in the desert, receiving private tutoring education while living in a town of roughly 20,000 people. There, his fam-ily experienced the violence characteristic of the revolution, marking Salvador Novo for the rest of his life. His father was a constant target, both as a Spanish immigrant and as a shop owner in a region dominated by land-owning oligarchs and monopolized businesses, several of which came from Novo's maternal side of the family. After his father died in the revolutionary period due to respira-tory health issues, Novo's mother became the head of the household and never remarried. Salvador moved with her back to Mexico City in 1917, enrolling at the Escuela Preparatoria Nacional to finish his studies. He remained in the city the rest of his life and became an important member of the loosely orga-nized Contemporáneos group of poets, playwrights, essayists, and graphic art-ists (many of them men engaging other men sexually) who were the brunt of the debates on virility and nationalism during the 1920s. During these years, the literary sphere was increasingly professionalized in the public sphere, and Novo began his career as a journalist and writer for newspapers and maga-zines from the 1920s to the end of his life, supplementing this income with several government positions that culminated in his becoming the Cronista de la Ciudad (Chronicler of the City) in 1965 and covered his work as the chief of publicity and publications in the Secretaría de Relaciones Exteriores (Foreign Relations Secretariat), the Secretaría de Economía Nacional (National Economy Secretariat), and the Secretaría de Educación Pública (Public

Education Secretariat) at various moments. Influenced by his collaborations with the theater wing of the Contemporáneos in his short-lived but significantly rich project of the *Teatro Ulises* (1927–1929), Novo's later cultural labor gravitated toward work with Carlos Chávez at the Instituto Nacional de Bellas Artes, establishing his own Teatro de la Capilla (founded 1953) on property he owned in the district of Coyoacán in southern Mexico City, where he lived for the remainder of his life.

Novo's biographical movements from city to rural *provincial* and back illustrate the changing (counter)culture of Mexico's early nationalist moments. First, the passage from a Porfirian childhood sheltered in the urban center to a revolutionary early adolescence in the violent countryside to come back for a post-revolutionary adulthood in the growing city provides a roadmap for a particular lettered experience of the material changes happening in the country. Second, the movement from early adolescence in rural spaces to an urban adulthood in the midst of rampant modernity (automobiles, telegraphs, cement, telephones, photographs, et cetera) gives contours to a (homo)sexual subjectivity; not only does Novo gain economic independence by transforming his vast and ever-expanding cultural capital into economic capital at literary and journalistic jobs, but more importantly, he matures (homo)sexually in a developing and ever-more technologized urban space.[21] Writing himself into *crónicas*, poems, opinion pieces, autobiography, travel journals, and scraps of notes, Novo defines his citizenship in modern Mexico by assembling a sexual body, acknowledging a homosexual impulse as an integral drive — a conatus, if you will — and weaves it within the material, literary, and cultural history of Mexico.[22]

Novo's writings evidence a constant contemplation on the material changes shaping Mexico City and the impact of these on his body and his sociosexual subjectivity, and ultimately how he himself can use his body to shape cultural reality around him. From *El Joven* (1923/1928) to *Pillar of Salt* (1943/1998) and the texts in between, Novo (re)assembles urban subjectivities from the very corporeal experience of seeing/gazing, being overwhelmed by storefronts and the "sexy" bodies of muscular bus drivers and mechanics, and speaking the desire through the body's orifices — a visual, sensorial, and pleasurable corporeal experience that in its expression dares to break unspoken sociopolitical norms. Like Cube Bonifant's and Nahui Olin's female freedom in the urbanized space, Novo's subversive actions in the bathhouse, the mechanical shop, the downtown apartment, and the public park are permitted precisely because they engage with technology and relations of consumption. He exemplifies a male-embodied counterpart to their female presence and freedom in modernized spaces since all of their subversive actions are permitted precisely by their engagement with new technology and novel consumption practices. I emphasize here that Novo stands out particularly as a virulent misogynist, in particular attacking women like Bonifant and Olin as liberated female citizens of the 1920s and 1930s, and yet I consider his sociosexual subjectivity countercultural in that it works to liberate a forbidden and criminalized desire through pleasure, textualized in his works through an unmistakable need to desire and feel. Unfixed onto a single object, the desire to desire overwhelms the homosexual bodies populating Novo's texts. I focus on the autobiographical *Pillar of Salt*, a text first documented in 1945 but not published fully until 1998 (Novo himself stipulated that the text could not appear in print until well after his death and that of everyone he wrote about, although he famously shared readings of his autobiography in private gatherings), as well as his very brief but extremely enriching collaboration with the working-class publication *El Chafirete* (1923), a gremial journal dedicated to the rising group of bus drivers, mechanics, ticket boys, and other men who were populating the city and making it move. Similar to Luis Felipe Fabre, I see in Novo's prose a sexual politics that emerges from the body as uncontainable and loud; while I will only briefly touch on his other prose texts such as *Ensayos* (1925) or *Continente Vacío* (1935), I want to underline how the sexual countercultures that Novo is textualizing populate his written life as a whole, even if just in flashes and glimpses. In doing so, he demonstrates a countercultural approach in the sense that he resists imposing a single notion of homosexual culture, working rather to draw lines of class, ethnicity, and racialization and how these mark homosexual bodies as singularized entities in the social ecology. My contribution to the debate on Novo's sexuality engages with Ruben Gallo, Salvador Oropesa, Brian Gollnick, and Robert McKee Irwin by conceptualizing Novo as a sexual citizen bridging social sectors in productive and counterhegemonic ways, subverting nationalisms while paradoxically literally building the nation in his various governmental positions.

I trace Novo's sexual biography less as exemplary or representative and more as intercorporeal assemblages where countercultural homosexual bodies come together through gradually increasing mutual pleasure, a navigation of consent, and ultimately an openness that belies the poetic metaphorization of one's acts. In the face of the subjectification of homosexuality as dandyism or effeminacy (in the upper classes) and criminality or deviance (in the lower classes), Novo's texts erode the normative understandings of homosexual acts by foregrounding a constant and explicit interclass *ligue* as well as sexual acts well outside the heteronormative paradigms of penetration. Pleasure, and especially mutual pleasure (with friends, lovers, or *ligues*), become the trademark of Novo's sexual snippets, and this serves to counterpoint the homonormative structurings that Ramos, Paz, and others so easily reproduce in their sexual politics. Urban consumption (of commodities as much as bodies) becomes sentimental/sexual education, assembling pleasure as a structuring machine of the sexual acts where class contact happens. Thus, Novo's engagement with the discourses that construct bodies — medical, melodramatic, pictorial, psychiatric — first denounce their medicalization and criminalization of homosexual bodies, and second serve to foreground the other strategies for construction of bodies Novo is documenting: bodies on and in machines, the sexual encounters of men (sometimes in plain daylight and public sight), and the mutual pleasure that underlies them all. The lines of class, ethnicity, racialization, and performativity are drawn in order to counterculturally assemble bodies, denying a homosexual culture in favor of homosexual pleasure.

Alongside Fabre's post-identitarian approach to Novo's sexuality, Robert Richmond Ellis's study on Latin American autobiography pushes for a consideration of *Pillar of Salt* "not solely for its affirmation of the homoerotic or because expressions of homoeroticism necessarily challenge heteronormativity, but also insofar as it *focalizes the broader social conditions of gender and sexuality*" (18).[23] These conditions appear ethically nuanced in the text when Novo's body perceives more than what could be named as such. Written in first-person memoir style, *Pillar of Salt* presents Novo's childhood, his sexual awakenings and various initiations, his schooling, and his first explorations of urban life up to his economic independence and the start of his life on his own terms. The text proceeds in temporarily lineal fashion, and yet critics such as Brian Gollnick have been careful to note the anti-Bildungsroman (a genre with which Novo must have been intimately familiar) character of his text; in this way, the autobiography comes closer to the picaresque genre, "emphasizing its hero's inability to assimilate as a critique of societal norms" (Gollnick 239). The sociosexual subjectivity that Novo constructs thus serves as an embodied entry point into the complex networks of men having sex with men, pleasure, and urban spaces. The process of socialization, from the institutional macho emerging from the murals and novels of the revolution to the literal building of the city, are revealed as the effeminate yet courageously sexual body of Novo moves alongside the racialized *mestizo* bodies of these new men.

When writing/speaking/directing about Mexican homosexuality — particularly in historical terms given the centrality of the dance of the 41 in intellectual histories — it is difficult to disentangle the strong connections that have been made between effeminacy and the homosexual body, particularly the dandy and the *fifi* in Mexican history. I anchor *Pillar of Salt*'s analysis in the intersections between performativity, homosexual desire, and homosexual acts, since Novo's self-critical understanding allows for a political nuancing. While never explicitly addressing his effeminate behavior, *Pillar of Salt* does provide ample opportunities for the performativity of gender to be explicitly seen as such, questioned and reevaluated; the text opens with Novo referencing his psychoanalytic readings and self-diagnoses with an "oedipal complex I am too cowardly to fully confront" (*Pillar* 47). The characteristic tongue-in-cheek tone that will mark the rest of the text situates his body as intrinsically sexual-erotic; these opening pages represent a textual self-birth and we see a body always already marked, whose "normal development stunted" (47).[24] His childhood was marked by the way "my mother dressed me with fanatical attention. She adored the curls she combed around my forehead; she made me purse my lips so my mouth would stay small; and, with the same inhibiting objective, she made me always wear shoes that pinched my natural development" (49).Writing in retrospect, it's almost as if the genderfluidity that characterized middle-/upper-class childhood in the late nineteenth and early twentieth centuries made evident for Novo the processes of gender subjectivation through visual performance, makeup, hair styling, shoe size, and lips. Continuing this corporeal subjectification, Novo's uncles would also parade their young nephew's beauty through the streets of Mexico City before they fled to Torreon. These multiple forms of performative, corporeal, and sexual violence are also critically represented by Novo himself, as the text presents complex understandings of gender and sexual desire as socially defined and constructed, while at the same signaling an erotic pleasure that is intrinsic to his body. In this way, his experiences pinpoint how and when his child body experienced gender subjectification, as well as when he first experienced erotic pleasure; psychoanalytic terminology is used here to playfully engage with the language in fashion, self-deprecating himself by participating in the medical institution and then skipping just outside of its bounds by hinting at other moments of erotic pleasure.

In the text, Novo demonstrates an awareness of how gender and sexuality serve to cross class boundaries and construct alliances (even if later in his life he will turn protofascist and classist to the extreme). Narrating his only cross-dressing experiences (that we know of), he says how much

> I liked then to transform myself, to dress like a girl or a woman. I played theatre games at home with the Greek boys [neighbors], and at night I insisted on going with the servant girls on their errands, so as to mix in with the "scruffy ones" who gathered to listen to the songs and *corridos* sung by a blind man who scratched at his guitar by way of accompaniment. It enchanted me to undertake these excursions in the early dark, wearing my mother's shoes, as though to challenge people to discover how I was shod, or invite them to find fault. (*Pillar of Salt* 64)

Playing with the idea of *transformismo* (itself an enriching way to understand gender fluidity outside the sometimes binary structure of gender transitioning), Novo is presenting a homosexual body constructing itself through an alliance of class. It is in these contexts that Novo's sexuality will begin to explore the territory of his own body just as he is wandering the town with the young domestic workers, mixing with the villagers in the darkness and feeling his body erotically charged as he is touched, gazed upon, urinated on, and caressed. His sociosexual subjectivity is anchored in a territory itself territorialized on his own body. For Elizabeth Grosz, the "body is involuntarily marked, but it is also incised through 'voluntary' procedures, lifestyles, and behavior" (*Volatile bodies* 142).[25] Novo takes the markings of gendered childhood with a socially sanctioned effeminacy and moves toward a *transformismo* that blurs the distance between theater and public life, playfully resisting any urge to remain in a single position on the gender spectrum. He wanders his childhood town with servant girls and mixes with the villagers in the darkness, recognizing the possibilities of more open social spaces outside the urbanized and symbolically ordered family house. As Grosz emphasizes, the body is never a blank or neutral entity, but rather is inscribed and marked by the "history and specificity of its existence" (142). Novo recognizes these gendered markings being inscribed onto his body in the childhood moments when cross-dressing was socially sanctioned, while in adulthood cross-dressing could only happen in private and the theater, never in public. This blurriness and instability are marks of countercultural bodies, a playful awareness of gender performativity and erotic desire related to but not equated to sexuality. Previously, Cube Bonifant signaled this playful attitude in her writings on the salon and conversations with herself; side by side, we can observe in Novo's and Bonifant's acts of gendering their bodies on a spectrum a subversion of the gender codes their bodies are subjected to while remaining firmly in their assigned gender positions. Their *transformismo* is mobilized more as a political act and a survival strategy, and less as an expression of an identity or a rejection of their assigned gender; this playful subversion assembles fluidity in the constellation of sex and gender, a key characteristic of countercultural bodies who refuse binaries of any kind.

From this vantage point, Novo's text reconstructs a critical approach to the performativity of gender in clothing, social behavior, and school subjectification, one that foregrounds the pleasure in performing gender no matter what identity is constructed; the fact that his body experiences physical pleasure with shoes, dresses, or makeup is key.[26] Upon arriving in Mexico City in his teenage years, his experiences move him to explore and test the limits of his own middle-class masculinity assembled in the intellectual circles of the times; it is here that makeup becomes a constant part of his life. He encounters the suited and well-groomed men (the *fifís* and the dandies who had been the object of critique during the last of the Porfirian years as symbols of decadence and corruption), the mustached and uniformed men of various revolutionary factions that regularly took over the capital, and the increasingly visible urban workers who populated the streets. In these embodied encounters, alongside the consumptions of so many other models of masculinity in literature and visual cultures, Novo begins disidentifying with masculinity itself through the erotic and sensual engagements with these bodies that smell, look, and feel so different than his. From the vantage point of his own homosexual desire and pleasure, the effeminate bodies of the *fifís* and dandies are not to be confused with homosexual bodies per se, and yet their modes of assemblages fascinate Novo and inspire him:

> Parading their distinguished, decadent insolence, the *fifís*, or dandies, multiplied like the daring mannequins in the windows of Butcher Bros., the tailor shop at the corner of Bolívar and Madero that set the tone for masculine elegance, and advertised its styles in the stereotypical drawings Carlos Neve: tight, high-waisted trousers that showed light-colored

hosiery, or elegant gaiters, and walking boots with rubber soles, short, tight jackets with a vent in the back, very wide lapels, and a single button. (*Pillar of Salt* 85)

First on the streets, and later as the *normalista* professors in his classrooms at the Preparatoria Nacional, Novo's encounters leave him with a fascination for the modern consumption habits that assemble these bodies; simultaneously, he critiques their existence as old-fashioned, unwilling to truly modernize, and above all consuming foreign culture without being critical of their consumption.[27] What matters is not so much the act of consuming as the uncritical attitude that depoliticizes consuming bodies and disconnects them for the national sphere where they are positioned.

Throughout the autobiography, Novo takes care to distance himself and his peers from the proto-mestizo masculinities being assembled in those years; the passages where Villa takes over Torreon are particularly scathing critiques of the "Olympus of Strong Men," and Novo takes care to poke fun at the urban masculinities that appeared in the wake of the revolutionary violence, more tailored and less violent. These *fifís* and dandies literally assemble their masculinities through habits of consumption characteristics of an urban middle class, and Novo differentiates his homosexual body from them by enacting what Brian Gollnick has described as "window-shopping," a modality of cruising that expands territories while resisting the capture of the purchase.[28] Wandering the same street as these *fifís* and dandies, Novo choses to gaze at the fashion products, admiring them while resisting the moment of purchase. Instead, he uses the experience of walking through the streets to assemble a sexual body expressing desire for other men, while also engaging with femininity through makeup and manicures. In this way, the flow of market goods creates a potential liberation from oppressive gender norms, particularly when the body remains in uncertainty before the moment of purchase. Once more, the processes of subjectification into normative masculinities (in family, school, and city) are transformed into processes of self-subjectivation; through the pleasures of a made-up body observing, touching, and smelling, Novo negotiates and follows lines of flight that queer his body, summing differences (gender, sexual, class) onto one corporeal territory. This countercultural pleasure in gender performativity, a highly erotic one that involves all the senses as well as being looked at, will characterize Novo's choices in dressing up the rest of his life, combining male elegance in toupees, suits, ties, and shoes with outlandish colors and makeup.

Novo's affective education is thus grounded in the consumption made possible by the development and modernization of urban markets, assembled with an erotics of pleasure that extends well outside the sexual encounter. While in Torreon and during his first years back in the capital Novo does have several sexual encounters with boys his age and with older men, it is the cinema that fully allows Novo to contour his desire outside the realm of (hetero)normative fantasies.[29] Escaping from the tedium of his overbearing mother and his greater family life, he finds solace in wandering the streets and sneaking into the cinema, "that evening escape and the refuge for the loneliness I knew so well" (92). The dark space of the cinema appears once more as a territory of class contact where gender normativity becomes fluid; the assemblage of image, sound, and bodies becomes too unstable for strict gender roles to be maintained. After seeing multiple films where heroes appeared in "nobility, strength and bravery," Novo finds himself in love with one of the studs, attempting to substitute the heroine on-screen with his own body. However, he feels humiliated, not because of his deviant desire, but simply because his desire appears so unique, alienated from a greater social territory populated with fellow homosexuals:

> I was humiliated, not by the thought of being *abnormal*; not by the fact of feeling for this man a desire and a passion that I was incapable of condemning, of considering as culpable; but rather by the fact that my feeling was without a doubt so singular, made me so unique, so strange in the world, that if my hero were to know of it, he would probably feel nothing but contempt for me, would humiliate me, hit me instead of kissing me. (*Pillar of Salt* 93)

This complex moment first serves to name a homosexual desire informed by the visual education of film, a countercultural process that will greatly develop as print and visual media expands in the twentieth century. Second, it provides Novo with a recognition of the gendered differences his body must navigate in a normative world, as well as the inability to have his unbridled desire expressed while remaining in the heteronormative structuring of society that the romantic couple embody. This moment happens in the Vicente Guerrero cinema, a space of interclass engagement where democracy is enacted upon paying a ticket to enter "basically a shed with uncomfortable seats, where everything smelled of the urinals, and the total silence of the films was punctuated by the notes played on the piano by an old, virtuously dressed señorita" (92). As in the village plaza I talked about earlier where he crossdressed as a strategy of navigation, this cinema is an interclass space where the cultural performance brings together people, allowing for the crystallization of a specific desire emerging from an erotic engagement with space, images, and bodies.

I want to take a moment to untangle the sexual, erotic effect Novo is constructing here and that characterizes (homo)sexual countercultural bodies. After this moment of awareness regarding his desire, Novo understand himself as a "developing character: with this search for pleasure in suffering, in exaltation through suffering" (93). Given his focalization on lower-class bodies, including graphic scenes of urination and other bodily fluids turned sexual, it would seem logical and ethical to signal a fetishistic approach where the middle class, educated, and urbanized homosexual body finds pleasure in experiencing sexual humiliation through interclass engagement, as well as in fetishizing bodies of lower-class men as objects to be consumed in a symbolic theater of social positions. I want to bring forward a specific scene from the town plaza in his childhood to trace the ways in which the erotic emerges in these moments, providing alternative readings that allow us to sidestep the symbolic theater of sexuality (and particularly the pornographic regime): "On one of these evenings, I was standing as part of a group listening to the blind man, when I felt something warm wetting my leg. I understood immediately what had happened: one of the 'scruffy ones' was urinating on me. But instead of moving away, or denouncing him, or protesting, I let him do it, seized violently with *sudden, indescribable, unfamiliar feelings of voluptuousness*" (*Pillar* 64).[30] These feelings, affecting the whole body as it encounters another body through the warm liquid that connects them, allows for a glimpse of an understanding of the erotic outside the paradigms of sexuality. While consent was not negotiated in the encounter initially, the pleasure that Novo experiences and the sensuality of smell, taste, and touch come together to assemble this moment that will mark his sexual subjectivation. In this way, Novo's mobilization of sexual pleasure prohibited to him as a man is like Nahui Olin's representation of female pleasure in her writings, paintings, photographs, and performances. These representations serve less to construct their identities as homosexual/female, and more to assemble sexual bodies through erotic acts that exist as legitimate in spite of their scandalous or prohibited nature. By naming and (re)presenting their pleasures in the face of prohibition, silencing, and criminalization, these countercultural citizens generate assemblages that serve their readers/consumers in eroding the sociosexual boundaries established in the *mestizo* nation; it's less of who I am (always a troubling question) and more of a what I do (alone and together). The erotic serves here to approach these embodied sexualities and sidestep the traps of identity-seeking to pin down bodies into strict categories.

More than sex, Novo's texts evidence a valuation of the erotic that appears influenced by the class positionality of the bodies he is encountering. As in the passage quoted above, the erotic appears for Novo in those instances when the structuring structures of heteropatriarchal desire are disrupted and the chaos of sometimes contradictory feelings is fully embraced; normative desire is continuously structured by psychological structures that are themselves reflections of political and social structures, and the erotic disturbs that process with waves of pleasure. As Audre Lorde states, "the erotic is a measure between the beginnings of our sense of self and the chaos of our strongest feelings. It is an internal sense of satisfaction to which, once we have experienced it, we know we can aspire" (105). The urination scene that disrupts his expectations and opens the door to a flood of feelings serves as the introduction to an erotic education that will continue in his encounters with lower-class citizens, as opposed to the penetrative and somewhat violent encounters with members of his own class. After that moment in the plaza, Novo experiences that "same fruition, that same voluptuousness *without a precise object*" (*Pillar* 67) with Trini, the bootblack son of the family cook in Torreon.[31] This experience of pleasure unattached to a precise object that nevertheless sparks it is a deeply countercultural act in that it disrupts the structuring of pleasure that culture codifies around objects (and bodies as objects). During the stifling summer heat of Torreon when everyone in town would take a siesta, Novo "would stealthily open the door, enter, and kneel down to contemplate him, empty of all thought, of any intention except to engrave in my own senses the image of his bare feet, his dark chest, his sweaty neck, and his peacefully sleeping face. I breathed in, as one more mystery, the spicy, acrid smell of his flesh" (67). Trini never reappears in the text, so this sensual representation is all the engagement that Novo shares with his listeners/readers. However, the brief scene is richly erotic, foregrounding the senses of sight and smell. The homosexual body being represented here is engaging in sensual acts where the dichotomy of passive-active or conqueror-conquered is sidestepped. The "deviancy" that Novo identified in his erotic pleasure in the plaza begins to take shape through this visual encounter, one where consuming another through the senses is more important than a sexual act itself — a sensual erotics mobilized against the penetrative normativity of the colonial nation-state that orders bodies into strict active-passive, dominator-dominated, top-bottom dynamics.

I emphasize these alternative homoerotics because Novo's proper "sexual" education is heavily nuanced by trauma and displeasure, particularly when he is situated in a middle-class context. While still in Torreon, he finds himself "seduced" by his upper-classmate Jorge González, ending up alone with the youth in a classroom after school. After kissing, Novo is horrified when he sees Jorge's "erect, reddened penis" (75), almost darting away except Jorge grabs him into another kiss. Jorge then masturbates himself until ejaculation next to the pinned-down and horrified Novo, who runs "from the room, confused, fascinated, disconcerted, torn between that infinite pleasure of that long, unforgettable kiss, and the anguish of the disgusting ejaculation" (75). Jorge and Salvador will find each other later in Mexico City, though they will not engage each sexually again. Novo's memory is vividly described in terms of the displeasure, the squeezing, the not letting go that marks this encounter as problematically moving away from consent, where the one-way pleasure that Jorge experiences hints at a greater violence at play in the (homo)sexual arena. Similarly, Novo's next sexual tryst with another schoolmate, now the twenty-year-old baseball coach Pedro Alvarado, is marked by displeasure and genitocentrism. Having seen Salvador and Jorge together, Pedro also "seduces" young Novo and convinces him to have an encounter before leaving Torreon to Mexico City. After agreeing, they both walk to Hotel Washington where Pedro enters first and Novo follows, guided by an old woman "visibly habituated to such diaphanous strategies, [who] looked at me scornfully" (79). This cursory evidence of a thriving (homo)sexual economy notwithstanding, Novo's description of the event echoes his moment with Jorge; under Pedro's "pressure . . . [he] let him do what he would" in an act that carried "not the slightest pain nor even the minimal pleasure" (79). Novo narrativizes the event as his equivalent of a virginal deflowering, and yet "similar to the slight discomfort I felt during the introduction of the enemas I was subjected to at home when I was sick" (79). Considering the class positionality of these three bodies, Novo's memoir evidences an understanding of middle-class male sexuality constructed around displeasure, discomfort, a vague notion of unspoken and unnegotiated consent, and, most importantly, a genitocentrism that prohibits any other erotic engagement beyond penetrative sex and an exclusive focus on the penis as the organ of pleasure.[32]

Shaped by the forces of heteronormative capitalism, Jorge and Pedro mobilize a desire to objectivize and consume Novo's youthful body, consummating a sexual act that in turn reifies their positionality as "men." However, Salvador's previous trysts in the plaza will lead him on different erotic paths once he and his mother move to Mexico, where he experiences the urban development and begins to shape his erotic desire through the affective consumption of cinema and the city, as analyzed earlier. With chauffeurs, mechanics, and other working-class men, Novo mobilizes a sexual agency that empowers both (or more) bodies in structurings of mutual pleasure, enacting a bilateral flow of erotic and sexual desire. I underscore the particular embodiments of chauffeurs and mechanics due to their technological becomings in these specific years; urban development (in the form of streets), technology (in the form of automobiles), fluidity (in the speed and distances that automobiles cover) and global capitalism (in the various commodities that come together to form automobiles) assemble and shape these particular bodies and their sociocultural milieu. Novo first encounters them when living in his uncle Paulino's house; after climbing the rooftop to admire the sunset over the city, he happens on the sleeping chauffeur lying on his cot outside his room.[33] As with Trini and the beggar in the plaza, Novo does not enter the space of a lower-class individual to give an order or reestablish a hierarchy, and in doing so he occupies the space with his ever-more marked homoerotic body. Upon waking and finding the youth leaning on the parapet, the chauffeur presses himself on his body and turns him to be face-to-face. He then "undid his buttons, extracted his penis, and tried to get me to touch it, as he watched me attentively. 'Do you like it?' he murmured . . . I contemplated its smoothness . . . its beautiful dark color, very different from the monstrous red of Jorge González's, which had frightened me" (100). I call attention to the softness, the low voices, and the explicit consent that the scene underlines; the man then leads Salvador back into his room to his cot, where "the pillow, his body, the rough face, his hard hands, gave off an odor of gasoline, which would long be associated with a pleasure I first truly experienced in that encounter" (100). This sexual act is marked by an erotic and ethical engagement where mutual pleasure is made explicit and where consent characterizes their action, even if it is necessitated by the class difference and the dangers that interclass contact present to the chauffeur. The erotic and sensual aspects of smell and touch, which had already appeared with Trini and the beggar, are now used to understand and engage with this modern urban subjectivity.[34] Novo's predilection for chauffeurs, which later in his life were joined by policemen, ties his homosexual experiences to urbanity; both of these bodies movie through the smooth and anonymous space of the city, crossing class boundaries as their vehicles move across the city, sheltered in the anonymity of their profession and uniforms. If female bodies are able to use technology as vehicles to literally and literarily traverse the city and contain their sexuality in a safe space, homosexual male bodies are able to engage in interclass contact in these more public vehicles, mediated by the economic exchange of tickets. And similarly to Bonifant (of whom he was no fan), Novo characterizes his engagements with explicit consent and mutual pleasure that, at the very least, trouble the constructions and experiences of homosexual acts as instances of domination and violence.[35]

Before focusing on the Mexico City *chafiretes* and bus drivers, I want to take a moment to explore Novo's ethical engagement with lower-class individuals subjectivized in other modern, urban settings to nuance this countercultural sexual exploration in the greater context of modernity and outside the geopolitical and ideological borders of Mexican *mestizaje*. During socialist Narciso Bassol's tenure as Secretary of Public Education between 1931 and 1934, Novo was hired to attend the VII Conference of Education in Buenos Aires, a voyage on which he visited Montevideo and Rio de Janeiro. Novo published his travelogue *Continente Vacío* (1935) as well as *Seamen Rhymes* (1934), a bilingual poetry collection with illustrations by Federico García Lorca, whom he met on that voyage in Buenos Aires.[36] He also explores new urban spaces from a queer and decidedly interclass position, participating in the queer world-making of gay cruising and sex. Upon his arrival in Buenos Aires, Novo encounters a policeman performing their military service who offers himself as a tour guide; an embodiment of the state, and yet not quite since Novo quickly identifies an uncommon Buenos Aires just underneath the surface, one he can't really resist: "cómo negarse a conocer desde ya un Buenos Aires poco común, que sin duda nuestro embajador y mis otros amigos ignorarían? [how can I deny myself exploring the little-known Buenos Aires already, an obscure Buenos Aires that no doubt our ambassador and my other friends do not know]" (Novo, *Continente Vació* 177). Cruising the streets, the pair hop on a public tram like the ones Oliveiro Girondo writes about and head to the policeman's house for him "to change into informal clothing." This veiled reason is quickly dispelled when Salvador obliquely describes: "no quiero que aguardemos a la hermanita. Prefiero imaginarla dulce, hacendosa, etéreamente desprendida de un poema nativo, alma de este budín, reflejo engreído de *este ropero que me hace, en su único ojo*, el reproche de una presencia inadecuada [I don't want us to wait for the younger sister. I would rather imagine her sweet, homely, ethereally taken from a native poem, pudding soul, vain reflection of *this wardrobe that gives with its one eye* the reproach of an inadequate presence]" (179). The one-eyed dresser and the nervousness at the arrival of the sister hint at a sexual encounter that will lead to an urban affair where the policeman leads Novo to the unknown Buenos Aires just under the surface, one known by men cruising the streets.

These hemispheric encounters give evidence of a sexual culture that brings men together in urban settings, one that historians of cruising such as Alex Espinosa in *Cruising: An Intimate History of a Radical Pasttime* (2019) or philosopher-activist Guy Hocquenghem in *The Screwball Asses* (1973/2010) highlight as an important political and socially inflected space of activity. More than Novo's body — which was regularly satirized by his enemies for his effeminacy, makeup, and mannerisms — I want to highlight how these sexual encounters serve as ephemeral moments of interclass alliances with hemispheric working-class men, moments that disappear without a trace except that of pleasure inscribed on the body of these men. In homophobic discourses of heteropatriarchy, sexual activity is symbolized to signify a male body that is somehow less than due to his being penetrated and a male body that is somehow more than due to his penetrating. The fleeting moments that Novo talks about, oblique as they are, push back against this homophobic discourse that underpins (Mexican *mestizo*) modern hegemonic masculinities. Novo did not hide himself in the closet; like Juan Gabriel decades later, he could easily have said "lo que se ve no se pregunta [what is seen is not asked about]" when questioned openly about his desires and pleasures. His textualization of sex — his sextualization, if you will — in specific places, with specific bodies, and performing specific acts where sexual desire gives shape to erotic worlds evidence a countercultural body that is not hiding and is also navigating the very real threats of institutional and physical violence inflicted upon "homosexual" bodies, from the violence of *redadas* and *razzias* to the transphobic and homophobic murders that continue to happen to this day. I highlight these moments of interclass sex that Novo subtly writes about to push back on the idea of a "closet" — which involved a denial of self in personal and political terms — and to add complexity to a notion of Novo as a consumer of Brown men.[37] These encounters, marked by the dynamics of mutual recognition and, above all, mutual erotic pleasure, give a glimpse into sexual cultures that cross class boundaries; furthermore, they provide examples of male, masculine, and virile bodies that are not reproductions of the exclusionary construction of hegemonic *mestizo* or national masculinities. These men, who also experience pleasure alongside Novo, become his friends, tour guides, drivers, chauffeurs, and accomplices, as well as his sexual partners; they are not objects of desire as much as subjects of pleasure in an urban sexualscape.

While the cities with their automobiles, machines, and storefronts were the central sexualscapes where Novo assembled his sexual desire and erotic expression, his more public life was increasingly as a member of that middle- and upper-class sexual community that Carlos Monsiváis names as the "world of sidelong glances," which included high-profile names and has been described as the gay ghetto of the time.[38] Gay ghettos emerged in Mexico City and other major metropolises in the aftermath of the global repression against sexual diversity kindled by the extreme violence of the Nazi regime against the Weimar republic. Built around class and racial privileges, gay ghettos become architectural and social spaces where middle- and upper-class men-desiring-men could and can come together to socialize, while remaining physically separate from one another.[39] In his seminal *Homosexual Desire* (1970), Guy Hocqueghem decries the ways in which the homosexual fronts in 1968 Paris are reproducing this logic of bodily separation, reinforcing the class dynamics that prohibit "proper" citizens from contamination by venereal disease or deviant desires. In Mexico during the years following the revolution, the urban and demographic growth allowed for the creation of these social and material spaces where middle- and upper-class homosexual men could gather and, given the strength of the heteronormative discourses around hegemonic *mestizo* masculinity, it seems inevitable that these men valued their sexual acts according to the hegemonic norms on sexuality. I call attention to these instances less to compare, measure, and qualify these sexual spaces and acts, and more to place them in erotic contexts that can serve to build strategies of countercultural homosexualities. The greater context of violence enacted by the state, its representatives, and the citizens it sanctioned cannot be understated when approaching these spaces, sociabilities, and the bodies that composed them.

In contrast, countercultural bodies construct themselves in and through dissidence with the normative social structures surrounding bodies, especially those that shape sexuality and erotic expression. Particularly in Hispanic cultures, the homophobic and misogynistic structures surrounding (homo)sexual acts run deep: "como el único cuerpo penetrable en ese imaginario colectivo es el de la mujer, el que un hombre sea penetrado es la mayor agresión posible a su virilidad . . . ha perdido su hombría, su estatus superior [the only penetrable body in this collective imaginary is that of the woman, the fact that a man is penetrated is the biggest possible attack on his virility . . . he has lost his manhood, his superior status] " (Saez 21). As a bottom who enjoys penetration, Novo mobilizes this erotic pleasure as a political tool. A countercultural homosexual who quickly discovered and used his ability to seduce and sexually consume any body he desired surrounded by a community of fellow homosexual men in a culture that constructed sex as a competition, Novo quickly gained a reputation for being able to take on penises no one else could. In a much critically commented and hilarious episode in *Pillar of Salt*, the Golondrina (the Swallow), a pillar in this 1920s gay ghetto and a pimp who procured young men from the lower classes for their consumption, locks Novo in a studio with an anarchist accused of bombing the American embassy equipped with "a tool so enormous, it was not easy to accommodate him" (Novo, *Pillar* 132). After leaving them for a moment, the Golondrina returns to confirm that Novo has completed the task and to address the rest of the witnesses at the gathering to proclaim, "the whole thing!" (132). Emboldened by this bottom prowess, Novo "determined to conquer a kind of championship" and would later take on Agustín Fink, famous in these circles for a penis "whose diameter positively matched a can of salmon" (143). While he was successful in his venture, Novo also suffered injuries that ultimately led to a rupture with his mentor Pedro Enriquez Ureña: the consequences of homosexual sex going public. In reading this episode, Robert McKee Irwin emphasizes the limits of Paz's definitions of Mexican sexuality, since it is Novo who actively seduces and engages with these two penetrators/conquerors/activos, pointing at Novo's queering of the normative understandings of (homo)sexuality that Paz writes about; Novo is definitely the subject and agent in these situations ("La Pedo Embotellado" 130). I echo McKee Irwin, and I underline how these scenes gain symbolic significance only in the context of competition that heteronormative masculinities mobilize; *and* I want to underscore the silenced yet present erotic pleasure that courses through Novo's, the anarchist's, and Fink's bodies as they engage each other: on the one hand, the insidiousness of normative masculinities embodied in this competitiveness, and on the other an erotic pleasure/pain that leads to a liberation from dominant cultural spheres, and in the middle a man who enjoyed being penetrated and felt no shame in being publicly named as the bottom.[40]

Contextualized in a moment when the medical-criminological category of homosexual was being solidified, Novo's writings reveal a constant use of this rhetorical device: publicly occupying the position and the stereotype of the bottom-pasivo and doing so with the pleasure of the position as well as the pleasure of parodying the whole signification system that gives meaning to that sociosexual position. His texts never directly name or engage with the sex-gender system itself — if anything, his journalism leans toward a slightly misogynistic attitude toward the social and cultural changes women were undertaking, and yet they constantly recognize their powerful influence as subjectivizing forces. The patriarchal Catholic morality underpinning the symbolic structure of the active-passive dichotomy with its valorization of the receptive anal partner as the only one committing sodomy, as well as the more modern patriarchal medical discourse surrounding "homosexuality" as a condition of the mind, surround Novo constantly. In the face of this constant homophobia, Novo's wit parodies the stereotypes of homosexuality that are emerging from this mix of cultural, medical, media, and religious discourses, particularly the misogynistic stereotype of the homosexual/pasivo/bottom as loud, melodramatic, effeminate, and overly sentimental. After breaking up a short-lived romantic relationship with a drama teacher Novo describes as seducing him with promises of giving him a major role in his new film, Salvador finds himself in trouble when the deeply emotional man accuses him to his uncle of "walking down the wrong side of the street . . . [and visiting homosexual bordellos" (*Pillar of Salt* 117). After the uncle questions him, Novo

> felt, and desired, death. The whole world went dark. The whole arsenal of my crimes overwhelmed in a single instant of absolute shipwreck, my total bewilderment . . . I went to bed like an automaton. I prayed for, yearning for death, and in

the pacifying states of insomnia, determined that the only way to save the situation was for me to kill Tovar Ávalos. I would go to see him early, earlier than on other mornings, before he even wrapped his hand around the razor with whose minute caresses he always began his slow toilette, while he was still in bed; I would take possession of the razor and slash his loathsome throat and his damned face, until I'd annihilated him, until I'd erased him from this world that didn't have room enough for both of us. (117)

While this passage drips with the affective and visual commonplaces of melodrama, from the unrequited love turned vengeful to the fantasies of violence and the hyperbolic adjectives in an attempt perhaps to mitigate the very real threat of social and economic punishment for his existence, Novo did not commit violence; upon simple confrontation, Tovar Ávalos begged forgiveness for his dangerous mistake of outing Novo and shamefully vanished from his life forever to avoid spreading the public sin of homosexuality, which often carried with it a punishment in the form of violence gleefully enforced by one or several young men eager to protect their limited construction of masculinity.[41] This ultimately reveals the very real danger that comes from inhabiting this identity and provides a sobering counterpoint to the hilarity in the passage above, which cannot be emphasized enough was read by Novo to his partygoers and close friends for decades before appearing in print, thus making it a deeply oral passage as well as symbolic. The descriptors, the emotional landscape of melodrama (falling in love, infatuation, unrequited loved, confessions, et cetera), and the theatricality often associated with homosexual identity construct a self-parodic Novo whose tongue-in-cheek reveals a body willing to test the limits (of social existence) and to expand them through pleasure and play. In this sense, *Pillar of Salt* codifies the bodies of men having sex with men into homosexual bodies, simultaneously subverting the notions of a single identity by continuously poking fun at and parodying the melodramatic aesthetics that have and continue to shape these bodies in the public discourse. Most importantly, he codifies these bodies as always potentially in danger of real violence, from the accusations and cultural violence Novo himself experienced to the real beatings, roundups, and murders these citizens face. Parody thus serves the ethical functions of making visible (and embodied) the joy and pleasure of queer existence and simultaneously underlining the constant violence queer bodies navigate in a patriarchal society, in the streets and bars as much as in the doctor's office.

By parodying these social, psychoanalytic, and criminological discourses, he reconfigures these masculine and homosexual bodies in a *mestizo* society by foregrounding the symbolic violence they experience. Historian Robert Buffington analyzes Mexican criminologist Carlos Roumagnac's work in Mexico City prisons during the nineteenth and twentieth centuries and traces how the criminologist was fundamental in establishing a field of study and an institution of criminology, mobilizing the texts of Spanish endocrinologist and sexologist Gregorio Marañón.[42] As Siobhan McManus has underscored, this nascent institutional criminalization of homosexual acts actually served to generate specific and concrete definitions of homosexual identities anchored in specific bodies, which slowly made their way into the public sphere through scandal, punishment, and stereotype. Perhaps intuitively aware of this, and undoubtedly put off by the criminalization built on this medical categorization, Novo evidences his knowledge and disagreement with the works of Marañón, whose writing circulated widely in Latin America in the 1920s and 1930s and was central in providing the medicalized understanding of sexual bodies that underpins past and current conversion therapies, rehabilitations, and social punishments through ritual violence. In *Continente Vacío*, he narrates his voyages as a cultural ambassador to South America, and while traveling aboard a ship he finds himself sharing a room with Mr. Buechlein, a tall and fit Nordic gentleman who disrupts Novo with his meticulous organization and his habits of early morning exercise. The Mexican writer uses these moments to reflect on his sexological knowledge:

> había tal diferencia de color y de calidad en la blanca piel de su cuerpo con la que revestía su cuello marchito y su rostro afeitado, rojo y duro, que yo pensaba, al ver su ausencia total de vello, en los estudios de Marañón sobre los caracteres sexuales secundarios, y no podía dormir tratando de recordar con precisión su teoría sobre la distribución del vello, que me parece demasiado general porque presumo que sus implicaciones endócrinas varían con las razas, y él habrá estudiado casi exclusivamente sujetos españoles, raza de que me vienen tan acusados
> [there was such a difference in the color and quality of his body's white skin with which he covered his burnt neck and shaven face, red and hard, that I thought upon seeing his total lack of body hair, on the studies of Marañon about the secondary sexual characters, and I couldn't sleep trying to remember with precision his theory on the distribution of body hair, which I found too general because I presume that its endocrine implications vary with race, and he must have studied exclusively Spanish subjects, a race which come to me so accused already]. (59)

Lying in bed and thinking of his Nordic roommate, perhaps the first such phenotype he has encountered, Novo starts reflecting on his own experiences while comparing bodies. He criticizes the limits of the Spanish sexologist for his biased approach to the diversity of human bodies. What is more, he carries out this critique while in bed and offhandedly treats this important medical source as a wandering thought before sleeping, unable to remember the details with precision. Thus, his presumption of racial and ethnic diversity as the grounds of his personal critique gives Novo more authority than Marañón to describe masculine bodies, giving us a homosexual body who can and does strike back at the discursive apparatus medicalizing and criminalizing him.

This experiential knowledge countering medicalizing discourse complexifies Novo's parodic narratives and gives nuance to his embodiment of *mestizo* nationalism in the form of state-sponsored arts, crafts, and propaganda of the postrevolutionary governments. After discovering the sidelong world of homosexual acts thriving in the modernized urban space (in bathhouses, dark alleys, bordellos, passenger trucks, and mechanical shops), Novo and his friends pool their resources to rent a studio together and have a place of their own, a locus for their sexual and social trysts. Visiting the exhibitions of rural and Indigenous-inspired pieces curated by Dr. Atl and by reading his *Traditional Arts in México* (1921), Novo, Xavier Villaurrutia, and their mutual friend nicknamed the Virgin of Istanbul find a small room in an office building on the corner of Donceles and Argentina, very close to the Preparatoria where they were still enrolled. Together, the trio decorated the studio

> with weavings, needlework, and other handicrafts. From the headboard of the "couch" we hung a small idol with large buttocks, which we called Saint Bollocks; from this "sacrificial perch," he presided over our scenes. And in a touch of extreme nationalism, I employed a small calabash as the most appropriate vessel for the Vaseline required for our rites. We purchased an earthen tea set, and took tea in the afternoon with thick cookies, fruit of the oven's womb, which I bought from the bakeries nearby, happy to have a home to call our own. (129)

This irreverent approach to Mexican nationalism (an early form of ethnic essentialism and commodification, perhaps) reveals nevertheless an engagement with the processes of nationalist subjectification. Taking it one step further, the trio of men queer this *mestizo* nation by using the calabash or *jícara* as a container for sexual lubricant, a ritual object that literally gives shape to the topos and territory of male sexual desire. The earthen tea set is also woven into a queer teatime when the trio and perhaps other men coalesce into a fleeting community of social and sexual deviants, a countercultural population anchored by their shared sexual desire.

Rather than engaging with a mediatized nationalism and accepting that mediation through the state, Novo and his countercultural accomplices use the material objects produced by this ideology and encounter these Brown bodies in a queer nation populated by countercultural sexual citizens.[43] In cocreating and populating this sociosexual territory, these men not only queer the models of masculinity and homosexuality, avoiding cross-dressing and effeminacy as the sole markers of queerness in lieu of a campy nationalism, but they also end up generating utopian spaces where different marginal citizens come together.

Thus, *Pillar of Salt* ends with a passage where Novo, Villaurrutia, Agustín Lazo, and Enrique Jimenez rent rooms in a building on Calle Brasil while the caretaker María and her family live in the rest of the building. Contrary to the old women in the Hotel Washington back in Torreon, who scorned Novo's sexual trysts with disapproval and disgust, María washes the soiled clothes of these young men and opens the door on their late-night encounters.[44] Taken together, the studios on Donceles and these rooms on Calle Brasil are markers of a utopic counterterritory free from the heteronormative structuring of bodies and behaviors, subversive territories where class divisions and moral codes are eroded by consent and participation in a community of economic peers. The young men rent the rooms, the woman stewards the building, and each know of each other's trysts, accomplices in their pleasures and economic support. This is not a place for them to cohabitate domestically to re-create a heteronormative home, but rather another locus of queer life, a temporary utopia where their sexual territories overlap and coexist, a singular point in a greater map of homosexual Mexico City that connects their lovers, nightclubs, dark alleys, bus stations, and quiet dark parks.[45]

This queering of space upending *mestizo* sexual morality is repeated in Novo's other texts, specifically when he writes about public spaces occupied almost exclusively by male bodies, such as bathhouses and car mechanical shops. As Víctor Macías González shares in researching the locus of the public bathhouse in Porfirian Mexico, as the city became more modernized, public hygiene would play a key role in its public architecture. Democracy may be an idealist value to structure modern life, and the need to survive the various vicissitudes of public health shaped the bathhouse as a space where modern citizens contested boundaries of class, race, and sexuality in the struggle to stay alive and healthy. The public bathhouse came to represent clean and ultramodern modernity needed to curb infections and diseases, a space where the bodies of men could be modernized first by being made visible and second by being manipulated in their behavior, hygiene, and performance (Macías González 29, 21, 33). While masculinity was contested in print and image during postrevolutionary Mexico, the bathhouse evidences the history of this contestation in a public space where the honor lines that divide classes can be undermined precisely by the class and racial mixings that occur in these spaces and generate horizontal networks of desire, eroticism, and visual appreciation. These bodies are removed — albeit temporarily — from their capitalist/productive roles as *patrones* and employees, and from their nationalist roles as *mestizo* men, in order to cohabitate a space where sexual subversion is always already just beneath the surface of the water, just behind the billow of steam, just around the dressing-room corner.

In "Motivos del baño," an article republished in *Ensayos* in 1925, Novo engages this newly urban space of the bathhouse in a complex manner, tackling its cultural significance in relation to legality, sexual behavior, and public cleanliness. He begins by noticing the novelty of the space in cultural terms (a historical blind spot that points more toward the homophobic silencing of queer sexuality than to a lack of writings on bathhouses, considering they were an important part of ancient Roman and Greek public life), and he uses that context to immediately connect this rhetorical instability with the precarious legal and social position of the bodies that occupy that space, perhaps subverting their hygienic purposes and generating a sociosexual landscape with other furtive men: "Es una molestia spiritual no conocer autor ninguno respetable que haya dicho una frase inmortal acerca del baño, porque los epígrafes dan fuerza y autoridad a los discursos como la cita oportuna de un artículo legal suele dar libertad a los presos, si sus defensores la hacen con tino y los jurados les creen [It is a spiritual bother not knowing any respectable author that has written an immortal phrase about the bathroom, because epigraphs give strength and authority to discourses just as the right quote from a legal article tends to give freedom to convicted men, if their defenders quote it with accuracy and the jury believes them]" ("Motivos del baño" 129).

This legal precarity hints at an all-too-close awareness of the potential violence that overlays this "silenced" space, an urban territory populated by bodies made vulnerable by being unable to be defended. The cultural vacuum in which this territory exists underlines the legal (and social) vulnerability of a deviant body, particularly one that behaves in a certain way. In the rest of the article, Novo stresses how although what makes the bathhouse celebratory is the cleanliness and hygiene it facilitates (in line with the nationalist tenet of social hygiene observed in *mercados municipales* with water fixtures and the economic support of sports), the space is so much more than that: "no es solo higiene, sino placer de la mirada y del músculo, exhibición de trajes untados de charol, en torsos ágiles y de graciosos gorros para vacío sobre orejas de concha nácar [it's not just hygiene, but also the pleasure of the gaze and the muscle, the exhibition of suits with patent leather, agile torsos and gracious swimming caps covering mother of pearl ears]" (129). His own existence in the space is marked by the hygiene that surrounds him, and ultimately it is defined by what he sees (and chooses to see) in the space: agile torsos, muscles, and half-naked bodies. He consumes these bodies with his gaze and, in doing so, redescribes them for his reader in a queer fashion, as subjects moving in the space and objects to be deliciously gazed upon with desire perhaps consummated. His keen eye zooms in on the rubber bathing suits and the funny swimming caps, also objects of modern technological progress. As rubber and industrial leather products, the emphasis on these accessories hints at the silenced history of fetishwear and they become a visual marker for the wandering erotic gaze of the young Mexican. In narrating the bathhouse as this liminal social space where some behaviors might go unnoticed, Novo assembles the bodies occupying it and his own body with theirs as bodies experiencing sensual pleasure (of water and slippery soap, of looking at and being looked at, of new fashion materials on the skin), and what is most important is they experience it together. What matters is this pleasure, which does lie in their hygienic- or health-related functions and yet goes beyond this ideological understanding of the space.[46]

So far, these sensorial and bodily pleasures that Novo is experiencing, perceiving around him, and textualizing have been diverse and obliquely erotic, barely explicitly sexual in nature even when confessed in the oral *Pillar of Salt*. Novo was contending with a hypermacho cultural and political field where every man wore a gun and physical violence leading to death, prison, or labor camps was a very real possibility — a reality that, albeit with punishments less violent, still underlies Mexican society. As Luis Felipe Fabre has brilliantly traced, informed by Paul Preciado's and Guy Hocquenhem's queer anal politics, the ethics and aesthetics of Novo and his fellow Contemporáneos are characterized by the centrality of the anus, as a real site and a contested symbolic site:

> The problem is not having an anus, as it is well-known that even the most macho of men have one. The problem is when the anus is made public. The problem is to say out loud what should remain secret, to open what must be closed. It is not in vain that the sphinx and the sphincter share a single etymological origin. As these anal poets articulate the multiple enigmas of the anus in their poems, they subvert privacy itself, that is, the social order those who call themselves revolutionaries would prefer to maintain. (Fabre, *Writing with caca* 13)

The cultural sphere of the 1920s and 1930s was highly dynamic with constant overlaps into the political sphere, and particularly its bureaucratic structures. Masculinity here was hardly a monolithic concept, as the Porfirian regime crumbled and the nascent militaristic state pumped out visual imaginaries of charros and other *mestizo* role models. At the same time, however, certain sectors were experiencing these rapid economic and social changes and responding in turn. Novo's unique position as an outlier of the cultural sphere, witty and quasi-child prodigy notwithstanding, placed him in contact with one of these sectors where masculinity was a thing to explicitly negotiate, assemble, and perform — a sector already familiar to him through his engagement with the chauffeur and his wealthy family's domestic employees: the modern world of cars and buses and motors.

To conclude Novo's (homo)sexualization of the urban corporealities populating Mexico City in these decades, I turn now to *El Chafirete*.[47] Published weekly throughout 1923, the popular newsletter was directed at the growing population of urban bus drivers and chauffeurs, young men who embodied the intersection of cutting-edge technology, spatial and class mobility, modernized consumption habits, lower-class masculinities, and youth cultures experiencing the first waves of state-sponsored *mestizo* ideology.[48] The editorial line of the journal was explicitly anti-union and instead celebrated the verbal and technical skills of this new labor force by emphasizing individual prowess, verbal skills, and economic autonomy.[49] Novo came upon this publication fortuitously and after visiting their offices in search of a job realized "a sure instinct had associated me with the founders of a weekly that brought them numerous easy contacts among their specialized readers: drivers and bootlickers" (Novo, *Pillar* 43). In his memoir, and most of all in the various poems and articles he penned for the weekly, Novo gives evidence of the homosexual practices of his fellow editors, writers, and readers; the journal maps a sexual territory where lower-class masculinities navigate the limits dictated by heteronormative masculinity by mobilizing an explicit and embodied deviant sexual desire.[50] I am not saying that *El Chafirete* and men surrounding it are radical sexual citizens, since the sexual politics we see in the weekly shows bus drivers and chauffeurs are strong, smart, and skilled enough to outwit traffic agents or to dominate their wealthy clients or employers demonstrate a conservative politics that undermines class solidarity and labor organizing by emphasizing individual power, running against a collective countercultural ethos. What I do notice and want to emphasize is the underlying anal pleasure that permeates the writings of Novo in this space, and that is hinted at in the actions of the other men around him, whether they be a driver fucking his wealthy client or a tryst between drivers in the bushes of a park. These shared anal pleasures run against the normative symbolization of penetration and transform shame into the empathy of *me as well*, I also experience this, leading into a shared politics of pleasure that makes visible experiences and runs counter to the cultural constructions of power established by patriarchy. As Saez and Carrascosa underline, the anus is the great metaphor of control over social systems.[51] Subverting this control (enforced by patriarchy through sexual violence, as Octavio Paz is so willing to universalize) through anal pleasure and, most importantly, the sharing of this pleasure, becomes a way for Novo to name what he is experiencing and witnessing in this potentially countercultural milieu of cars and workshops. His writings describing lower-class masculinities are the voice of an elite and cosmopolitan man, yes; and they are assemblages of masculinities emerging in conjunction with the bodies he is representing. The sexual freedom, the spatial and sexual autonomy, and the stark individualism of the singular drivers the weekly celebrates in text and contests come together around Novo (and perhaps other men) to form a collective based not on class solidarity as much as on shared experiences of sexual pleasure that cut across class, race, and ethnic boundaries through an assemblage with technology.

The general tone of *El Chafirete* is saturated with *albur*, the popular Mexican form of double entendre charged with sexual innuendo often mobilized to showcase (verbal) dominance over an interlocutor who does not understand (due to a class or social difference, typically) or is unable to respond. Typically understood as another tool of sociosexual oppression, particularly when mobilized against sexual minorities such as sexually active women or homosexual men, the *albur* has also been observed as a verbal tool for "breaking the alienating hegemony of dominant culture and society" (Limon 478). In an exclusively homosocial context, the *albur* becomes a way to make visible what cannot be spoken about directly (homosexual desire) and a way to mark the navigation and challenge of the gender norms that structure these male bodies (homosexual sex). Seen through this subversive potential, a *pasivo* politics coalesces in the weekly, perhaps evidencing only Novo's pleasure, and perhaps signaling a wider countercultural consciousness that is distancing itself from the "image of the bottom being violated and violently ripped open" (Cervantes-Gómez 337). While *albur* is mobilized in the weekly as a way of establishing social dominance, particularly when drivers are engaging with upper-class clients such as *fifís*, there are many instances where the *albur* becomes the rhetorical strategy naming a deviant desire and the acts that embody it. Often, the *albur* becomes a way to name the bodily reaction that marks the shared sexual pleasure, whether a moan or an ejaculation, without necessarily degrading the bodies to a domi-nator-dominated dichotomy. The journal also published important informative sections, such as open letters to the traffic director "Ingeniero Margáin," or a comic strip titled "Cómo evitar accidentes" illustrating common traffic mistakes chafiretes needed to learn to avoid (in itself already evidencing an "organic" urban traffic education generated by these modern subjects themselves and not a state authority or institution) and, most importantly, advertising for auto parts and a space for complaints about urban developments. Together, this commu-nication with authority figures, self-education, and the presence of the market evidence the weekly as a vehicle for urban subjectification (a how-to on becom-ing a proper *mestizo* citizen) *and* a space for community around modern con-sumption habits and highly sexualized lower-class masculinities.[52] However, the bulk of the published text in the weekly consisted of comic sections such as "Lo que no hace un chafirete [What a driver does not do]," which educated through humor; poems and short stories obliquely recounting sexual exploits throughout the city; a yearlong contest on "¿Cuál es el chafirete más feo? [Who is the ugliest driver?]," evidencing a population interested, if only through humor, in their aesthetic appearances, a trait that remains a marker of the ste-reotype of the urban bus drivee with a comb and a mirror in their pocket; and a recurring section titled "Retratos mentales" where Novo interviewed drivers and playfully textualized their sexuality, playfully hinting at their homosexual acts without constructing a social identity, that is, "outing" them.

Radiador was Novo's most-used pseudonym in the weekly, though he also was known to have been Juana Inés del Cabus (the caboose, the last car of a train or metro that would later become the most well-known cruising spot in urban Ciudad de México), Garcirrastro de la Viga (a play on *viga* or beam, phonetically close to *verga*, cock, or main mast of a ship, as well as Garcilaso, the famous Golden Age poet) and Mamado Cuervo (a play on *mamar*, to suck, and a jab at Amado Nervo, established poet at the time).[53] Opening with the motor radiator, the writer uses a style dripping with sexual innuendo in an exchange of fluids and the effects of overheating/overexcitement that has now become characteristic of popular masculine speech (the *albur*), but that may nevertheless seem innocuous for an unwitting reader. The motor vehicle provides Novo with an assemblage relating his body to a lower-class public with whom he can engage with sexually without the repercussions of social violence. However, rather than mobilizing literary references to his reader, Novo's main persona was a reference to a mechanical object: a car radiator. In a section titled "Decálogo del camion," the writer lists the ten essential parts of the new machines speeding through the streets, beginning with the most important of all: "yo voy a la vanguardia de todos ustedes. Si me caliento, les salpico el parabrisas. Existo en todas partes y, para enfriarme, me destapan. Y he óido lo que dicen todos ustedes, camiones de México [I go at the vanguard of everyone. If I get hot, I splash your windshield. I exist everywhere and to cool me down, you open me up. And I have heard what they say about all of you, buses of Mexico]" (Num. 12, June 10, 1923). The mechanical object becomes a metonym for Novo, not as an individual but as a collective, a body who experiences desire and satisfies it with the help of those other men. Innocently read as a car part, the radiator drips with sexual innuendo in the exchange of fluid and with the social effects of overheating and overexcitement. As the taxi becomes a part of the machine-body assemblage where Cube Bonifant can express a sexual female body, for Novo the vehicle becomes a part of the homosexual machine-body, particularly the one who is penetrated, who is unable to contain himself, and who knows other men and what they say (and do). Most importantly, in the shifting landscape of masculinities, Radiador sees himself at the vanguard of everyone, perhaps speaking to a wider cultural sphere than the intended reader audience of the weekly. He textualizes an explorative body who navigates the city, fully up to date on what every other *camión* is saying, empowering himself to answer back — a sexual body assembled with technology exchanging bodily fluids, armed with a mastery of wit and double entendre that makes him (and, by extension, perhaps other *pasivos* around him) as dangerous subjects to attack or ridicule.

In this textual representation of *chafirete* and mechanics' bodies as sexual agents who mobilize their sexuality for pleasure as much as for weapons of resistance toward upper-class citizens, "the urban landscape emerges as an arena of desire" (Gollnick 241). The spatial and sexual mobility that characterize these bodies charge the landscape with a homoerotic and homosexual energy that exists outside of the sidelong world of middle- and high-class men Novo engaged with socially in his cultural community.[54] Critics have noted how these urban working-class bodies coexist with the sailor, another highly sexual male body Xavier Villaurrutia epitomized in his poem "Nocturne: The Angels," where the sailors Villaurrutia engaged with in his visits to Los Angeles are transformed into angels. What matters here is that this sociosexual sphere exists somewhat visibly, not in whispers and sidelong glances as much as in known cruising spots (parks, docks, buses, certain street corners) and in a somewhat publicly accepted manner, albeit if only by the men who occupy these spaces. Ultimately, consent and mutual pleasure mark these sexual territories as something more than survival strategies for the criminalized and pathologized homosexual bodies who create them.

El Chafirete thus displays a working-class (homo)sexuality that mobilizes sexual prowess as a strategy to resist state oppression, and a strategy that begins with pleasure. In their issue number 14, published on June 25, 1923, the headline reads: "¡Me he de echar a un vigilante desde la raíz hasta el hueso! [I will take down a watchman, from the root to the bone]." The images conjured by *echar, raíz,* and *hueso* play with the act of consuming in a sexual sense and mobilize popular refrains to reassemble them with deviant sexual acts; *echar* is a verb commonly used to describe the successful pursuit, seduction, and act of sexual intercourse (as opposed to the more popular English translation *to get laid,* which implies a certain passive reward), *raíz* meaning root visually connotes taking something wholly as in swallowing to the root, and *hueso* meaning bone visually refers to an erect cock. The headline introduces a short poem meant to jab at the *mordelones,* traffic agents called "biters" for their action of taking bribes to avoid fines (this term remains in use, with *mordida* being the commonplace word for a bribe). The poem reads:

> me he de echar un vigilante
> desde la "raíz" hasta el huezo
> Me he de echar un zopilote
> más que me duela el gañote

> [I will take down a watchman
> from the "root" to the bone
> I will take down a vulture
> though my throat may hurt]

(*El Chafirete*, Num. 14, June 12, 1923)

The vigilante or traffic agent becomes a body to be consumed by the poetic voice, standing in perhaps for Novo or perhaps for someone else. What is striking is the act of penetration, in this case oral sex, described as an act of power negotiation; gañote means throat, and the poem is describing the prowess of the poetic voice able to swallow a hard cock to the base, the pleasure overriding any potential throat pain. The body gains power over the traffic agent precisely through this act of penetration, countering all the normative definitions of a penetrated body as abject, dominated, and powerless. More so, the poem is a queer parody of the popular song "El Durazno," whose lyrics read: "me he de comer un durazno // desde la raíz hasta el huezo // no le hace que sea güerita // sería mi gusto y por eso [I will eat this peach // from root to bone // it doesn't matter if she's blonde // it's my desire and that's all]."[55] In the previous chapter, I analyzed the *corrido de las pelonas,* which parodied various registers of popular music and attempted to resignify their misogynistic attitude in the face

of an increasing presence of women in the public sphere. Here, Novo resignifies the patriarchal and heterosexual structure of the popular song into a highly
explicit homosexual parody. In doing so, he transforms the traffic agent into
a sexual object while also describing the body of the consumer as strong and
willing to navigate pain to obtain pleasure — hardly a weak, effeminate, or
powerless body in any way. In the background, pleasure can be testified in the
erectness of the vigilante's cock, hardly a noncompliant subject in the sexual
scene before us, and while consent is difficult to be evidenced in this fragment
(or in the other fragments where Novo engages with other working-class men),
I understand these social encounters within the general framework and history
of interclass homosexual relationships in Mexico and beyond. Specifically in
Mexico, this is manifested in the dynamics of *chacales*, *ramones*, and other
gender stereotypes that are mobilized to understand men (typically younger,
Brown, and working class) who have sexual or social encounters with men in
exchange for something, from a beer at the bar to economic payment for goods.
In texts such as Luis Zapata's *El vampiro de la colonia Roma*, Antonio Pacheco
Zárate's *Centraleros*, or Elvis Guerra's *Ramonera*, these social subjects appear
in their social complexity as subjects who coexist with homosexual men while
they reject this identity and indeed practice more normative forms of social
behavior; although tempting to understand them with the notion of the closet,
I resist this easy explanation of them as men with internalized homophobia
and want to signal their potential pleasure in their encounters with other men.
Ultimately, though, there is no textual evidence of this pleasure in most of the
texts, since the focus tends to be on the subject who initiates, seeks out, and
sometimes pays for the encounter.

Shared pleasure marks the bodies of both the chafiretes that Novo writes
about as well as his own body, assembling a sexual community that crosses
class boundaries and becomes a ubiquitous aspect of the modern city.[56] In the
"Eglogas de Garcirrastro de la Viga," Novo uses the (neo)baroque poetic form
of the eclogue to describe an encounter and dialogue between two men who
masturbate alone and together. The bucolic setting typical of this poetic form
is transformed into an urban landscape of streets, speeding cars, new buildings,
and public parks; the pastoral characters become two *chafiretes*, Patricio sleeping in his garage and Sinforoso wandering the Alameda park while "torciendo
el paso por su verde seno [twisting his step down the green path]" (*El Chafirete*,
Num 20, August 6, 1923). The poem constructs an image of Patricio having
a wet dream and ejaculating in his sleep, while Sinforoso's wanderings are a
reference perhaps to the homosexual cruising for which that particular park was
known. However, he is unable to find a companion, and thus "de puro contento
// con Manuela y Ana me recreaba // hasta que aceite grueso discurría // y todo
yo me mojaba [out of sheer joy // with Manuela and Ana I would re-create
myself // until thick oil spilled out // and all of me was wet]." He calls out for
Patricio to join him, and the other man does so while the poetic voice watches
them voyeuristically, able to understand and name their hidden desires even

if the two *choferes* don't name it themselves. Their encounter is broken by a policeman who sees them and runs to catch them, but the two men are too fast to get to their buses and escape quickly into the dusk. While the baroque style of the composition is interesting as a subversion of a classic form in Spanish poetry, Novo was also known to parody Sor Juana Ines's sonnets and other popular poetic forms as a joke and a playful jab at the "seriousness" of poetic traditions. I am more interested in how the poetic voice describes these sexual bodies of two men caught in the throes of intense erotic desire. They appear as commonplace in the urban space, occupying the garage, the public park, and the urban bus as familiar spaces. Their powerful desire, literally overflowing their bodies in an uncontrollable manner, evidence a network of bodies and spaces beyond Novo's individual body, even if he is the one to see and name it in writing.

Salvador Novo would go on to become an important cultural bureaucrat in Mexico's cultural sphere, being named the Cronista de la Ciudad (Chronicler of the City) in 1965 after occupying important publishing positions in the Secretarías de Relaciones Exteriores, de Economía Nacional, and de Educación Pública. While his early texts reveal a young man caught in the waves of progressive modernization and iconoclasm characteristic of the avant-garde movements of the early twentieth century, Novo would increasingly occupy a conservative political position. He would infamously be remembered for siding with the authoritarian government of Gustavo Díaz Ordaz during the violent events of 1968 in Tlatelolco and for calling for the quelching of student unrest. History would remember him as the ultimate elite homosexual, a provocative and scandalizing dandy with refined taste and a sharper wit whose refined mannerisms carved out a space for his homosexuality. This fearless performance of sexual identity in the face of a violently normative *mestizo* gender order revolving around the *macho* figure gains even more political weight when his sexuality is read alongside that of the other Mexican men he describes in his texts, queering both idealized *mestizo* masculinities and lower-class masculine bodies.[57] The shared pleasure in these textualized sexual encounters implode the narrow sexual politics of the active-passive Mediterranean complex as well as Octavio Paz's later theorization of Mexican sexuality as violent domination through the Chingada complex. The anal and oral pleasures that Novo writes about assemble a series of masculine sexual bodies moving through the city and complexify what critics have described as instances of class consumption; while Novo undoubtedly had a predilection for lower-class bodies of policemen and chauffeurs, the pleasure these men experience alongside Novo and other men allows for a glimpse into a sexualscape where consent and mutual pleasure become the catalyst for ethical sexual relations of a more horizontal desiring structure. Against a symbolic understanding of sexuality that places bodies in strict symbolic positions associated with power, these instances of pleasure and bodily engagements construct a homosexual body outside the narrow confines of normative ideologies. Novo and the other homosexual bodies explicitly resist the powerful medical, criminological, and psychoanalytic discourses that contain them in discreet and neutralized positions under the control of the politically authorized heteronormative citizens who mobilize these discourses. Like the *chafiretes* speeding from the traffic agents and like Novo offhandedly rejecting Freud and Marañón while dozing, these bodies are powerful in their desire and they anchor it in each other, naming their pleasure through acts without shame; in doing so, they weave a sexual history that continues to shape the countercultural sexual politics of Mexico today, in metro cars, quiet public parks, and homosocial bathhouses.

The Neobaroque Desert: Humanimality and Queer Utopian Nationscapes in Abigael Bohórquez's Theater

While Salvador Novo was perhaps the most audaciously campy homosexual writer in postrevolutionary Mexico, he was not the only one writing about explicit sex. Abigael Bohórquez was born in the small northern city of Heróica Caborca, Sonora, in 1937 and lived his childhood years in this northern state under the care of his single mother and his grandmother. He received primary education in Caborca and Gadsden, Arizona, later working in the Civil Registry in San Luis Río Colorado, an important mining town. In 1955, he migrated to the Mexico City metropolitan area. By the 1950s, the Mexican capital was experiencing the high point of the economic growth spurt retroactively named the *Milagro Mexicano*, the postwar period between the mid-1940s and the early 1970s when economic policy changes, infrastructure development (roads, dams, irrigation systems, and public housing), and internal migration accelerated the modernization of the cityscape.[58] Joining this migration, Bohórquez studied theater in the Instituto Nacional de Bellas Artes (cofounded by Salvador Novo) and began his lifelong (albeit culturally silenced) publishing and playwriting career. Like Novo, during the 1960s he held cultural positions in various governmental departments, including the Secretaría de Relaciones Exteriores. However, unlike Novo, his radical leftist politics aligned Bohórquez closer to writers such as José Revueltas and, coupled with his outspoken homosexual desire emerging during global sexual liberation, caused him to be shunned from major cultural spheres. From the 1970s onward, Bohórquez moved to Milpa Alta, one of the southernmost districts of Mexico City with a strong Indigenous presence. For the remainder of his life, he worked in the Instituto Mexicano del Seguro Social (IMSS) in various cultural departments, using the stages provided in this public health/public education forum to stage his theatrical production in small venues in the metropolises and across the country. He moved back to Sonora in 1990 to continue working as a cultural promoter for the IMSS and passed away in 1995, leaving behind perhaps one of the most explicitly homosexual and poetically complex representations of homosexual desire and theater in Mexican cultural history.

Although a prolific writer with over twenty titles of poetry and theater, for decades Bohórquez did not receive critical attention outside of a small group of female academics from various cultural institutes in Hermosillo, Sonora, many of whom were close friends with the outspokenly homosexual poet. In recent years, Mexican and US academics have begun to focus their attention on his poetic works, including Andrew Gordus, Ismael Laris, Iván Figueroa, Gerardo Bustamante Bermúdez, Miguel Manriquez, and Christina Karageorgou-Bastea, all of whom have approached his poetic oeuvre through the lens of homosexual and political poetry in the tradition of neobaroque poetry in Latin America. However, Bohórquez's rich theater production has not received much critical attention aside from Bustamante Bermúdez's recent anthology of Bohórquez's many dramatic works, which joins Hugo Salcedo's introductory essay from a 1992 collection. I emphasize this theater production not just because of its prolific span from the 1950s to the 1980s, but also because of its unique staging across Mexico in small venues, particularly those related to the cultural departments of the Instituto Mexicano del Seguro Social where Bohórquez labored for years. These stages allow for an understanding of theater as an educational platform, a communal space, and an artistic space to explore new and alternative social identities emerging as the country developed. Furthermore, the particularities of these stages allow for the visualization of social identities that don't tend to make it to the artistic scene of more canonical theater until much later, figures such as sex workers, transvestites, young migrants, young single women and mothers, children, and other marginalized citizens.

Bohórquez began his literary career in the 1950s, the same decade that saw Carlos Fuentes's *La region más transparente* (*The most transparent region*), Juan Rulfo's *Pedro Páramo* and Luis Buñuel's *Los Olvidados* (*The young and the damned*) appear, all cultural texts that epitomize the dreams and failures of the *mestizo* state national project. Experiencing the sentimental and affectual education (or subjectivation) of this project through Golden Age cinema and stronger educational and public health institutions, Bohórquez's work allows for an understanding of homosexuality that builds on Novo's first encounters with modernity. Both are authors who were outspoken in their sexual desire in literary works and in their public personas.[59] However, Bohórquez's homosexual representations in poetry and theater showcase an already urbanized subjectivity that does not negate or deny the sexual landscape of the northern desert provinces; a sociosexual subjectivity that lives both in the urban motels and in the quiet and expansive desert or the milpa. These representations engage with the silenced history of rural homosexual practices alongside the realities of urban migration and the criminalization of homosexuality that demanded facing the authorities while remaining elusive and safe. While some have read Bohórquez's open sexuality and choice of desert landscapes as a form of self-exile, I see in his literary works a mobilization of rural homosexualities and femininities — through queer and female bodies — that produce counter-cultural bodies directly engaging with the cultural paradigms of both homo-sexuality and national masculinities, particularly in his theatrical works where characters are often asked to act in parodical imitations of national iconic actors like María Félix or Pedro Armendariz.[60]

My argument here is that Abigael Bohórquez uses poetry and theater to stage queer utopian nationscapes through a neobaroque aesthetics where the urban and rural geographies of the nation are populated by humanimal intersubjec-tivities. These alternative and utopian modes of being Mexican shape humans in relation to animals around them (horses, coyotes, snakes), to the mineral formations surrounding them (mountains, rocks, cliffs), and, critically, to the cultural institutions that are projecting ideologies onto them (performances of femininity and masculinity in film). These intersubjectivities then become ways to resist existing in marginality and exclusion and push these characters and bodies to demand a social and political recognition of their presence in the nation. By shaping these bodies through a neobaroque aesthetic made up of syn-tax, vocabulary, images, and specific literary references, Bohórquez generates countercultural bodies that reject exclusionary notions of nation and chose to exist rather in networks of class, race, gender, and sexual relations that connect and expand Mexican understandings of queerness beyond the more normalized urban, homosexual, and cis-male definitions. Taken together, these bodies (rev-olutionary men, housewives in the desert, homosexual shepherds, men in trysts in motel rooms, et cetera) appear on the poetic space and stage as utopic agents who provide glimpses into an alternative construction of Mexico; the open and explicit representations of homosexual desire become the foundational acts of another nation, inclusionary in its intersectional feminist alliances with other marginalized human and nonhuman bodies beyond its sexual limitations.

Previous criticism has emphasized the aesthetic particularities of Bohórquez's poetry as regionalizing and as politically committed in its explicit references, and building on the work of Miguel Manriquez Duran, Silvestre Uresti, Iván Figueroa, and Christina Karageorgou-Basta, I propose a reading of Bohórquez's literary oeuvre as a staging of queer utopian nationscapes. By this I mean both the literal staging (scenery, mise-en-scene, geography, and place) as well as the characters and their performance in this space. In his poetry and theater, these characters often present humanimal intersubjectivities, their humanity inextri-cably entwined with the existence and contours of animal, mineral, and material culture surrounding them. Finally, these queer utopias are queer both in their gender-sexual expression where dissident desires make themselves explicit as well as in an aesthetic sense where a neobaroque style defamiliarizes language through syntax, vocabulary, and poetic tropes.

This approach to Bohórquez is informed by my own experiencing of his the-atrical work when I was a teenager in *preparatoria*/high school and attended a staging of one of his lesser-known educational short plays at the cultural center in Hermosillo, Sonora. The small theater was sparsely occupied, and the stage

was a rather makeshift scenario, the costumes simple and unable to really identify the characters; a trio of actors played out a short scene related to domestic
violence and institutional intervention. The context of the play was educational
more than artistic, and, nevertheless, between the dialogue with local vocabulary, the sparse staging, and the intimate setting, the play generated a brief
utopia where the production and audience came together to understand a different world, one where domestic violence was spoken about, acknowledged, and
navigated through emotional and social support. While wary of blindly apply-
ing José Esteban Muñoz as a Latinx theorist to a Mexican context, his approach
to queer temporalities is useful to tease out the ways in which Bohórquez uses
forms of temporalities to disturb the order of the nation. For Muñoz, utopia is
a politically relevant tool that allows for the consideration of queerness "as a
modality of ecstatic time in which the temporal stranglehold that I describe as
straight time is interrupted or stepped out of" (*Cruising Utopia* 32). This idea
of breaking out of straight time, coupled with the social aspect of queerness that
ultimately relies on relationality, generates these spaces (theatrical, emotional,
psychological, and poetic) where countercultural subjects can come together.
That day, my teenage self witnessed two women on stage support each other as
they navigated, denounced, and fought back against domestic violence, *and* I
also came together with the rest of the audience in a complicit space we knew
was different than the one outside the theater. Queer utopic nationscapes not
only exist on paper, but they are also generated in the ecstatic moments when
readers and viewers engage with them, breaking the temporal boundaries of a
nationalist *mestizo* temporality.

This utopian reading compliments and runs parallel to a neobaroque aesthetics, often defined as "an alternative modernity that eschews breaking with the
past for re-creating the past, in the neobaroque, to create means to re-create"
(Kaup 21). This aesthetics forms a nationscape identified with the nation itself
(through characters such as revolutionaries and spaces such as the rural deserts)
while nevertheless being marked with alternative and novel significations tied
to a countercultural milieu of sexual and social dissidence. In a similar vein,
Bolívar Echeverría signals how the baroque seeks to revitalize classical canons
through an ambivalent process in which the reworking of certain themes is
confused with new meanings.[61] While remaining squarely within the historical period of the New World Baroque during the colonial period, Echeverría's
analysis nevertheless provides an understanding of the (neo)baroque ethos that
speaks to the poetic expressions of neobaroque Latin American writers such
as José Lezama Lima, Néstor Perlonguer, or Eduardo Espina. To the erudite
and poetically referential style of these writers, Bohórquez contributes a neobaroque aesthetic shaped by the visual regimes of the Mexican Golden Age
of film and the erotic landscapes of Mexican homosexual men, using these to
articulate alternative nationalisms that tie back to the colonial/baroque period
as much as they look forward to the urban futures ahead.

Critics such as Miguel Manriquez Duran, Silvestre Uresti, and Iván Figueroa (all of them focusing on his poetry) have approached Bohórquez's work as regionalizing (focusing on the rural as regionally separated from the rest of the nation), aestheticizing (focusing on the aesthetic dimension of his work as separated from a political dimension), and corporally marginalized (focusing on how his work includes bodies typically excluded from the nation, such as homosexual men or female prostitutes). Bringing these approaches together and extending them, I propose a reading of the playwright-poet from a neobaroque angle that highlights and connects these threads in a more ethical and contingent oeuvre. I understand the neobaroque particularly as Mabel Moraña has described it as "an assemblage of power and resistance, identity and difference, rationalist excess and sensorial extravagance [that] are articulated, from the beginning, in the overcodified registry of baroque aesthetics" (Moraña 242). This assemblage, another form of countercultural aesthetics that remains in the uncomfortable place of poetic beauty and symbolism coexisting with political critique and social dissidence, can be seen over and over in Bohórquez's oeuvre working against the grain of institutional modes of cultures, literally (where these books were published and circulated) as well as figuratively (in the topics and treatments he explored). Furthermore, these queer Mexican neobaroque assemblages from the desert become ways to resist a more elitist and exclusionary understanding of culture as they engage with a recoding of baroque aesthetics, which historically values an "elite" education with erudite references over a more popular mode of the baroque. Like Novo in the rare poems published under the pseudonyms of Juana Inés del Cabús and Garcirrastro de la Viga, Bohórquez uses the neobaroque as an articulation, "a hookup, a historically and socially contingent linkage between disparate phenomenon, that is historically forged and broken over time and across cultures" (Kaup 6). These hookups bring together a specific syntax and style with vocabulary and references that relate to popular film and street slang, anchored in the imaginary nations lived and breathed by working-class citizens and anyone subjectified within the *mestizo* nation. This accessibility makes their cultural projects distinct; rather than generating an elitist artistic project or persona to be discussed and circulated in the cultural sphere, they generate poetic and corporeal assemblages that can be consumed by modern Mexican citizens and recirculated as dissident desires, now named and poetically expressed.[62]

This neobaroque aesthetic permeates Bohórquez's oeuvre and generates a lyrico-political discourse anchored in the everyday experiences of the average Mexican citizen of the time, particularly the working-class citizens consuming Golden Age film, linguistic migration in the form of the *bracero* and *pachuco* migrants flowing to and from the United States as well as stemming from his border experiences, and state nationalism through the educational system.[63] By invoking this aesthetic through a countercultural framework, I want to place Bohórquez in the cultural milieu in which most of his work was produced and published — mainly Mexico City and small university presses — and in relation to the multiple fronts in which he declared an explicit and committed political position. Countercultural bodies produce, negotiate, and mobilize difference by following lines of flight and escape, questioning the implicit limits of culture and politics in order to explicitly state the social structuring process of gender, sexual, ethnic, racial, and national norms.[64] In doing so, they mobilize an erotics of politics, an understanding of politics as an arena of the erotic in the bodies that are experiencing and are motivated by sensual pleasure and stimulation, and not as much by ideas or slogans. This erotic of politics is grounded in the corporeal existences of the poetic persona and characters, where the body becomes the way of engaging with and subverting national narratives and traumatic events that end up placing gendered bodies in fixed social and sexual roles.[65] This staging of sexual alternatives produces a national landscape where the figures of the revolutionary, the urban policeman, the flaneur, and the housewife coexist with the general male bodies experiencing homosexual desire, thus engaging with and expanding the limits of legitimate/normative citizenship. From this countercultural, political, and aesthetic angle, Bohórquez's textualization of rural and urban men experiencing homosexual desire and carrying out homosexual acts becomes an active resistance of an identitarian construction of (urban) homosexual identity and subjectivity. Rather, these bodies coexist in a national space populated by other (national) bodies. Thus, he generates models of homosexuality that defy the active-passive construction, while also resisting being genealogically tied to the dandies, *fifíes*, the 41, the Contemporáneos, and other elitist representations of homosexual desire. While the relational queer utopias that Bohórquez constructs do sometimes include such figures as Langston Hughes, Federico García Lorca ,or even Salvador Novo, their appearance is tied to their corporealities (Black, queer, and sexual); Novo is remembered as a homosexual flaneur and a *maese* of Coyoacán rather than a cultural authority. These queer icons appear, then, in relation to other spaces such as motels for brief sexual encounters and bathhouses, generating a queer utopia represented through neobaroque aesthetics that anchor the nation in concrete space as well as time, while questioning the limits imposed by a nationalist mythos of desire.

The humanimal intersubjectivities that populate Bohórquez's queer utopian nationscapes are not bound to a single poem, anthology, or play. They are geopolitically situated, often appearing in relation to a specific region, historical moment, street, or house, or even a specific bedroom, kitchen, or motel room. Their vocabulary and syntax — as well as that of the poetic or theatrical voice that orders the space around them — appear in a neobaroque style and structure where the tropes and wordplays of sylvan and other Golden Age genres fuse with the bodies of Mexican countercultural citizens: homosexual men, liberated women, rebellious youth, and others. For the remainder of this analysis, I will focus on the two theatrical poems *La madrugada del centuaro* and *El círculo hacia Narciso*, both award-winning and staged and published in the 1960s, and the poetry collection *Digo lo que amo* (Federación Editorial Mexicana, 1976). However, this queer utopic counterculture can also be seen in his other poetry and theater, such as *Memorias del la alta milpa* (1976), a poetry collection that brings together his everyday life experiences living and working in Milpa Alta, a southern metropolitan district with the historic highest concentration of Nahuatl-speaking peoples, with his poetic encounters with other global queer writers such as Langston Hughes. In this poetic landscape, homosexual desire is expressed alongside a Nahuatl vocabulary that does not appropriate through an essentializing lens so much as serve to construct a specific geography marked by class and racialized oppression, the words themselves building a material reality full of embodied speakers. In *Abigaeles, poeníñimos* (Instituto Sonorense de Cultura, 1991), he speaks to and from a child's poetic perspective, using the Christmas pageantry of popular *posadas* and *nacimientos* to reimagine a neobaroque nationalist stage. The short poetic format and the vocabulary of children's poetry expresses a utopic revisioning of the literal staging of culture and religion; as in the more contemporary Argentinian performance artist, writer, and activist Susy Shock's *Crianzas* (2016), the child narratee who is listening to poetic voice becomes a powerful way to interpellate the reader to reimagine the present. Finally, in *Navegación en Yoremito* (Universidad de Sonora, 1995), his poetic style is a confusion of verses in baroque Spanish, Nahuatl, and English that express dissident sexual and social desires. The (neo) baroque vocabulary, orthography, and grammar places the queer, homosexual, and dissident bodies in an expansive time and space, simultaneously claiming existence in the political here and now and in the historical past, an act of defiance in the face of heteropatriarchal erasure.

The one-act play *La madrugada del centauro* appeared in 1964 after being awarded a prize in the Segundo Concurso de Creación de Obras en un Acto organized by the UNAM (Universidad Nacional Autónoma de México). In this context, the centaur is an expansively polysemic figure: a reference to Pancho Villa as the revolutionary *centuaro* del norte, a reference to the mythical Greek healer and teacher Chiron, a symbol of subjective intercorporeality, a stand-in for queer desire as monstrous, and more. The play is contemplated to be staged in the open and calls for as little scenography as possible; "la acción transcurre de anochecer a amanecer de un día de desposesión en un lugar del agro mexicano [the action takes place from sundown to sunrise on a day of dispossession in some place in the Mexican countryside]" (19), signaling a geopolitical situating in rural poverty and dispossession. The plot centers on the death/homicide of Floriano, a rich landowner with aristocratic background who married Lila only to confine her to his rural arid property, where he visited only to procreate while spending most of his time in the city gambling and buying sex. His progeny in the forgotten ranch is Aldebarán (the eldest), Golondrina, and Sagitario (the youngest).[66] Each has experienced a particular form of patriarchal violence: Aldebarán's fiancé Lucila was raped and exiled by Floriano, and Golondrina's betrothed José was murdered in cold blood by the father. During the night's events, Floriano discovers that Sagitario has been having carnal relations with Galana, his mare, a symbolic stand-in for a feminized male youth. After punishing the young man and threatening to place the animal with the stallions, Floriano dies accidentally in a stampede of bulls. Rather than allowing Galana to suffer the sexual violence his father is inflicting upon them, Sagitario literally jumps the gun and shoots Galana, sparking the stampede that kills Floriano. Even though the whole family had been plotting during the play to eliminate Floriano and take control of the land to end the dispossession and extractivist economy of Floriano and maintain their survival in the harsh ecosystem, once the patriarch is dead Aldebarán steps into his shoes and becomes the patriarch himself, evicting and exiling the rest of the family from the land under pain of death. The sociosexual imagery of the play is nuanced with multiple meanings and constantly signals the various structural oppressions of heteropatriarchal capitalism. The family here is used both as a political structure to point at the construction and nature of the state, as well as to frame the historical events that shape Mexican families and point at their survival strategies in the face of revolutionary and state violence.[67]

The central character of this family drama cum caricature of state power is undoubtedly Sagitario, the youngest and only character to openly resist his father's violence and the one who is punished on stage, the body who symbolically receives the heteronormative male violence and pushes back, as well as the centaur of the play, in his self-conceptualization and in his sexual acts. In its representation of violence, the play speaks to the history of the revolution and the waves of heteronormative violence mobilized by the PRI regime in its wake. Through the central taboo acts of human-animal relations, the play mobilizes sexuality as a political tool; rather than representing literal homosexual desire, the extremely dissident sexual practices serve to symbolically place us in the terrain of the taboo. According to sociologist Christie Davis, sexual taboos function to give shape and strength to political-social structures; the persecution of certain acts serves to reinforce the identitarian boundaries of a specific group while also maintaining a hierarchy based on military or religious order often enforced with physical violence.[68] In the face of the historic and continuous criminalization of homosexual bodies, representing dissident desires through a taboo structure becomes a way to re-present homosexual bodies and desires without entering into the terrain of homosexual identity tied to criminalization and persecution. The sexual pleasure that Sagitario embodies and speaks about on stage is a way to name the "significado de la vida terrenal [meaning of an earthly life]" (Manriquez 26) and transforms the mythical character into an emblem of sensual pleasure where "el instinto visceral se impone; no hay grandeza sino inflación del yo que se pierde en la embriaguez del sexo [the visceral instinct imposes itself: there is no greatness but an inflation of the I that loses itself in the inebriation of sex]" (Salcedo, "Claves" 115). I see in Sagitario an erotically powerful character whose pleasure is not exactly represented visually on stage, and whose desires become political structures that end up building his subjectivity in relationality with his mother and sister, as well as with the land around him. His is the body that receives the physical violence of Floriano on stage (while sex is too taboo to represent on stage, physical vio-lence is perfectly reasonable to be embodied in heteropatriarchal society), and as Floriano beats Sagitario he invokes religious scripture to condemn the young man and further cement his moral structure spiritually. Ultimately, Aldebaran changes his name to Ruiz III after casting out Sagitario and his family, rein-stating the heteropatriarchal order even though it is Sagitario who is directly responsible for Floriano's death. Thus, the Mexican Revolution lays the back-drop for this night's action, a foundational moment for *mestizo* nationalism whose exclusionary nature is revealed for what it is: a sexual and racialized social order built on the appropriation of violence by the state after an initial explosion of rage by dissident citizens.

As a centaur and a sexual dissident, Sagitario exists in a greater cultural tradition of embodying political resistance through the monstrous. Sustained in an interdependent ethical network/rhizome of familial support as he protects and is protected by his mother and sister, Sagitario's radical sexuality is also in itself a political structure of care, as Galana has been under his care since birth. Sagitario's shifting body harkens to a tradition of representing queer-ness through the figure of the monstrous that in the Hispanic world includes Federico García Lorca, and beyond includes figures such as Mary Shelley's Frankenstein.[69] In his work on homosexuality and horror film genres, Harry Benshoff signals how queerness "is a narrative moment, or a performance or a stage which engages the oppressive binaries of the dominant hegemony" (4), where the semantic figures of the "monster" — radically outcast by a heter-onormative society with little to no chance of redemption — become a way to understand the lived experiences of queer bodies around us. Sagitario is thus a double monster, a sexual deviant on the one hand and a social saboteur that choses to ally himself with the women around him on the other. Bohórquez's bestialization of Sagitario distances the understandings of queerness from a fully urban tradition of homosexual acts, anchored now in the rural regions, and presents a version of queerness where social exclusion — while traumatic and violent — does not culminate in alienation and solitude: a queerness built on and sustained by community. Furthermore, in the face of the political structures of punishment, Sagitario, Lila, and Golondrina build a community based on forgiveness and redemption where alliance and support shift the guilt of Lila in surrendering to Floriano's violence throughout the years into a current and future network of support and survival.

This countercultural community coalesces in the provincial regions of Mexico, anchored by a series of geographical and cultural markers that weave the Sonoran Desert into the revolutionary nationscape. This geography is set apart from the *mestizo* camposcape by the distinct conjunction of its materiality and cultural uses with an economic history and reality of dispossession; against the timeless qualities of the mestizo *camposcape* as an eternal repository of ide-alized indigeneity alienated from a material reality, Bohórquez presents an (agri) cultural geography populated by men and women with physical, emotional, and sexual needs, desires, successes, and shortcomings.[70] Bohórquez further queers this landscape by populating it with explicitly, openly, and celebratorily sexual bodies, male and female; these do not appear as sexualized objects of a male gaze, but rather as sexual and erotic agents who desire and decide, especially in the face of oppressive violence that seeks to punish and control them. In the opening scene, Lila and Golondrina are cleaning *lentejas in bateas o coritas*, woven pots characteristic of the Comcáac peoples, while Sagitario splits *mesquite* and *palofierro* firewood, both trees native to the region. These markers, which in the sparse scenography are meant to be imagined rather than visually represented, already present an erotic and embodied engagement with regional specificity, an engagement where their bodies are touching, smelling, tasting, and ultimately shaping the material conditions around them. The two women remember "una antigua conseja regional" and their interlocutions narrate a retelling of the biblical couple Joseph and Mary now existing in the Sonoran instead of the Egyptian Desert, eating *higos, chile verde, carne machaca, horchata de melon*, and *bichicoris*, all food items characteristic of this region. The linguistic precision of these markers serves to construct a regional identity, and coupled with the religious narrative, they become subversions of the heteronormative power structures of both Catholic and national political structures. From the opening, the holy family of Mary and Joseph provide a structure to understand the holy family of the *mestizo* nation, as well as a structure of power that Sagitario will challenge and undermine. In their interlocutions, Lila and Golondrina begin to resignify the Virgin Mary as a stand-in for the daughter herself, and the murdered fiancé is reborn in the place of Joseph when Golondrina, her voice "quebrada por el llanto [broken by laments]" (22), interjects "y María y José, bebiéndose, enlazados, // fueron entre la vid y el trigo y la solana // a procurarse un beso . . . de pinole [and María and José, drinking each other and entwined // went between the grapevine and the wheat and the solarium // to give each other a kiss . . . of pinole]" (22). These substitutions radicalize religious and cultural narrative; the suffering of the Virgin Mary is recast into the suffering of Golondrina for the murder of José, the Catholic imaginary used to understand patriarchal and nationalist violence. While her suffering is typically assembled with the justified sacrifice of Jesus for the sins of humanity, in their retelling Golondrina and Lila use Mary's suffering to make sense of the senseless murder of José. In doing so, Golondrina's body is assembled as a religious body experiencing piety and sacrifice, a desiring body, and, above all, a political body seeking to release her rage onto the person who committed the murder that is causing her pain.

Thus, while the desert has typically been understood as a marker of isolation and abandonment experienced by Bohórquez due to his own marginalized status and representative of the marginalization experienced by those provincial regions as a whole, I believe this particular utopian camposcape is speaking of a richness, abundance, and relationality that is politically relevant.[71] In this play in particular, and time and again in other poetic works, the desert appears as a productive (in the sense that it produces identity and existence) and expansive (in the sense that it contains more than can be represented) assemblage that subverts the exclusionary nationalistic construction of Mexico; it is less of a marginalized storage of refuse and more of a source of subjective and material support. By assembling the northern spaces of Sonora with the foundational moment of the *mestizo* social order (the revolution) and populating it with sexual bodies, *Madrugada* generates a utopian geography of neobaroque possibilities "where the simultaneities of multiple cultural times open a space full of potential and common grounds" (Moraña 263). These multiple temporalities serve to further queer the narratives of the nation predominant in the reimagining of Mexico through the geographical lens of its rural regions; rather than contain an essentialized past, they contain multiple temporalities that include both the Catholic heritage of Jesus, Mary, and Joseph and Indigenous and autochthonous culture in the form of material objects, names, and sometimes bodies.[72] What ultimately matters is the coexistence of these temporalities in a single space, even if it is sometimes in conflict or contradiction, remaining open in the possibilities and encouraging the reader to resignify the space around them in complicity and alliance.

In this already countercultural space containing multiple temporalities and cultures, Sagitario's relationship with Galana provides the ultimate queering of nationalism, constructing a Muñozian utopia embodied in humanimal intersubjectivities. I use this term to understand expansive and inclusive subjectivities whose embodiment cannot be contained to a single organism; it serves to highlight the ways in which our "human" subjectivities are always already humanimal in the interactions and it assemblages with a mind-boggling number of bacteria and other life forms in our biome, as well as highlights the relationality between the "human" body and the environment surrounding it, beyond nutritional needs and looking toward the emotional, psychic, spiritual, and cultural relationships that make up our existence. Analogous, though not the same as the deleuzo-guattarian notion of becoming animal, humanimal intersubjectivities allow for an understanding of politico-social subjectivity running against the grain of liberal, individualistic, and anthropocentric conceptions of the citizen; their relevancy today highlights the countercultural history of Mexico and sheds light on current contemporary citizens challenging the strict boundaries of nationalist and capitalist subjectivities. Sagitario self-reflects on this subjectivity multiple times in the play, and in his longest and most poetic interlocution on stage, he speaks of his belief:

> En algún tiempo fui centauro y ahora vivo de un recuerdo. Cuando tú relinchas, Galana, me sacuden los siglos y un desbridado deseo despierta en mi memoria viejos abuelos de cascos cogelones. Entonces, soy el centauro que resucita para domar potrancas. Soy tal vez el último hijo de los hombres destinado a aliarse con tu raza, pero habrás sido al menos la más bella y yo el más feliz

[Some time ago I was a centaur and now I live from a memory. Galana, when you neigh the centuries shake me and an unbridled desire awakens in my memory the old hotblooded grandfathers with heavy hooves. Then, I am the centaur come back to life to take colts. I am perhaps the last son of the men destined to ally themselves with your race, but you will have been at least the most handsome and me the happiest]. (Bohórquez 23)

This centaur, although a real reference to an already corporeally inclusive body, is more than a symbolic fusion of Sagitario's and Galana's bodies (Bermudez, "Introducción" 31). To read it solely as this single moment of sexual union undermines the sociosexual and erotic components of this humanimal intersubjectivity. Rather than a purely sexual encounter, Sagitario's centaurhood is grounded in a series of erotic and political relationalities: first, in his ethical structure of caring for Galana since his and her childhood, a loving and caring relationship of mutual interdependence; and second, in the redirection of the typically violent nature of centaurs (Chiron was the exception to the rule, and even then he is a mythological figure prone to extreme acts of violence) toward a resistance to the pre- and postrevolutionary heteronormative political order. These relationalities transform both Sagitario and Galana into an embodied anticommunity built on alliance, mutual care, and support, where he provides food and physical care while she provides emotional stability and safety for his expression.[73] I consider it important to understand Sagitario's desire at face value, while at the same time understanding it symbolically in the context of its material and cultural production; his zoophilia signals marginal desires, bypasses urban constructions of homosexual desire and acts, and ultimately points at a series of commonalities in lived experiences across both rural and urban citizenries in their care for each other and for other animals.[74]

In this humanimal intersubjectivity, the body of Galana isn't seen on stage, and her theatrical presence is aural with whinnies and other noises off stage when Sagitario cleans her stall and bathes her. This (dis)embodied presence activates other regimes of the audience/reader's sensorium and catalyzes the imagination toward a liminal space where previous social experiences can fill in the details. Surrounded by the violently heteropatriarchal space of the nation, Galana can thus become an affective refuge for anyone and everyone, as she is a physical, corporal, symbolic, and affective refuge for Sagitario: "tú eres como un cuarto tibio. Como en cuarto que siempre invita a entrar en él. Como un cuarto que se hizo para mí y que me pertenece desde que se levantaron sus cuatro paredes [you are like a warm room. Like a quarter that always invites me in. Like a room made for me and that belongs to me ever since its four walls were erected]" (22). The poetic alliteration of the "c" (/k/) sound creates a sonic space (a baroque poetic technique) and then gives way to a more complex confusion of images: cuarto as room and refuge, a territory to be explored and occupied; and cuarto as a horse's hind quarters, now a sexualized body and another territory to be relational with. Galana is an affective territory as well, a space where the emotions and desires unable to be expressed in any other way in the outside striated territory of heteropatriarchal violence controlled by Floriano can be released. The physical-corporal space of their taboo relationship is revealed to contain within many plateaus, and sexuality is hardly the most important of these territories, giving way to emotional and sensorial relationality.

These "cuatro paredes" are also example of the political claiming of space and existence that queer dissidence creates, a productive and expansive position-taking that lies in saying "I exist in this world and there is space for me." This is the ethos of Bohórquez's entire oeuvre, speaking from a body that first of all claims existence, and then expresses explicitly a sexual dissidence in the face of heteronormative violence that denies its existence and then furthermore establishes political dissidence in the face of homonormative violence that denies its existence. Bohórquez's queer experiences are those of a migrant and a cultural outcast due to his openly revolutionary and leftist positionings in the decades when the PRI state and cultural apparatus was violently vigilant. His cultural bureaucratic positions in the various IMSS (Instituto Mexicano del Seguro Social) health departments evidence an exclusion from the cultural sphere that may have been motivated by his tense encounters with Carlos Monsiváis, Salvador Novo, and other cultural figures. Thus, he is another unlikely bedfellow in this study who serves to exemplify how counterculture is not contained by ideologies or political camps, but by practices that are shared across different social groups and individuals. Ultimately, though, this claiming of existence, space, and subjectivity is powerful enough in itself, coming from a Brown homosexual body unashamed and unafraid to express his desire, in any form it may come.

In contrast with his siblings' thwarted relationships (Aldebarán's love interest, Lucila, is kidnapped, raped, and abandoned by Floriano, while Golondrina's betrothed, José Manuel, is murdered on a hunt under orders of Floriano), Sagitario's relationship with Galana assembles a queer temporality, a nonreproductive utopic nationalism that strongly resists the reproductive futurity demanded by heteropatriarchal capitalist societies.[75] This temporality appears in glimpses in Sagitario's monologue where he states his continual adolescence, engaging in bestial acts that may characterize rural sexual education and choosing to remain in that milieu. Again, the symbolism here of homoerotic adolescent encounters and exploration as temporary stages of sexual development is clear and directly recognizable by readers and viewers. The underlying reference to youthful homosexual exploration from which a man in the country "grows out of" is hardly veiled in the symbolic humanimal intersubjectivity that is Sagitario the centaur. It would seem that Sagitario's merciful killing of Galana, instead of letting her be sexually ravaged by every stallion under orders of Floriano, might dissipate this temporality, and yet Sagitario's choice and action itself is another manifestation of queer resistance that Aldebarán and

Golondrina did not muster in their individual violations.[76] At the play's end, when Aldebarán has exiled the remaining family, it is Sagitario who holds the final words, "por supuesto que volveremos a vernos. Habrá guerra" (43), signaling this power of resistance embedded in his queer body. These words are spoken as Aldebarán's men are literally pushing them off stage with rifles, and in the empty space that is left the audience becomes witness to and participants of a queer temporality always already present around them, populated by outcast men and women who seek refuge from the violent *mestizo* social order. In this open space, the utopic function of the text is "enacted by a certain surplus in the work that promises futurity, something that is not quite here" (Muñoz, *Cruising Utopia* 7), and yet something that is quite visible and tangible and that promises to be within reach *if only* we reach for it. The revolutionary ethos of temporal rupture — which the *mestizo* nation seeks to capture into a capitalist, heteronormative, and racialized state organizing society through violence — breaks through with Sagitario's desire and will to action.[77] The final words as their bodies disappear off-stage speak directly to the audience: "esta es, pues, una historia de historias. . . . Pero, si nuestra pobre historia, fuera la de usted, señor . . . .Usted, ¿qué haría? [this is, then, a story of stories. . . . But if our poor story were yours, sir . . . you, what would you do?]" (42). This open invitation becomes a staging of alternative actions pushing back against the rejection from the nation, an invitation that in a Brechtian move (or, more appropriately, a Boalian gesture reminiscent of theater of the oppressed) opens the dramatic space to the whole of society, inviting a reimagining and reshaping of social relations.

For Bohorquez in his oeuvre, and in particular in theater, queerness becomes an embodied tactical vantage point from which to observe the violent exclusion practiced by the normative *mestizo* nation-state, and a positioning from which to resist, reconvene, and redefine both gender and national norms. The humanimal intersubjectivities that Sagitario, Lila, and Golondrina embody in their relationality with the animals, the crops, and the desert environment slowly sediment into a countercultural community of resistance and survival. These intersubjectivities do not always have to humanimal to be queer, and Bohórquez explores other queer and campy masculinities in the context of the revolution. In the third play published in the *Primera reunión de teatro breve* (1992), he delves into the violent aftermath of the Mexican Revolution as it redistributed wealth from a landowning to a peasant class (in the best of cases) and a military class (in the worst of cases). Grounding itself in ancient Greek mythos, the satire in three acts *El círculo de Narciso* tells the story of Casandra, Olivia, and Álvaro as they gather to mourn the death of their mother. Hailing from a wealthy landowner class, Álvaro hasn't seen his sister in years after marrying Claudia, a woman from a lower-class upbringing, and choosing to ally himself in his lawyer profession with the working classes. Casandra and Olivia, however, seek to maintain the family's wealth and the funeral night becomes an evening full of class tensions among the four of them. Fatedly, the revolution comes knocking on their door that night of mourning, literally in the form of a general, Felipe, who leads a troop to expropriate this family's wealth. Old class and gender wounds come to the surface, as Felipe is the brother of Arturo, who long ago wooed Olivia and was driven to suicide by her and Casandra's cruelness as they flirted and teased him without ever intending to lower their class positionality by actually engaging with him. The play explores these tensions and continues the use of sexual metaphors and sexual histories to stage class exploitation in the wake of the revolution. Toward the end, after taking control of the old hacienda house, Felipe is about to leave the captured women with his troops, lasciviously waiting off-stage, when Olivia escapes from his grasp and proceeds to pull out a revolver, shooting Casandra and then herself. The play closes on the two remaining revolutionary men embracing each other in campy drag while performing a short scene imitating movie stars. As with *La madrugada*, suicide and murder become strategies to navigate the sexual violence imposed by a military revolutionary social order, as acts of violence performed by a political and social subject too marginalized to move in any other action easily. Self-violence serves to underscore the extreme and institutional violence of the state apparatus.

I highlight this particular play because of its engagement with Golden Age film aesthetics and ethics in order to construct the theatrical stage and communicate with its audiences. The epigraph of the play reads: "a Inés Martínez de Castro, a las *heroínas inmarcesibles de la televisión y a los caudillos cinematográficos de la Revolución*, esta anécdota de la vida real [to Inés Martínez de Castro, to *the unfading heroines of television and the cinematographic leaders of the Revolution*, this real life anecdote]" (186). The play opens in a visual milieu populated by the likes of Dolores del Río, Pedro Armendariz, María Félix, Emilio Fernández, and other actors and actresses who would embody revolutionary generals, peasants, and fighters with melodramatic and campy performances during those golden midcentury film productions. This aesthetic would come to dominate the (self)imagination of Mexico, within and without the country as these films circulated and continue to circulate in the US and the rest of Latin America; thus, especially for a more popular audience whose references may be more from the TV and film screen than a cult history of theater, the play speaks to a particularly idealized aesthetic that is shared across the continent. Furthermore, it was through this aesthetic that *mestizo* Mexico was cemented in the visual imaginary through the films of directors such as Emilio "el Indio" Fernández, Julio Bracho, Ismael Rodríguez, or Fernando de Fuentes, among others. The same transnational relations in economics and aesthetics from which counterculture emerges allow for an understanding of the "provincial" staging of the Mexican Revolution as a current event, a shared reality with which viewers both from Mexico and outside (in particular, the border regions) can identify with and understand. For these reasons, the short play is an example of how to use cultural aesthetics in a countercultural way, mobilizing camp aesthetics as a way of subverting and dialoguing with an audience who recognizes these tropes and characters.

While the short play depends on the virile representations of revolutionary men so often encountered in the bodies of actors Pedro Armendáriz, Antonio Aguilar, or even Marlon Brando, the shocking finale reveals not only the violent self-determination of female self-defense, but especially the campy nature of gender performance in general and the culture of drag specifically. Particularly relevant for US readers today in a political landscape where drag and female impersonation has become a target for conservative political organization in the country and for readers in Mexico where drag is emerging as a discourse to express political critique and social discontent, the final scene is a biting commentary on the power of performance and its central place in the construction of a *mestizo* masculine-centric order, where cross-dressed male-identified bodies become the building blocks of the postrevolutionary political order. In the instant after Olivia shoots Cassandra and then herself, Felipe Landeros turns to his sergeant Asúnsolo, the script indicating:

> Sobreviene un instante de desconcierto. Landeros y Asúnsolo quedan mirándose profundamente, acariciándose con los ojos. Asúnsolo se delicadiza, sin afeminarse grotescamente. Camina. Se agacha, quita las joyas, pendientes, collares de las muertas, se adorna con todo lo que puede. Sonríe a Landeros. Se le acerca, Landeros lo abraza de la cintura y Asúnsolo sólo le dice, con voz de María Félix
> Asúnsolo: Ya fui mucho la guacha, defeña, chinguen a su madre. Bésame, Felipe. La revolución es la revolución.
> [There comes a moment of confusion. Landeros and Asúnsolo look at each other deeply, caressing each other with their eyes. Asúnsolo becomes delicate without being grotesquely effeminate. He walks. He leans down, removes the jewelry, earrings and necklaces from the dead women, adorning himself with everything he can. He smiles at Landeros. He comes closer to him, Landeros takes him by the waist and Asúnsolo just tells him, with the voice of María Félix
> Asúnsolo: I have been too much the city girl, the girl from Mexico City, go fuck yourselves. Kiss me, Felipe. The revolution is the revolution.] (113)[78]

Suddenly, these two manly and virile revolutionary men who had entered the stage and the domestic space with the promise of revolutionary violence are transformed into a homosexual couple imitating already-campy performances that seek to imitate actual historical events — the imitation of an imitation of an imitation. Their ultramasculine and machista subjectivities that seem to have sprung up from the pages of Mariano Azuela, Martín Luis Guzmán, or Carlos Fuentes are suddenly transformed into a gender-bending spectacle, Asúnsolo's campy yet not grotesque feminization a reconfiguration of their

sex-gender revolution as THE revolution. What is more, these campy revolutionaries are in themselves assemblages of modernity and industrialization
as they emerge from an entertainment industry that strives to distribute products associated with the ultimate tool of modernity that is the cinema. María
Félix, the 1940s movie star who would go on to become a camp diva queen of
Mexican and Latin American homosexual circles to the point of living posthu-
mously in the form of a drag character names La Roña in honor of her nickname
la Doña, is now transformed into an over-the-top performance of femininity as
counterpoint to a masculinity grounded in violence. Humor is embodied in a
gender-bending body that denounces the violence at the core of postrevolutionary *mestizo* society.

The countercultural community that coalesces in the theatrical space is thus
activated in the audience/reader-performer/writer relationship, a complicity
that depends on shared social codes and experiences in order for the parody to
function: both a recognition of a historical violence in the wake of the revolution and a humorous refusal to reproduce that violence, providing an alternative
line of flight through a performance of camp. Profoundly baroque in its multiple citations, Bohórquez here signals how "recycling, pastiche, fragmentation,
and simulacrum intervene the territory of cultural and historical memory, and
reactivate it in combinations that are, at the same time, evocative and parodic"
(Moraña 253). In the bodies of Sagitario, Asúnsolo, and Felipe Landeros, the
revolution *is* the revolution, a sex-gender revolution that refuses to reproduce
the sex-gender violence and chooses to laugh at the self-described virility of
these two men, who threaten with sexual violence in their roles as revolutionaries and yet who, in the face of actual violence, respond with cross-dressing.
Thus, it is less that their queerness directly constructs an alternative social order,
and more that their cross-dressing and radical sexual desires make hypervisible
the latent violence of the postrevolutionary state, and their campy performance
allows for a more quotidian understanding of the ways in which this sex-gender
violence is reproduced in film and popular media.

As a way of concluding this very brief overview of Bohórquez's homosexual countercultural bodies experiencing deviant desires and embodying other
worlds of pleasure and community, I turn briefly now to *Digo lo que amo* (*I
say what I love,* 1976), his coming-out anthology, and, in particular, his poem
"Primera Ceremonia." A landmark in homosexual and queer poetry, although
unrecognized for a few decades, the poetry collection engages with multiple
aspects of homosexual desire, homosexual culture, and Bohórquez's personal
and individual experiences. Some of the poems are set in an urban space,
such as "Aprehensión," "Descaración previa," "Reconstrucción del hecho,"
"Sentencia," "Cuerpo del deleite," or "Trilogía policiaca," all of which reference in their titles the close relation between criminalization and homosexual
desire, flirting with the images of an arrest, a crime scene, a body of evidence,
and a threesome with police officers. These close connections already reveal
a recognition of the ubiquity of homosexual desire across male bodies of all

classes, ethnicities, and professions, and with this recognition an acknowledgment and celebration. As with Novo, the recognition of the criminalization processes that institutions advance with their diagnoses and imprisonments does not negate the fact of the homosexual desire existing and being acted upon, no matter the social "identity" that is constructed (or not) out of these acts, and especially no matter the criminal consequences of enacting their desires.

The bodies that appear in these poems occupy marginal and vulnerable positions with regard to the bodies of the policemen that surround, capture, and imprison them, and their desires are nevertheless also mirrored by these same policemen, pushing the readers to consider the ubiquity of homosexual bodies. In the face of exclusionary identity politics where certain bodies are prohibited from feeling certain desires due to the constraints of their identarian gender prisons, this paradoxical representation reveals a more complex understanding of sexuality, desire, and identity where power and its abuses take center stage, as opposed to an uncritical reconstruction of sexuality. In the same vein, the poetry collection contains "Tlamatini" — a Nahuatl term meaning "he who knows something, a wise man" — as a eulogy of Salvador Novo written upon his death where Bohórquez explicitly assembles Novo with his sexuality and his daring imagination creating valuable things, a foreshadowing of what Luis Felipe Fabre has described as Novo's writing with caca (shit). Bohórquez writes how he and other homosexual men mourn Novo's death as "ataviamos, nos enriquecemos // con tus pertenencias: cíngulos // crótales, diálogos, lenguas de obsidiana, una calle. // flores cogía el de coyohuacan. // pájaros cogía. pájaro en mano [we dress up, we enrich ourselves // with your belongings, badges and girdles // rattles, dialogues, obsidian tongues, a street. // flowers he picked from coyohuacan, // birds he picked, birds in one hand]" (*Digo lo que amo* 26). Novo is reconfigured into a creator of beaty whose words, ideas, concepts, and desires become valuable objects to decorate other homosexual bodies, his poetic-ethical-sexual labor a transformation into beauty as he explores the city, maps bodies, and assembles territories for Bohórquez and other homosexual men embracing their sexual desires freely.

While the collection gives the reader a sample of homosexual desire expressed in different bodies, intersectionally defined by race, class, skin color, language, and even profession, I want to focus on the poem "Primera ceremonia" for the remainder of this analysis. Aside from its poetic qualities, this is the poem that Bohórquez most rewrote during his career, infusing it each time with neobaroque, Indigenous, and rural poetic qualities until its last publication in *Navegación en yoremito* (1993). "Primera ceremonia" describes a sexual encounter between the poetic voice — age and profession undetermined — and a youthful shepherd he encounters in the open field. The poem opens with a series of neologisms that tenderly describe the two male bodies with reminisces of the wind's breeze, spring's glow, joyful glee, and doe-like tenderness; the two bodies appear in a bucolic and pastoral environment that even in this first appearance is already reminiscent of the sylvan poetry of a Hispanic tradition going back to precolonial times. Thus, "primaverizo yaces, // deleital y ternúrico, // y nadie es como tú, cervatillo matutinal,// silvestrecido y leve [springlike you lay, // delightful and tender, // and no one is like you, fawn of the dawn // wildling and slight]" (*Digo lo que amo* 10). The young man seems to sleep while the other man gets closer, and his opened eyes reveal a shared desire that invites; as the poem progresses, the two men engage each other erotically and sexually to generate another form of intercorporeal subjectivities, their sexual pleasure intertwined with the dirt and the air and the flowers and the grass, and the technology around them. These natural and technological references become assembled to their intercorporeal subjectivities, their shared sense of self that is redefined momentarily during their encounter to continue existing in this reshapen way once they part. The poetic voice describes the youth as "tu sexo, // húmedo, cálidamente eléctrico, madero victorioso . . . y tu cuello miro que pulsa las cuerdas // del corazón, no sé si el tuyo, el mío [your sex, // wet and electrically warm, victorious wood . . . and your neck upon which I see the pulsing of the cords // I know not if of your heart, or mine]" (*Digo lo que amo* 10). This electric sex, a victorious wood, are images that speak to virility interwoven with the tenderness of a neck, veins pulsing with a shared desire that cannot be pinpointed to a specific body. And the youth continues to transform, becoming with the natural space of the pasture and the field and becoming nature, "tu modo de ser tú casi me lame, // calor de perro, ojos de ganso, hermano de caballos [your way of being you almost licks me, // heat of the dog, eyes of a goose, brother of horses]" (11). Once again, humanimal intersubjectivities appear to populate the space of the nation, a becoming- animal that occurs in a flash and a spark of desire, and yet that remains embedded and sedimented in the body itself.

I bring this poem forward not only for its neobaroque aesthetics, but also and mostly for its sexual ethics that break down the paradigms of (homo)sexuality as conquest, violence, dominion, and extraction of pleasure, paradigms that mark the so-called Mediterranean scheme and ultimately characterize sexuality under colonialism and capitalism. The poem ends with the culmination of the sexual encounter, an exuberance that overflows the bodies of the two men and the verses themselves, words breaking down and breaking apart all kinds of dichotomies as sensations, feelings, emotions, and bodies meld together in an expansive understanding of pleasure. Symbolically, this confusion of pleasure is already a marker of liberatory sexuality, an erotic blueprint for a mapping outside the limits of one's own skin. Linguistico-poetically, the contrasting and sometimes contradictory words Bohórquez uses generate antitheses and paradoxes that complexify desire and pleasure outside the strict and rigid containers of active-passive, man-woman, penetrator-penetrated, dominating-dominated, et cetera; both bodies occupy both and all positions and places, their territories unwilling to be separated, mapped, and inscribed:

rindo el sentido.
tómame.
deshónrate, sométeme, contrístate, obedéceme,
enloquece, avergüénzate, desúnete, arrodíllate,
violéntame, vuelve otra vez, apártate, regresa,
miserable, amor mío, lagarto, imbécil, maravilla,
precipítate, aúlla.
de pronto, tú, el relámpago,
abierto, florecido, restallante,
arriba, abajo, encima, ¿dónde?
hiendes la oscuridad
y adentro:
llueves.
[I give up meaning.
take me.
dishonor yourself, make me submit, sadden, obey me,
go mad, be shameful, unjoin yourself, kneel,
violate me, come again, remove yourself, return,
miserable, love of mine, lizard, imbecile, wonder,
precipitate upon me, howl.
suddenly, you, the flash and lightning,
open, flowering, cracking,
up, down, on top, where?
you cut open the dark
and inside
it rains]
(11)

The imperative verbal mood fluctuates between a command, a request, and a desire, sometimes giving them to the youth in a reordering of the space and their bodies, and sometimes expressing a desire from within the poetic voice's body. The rapid movement between misery and joy, between lizard and idiot, between madness and pleasure, begins with a giving up of sense, a willingness to be taken and to take, to be dishonored and to dishonor, to be submissive and to be dominant. This movement acknowledges the existence of a sexual spectrum with poles of tenderness and violence, of domination and submission, of penetrator and penetrated; and yet, the poem refuses to stay within a single unique point on this spectrum and presents rather these two explicitly male bodies with virile masculinities fluctuating, transforming, becoming. As Palou states in his "Instruction for undoing the mestizo," "the constant making and unmaking of oneself is, in fact, the only way to negotiate with the demands of the symbolic order, with the destabilizing presence of the real and the imaginary projection" (323). As these two bodies — and Bohórquez's other bodies in his theater and poetry — dissolve into each other momentarily, they counter normative understandings of homosexuality as active-passive; I emphasize this dynamic because this dichotomy is still current in academic and popular approaches to sexuality and is currently being challenged and reshaped by academics as much as activists, podcasters, content creators, and queers on the streets. Thus, anticipating these global countercultural queer bodies, and in line with French queers such as Guy Hocquenghem, Bohórquez constructs (homo) sexuality as a fluid spectrum where bodies move as they please, united by a shared and mutual pleasure that erotically cements their subjectivities while keeping them autonomous from one another.

I began this chapter understanding the history of homosexuality as a sexual act, an urban and rural culture, an erotics, and a politics. I would like to conclude these two case studies by way of underscoring their daring existence in a hypermasculine and violent society where gay-bashing and homophobic murder are sadly still commonplace; in speaking their desires, their pleasures, and their experiences openly and explicitly, these authors open countercultural space where readers and audiences can reshape their/our own cultures, perhaps moving away from the culture of normativity, capitalism, and colonialism. In these writings, "the evocation of himself, with this ability to recapture experiences of delight, and the presentiment of horror on the part of his readers, who merely by casting an eye on his pages become his accomplices" (Monsiváis 42), as Carlos Monsiváis states about Novo, the authors transform reader into accomplices of an already existing and populated alternative nation. Non-queer citizens are invited to join this homosexual space, generating textual communities that are sentimentally and sexually (re)educated outside of heteronormative models; let us not forget that Novo would regularly read from his autobiography in private parties well before it was published, and Bohórquez would stage homosexuality and sexual dissidence in theatrical stages, his audience physically gathered in a shared space and time.

Mexican gay history tends to describe the postrevolutionary decades of the 1920s and 1930s as one of gay ghettos in the aftermath of the violent persecution of the 1901 ball of the 41 and caught in the homophobic violence mobilized by the revolutionary intellectuals in their construction of nation. However, both Novo and Bohórquez testify to another history, writing about a (homo) sexual culture that extends outside of the metropolis and, even within it, that extends into lower as well as higher classes. Instead of a closed community that protects itself through silence and closets, their texts push us to consider the male and other bodies that already lie on the outskirts of the *mestizo* nation: workers and mechanics, shepherds and cowboys, bus drivers and policemen. In this sense, they seek to belong less to a "homosexual" community named by criminalization and psychological diagnoses and consisting of "searches, scorn, and social harassment" (Monsiváis 44), and more to a series of sexual and erotic communities built on ethical and consensual pleasure, mutually experienced in a silenced but not exactly hidden or ghettoized space. These texts thus provide an alternative countercultural history of male sexual desire and allow for a more nuanced reshaping of queer sexualities in contemporary Mexico. Homosexual bodies become assembled as queer bodies, connected to networks of desire that cross lines of class, nationality, language, and species.

These erotic bodies build anal politics, politics of inclusion and reciprocity, politics of care both individually and communally, and politics of reciprocity and mutual recognition. Their texts become machines of subjectivation "that counter the 'war machine' of postcolonial modernity: subjectivity is polyvocal and composed of multiple strata that cover and exceed language" (Moraña 262). Their bodies cannot be contained within a category, a concept or a word, and their erotic and sexual desire provide pathways for lines of flight to emerge, to transform their bodies into unknown territories where they encounter one another. In their texts, the streets of Mexico City and the fields of rural Mexico become countercultural nationscapes, spaces where queer citizens express their sexual desires and construct utopian spaces with promising alternative modernities, where the heteronormative violence of the nation-state is pushed back against and rejected, where they may come together to exist albeit for a moment before merging back into the shadows to reappear once again.

For the homosexual citizens of the 1930s through the 1960s (before the eruption of student activism and gay liberation/gay activism movements), their expulsion from the *mestizo* nation catalyzed a series of productive corporal assemblages where lines of class, race, gender, and sexuality crossed under the aegis of shared pleasure. In following their pleasure, these countercultural men constructed communities that revolved around technology and cruising and that noticed the material changes in the world around them and changed with them, carving out niches of sexual, erotic, and social pleasure to be shared. In representing these national bodies that experience pleasure, Bohórquez and Novo follow on what Bonifant and Olin represented in their characters and self-representations; their "nationality" emerges from their immediate contexts, their bodies contained and signified by the narratives of nation and *mestizo* society. Simultaneously, their bodies are countercultural in their initial dissent with gender norms that catalyzes a transformation, a becoming; the imposed identities of *mestizo* normativity (colonial, capitalist, and supremacist structures) are not just rejected or repressed, but rather transformed by their erotic engagements with technology and each other. They are countercultural bodies that find each other in a glint of desire and a gesture of complicity, and whose solidarious actions sediment over time into countercultural territories overlapping with the *mestizo* nation, layers of reality visible for the knowing and accomplice eye that nevertheless remain invisible to the normative *mestizo* citizen, places like the cruising parks and Sanborns restrooms where men know how to find pleasure, and each other.

Between Bodies That Desire
and Bodies That Consume

The previous chapters have explored how countercultural bodies experience desire and are moved by these desires to occupy the city and the national space, to express their pleasure and joy, and ultimately to find each other through their desire — bodies that feel and sense, that touch themselves and each other, that experience desire and, through that desire, are able to *be* in the nation and the city. They are the bodies of women and homosexual men that were historically rejected from the nation and social fabric and that through feeling their desire can enter this social space and occupy the nation in both literal and figurative terms. Desire is a force that floods a body and pushes it to move, to situate itself in a series of relations, to find other bodies and touch and feel them. Bodies that desire are bodies that move, and countercultural desires move bodies in countercultural flows, pushing us to flow across the city in forbidden avenues and dark streets, to walk shadowy alleyways and dark parks in search of our pleasure and each other. Desire literally shapes the paths we walk in the city and the nation, and countercultural bodies emerge when these desires are enacted upon and expressed with each other.

I will turn now to how bodies consume and how consumption becomes a way to anchor desire into an object and to allow that action to reshape the body. Countercultural bodies consume in countercultural fashion, disrupting the apparently transparent transactions of economic payment in exchange for a product. Countercultural consumption goes beyond this to also include the consumption of music, food, substances, fashion, clothes, and even specific sexual and other embodied actions. All bodies consume, and countercultural consumption is characterized by an ethics of transformation, a modality of consumption that allows for the changing and reshaping of the body through the act of consumption. Consuming bodies are those that emphasize their consumption as their path of transformation, where consumption is not meant to satisfy a desire as much as to transform that desire and, through it, the body itself. Consuming bodies break the limits of national, colonial, gender, racial, and other identitarian markers that seek to define themselves by not consuming, by being essentially defined through some intrinsic and mystified meaning. Rather, consuming bodies are those that use their consumption as ways to generate and build subjectivity relationally, consumption becoming a modality of relation that allows for their transformation into something else, something perhaps unknown but not unreachable. To consume is to know, and to know is to consume.

Chapter 3

Bodies of Knowledge, Psychedelic Journeying, and the Writing of Space

The Liberatory Countercultures of Margarita Dalton and Parménides García Saldaña

Soy y soy la conciencia en cada célula.
[I am and I am consciousness in every cell.]

— Margarita Dalton

Mexico City, 1974

Youthful figures — long-haired young men with bell bottom pants and young women in short miniskirts and colorful blouses — walk quickly and furtively down the street, looking back over their shoulder to make sure they are not being followed as they disappear into a discreet door at the side of a building that opens onto a dark staircase leading into a basement. As it opens, faint sounds of electric guitars and drums sneak out onto the streets, threatening to blow their cover. It's been a few years since 1968 and everyone knows just how violent the Mexican state can be, even if these young men and women are not doing any student organization and are just dancing, drinking, and smoking in a sleazy makeshift basement rock venue. They're gathering here because the latest bands from Tijuana and Durango were rumored to be making appearances in *hoyos funkies* across the city and their fans are hoping to catch them playing. The basement venue is dark and damp, but the bodies of the youth filling the space are anything but dampened; their colorful blouses and shirts hug their torsos, and the men with long hair are shaking their *melenas* as they dance

131

with the women in short skirts and high heels. Together, they are breaking the stereotypes of gender and nationality that encase their bodies while singing and dancing in Spanish, listening to the latest song by the Dug Dugs, "No te asustes, es solo vivir [Don't be scared, it's just living]," as the chorus encourages them to enjoy their life in the face of the constant violence that surrounds them. For a moment, their bodies swerve and flow in the music and their lives are marked by a politics of joy that cannot be contained either in the organized politics of student activism and its violent responses or in the strict gender roles of their parents waiting for them at home. For a brief moment, it's just about living.

Avándaro, Valle de Bravo, 150 km from Mexico City, September 1971.

Thousands of young men, women, and other gender dissidents stream from Mexico City to the Avándaro Gold Club, where organizers called for a Festival de Rock y Ruedas, a two-day music and automobile festival. It has been two years since Woodstock happened in the town of Bethel near New York City, and since the 1969 Harlem Cultural Festival that has come to be remembered as the Summer of Soul. For two days, the valley in central Mexico is full of a youthful culture that refuses to be squashed by the violence of the state, still fresh from the Jueves de Corpus massacre that same summer. Many of these concertgoers bring with them psychoactive substances such as LSD (lysergic acid), *yesca/yerba/mota* (cannabis), peyote, and mushrooms, and many more of them have taken these substances before and are ready and excited to share them with their peers and friends. Gender roles are disturbed, torn down, and reformulated in a communal space where, even if briefly, a politics of care emerges as women take the stage to undress themselves and challenge normativity with their joy. Perhaps one or more of these women has taken an acid trip in the previous years, perhaps participating with Salvador Roquet in one of his radical therapy circles in the capital or perhaps with a friend who had traveled to London or California and brought back some of the strange stuff called LSD, *ácido lisérgico*. In any case, for a couple of days the festival grounds were a radical liberatory territory where the concertgoers, some of whom had walked for days to reach the space, became a part of alternative territories, their *mexicanidad* shifting and transforming amid the sounds of rock and roll, the screams of fans, and the clouds of cannabis smoke. Their bodies are the first territories of these new worlds emerging around them — territories they have learned to explore, undress and dress up, and communally rename as they come together to consume substances, music, and each other. The freedom in these consumption practices and their ethics of sharing joy will be carried with them when they go back to the city, to their parents' house and their national lives. But for now, they dance and laugh.

This chapter focuses on the liberatory actions carried out by youth in the territories of their bodies, through consumption of rock and roll as music and ideology and the consumption of psychedelic/entheogenic substances, seen in the journalistic texts of Parménides García Saldaña and the fictional work of Margarita

Dalton. I approach these writings and the events they describe, typically seen exclusively in the framework of a sociological understanding of counterculture, through a focus on the micropolitical-molecular actions and their effects on the bodies of these youth; in other words, through a focus on their erotic engagement with the world around them and the ways in which these emerging erotics shaped their political action.[1] I use erotics here in the widest sense of the word to capture not only the embodied sensations of pleasure catalyzed by a sexual encounter, but also the embodied sensations of pleasure/pain that emerge in situations of contacts between bodies, and between bodies and substances; that is, the feelings, emotions, and sensations that emerge as bodies come together and rub on each other as they play a sport or watch a sport being played, or when bodies rub on each other as they board a city bus or a metro car, or when they walk down a busy crowded city street, their eyes inundated with commodity objects and advertising as their noses are overpowered by the smell of food, perfumes, and body odors, and their skin is stimulated by the touch (or not) of other people as they pass each other. In many ways, it is during these years that seeds are planted for the contemporary focus on bodily autonomy, affect, and care in the realm of feminist and dissident politics in Mexico.

The journal articles of García Saldaña and the short stories, novels, and children's book of Margarita Dalton endeavor to tackle social issues and radical change in ways that center bodies as the first territories of these changes. Whereas earlier and more culturally legitimized authors such as José Agustín, Gustavo Saínz, or René Avilés take on a more normative (in the sense of Pierre Bourdieu's understanding of the rules of art) position of iconoclasm against the bourgeois norms of the urban middle class, Dalton and García Saldaña utilize literature and journalism as creative spaces where bodies are (re)engaged, (re) defined, and (re)articulated in novel personal and collective forms. They are less interested in signaling the pitfalls and limitations of their parental and social figures, and more in using texts to generate embodied assemblages engaged in the practices of community-building and even nation-building at times. Their texts thus (re)present new sociabilities, pointing out the shortcomings of *mestizo* sociability and its dependence on heteropatriarchal gender performance and caste-structured relationships of more-and-less power to showcase the changes these young men and women are embodying. For Margarita and Parménides, global counterculture (that is, rock concerts, communes, acid trips, music records and stores, pop art, fashionable philosophy and other academic texts, and educational campaigns both institutional as in Cuba and structureless as in the consciousness-raising sessions that marked the decade) becomes a language they can fuse with national issues and problematics (that is, student activism, how to engage with an increasingly violent state) in order to establish other lines of flight for the growing urban population. They seek less to escape their immediate political surroundings than to reengage with them in alliance with the other marginalized bodies they see around them, particularly in their middle-class environs.

The two scenes I fictionalize at the start of this chapter bookmark two of the spaces where these lines of flight were enacted; libraries, communes, private house parties, bedrooms, street performances, student marches, tiny rock concerts, and film screenings were among the other sites where bodies were being reshaped, as well as in the quotidian encounters with each other on the streets and the newly inaugurated Metro system (1969). The vignettes hopefully provide the context for the lines of flight the authors in this chapter will follow, lines provided by substances and rock music, avenues of escape that become accessible in the act of consuming counterculture. Paradoxically, the process of consumption itself will end up strengthening the product — especially when the product is criminalized as in substances or music — making its presence more available in the greater symbolic market and paving the way for later neoliberalization of counterculture as a mark of global cultural capital, a commodity to be traded freely in the markets of music and arts in the late 1980s and 1990s as new age and other neoliberal ideologies emerged. In the 1960s and 1970s, however, cultural producers such as García Saldaña and Dalton could communally drop acid, collaborate in journals such as *Piedra Rodante* or *Yerba*, publish novels, and foment community-building in *hoyos fonkis* (underground rock concert halls) and communes, generating alternative spaces within the symbolic and real *mestizo* nation.[2] In the texts I analyze in this chapter, these two authors mobilize their and other bodies as platforms of biochemical change (Dalton) and as positioned embodiments in male-dominated cultural spheres (García Saldaña). Through their explicitly and self-reflexively gendered (re)positionings, their embodied experiences of modernized urbanity, national cultures, and alternative states of being assemble new citizenship models that seek to be less hierarchical oppressive and move toward relationality and horizontal structures of power. This chapter is divided into three parts: a short introduction and contextualization of youth culture in its diverse manifestations, a literary and cultural analysis of Margarita Dalton's novel *Larga Sinfonía en D y había una vez* through the lens of the psychedelic and countercultural studies of the time period (1950s to 1970s) and feminist ethics particularly around bodily autonomy and female erotic and sexual pleasure, and a literary-sociological analysis of Parménides García Saldaña's journalistic texts focused on the ethical repositioning of male bodies in countercultural spaces.

Enter Youth: The Dynamic Landscapes of Counterculture in the Mexican Midcentury

The postwar culture of midcentury that peaked in the global countercultures of the 1960s was radically changing the previously established social roles. While young men and women had been an active and important part of society for centuries (from soldiers to secretaries to urban workers), the burgeoning educational and economic institutions became key in formalizing what we now identify as youth culture: youth as students and youth as consumers began to take more important symbolic and social roles. In the specific context of Mexico, the postrevolutionary decades experienced not only the solidification of its educational and political institutions, but also the development of strong entertainment industries during the height of the Golden Age films of the 1940s and, especially, the burgeoning of cultural institutions in literature. In all of these, the figure of the *mestizo* became an ever-present signifier that served to coalesce the at times chaotic and contradictory multiplicity of bodies populating the streets. I don't intend to reproduce a gender binary in this understanding, and I hope rather to signal how the *mestizo* ideology is founded on a gender binary that negates the existence of other bodies, as well as any diversity within the two gender roles in themselves. Ultimately, it will be these changes that countercultural bodies mobilize in these decades in their struggle to liberate, signify, and socialize themselves into alternative nations.

As the decades progressed once the dust of the revolution settled, the diversity of female experiences (soldaderas, secretaries, writers, painters, poets, teachers, domestic employees, sex workers, and many, many more professions), whose possibilities were opened explosively during the contested years of the 1920s, slowly gave way to specific feminine roles to be expected and embraced by *mestizo* women: on the one hand, the figure of the mother embodied in the revolutionary murals, as well as in the constant representation of Frida Kahlo as a (failed) mother and ultimately in the technologies of advertising that promoted "good" and bad girls; and on the other hand, the figure of the *mestizo* woman as a preferably rural teacher (a desexualized variant of the mother of the nation), a subjectivity that began in the educational campaigns of the 1930s under socialist Secretary of Education Narciso Bassols and that was quickly solidified in propagandist films such as *Río Escondido* (dir. Emilio Fernández, 1947) and *Rosaura Castro* (dir. Roberto Gavaldón, 1950). Mothers and teachers stand in opposition to sexual and sexualized women, who were contained within the spaces of the cabaret and its various iterations. Explicit and overt female sexuality was condemned in popular films such as *La mujer del Puerto* (dir. Arcady Boytler, 1934), *Aventurera* (dir. Alberto Gout, 1951), or *Salón México* (dir. Emilio Fernandez, 1949), where female desire was seen as dangerous to the fabric of the nation and must be contained on the cabaret stage, always surrounded by men who protect the space and those enter it. *Mestiza* femininity, especially when assembled with the Catholic *Tres Marías* complex that uses the Virgin Mary, Mary Mother of God, and Mary Magdalene as three models of femininity to be celebrated and condemned, is transformed into a subjective position marked by exploited labor, repressed sexuality, and social subservience to the men around them.

On the flip side, *mestizo* masculinity developed into static models of being men grounded in relations of property toward female and othered bodies, relations that could and would be enforced through extreme violence. Anchored in the representations of violence of revolutionary fighters as can be seen in the *novela de la revolución* and its more contemporary variations, from Juan Rulfo's *Pedro Páramo* (1955) to Carlos Fuentes's *La muerte de Artemio Cruz* (1962) — highly critiqued by Marxist writer José Revueltas in *El luto humano* (1943) — *mestizo* masculinity was mediatized in films that epitomized the *macho* mexicano and transformed the hero figures of Pancho Villa and Emiliano Zapata into rural and urban variations in the bodies of Pedro Infante, Pedro Armendáriz, Jorge Negrete, and others. The male urban workers would be psychoanalyzed by Samuel Ramos in his *Perfil del hombre y la cultura en México* (1934) and later by Octavio Paz in *El laberinto de la Soledad* (1950); these stereotypes were sedimented alongside the more visual and popular representations of masculinities into inorganic assemblages of *macho* virility and behavior subjugated to ideological constructions. In the urban contexts where women's movements were closely watched and preferably tied to a specific economic reason while men roamed the streets freely, the increasing and exponential urban growth of Mexico City and other cities — visualized and mediated in *Nosotros los pobres* (dir. Ismael Rodríguez, 1948) or *Los olvidados* (dir. Luis Buñuel, 1959), to quote two ideologically opposed representations — paradoxically solidified *mestizo* gender norms while simultaneously providing the material conditions for their erosion. Gradually, spaces where the bodies of lower-class male citizens could sometimes engage with middle- and upper-class bodies with the aid technologies and cultural situations where class differences were set aside in pursuit for pleasure, presenting possibilities and opportunities for alternative sexualities and subjectivities to be constructed. However, I cannot emphasize enough how this happened in the all-encompassing shadow of virile *mestizo* masculinities, ideas of *macho* subjectivity that were generated and echoed in the film and cultural industries and institutions. How to be a man was a particularly protected normativity, and one that in Mexico was closely watched by the forces of state ideological apparatus, market consumption, and fashion.

Though these processes started in the 1950s with the increase in university student populations and other youth occupying the city, by the 1960s the changes were too significant to be controlled by ideology or institutions. Even as the subjectifying forces sought to stratify Mexico City into specific gender, class, and racial roles — as can be observed in the film *Los caifanes* (dir. Juan Ibáñez, 1967) — the growing urban sprawl smoothed the city, creating flows and engagements where bodies were difficult to contain in exclusionary roles. By the 1960s, Mexico and the rest of Latin America were riding the waves of political changes sparked by the Cuban Revolution. The entrance of Che Guevara, Camilo Cienfuegos, and the rest of the *barbudos* into Havana in 1959 inaugurated a decade of resistance on all fronts that reverberated across the continent. It is not coincidental that fifteen years later Operation Condor and the War Against Drugs began to ravage the region, in particular its more leftist governments and the rural areas where guerillas and paramilitaries were taking refuge. In Mexico, the events of the Cuban Revolution served to reignite the potentialities opened by the event of the Mexican Revolution, many of which had been captured by the depoliticized imaginary and the romantic/idealized aesthetics promoted by the entertainment industry of the 1940s.[3] Suddenly, the labor struggles of the railroad workers of 1958 to 1959 were recast in light of much larger political struggles, and the nascent student and medical professional movements began to take shape in a much wider hemispheric and global context; students were seeing themselves rise up in protest and cultural production all across the continent. All the while, young men and women continued to leave their homes in search of education, work opportunities, new commodities, and especially opportunities to have fun, experience pleasure, and challenge their social/gender norms.

Youth in Mexico City found themselves in a very particular historical moment during these midcentury decades. The Universidad Nacional Autónoma de México (UNAM) and the Instituto Politécnico Nacional (IPN) had been educating middle-class youth in their sprawling modernized locations for well over a decade, their new campus effectively serving as gravitational centers of institutional education for a growing youth and, perhaps more importantly, becoming foci of politicized student activities that connected them with their peers in Europe and the United States.[4] During the 1950s in particular, the *universitarios* and the *politécnicos* created institutional networks grounded in the solidification of university sports. In previous decades, sports and other extracurricular activities and groups had been coalesced under the aegis and watchful eye of state programs.[5] However, as schools grew and their sports programs developed, the youth found in them alternatives to come together and use their bodies for other forms of pleasure. And as these groups — and their fanbases and cheerleaders and spectators — grew, more and more youth from across the universities came together outside the closed walls of the classroom, and they learned from and about each other in the process. In the 1960s, youth suddenly saw themselves flooded with revolutionary influences that pushed them to participate in educational campaigns in Cuba, found national rock groups singing in Spanish, create troops of street theater and enact performances across the city, and ultimately begin to question more widely the role of the state and the family in the formation of a modern cosmopolitan society.[6] This was the first generation of Mexican citizens to grow up during the so-called *Milagro Mexicano*, and as such they experienced the bountiful expansion of Mexican markets during the 1940s through the 1960s. Postwar economic growth was marked by an ever-stronger dependency on the US economy, as well as a closer contact with US culture not only through commodity products but also through the migrants coming back from working in the fields during the US Bracero program (1941–1964), and the establishment of entertainment industries modelled after their US counterparts.[7]

Mexico City in these two decades faced intense modernization and urban growth as its position as the central node in a national communication network grew exponentially along with national development across the territory.

Thus, and in a continuous feedback loop that absorbed cultural production from its *provincias*, whatever was produced in the capital quickly spread throughout the country as radio and telecommunications networks were established. These communication networks became increasingly centralized, with the Azcárraga family that had already shaped radio communication in the 1930s taking more control of the television and media networks with the establishment of Telesistema Mexicano (later Televisa, Grupo Televisa and now TelevisaUnivisión) in 1955, combining the already existing TV stations into a centralized network. It was through these channels, closely associated with the government in place, that official state-sanctioned consumption of foreignness occurred, such as learning to *agogo*, *swing*, and *chachachá* as signs of cultural competency and an accumulation of cultural capital that symbolized modernity. These rhythms and their aesthetics became part of an increasingly diverse vocabulary of global consumption. Musically, transnational record companies such as RCA Victor and Columbia Records were quickly catching onto the economic success of rock and roll rhythms, pushing local musicians in Mexico to produce *refritos*, the Spanish-language translation of English pop hits. Early rock films of the late 1950s and early 1960s were important rearticulators of national folkloric traditions in modernized vocabularies, their box-office success serving to "domesticate foreign cultural influences and promote homegrown musical talents" (Price 36). Their didactic impulse, as Brian Price has closely studied, is important; these films —loose adaptations of Hollywood plots to Mexican geographies — showcased a variety of Mexican rock bands and sanitized their rhythms, and, above all, they served as pedagogical tools to learn how to dance, how to listen, and how to perform these new rhythms, usually in a space sanctioned by the state through the reproduction of specific gender roles that reinforced male freedom and female commodification.[8]

As rock made its appearance on theater screens, TV screens, and radios and became a rhythm and style more understandable in the national context, youth across the country slowly adapted it as a style to further express rebellious and antiestablishment attitudes. Eric Zolov describes this rearticulation of rock as a wedge that increasingly drove deeper into the national fabric and imagination, separating populations by musical taste as well as political and social attitudes:

> Rock music thus served as both wedge and mirror for societies caught in the throes of rapid modernization. Rock was a wedge in the sense that it challenged traditional boundaries of propriety, gender relations, social hierarchies, and the very meanings of national identity in an era of heightened nationalism . . . yet rock was also a mirror reflecting the aspirations and anxieties of societies in pursuit of an elusive sense of "first-worldism," whether in emulation of or competition with its standard bearer, the United States. (*Refried Elvis* 10)

Especially influenced by the multicultural and bilingual contexts of the northern regions, bands in places like Durango and Tijuana started to sing in English to express their dissident sexual, romantic, social, and political desires.[9] *La onda chicana* emerged when these bands moved to Mexico City and became part of a wider countercultural movement in the capital, culminating with the historical Avándaro concert of 1971. In the filmic sphere, the radically different attitudes the youth were exploring became too much for the studio productions with ideological limitations, and the visual representation moved toward the small and experimental format. The *Primer Concurso de Cine Experimental* in 1965 saw the release of the hyper-experimental *La formula secreta* (dir. Ruben Gámez), where rapid cuts and radical angles were coupled with a poem by Juan Rulfo read by Jaime Sabines. This prompted young directors and producers to begin searching for alternative ways to finance, produce, and release their films and bypass a stagnating industry. In the process, they found in these experimental, low-budget, and self-organized film spheres a way to avoid ideological limitations due to the close ties between the media and film industries to government officials and syndical politics. Thus, youth in general as well as countercultural youth with more radical tastes in music, fashion, and gender politics began to form alternative circuits of distribution and new habits of consumption, going deeper underground as violence increased with the only recently acknowledged Mexican Dirty War against guerrilla groups and social organizers. Rock thus became increasingly both a commodity for the film and music industry seeking to sell products and a form of resistance for the rebellious youth who refused to conform to capitalist, nationalist, and patriarchal regimes.

In the literary spheres, three books appeared that were quickly becoming the pillars of Mexican letters: *Pedro Páramo* (Juan Rulfo, 1955), *La region más transparente* (Carlos Fuentes, 1958), and *Laberinto de la soledad* (Octavio Paz, 1950). In the midst of this, youth authors proliferated with a diversity of literary styles, from the eroticism of Juan García Ponce to the poetic realism of José Emilio Pacheco, the cosmopolitan protofiction of Salvador Elizondo, the journalistic style of Elena Poniatowska, the quiet and unceding feminism of Julieta Campos writing à la Monique Wittig, the historical realism of Fernando del Paso, and of course the playful and cheekily youthful style of José Agustín, Parménides García Saldaña, Gustavo Saínz, Margarita Dalton, Enrique Marroquín, and others. What characterizes these authors as a generation is a youthful response to the intellectualization of Mexican culture and reality that generates alternative styles grounded in rebellion (sometimes quietly social, sometimes openly political) and a resistance to quietly accept the hegemonic order of nationalism as unquestionable reality; a consumption of local and foreign popular culture and especially rock and jazz music; and a resistance to forms of patriarchal social norms, sometimes seeking to reform them by expanding visual and linguistic vocabularies and sometimes seeking to reject them outright by exposing the symbolic violence characteristic of patriarchal regimes. Although there was never an organized literary movement as such among this generation, the more playful and iconoclast writers such as Agustín, García Saldaña, Saínz, and Dalton became known as the *Onda* movement in contrast to a more "formal" approach to writing.[10] A greater argument can be made that the *Onda* provided the growing middle-class with an aesthetic opportunity to storm the elite walls of the lettered city, since before its appearance in the latter 1960s, "the literary field was restricted to the upper and middle-classes that had been the beneficiaries of the economic development of previous decades" (Viera 148). In particular, José Agustín, Gustavo Saínz, and René Avilés use the literary spaces of short stories and novels to take on a decidedly iconoclastic position against the ruling norms of the urban middle class. In their texts, youthful bodies and, in particular, young men appear as territories of resistance to their parents' or society's norms, sometimes explicitly addressing the shortcomings of the *mestizo* sociability and sometimes focusing on mobilizing foreign influences to construct alternative representations of (male) bodies.

In this cultural context, the writings of García Saldaña and Dalton emerge as examples of other ways of writing and imagining, tackling social issues in other ways that sometimes seemed less bombastic or iconoclastic and yet tended to disrupt gender and social politics in much deeper and significant ways. In their texts, bodies appear as novel assemblages already engaging in practices of alternative community-building, and sometimes even nation-building; they bear witness, explore, and reconstruct new sociabilities. For these authors, global counterculture (that is, rock concerts, communes, acid trips, music records, pop art, fashionable philosophy, academic texts and the whole cultural mélange that has been named retroactively as such) became a language they fuse with national issues, problematics, and realities (that is, student activism, how to engage with an increasingly violent state) to generate other lines of flights for the growing urban population. Ultimately, the urban reality with this celebration of youth through rock music and film as well as literature written for and about youth was not all peaceful; in the same period, the Mexican government responded ever more violently to multiple labor strikes, including the railroad workers strike of 1959 (textualized in Fernando del Paso's novel *José Trigo* from 1966) and the medical workers strikes of 1964 to 1965, not to mention the later violence against students. This paradoxical support of both cultural and economic modernization and "progress" while simultaneously violently suppressing any dissent became the organizing principle of the state and its institutions.[11] In Mexico, the state responded by establishing closer relations to paramilitary groups, at times even training them as with the infamous Brigada Olympia, responsible for the 1968 Tlatelolco massacre and other repressive events. At the same time, through its funding of film and media projects, the state increasingly enforced a depoliticized consumption of rock and other youthful ideologies, as can be seen in the film *Bikinis y rock* (dir. Alfredo Salazar, 1972), itself a remake of *A ritmo de twist* (dir. Benito Alazraki, 1962). I will return to this context in the next chapter, and I emphasize this underlying political violence and economic-social control now to build a context to better understand the liberatory actions of Margarita Dalton, Parménides García Saldaña, and other youth in these decades, particularly as they speak to the state and paramilitary violence that characterizes Mexican realities today.

Given this history of state violence that shaped these decades, especially the extremely repressive actions of authoritarian governments in 1968 and 1971 directed at students and the rest of the 1970s in the Dirty War, which tended to target young guerrilla fighters and left-leaning youth, it is difficult to approach youth culture at this time without focusing on, idealizing, and centralizing their politically engaged actions.[12] The approach to youth I want to take centers more on the micropolitical actions of these youths, as can be glimpsed in the texts of two authors. These quotidian actions are places where youth reshaped their bodies and explored avenues of being as well political and social organizing, which is particularly relevant today when the nation-state is paradoxically more powerful than ever while being more questioned than ever as a subjectifying force. Counterculture is typically understood as a sociological category used to describe certain youthful behavior and activity, especially during and after the radically liberating global 1960s; keeping that in mind, I want to underline what historian Christopher Dunn has emphasized as the core tenets of counterculture no matter the geopolitical location of its emergence: "self-critique, disengagement from organized politics, and a reorientation toward personal behavior" (*Contracultura* 2). This drive for personal transformation — from the immediate territory of the personal body to the collective territories of family, friendships, relationships, and social structures — engages the bodies of these countercultural youth from the nationalized subjectivities that are projected onto them. It also grounds their bodies in their resistance and their specific actions to push back on the biopolitical control enforced by the institutions of family and the demands it makes on the binary gender division, and by the institutions of state and the demands they make to shape male bodies into compliant *machos mexicanos* as good soldiers and workers and to shape female bodies into compliant women who serve the nation in the home and in their reproductive functions.

In this context of (sometimes violent) repression and (sometimes violent itself) liberation, many of these youths anchored their actions in what we now name as bodily autonomy, or the autonomy to remake their bodies as they saw fit, from fashion to hair length to sexual choices to, ultimately, the consumption of psychedelic/entheogenic substances such as lysergic acid diethelamide (LSD), psylocibin (mushrooms), and cannabis (marijuana). In Mexico, this consumption was a site of contestation and debate, as were the processes of consciousness-raising that emerged in university settings; some called these acts a form of mental colonialism while some celebrated them as liberatory practices in and of themselves. Whatever the case, the fact remains that youth were steadily gaining, developing, and practicing radical bodily autonomy, pushing against the normativities of nation and market.[13] The process of

consciousness-raising, which feminists, hippies, gay activists, civil rights leaders, and more were practicing, centered personal transformation as the starting
point for political transformation.[14] In Mexico, alongside the strange psychedelic rock of The Doors, Creedence Clearwater Revival, and The Beatles as
well as local bands such as *La Revolución de Emiliano Zapata*, *Los Dug Dugs*,
and *Three Souls on My Mind*, these substances became a way to establish a
different set of habits, patterns, and behaviors that connected these local *mestizo* bodies undoing/redoing themselves with youth in the global counterculture. For authors such as Margarita Dalton and Parménides García Saldaña, the
consumption of these substances was greatly informed not just by their *set* (that
is, their specific mindset and that of their characters and they ingest them), but
especially by their *setting* (that is, the surrounding social context in which they
chose to consume and relate to). Thus, the act of consuming a hallucinogen,
listening to rock music, and coming together with other youths becomes a way
to generate alternative sociabilities where equality and democracy move away
from a liberal notion of political subject and are rather grounded in the embodied experience of communal citizenship, collective living, and a recognition of
and an explicit engagement with the class differences (and occasionally conflict) inherent in countercultural spheres and rock music, where sometimes very
different classes, genders, ethnicities, racial identities, and linguistic identities
come together in the same space.

Larga Sinfonía en D y había una vez: Transatlantic Trips and Psychedelic Journeys

No known culture has ever deployed such a vast
pharmacopeia of substances for getting high, getting healthy
or just plain coping as modern Western civilization has.

— John Strausbaugh

The year is 1968. Three youths from widely different geographies and cultures
come together in London to explore their own psyche by ingesting lysergic
acid diethylamide or LSD, doing what youth across the globe are doing. Sitting
around a living room coffee table, they ingest the substance while staring into
each other's eyes, seeking to further bridge their differences that span ideologies, geographies, gender and racial identities, and ultimately their bodies. Thus
begins an exhilarating and literarily innovative journey narrated in Margarita

Dalton's novel *Larga Sinfonía en D y había una vez*, their acid trip distributed across ten chapters and ten hours arranged in nonchronological order. The novel explores pop art and visual representation in the age of mass advertising, social revolutions, and armed resistance in the age of nonviolence and nuclear threat and presents itself as a multilayered text with several encoded texts hidden within its typographic experimentation. The text culminates, if one could describe this reading experience as culminating in the classical narratological sense, in the detachment of personal identity from the experience of a singular and isolated body and the alternative assemblage of identity to a collective experiencing of bodies together. The novel was first published in 1968 in the context of a literary contest ("Seis primeras novelas en competencia de jóvenes escritores mexicanos") organized by Editorial Diógenes with the intention of encouraging new literature, and while it was favorably reviewed by critics at the time and later, it did not circulate beyond that initial publication and has been treated as simply another manifestation of *Onda* literature to be archived. It was republished in 2022 by Editorial Lumen, a part of the major publishing house Penguin Random House and distributed in both print and ebook, mostly because of a dedicated readership that labored to have it reappear from its quasi-cult status circulating in xerox copies and pdfs.

Margarita Dalton was born in 1943 and raised and educated in Mexico City. She is the sister of Roque Dalton, a famous Salvadorean poet and revolutionary from the 1960s who grew up in El Salvador and died during the armed conflict to become one of the Latin American left's martyr poets. After finishing high school in Mexico City, she eloped with her then-husband José Agustín to participate in the alphabetization campaign in Cuba, which managed to reduce illiteracy from 77 percent to 3.9 percent in under two years from 1961 to 1962, in part thanks to the regional support form youth across Latin America who answered the call from Fidel Castro and the *barbudos* to reshape Cuba. Dalton chose to remain in Cuba for a period afterward and earned her bachelor's degree in history from the University of Habana in 1966. She then moved to Accra in Ghana in 1967 and, after a brief stay in France and Europe during 1968, moved back to Mexico establish a commune in the state of Oaxaca named *El Vergel*. It was during her time in Europe that she wrote and published *Larga sinfonía*, sending it back across the ocean to appear in print before her return — a literal object of world-making in its material life. The commune in Oaxaca served as a gathering place for several countercultural icons of the time, including the Catholic priest Enrique Marroquin (Agustín, *La contracultura* 81). After the commune disbanded, Dalton pursued and received a doctoral degree in history from the Universidad Central the Barcelona (1982–1985) and returned to Oaxaca where she has produced ample anthropological, sociological, and historical texts relating to the region and focused on women's participation in society. She now lives there and has been the director of the CIESAS (Centro de Investigaciones y Estudios Superiores en Anthropología Social), continuing to collaborate with the Centro and other organizations in Oaxaca and Mexico since the late 1970s.

During her creative trajectory, Dalton published the mentioned novel, short stories, children's literature and poetry collections, as well as being the translator of several of Adrienne Rich's texts into Spanish.

Larga Sinfonía en D (*LSD* from now on) is a text that centers lysergic acid experiences of three youth and therefore exists in a greater milieu of Mexican and global literature around these topics that include *Pasto Verde* (Parménides García Saldaña, 1968), *The Electric Kool-Aid Acid Test* (Tom Wolfe, 1968), *Fear and Loathing in Las Vegas* (Hunter S. Thompson, 1971), *The Door of Perception* (Aldous Huxley, 1954), and, more recently, *Circa 94* (Fran Illich, 2010) and *Taipei* (Tao Lin, 2013). Although this literature is easy to dismiss as socially disconnected, artistically innovative, and sometimes playful experimentation, these and other texts involving the use of and reflection on psychedelic/entheogenic substances are part of a lineage of Western writings that engage deeply with the psychological and political relations of substances and humans; Walter Benjamin's *On Hashish* (1927–1934) and William James's writings on nitrous oxide stand out. Self-aware of this global ecosystem it's a part of, *LSD* references and engages with philosophers such as Plato, Marshal McLuhan, and Chairman Mao as a way of inserting itself into a global youth culture emerging across continents.[15] In this way, the novel speaks to and of a historically situated youth culture and reconnects itself (particularly with the new editions coming out in 2023) with a globalized and planetary consciousness that sees the limitations, pitfalls, and devastating effects of colonial consciousness epitomized in the Self/Other binary that underpins the universal subject of modernity. In doing so, the novel radically proposes intercorporeal subjectivities, embodied and experiential knowledge, and political actions anchored in and emerging from the liberation of consciousness and body.

Larga Sinfonía en D bridges the ritualized and sacred consumption of a substance with the political and social liberation of oppressed peoples, particularly when considered alongside the historical lineage of female wisdom-keepers in the temples of Eleusis and the Mediterranean where psychedelic wine (*kykeon*) and other concoctions were offered to elite members of these cultures before the rise of Christianity and the violent monopolizing of psychedelic experiences by the emerging Catholic Church. Radical already in this act of taking a substance out of the medical room or the temple, the novel uses three very different characters to explore the different paths of social and sexual liberation anchored in their different corporealities, which, although distinct, emerge as shared bodies from which relational subjectivities are assembled. I argue that *LSD* offers a roadmap for what the liberation of consciousness looks like in relation to historically and political situated struggles, where substance use becomes paradoxically a way to strengthen the bonds of bodies with their context rather than tools of escapism or bourgeois recreation. Following Walter Benjamin's approach to substance use in the experiments he led with other Frankfurt school philosophers and their use of cannabis and morphine, I see in Dalton's work a cultural undertaking of liberatory consciousness-building, an exploration of what it means to liberate one's body from one's immediate political, social, economic, gender, and other constraints.[16] In particular, I focus on the cultural constraints of art and aesthetic representation in times of capitalist hyperproduction and consumerism (pop art), the political-social constraints of revolution understood only as male-centered "macho" violence in the context of Cuba and other postcolonial uprisings across the colonial globe including civil rights in the US and Europe, and the gender constraints that police both male and female bodies and the relations that may be constructed between them outside of heteronormative and compulsive monogamy. Without attempting to be exhaustive, I will approach this liberatory roadmap by paying attention to how the lysergic experience informs first the aesthetic devices, second the representations of gender and sexuality, third the embodied sensations and sensorial world-building the characters experience and undertake, and finally the temporalities the novel mobilizes as it disrupts the normative temporalities of capital, colony, and revolution.

Before continuing with the textual analysis, a brief contextualization of psychedelic studies then and now: Synthesized first in 1938 from the ergot fungus by Swiss chemist Albert Hoffman as he searched for analeptics to treat respiratory system illness, LSD appeared on the world stage fully in 1943 when the chemist accidentally ingested a minuscule amount and had to head home on his bicycle, experiencing the first "trip" in the world in the process.[17] After discovering its psychoactive effects, Hoffman and Sandoz Laboratories promoted the substance as a therapeutic and research tool, sending it to therapists, doctors, researchers, and laboratories across the world. From 1945 to 1970 (the year when US President Richard Nixon signed the Controlled Substance Act and initiated the War on Drugs, aka the War on Plants), LSD was explored in many settings and formats as a therapeutic and research device. I particularly underline the history of psychiatrist Salvador Roquet in Mexico City and the history of Alcoholics Anonymous and the twelve-step programs that emerged from psychedelic therapy sessions in Canada and the US. I will explore the details of these therapeutic modalities later in the next chapter, and here I want to focus on the rich intersections of psychedelic research and religious studies, in particular through mysticism. Early in the mid-sixties, psychologists Walter Pahnke and William Richards developed a Mystical Experience Questionnaire based on the previous research by William James, W. T. Stace, and other psychologists to categorize, identify, and describe a mystical experience across cultures and religions. Pulling from their participation and collaboration with psychedelic research in the US and Europe, such as the Good Friday experiment and the Johns Hopkins teams, this questionnaire explored the categories of (a) unity, (b) transcendence of time and space, (c) deeply felt positive mood, (d) sense of sacredness, (e) objectivity and reality, (f) paradoxicality, (g) alleged ineffability, (h) transiency, and (i) persisting positive changes in attitude and/ or behavior.[18] In observing these categories in mystics across different cultures and how the subjects and participants described their experiences in the various experiments under a psychedelic mystical state, Pahnke and Richards (who would later become one of the pillars of contemporary psychedelic studies after the decades of darkness when this research reemerged in the late 1990s) provide a blueprint to understand the deeply impactful psychological, individual, social, and political effects of psychedelic substances in a specific (set and) setting. In the analysis that follows, I want to keep in mind these categories of psychedelic experienced and explore how they inform the aesthetic and embodied representations of the LSD experience as the characters navigate their individual and collective gender, sexual, and political revolutions.

Returning to *Larga Sinfonía en D*, the novel was written upon a friend's insistence to textualize and share the experiences lived in the countercultural milieu of the decade. As can be observed in the carefully chaotic restructuring of the ten-hour trip, the novel re-creates a psychedelic-mystical experience that catalyzes profound psychological changes in the characters and reshapes their relation and commitments to social revolution, gender revolution, experimental and political art, and social formations. Thus, and particularly in the literary context of a popular literary series that included other drug narratives such as Parménides García Saldaña's *Pasto Verde*, the novel was indubitably read as a countercultural text whose political engagement is to be found under, within, and shaped by the psychedelic experience itself. Emerging from Dalton's own political experiences during her deeply committed activist engagement in the 1960s, the text explores a series of political actions that remain just under the colorful and sensorial overwhelming experience. In its narrative structure, the novel continues the tradition of the Beatnik narration of self-discovery through voyage (physical in Jack Kerouac's *On the Road* or spiritual in Allen Ginsberg's poetry, especially *Howl*), bringing together three characters who travel the world to find themselves and each other in this global metropolis.[19] In this way, the road trips and physical journeys are less voyages of discovery and more templates to understand the psychic, emotional, and inner social journeys and changes that the characters undergo. While the characters are experiencing and describing the effects of the substance, the narrative voice itself begins to textualize the psychedelic experience: the text is suddenly separated into three simultaneous columns of narration, words appear to float off, and capitalized letters sprinkled throughout the text tell a short story.[20] Coupled with an unfixed narrative focalization, Dalton presents a text that refuses to universalize a particular perspective (so often gendered as male); even though both Roberto and Martin are autonomous characters, they are subjugated to Ana in the sense that her "trip" is the one around which theirs gains meaning. In a wink perhaps to Albert Hoffman, whom she attempted unsuccessfully to visit in 1967, Dalton writes about a trip that moves through space, time, and history without leaving the physical space of a few city blocks.

The experimental novel utilizes these aesthetic devices first to textualize and represent in a more embodied manner the effects of the psychedelic substance on the characters and narrator, and second to impact the reader's own experiences as they force them to engage with the text, finding references and deciphering hidden messages: literally reading between lines and sometimes following the words off the page. The first of these aesthetic devices the novel proposes against the violently masculine-centered narratives of both psyche-delic and revolutionary literature is a radical act of reimagining; this is not an illuminated voice that knows and will reveal secrets, but a voice that invites readers to deconstruct the world with the text.[21] It is up to the global subject to reject the normative structures of appropriation that characterize Western cul-ture's contact with other cultures. For this reason, the first words of the novel are a "recommendation":

> Ante todo este libro debe leerse con los ojos abiertos
> todo este libro debe leerse con los ojos abiertos
> este libro debe leerse con los ojos abiertos
> debe leerse con los ojos abiertos
> leerse con los ojos abiertos
> con
> los
> ojos
> abiertos.
> [Above all, this book should be read with open eyes
> all this book should be read with open eyes
> this book should be read with open eyes
> should be read with open eyes
> read with open eyes
> with
> open
> eyes].[22]

First, this technical repetition anticipatorily places the reader in the synesthetic space of seeing the sounds. The recommendation re-creates a record-player nee-dle skipping, while underlining the specific mode of reading the text is demand-ing as a worldly novel (re)creating a world through countercultural aesthetics. In other words, the recommendation generates an ethics in its aesthetics, an aesth-ethics that guides the reader in their experience of the text. Later in the novel, this countercultural ethic is vocalized in the statement "existe la posib-ilidad de *desaprender* [the possibility to unlearn exists]" (108) and described as being born into and living in a room with no doors until one day a door appears, but the reality outside (which does not deny but rather expands and complements the reality inside) cannot be appreciated unless one opens their eyes. Characteristic of the psychedelic experience as studied by psychologist William James (the noetic quality of the mystical experience) or neuroscientist Robin Carhartt-Harris (the diminution of the default mode network in the mind/brain), Dalton emphasizes the agential position of the worldly subject during this moment of mystical neurodiversity, a subject who intentionally unlearns the norms imposed by the hetero-colonial-capitalist society that surrounds them.[23]

Current psychedelic research at UC Berkeley, John Hopkins, Imperial College, and other places, as well as the rich history of underground research carried out in hiding for decades, point toward the existence of a multiplicity of states of mind and neural states of being; psychedelic states continuously appear in different studies as those states where the mind most resembles a childlike state of being with its capacity to observe, take in information, witness without mediation of social norms, and imagine possibilities.[24] In other words, there are states of mind where (un)learning can happen most readily, with neural plasticity at a certain peak during the psychedelic state.

After this "recommendation," the novel introduces the three characters. Roberto is the twenty-seven-year-old middle-class student from Mexico City who travels to London to escape political persecution after his reckless participation in certain student demonstrations and training in urban guerrilla warfare; to calm things down, his parents send him off on a summer vacationing in London. There he meets Martin, a twenty-six-year-old Australian painter with whom his friend connected him to find a place to stay in the city; Martin is already hosting Ana, a twenty-four-year-old woman from unknown origin. After talking among the three of them and sharing urban experiences that are hinted at but not fully told, Martin — the initiated one — offers to share with his two new friends the secrets of lysergic acid, noticing typical youth problems in his peers and inviting them to join him on an acid trip. The novel then proceeds to narrate their experiences from 1:00 p.m. to 10:00 p.m., each chapter covering the events of an hour while being ordered in a nonchronological manner, forcing the reader to not only struggle to understand what is being represented in each chapter but also to reconstruct the text physically.[25] The three listen to music in the apartment, head out for a stroll that takes them to a supermarket and a florist shop on their way back, hail a taxi, and continue tripping in their apartment until late at night. As the characters progress into this psychedelic state, the narrator's voice itself begins to present symptoms of the substance, separating the text into three simultaneous columns of narration to delve into their psychologies, or wandering all over the page with the text refusing to be in a straight and contained line, or hiding capitalized words in the novel to form an alternative short story (the once upon a time of the title), as well as the more stereotypical changes in perception and sensation that the narrator also perceives and cannot avoid. By constantly shifting the focalization from narrator to characters, Dalton constructs an aesthetic experience that refuses to centralize a single (masculine) perspective; while the narrator's gender is unspecified in the third-person omniscient voice, the novel nevertheless centers a female experiencing of the world through Ana, the characters whose trip will end up "ordering" the experiences of the other two around her, centripetally gathering their psychic wanderings into her sphere. The characters all experience deep and profound change in the novel; Roberto will resignify his relationship to political action through violence, Martin will reapproach his artistic practice as explanatory, and Ana will redefine/reconstruct her gendered subjectivity. In a particularly striking scene, the trio enter a flower shop and Ana finds she can understand the flowers' language and their biological workings. What is more, by presenting multiple views of/from three very different countercultural bodies (the artist, the revolutionary, the sexually liberated woman), Dalton constructs a diverse countercultural sphere that remains multiple and sexual in liberatory and productive terms (that is, not commodifying either sexuality or diversity into a specific fetish object to be circulated).

This psychedelic experience in a worldly setting becomes a momentary rupture in the fabric of space and time imposed by the normative forces of capital and nation, particularly through literary and advertising narratives. During the seventh hour after ingesting LSD, the trio begins to integrate their singular and shared experiences and they call attention to the limits of rational thought expressed in writing: "solo los que no han sentido la necesidad de despojarse del pensamiento, son los que se sienten tranquilos y repasan la palabra escrita [only those who have not felt the need to dispossess themselves of thought, those are the ones that feel at ease and go over the written word]" (14). This paradoxical critique of the written word, including literature, ultimately points to the powerfully decolonial move to explore other modes of knowledge construction. Philosopher Vittorio Morfino, speaking from the plural temporality that characterizes Western modernity, describes knowledge as neither the production nor the reflection of the real object (in this case, the lettered word in relation to the world), but as the production of a "concrete-in-thought, starting from the transformation of an imaginary material which is always-already given as structured, then generating a radical discontinuity with it" (4) — an ethical discontinuity with the histories of representation and a momentary unworlding that provokes in the reader an imagination of other worlds and other modes of being and thinking and knowing. This discontinuity is woven in the text also through the epigraphs that mark each chapter, situating the novel between Lewis Carroll, the Beatles, Marshal McLuhan, Bob Dylan, and *New York Times* clippings that are focused on signaling the cultural use of the psychedelic experience as a radical democratization of Western culture. Alongside the classic psychedelic text *Alice in Wonderland*, Dylan's *Song to Woody* articulates the political commitment of youth facing the challenges of revolution and nonviolence, while George Harrison's *Within You Without You* and Lennon and McCartney's *I Am the Walrus* frame the spiritual journey and the psychic unwinding that journey necessitates. Taken together, these epigraphs are woven into the text as aesthetic devices that guide and contextualize a setting existing outside the temporal and spatial boundaries of London, connecting youth across the globe in a series of shared experiences in which acid trips are just one.

My argument is that *Larga Sinfonía en D y había una vez* is much more than a novel about drug use or just another example of youthful "literatura de la Onda"; it is a novel that utilizes LSD and subjective liberation to generate possibilities and imagine utopic futures for Mexican and global youth. By connecting the changing local social context (Mexico City in the middle of student organizing and labor struggles) with a much larger global context (London in 1968), the novel blurs the geopolitical boundaries; the seas of references that populate the text finish undermining these boundaries and generate sociopolitical territories that reach across oceans. Contrary to the Mexico City–centered *Onderos* (José Agustín, Gustavo Saínz, and others), Dalton participates in a greater countercultural flow where "contact and communion with cultural others was, of course, a common desire among countercultural youth in many contexts. At that time, North American hippies traveled to Mexico often in search of hallucinogens traditionally used in indigenous religions" (Dunn, *Contracultura* 109). By moving the characters and action to London — a central space in the global countercultural sphere, the starting point for the mythical journeys into the East — without disconnecting them from their places of origin (Mexico City, Sydney, and the home), Dalton decolonizes the countercultural gesture and instead asks (and answers): What does the global Southerner have to say about substance use, student activism, and global counterculture, especially in the face of violent authoritarian responses from those in power (such as in Mexico, Brazil, Chile, Argentina, Uruguay, Colombia, and the US)?

These geographical displacements in turn give way to a series of aesthetic reflections and interventions that expand canonical youthful *Onda* texts such as *La tumba or Gazapo*, where the problems of middle-class male youth from Mexico City are the central themes (á la mainstream Beatnik texts). For Dalton, visual art is a way to understand the problematics of representation in general as visual media accelerates in the age of mechanical reproduction; following Benjamin and McLuhan, pop art appears in the novel as a central preoccupation of Martin. In his words and understanding, pop art contains a liberatory practice insofar as it breaks with the artistic canon by explicitly recognizing and engaging with the market and art itself as a consumer product. Hallucinogens, which make visible the sometimes-hidden economic and social relations that bring together humans and nonhumans into a global social fabric, are the tools that Martin uses to make explicit for the reader how the boundaries between art and non-art are blurring in times of hyperconsumerist visual production. Thus, the novel underlines the impact the market has on contemporary culture, and it does so by taking the characters to a literal supermarket, this new emerging social space that becomes the gestation chamber of a powerful consumerist society. As they walk toward the supermarket and look at their surroundings, the trio realizes "hemos copiado la naturaleza tan bien que ahora no es más ella, sino la semejanza de nuestra copia. ¡Qué gran preocupación la del árbol por parecerse a un cuadro de Renoir! [we have copied nature so well that she is not her anymore, but the reflection of our copy. How the tree worries to resemble a painting by Renoir!]" (Dalton 31). Since art (and advertising companies) have concentrated their efforts in realism and natural depictions of a "real" world, that same artistic language is incapable of depicting current society, and its depictions appear as violent psychological interventions that must be guarded against; at some point, the characters cover their eyes to hide from the violently screaming billboards that want to get into their heads. These representational dead ends and cages reveal that another form of communication is needed, one that is nonrepresentational and nonlinear perhaps, and when they finally end up going into the supermarket, they are bombarded with what is now true art: an actual can of tomato soup sitting on a shelf alongside hundreds of other cans. In other words, rather than reveal the hidden essence of a psychological or commodity interior, art must reveal the external connections that make up this object and transform it into a commodity product.

In characterizing the Brazilian counterculture of the 1960 and 1970s, Christopher Dunn specifies how their actions were "micropolitical activities oriented towards subjective, interpersonal experience" (*Contracultura* 37). In a similar way, these micropolitical actions of visiting a supermarket and a florist, engaging in nonmonogamous relationships and transforming their bodies/consciousness at will become points in a utopic assemblage of Mexican and global youth that crisscross substance use, rock music, fluid sexuality, student activism, regional political changes, and more; in the end, these actions push the characters to relate to each other and their social struggles in micropolitical engagements rather than grand macropolitical gestures that so often become spectacle (see Che Guevara's picture taken by Korda). I emphasize this model of assemblage to understand what the text is doing in aesthetic and ethical terms to draw a distinction between it and other *Onda* novels where literary and cultural references are crude strategies of extraction and accumulations of symbolic and cultural capital. In contrast, Dalton places these references in "low-key" ways, identifiable only to the well-versed reader familiar not with the references themselves but with the substance and its effects, freely mixing figures such as Bob Dylan, Plato, and McLuhan as recognizable figures for someone "in the know."[26] Brazilian critic María José de Queiroz signals how the rise of drug literature (or literature that defies the "normal" mode of narration/textualization of experience) is to be understood as a phenomenon that occurs when artistic and moral dogma is radically questioned; when realism is suspected as a mode of access to "reality" beyond, an alternate mode of writing emerges (49). In this sense, *LSD* inserts itself in a global milieu of writing modes that seek other ways of narrating experience and life under global capitalism and revolutionary contexts.

By presenting the text as an experimental novel, Dalton goes further than the *Onda* writers and renews Mexican literature as global literature. The major stylistic innovation already mentioned is the transference of the substance's effects from the characters to the narrator and thus to the text itself. Though the avant-garde of the early twentieth century had already carried out more and extremely wild stylistic innovations and experimentations, tied in the Mexican context to the use of technology such as with the Estridentistas in the 1920s or José Juan Tablada's calligrams in the 1910s, Dalton and other writers such as García Saldaña stand out in their explicit use of a substance to generate these alternative psychic and social states within the texts themselves and further stylistic innovation. In other words, "by intoxicating their narratives, these authors destabilize their characters' voices and open up their texts to a discursive mirroring through which the underground master narratives of liberation become transparent to their readers" (Viera 157). As with the automobile technology for Cube Bonifant or the street/urban technologies for Salvador Novo, lysergic acid (a synthetic substance, albeit with a long and rich cultural history that goes back millennia) becomes a technology to be used by and absorbed into the body to reengage with consumerist and nationalist subjectification processes. The substance catalyzes the representation of intercorporeal bodies in the characters and the reader-text relations, while the novel generates a textualized embodiment — a corpotext — of a fluid, dynamic, and on-acid narrator.

Perhaps the most interesting aesthetic device that Dalton mobilizes throughout the novel is the *mise-en-abyme* carried out by the capitalized words throughout the text. If these words are picked up by the reader and arranged in order of appearance, they create a short one-page "summary" of the psychic, spiritual, psychological, and revolutionary journey the trio undertake; this is the aforementioned "y había una vez [and once upon a time]" that the novel's title hints at. In the novel itself, Ana considers the symbolic power of language and literature in creating confusion in the act of communication and states how "si pudiéramos evitar tantas letras y leer solo las mayúsculas se podría acabar un libro en diez minutos, y sabríamos lo esencial, seguramente [if we could avoid so many letters and read only the capitalized letters we would finish a book in ten minutes and surely know all the essentials]" (Dalton 133). Countercultural theorist Joseph Berke stated in 1969 how "the destruction-destructuring of the system in people is fundamentally a political event" (34).[27] If the novel is understood as a textual body, the aesthetic transformations become, then, a political act in that they push back against the normativities of Western and colonial artistic production; these are not avant-garde innovations as much as interventions of a body of culture. Particularly within the Mexican literary and cultural sphere, the changes that occur within the characters' bodies serve as mirrors for the changes that are occurring within the text itself. By placing these words throughout the text, Dalton de-structures even more the literary system she is participating in, especially when considering *Al calor de la semilla*, her book of short stories published before, and her works published after *LSD*. It is not enough that she is including lyrics in English, talking about pop art, or even narrating a drug experience; the embedded short story motivates the reader to de-structure their own reading experiences, taking it one step further than Cortázar in *Rayuela*'s chaotic chapter order. The reader must disentangle the words, arrange them, and read them *after* having experienced the novel as a whole; this aesthetic device demands a close reading initially and later rereadings.

This extreme playfulness with the typographic structure of the text (which also at times abandons the horizontal line across the page to wander or present multiple views on a single page, or switches between narrators within the same paragraph one word at a time) can be understood in literary terms as the textualization of a predictable and well-known lysergic effect, the expansion of consciousness beyond the ego-centered self. In this sense, psychologist Ralph Metzner has pointed out how "one does not see hallucinated, illusory objects; rather, one sees the ordinary objects but also sees, knows, and feels associated patterns and aspects that one was not aware of before" (34). The short story, the typographic jumps, and the narrative cuts all serve to push the reader to thread these words, to see the ordinary and traditional novel (because ultimately the novel is a pretty standard trip report, albeit typographically intervened), *and* to see and feel the patterns that underlie these representations. Thus, like when the characters go to the supermarket and see the vegetable and soup cans *while simultaneously* visualizing a critique of pop art and consumer society, the novel pushes the reader (and particularly the reader experienced with LSD and other substances) to practice this double vision. This consciousness expansion results in the practice of embodying knowledge; instead of reading or discussing philosophy or art theory, the characters obtain insight and knowledge about themselves and the world around them precisely through this embodied experience, textualized through aesthetic disruptions, interventions, and re-presentations.

These aesthetic devices, from the narrative voice to the typographic choices and more, end up exploring literary paths that diverge from the main Ondero writers, although their general political and generational preoccupations are also marginally present in the text. The choice of time and space (London 1968) allows for a reading of the text in dialogue with a transnational artistic, social, and philosophical context worried more with critiquing and overcoming the multiple modernities of Western societies and their shortcomings than with breathing life into an old or creating a new middle-class urban identity.[28] By reading into the dense network of aesthetic innovations and cultural references that include musicians, authors, social movements, religious figures, philosophers, artists, and more, the text is disconnected from the specific Onda geography and united with a more global literary and cultural sphere. It is not only the space that is aesthetically re-created through the eyes of the characters and the narrative voice, but also the bodies of these characters that are transformed and then returned to their social contexts. Bodies that are reassembled after their psychic and physical trip, as these substances are absorbed and woven in these embodied Mexican and global youth subjectivities. Specifically in the Mexican context, the novel then becomes a substance-mediated approach to the consumption of international counterculture in general, providing a "blueprint" for the Mexican readers not on how to consume LSD, but rather on how to approach and consume counterculture *through* the biopolitical act of transforming and modifying one's body chemistry for a few hours, no matter the substance. This bodily autonomy thus lies in the choice that is continually reiterated in the novel, not in an idealization of the substance itself.

A central theme that repeats throughout the novel is the questioning and reimagining of revolution in the global context of postcolonial actions throughout capitalist geographies. *LSD* proposes first an interior re-evolution of the psyche as the paramount political action, and it does so in the representational space constructed through signification that critic Pheng Cheah signals.[29] London as a capitalist capital of the world and Mexico City as a revolutionary capital (in the context of student movements, labor strikes, and state violence that marked 1968) are spatially remade through the active experiences and remembering of the trio in both of these metropolises. In other words, as the characters move physically in the space of London and psychically in the spaces of Mexico City and Sydney as postcolonial metropolis, they remake these spaces of their past, present, and futures by reimagining themselves in them, not only in the future through their shared dreams but also and most importantly in the past through their individual trips. The memories of Roberto in his childhood exploration and young adult revolutionary actions (including the training with guns and military action) are reshaped into alternative representations of revolution where non-violence appears as an ethic, especially when it cannot be imperatively enacted in the face of militarized state violence. In a similar way, the childhood memories of Martin bring forward an alternative way to inhabit the social spaces he moves in as an adult, his memory of swimming and snorkeling in the reefs of Australia now informing his representational movements in the art circuits and countercultural spheres of London. Ultimately, during their psychedelic experience, the artist, the revolutionary, and the feminist realize they "do not merely inhabit social space as passive subjects but can actively participate in making it" (Cheah 85). The ten hours documented in the novel insert the characters (and the readers with them) in a globalized space where their presence impacts the space around them as much as the space impacts their own imaginings; their actions reshape the world around them, thus empowering the youth to continue participating in society in micropolitical action.

What I find most interesting about these representational strategies is not space itself — already a radical reimagining in the context of a psychedelic experience — but the representations of gender, sexuality, and revolution as they appear in the territory and space of bodies, skin, and flesh. In this spatial territory, *LSD* brings forward a series of encounters with themselves and each other that continuously mark the boundaries of normative genders, sexualities, and revolutionary action on their bodies and that ultimately works toward untethering these boundaries while refusing to offer fixed alternatives. Similar to the anti-accumulative collection of references that generate the assemblage of the text, *LSD* showcases sexual liberation as one of the core tenets of counterculture, promoting an ethical and consensual sexual engagement even under the influence of the substance itself, contrasting in this with Gustavo Sainz's *Gazapo* or *Obsesivos días circulares* (1969), and even with José Agustín's *Se está haciendo tarde (final en laguna)* (1973), where substances quickly and definitely lead to dangerously unethical and potentially nonconsensual sexual relations. Here, the set and setting serve to catalyze the substance's potential in terms of sexual liberation, and the nonverbal and verbal communication between the characters underline the negotiations of these relationships; more than the act itself, it is the process of liberation that sexual revolution promises that interests the narrator and the text.

In the text, the three youth coalesce in their bodies three distinctly gendered positions of resistance and revolution: the armed struggle with its ethics of social action and the psychological struggle with an ethics of individual action, embodied in both Roberto and Martin respectively, and the liberation struggle of feminism as it renegotiated gender norms in domestic, public, and revolutionary spaces, embodied in Ana. In this way, Dalton bridges the preoccupation of social change that youth were facing across the globe in the many different armed struggles with an understanding of counterculture as self-development and radical bodily/subjective autonomy. This tension between individual-collective struggles will in turn provide the backdrop for the various gender revolutions each of these characters face as they navigate their relationship with themselves and each other; for example, while Martin celebrates the use of lysergic acid as way to enlighten society, Roberto demands specific actions such as taking down a specific government. As their trip progresses, however, both discover fundamental flaws in their philosophies, paradoxically both anchored in their colonial masculinities that are being challenged. Martin realizes that by demanding *everyone* take lysergic acid, he is prescribing a socially normative event to change the individual, imposing his own will over everyone's and reestablishing a normative order with punishment and reward.[30] On the other hand, Roberto realizes that the use of overviolence against the state will inevitably create more violence, but he is confused as to what course of action to take; however, his commitment to the cause and the end goals of collective liberation is strengthened in particular by a critical awareness of the impact of violence, physically and psychologically. In a similar yet unique way, Ana embarks on a psychic journey that unfolds in time and space while remaining within the boundaries of her skins, gender becoming the way in which she gives meaning to a series of experiences the trip brings forward. Her familial relation to her single mother, her social relation to a professor, her friendship with Martin, her sexual relations with Roberto and Martin, and her own sensual relation to her own body through each of the senses applied to herself (how she sees, smells, tastes, touches, feels, and hears herself) all mark Ana's reengagement with herself as a revolutionary agent, a subject of her own desire and will and not just an object of *his*tory or circumstance.

Embodying these revolutionary genders is not just a matter of reshaping the bodies themselves, and Dalton expands the representational space these three characters are moving in by continuously reconnecting them to the revolutionary representational space of dissident and countercultural youth across the globe. In the face of Western societies that have emerged out of strict and exclusionary nationalisms (such as Mexico), the novel creates a space-time and characters that fluidly move into the flows of globalization, albeit through the channels of commodity capitalism. The gendered subjectivities of the trio thus exist in a shared space, and the epigraphs for each chapter that weave the *New York Times*, Dylan, Lennon, McCartney, Lewis Carroll, and McLuhan serve to draw the contours of this revolutionary space. While appropriation is a common literary technique the rest of the *Onderos* such as José Agustín, Parménides García Saldaña or Gustavo Sainz used, here Dalton uses these lyrics and symbols in a slightly different way that engages with the characters bodies' in much deeper ways; the lyrics are songs that are played in the apartment, and the newspaper clips and quotes come from books and newspapers lying around in the apartment. What is more important is that these characters are transitioning in this space, moving from and into multicultural settings; in the case of Roberto, his explicitly Mexican masculinity is challenged time and again by this erosion of heteronormative values, best exemplified in the crisis he experiences in the bathroom mirror after seeing a sexual act between the other two youth and in remembering his own involvement with them. Sexual liberation becomes a marker for a different Roberto, a young Mexican man who has now incorporated these experiences into his own body and takes them back to a national and regional context. By undertaking these small yet deeply meaningful changes in their (gendered) bodies, the characters incorporate foreignness directly into their existence through the consumption of the substance, in the process generating intercorporeal bodies that defy the strict notions of gender and sexuality under a colonial-patriarchal order. Bodies that consume become bodies that transform, and the transformation gets carried back to their reality and national space.

While the trio met before the events of the novel and socialized and embarked on a sexual relationship before taking LSD, I consider the substance to be the catalyzer of their revolutionizing gender, in the context of a critical and political use. Throughout his research on traditional and current Mesoamerican cultures and their relations with different plants and fungi in ceremonial, social, and spiritual rituals, anthropologist Peter T. Furst stresses the differences this practice has with Western, modern recreational uses.[31] Particularly given the mediatic and social evolution that a substance such as LSD has had for the past century, with figures such as Timothy Leary and the US hippies as the poster children of LSD, it is not surprising that a modern substance user views LSD more as a moment of entertainment or recreational exploration than a political attempt to question or alter cultural reality, much less using it specifically to construct alternative social organizations or collectively shape political action, not to mention ritualistic mystical uses. Thankfully, this is changing not only with the surge of medical and therapeutic research, but also with the decades of underground therapeutic and political uses of psychedelics coming to the surface. Since the 1960s, however, LSD and other substances were valued as therapeutic and political tools, and under a certain *set* and *setting* as psychologist Ralph Metzner and others have demonstrated, lysergic acid can serve to attain a certain experience that takes the individual into a different sense of body and society, similar to the effect of some initiation rituals as they prepare the person to reenter society on different terms after a full transformation. It is with this in mind that I want to understand the revolutionary uses of LSD in the novel as it engages with gender and sexuality, a countercultural use that speaks of political motivations and a desire to radically transform the world around them, starting with their bodies. The effects of lysergic acid on the characters and narrator, then, are not simply modern textual literary innovations existing in a literary tradition but are also a countercultural catalyzer in and of themselves, documenting how these characters are transforming themselves and allowing for (youthful) readers to transform themselves in the process. That is, if lysergic acid (whether consumed or read about/in) allows for the characters to "shake off" and unlearn (gender and sexual) norms to reshape their realities and achieve a certain "liberation," then it serves to say that they are revolutionizing lysergic acid as much as it is revolutionizing them.

As the process of "unlearning" continues during the novel, the social injunctions associated with normative gender roles are also disturbed, reexamined, and ultimately rejected. The concept of revolution itself is transformed, and given the context of armed struggles in Latin America as well as social movements led by students, this is less of an idealistic struggle than a concrete practical discussion with implications for bodies on the front lines of political struggles. In the critical discussions the trio holds during the lysergic state, revolution is transformed from a radically violent and armed fight celebrated by Roberto into a more inclusive and countercultural stance, a shift in both tactic and territory toward an interior that contains the exterior of society. As countercultural theorist Joseph Berke stated in 1969, "the structure is ourselves. The revolution is ourselves. The revolution is the revolution" (18). Thus, Ana states "encore la revolution! Ahora viéndole todos sus trucos y por lo mismo con más consistencia. ¡Hay mucho motivos para hacerla! Estoy dispuesta a luchar en la única forma que considero eficiente [encore the revolution! Now seeing all its tricks and therefore with more consistency. There are so many reasons to do it! I am willing to fight in the only way I consider efficient]" (Dalton 22). Thus, resistance and even armed struggle are accepted, and yet this is also recognized as a futile and limited attempt, a symbolic bullfight where the fighter is not the matador but the bull, caught in the arena set up by the state. Roberto states he now understands how his rebellious actions against the state make him into the bull, where he stands against the bullfighter and yet has "menos oportunidades que él, pero me lanzo al ruedo. Hoy comprendí que hay muchas cosas necesarias de las que no puedo desojarme y *no quiero* perderlas. Si te gusta la expresión, forman parte de mi macrocosmos [fewer opportunities than him and still I go into the ring. I understood today there are many necessary things I cannot get rid of and I don't want to lose them. If you like the expression, they are a part of my macro cosmos]" (23). Even if ultimately violence is accepted as a legitimate avenue to push back against a repressive and colonial state, it is now understood through a critical lens.[32] It is striking that Dalton understands this particular position in the year of 1968 *before* the events at Tlatelolco, and well before the Jueves de Corpus; in other words, well before the Mexican state appeared in the public lens as the real matador willing to enforce violent and paramilitary repression in the name of protecting society. It is also important to note that Dalton writes from her experiences participating in the rebuilding of Cuban society during the literacy campaigns, land reform, inclusive marriage, and civil law reforms of the early 1960s in the socialist island. Thus, especially for (youthful) readers who approached this text after the violence of Tlatelolco, the figure of Roberto provides an avenue of political resistance that is grounded first in the personal body, a transformation of the self that radically redefines masculinity and especially disengages masculinity from the enforcement of violence: a subjective strategy that in Mexico dates back to the colonizer masculinities of Hernán Cortes and other conquistadors, moves through the independence fighters of the nineteenth century, and is updated with the revolutionary figures and heroes the *mestizo* postrevolutionary state celebrates. Roberto's masculinity is reshaped without being rejected and supplanted with a washed-down version of Orientalist pacifism or nonviolence; his lysergic acid is revolutionary in that it allows him to understand his subjective reshaping as an act of rebuilding, followed by an active positioning in the margins of society through guerrilla engagement.

Ultimately, the use of lysergic acid also becomes a catalyzer for the emergence of other states of consciousness, some of which remain accessible to the characters post-trip as Martin explains and as Ana and Roberto are eager to explore as they return to their homes of origin. These other states of consciousness also serve to signal the crisis in the experiencing of life under contemporary consumer capitalism; these countercultural bodies can resist these subjectification and epithumogenetic processes thanks to their choices and acts of consumption. Particularly in the face of current contemporary capitalism and the deep psychological effects of individualism, social and economic alienation, and consumerism, these liberatory practices are important and must be considered alongside the findings of psychedelic therapy nowadays. This embodied knowledge attained through a psychedelic session instead of (only) through philosophical readings or political praxis is a manifestation of a much larger and multifarious countercultural phenomenon that seeks to bring about sociocultural and political change *from* the body, springing from knowledge contained in the body itself through its movements and relations with the world. For bodies of culture and bodies of color and bodies of gender, this centralization is doubly important since it serves to also validate, legitimize, and value their existence as bodies different from the normative Eurocentric body so often taken to be the paradigm of human existence.

This embodiment of knowledge and experiences through a sensorial world-building that is anchored in the physical bodies moving in time and space and not in romanticized ideals of peace, love, revolution, or justice will shape the events in the novel and give nuance to the events experienced by youths across the globe in these decades. In his exemplary work *The Making of a*

Counterculture (1969), Theodore Roszak describes (American) counterculture as a segment of a (mostly young) generation who "see, and many who follow them find the vision attractive, that building the society is not primarily a social, but a psychic task" (49); in other words, a "mode" of achieving social change and maybe revolution, not by social means and organization as much as by psychic and individual transformations, leading to changes in conceptions of society, in turn shaped by culture itself. Also, in approaching the global countercultural youth, Gila Hayim points out how the "regaining of 'authentic' experience amounts to an undoing of culture. It is first of all a disengagement from that form of socialization that endorses a 'shared solution' predicated, as we have noted earlier, on the structure of violence" (112). In other words, the singular, sensual, sensitive, and sensory experiences of being (always already a danger to the normative political order in its disruptive potential) become the ways in which youth (and our trio of characters) can redefine their political existence and provide a theoretical-political foundation for their "peace and love" and "flower power" discourse of revolution and resistance. As simple as this idea might seem, in the context of (normative and phallocentric) countercultural production, *Larga Sinfonía en D* is proposing a radical alternative that not only critiques capitalist and colonialist social structure, but also provides avenues of liberation for its characters and readers. In contrast, it is interesting to note that typical "canonical" *Onda* and US countercultural characters are constantly places in social environments where the individual dissolves into an undefined and defaced mass in a best-case scenario or self-destructs in acts of suicide in the worst-case scenarios.[33] At the end of *LSD*, Roberto decides he is ready to go back to Mexico and continue revolutionary resistance with a renewed political consciousness now anchored in his own body and not some foreign ideals. The focus of the novel is on how the physical changes catalyzed by the substance, by the rock music they listen to, and by the art they surround themselves with become the ways in which a countercultural ethos is woven into their bodies.

While the novel clearly makes connections with ancient Mesoamerican, Greek, and Hindu societies and their uses of entheogens such as mushrooms (*amanita muscaria*), ergot (LSD), ololiuqui (morning glory seeds), and others, I consider it more enriching to read it alongside the more modern approaches that study the effects of lysergic acid as a catalyzer of alternate states of consciousness that closely resemble the Western variations of mystical experiences.[34] In doing so, I resist romanticizing countercultural contact with Eastern philosophies, something that in later decades would allow for an easier commodification of "hippie philosophy" as a lifestyle, aesthetics, and ethics easily packageable and sellable as a westernized version of Indian thought. In the novel, Martin encapsulates these connections to reveal the historical lineage the trio are a part of, without necessarily containing their experiences to these traditions:

> ¿por qué quieren negar que Platón descubrió lo mismo en su noche de misterios? Eleusis suena a claridad, ¿no es cierto?

Fue por el mes de septiembre cuando nació su mundo de las ideas. Porqué queremos demostrar que somos los descubridores del ácido, olvidando que por siglos ha dominado los bosques húmedos, donde hadas, duendes, girasoles y gnomos se han reunidos en círculos alrededor de los hongos, cantándoles y alabando su naturaleza cotidiana de 'Carne de Dios.' Roberto debería comprender esto mejor que yo. Los hongos en mi pintura no son otra cosa que la representación histórica de la música. Son mi larga sinfonia.

[why do they want to deny that Plato discovered the same thing in his night of mysteries? Eleusis sounds like clarity, does it not? It was around the month of September when his world of ideas was born. Why do we still want to prove we are the discoverers of acid, forgetting that it has dominated the wet woods for centuries, where fairies and elves and sunflowers and gnomes have gathered in circles around the mushrooms, singing and praising their quotidian "Flesh of the Gods" nature. Roberto would understand this better than I. The mushrooms in my painting are just the historical representation of music. They are my long symphony.] (Dalton 150)[35]

In this way, Dalton points toward the ancestral and traditional uses of lysergic acid and other entheogens, distancing the experiences in the novel from a purely "recreational" afternoon with friends. What is more, this fragment hints at a whole pharmacopoeia on a global scale, working to deprioritize any singular mode of achieving a hallucinatory, psychedelic, or mystical state, effectively legitimizing a Mexican curandera alongside a Greek philosopher. Of the modern approaches to psychedelic experiences, those of Aldous Huxley in *Heaven and Hell* (1956) where he draws parallels between his experiences with mescaline and the experiences described in medieval mystical poetry opens a path of exploration that traces mystical experiences across ages.[36] Following this line of thinking, Pahnke and Richards's studies focused on the mystical experience, whether catalyzed by entheogens, through meditation or other practices, or spontaneous. They enlist the previously mentioned nine categories to describe these experiences, and their questionnaire remains relevant today, providing guidelines in contemporary studies. By no means do these nine categories appear in a specific order in every single mystical or lysergic experience, and their appearance in certain moments in *LSD* serves to exemplify how — for the characters, the author, and the readers who engage with the text — the experience resembles more a mystical/lysergic acid than a mere recreational trip.[37] Through their embodied experiences that solidify their intercorporeality, these mystical categories serve to understand and redefine the subjective existence of the three characters.

Anticipating what Pahnke and Richards systematized in the mystical experience studies, Walter Benjamin explored the uses of substances such as hashish and opium earlier in the century while in the city of Marseilles. His experiments led him to trace one of Pahnke and Richards's key postulates about the mystical experience: the sense of unity with the immediate context surrounding the subject and, beyond that, unity with the cosmos itself.[38] Within the novel, this theoretical knowledge becomes embodied and thus allows for the grounding of these abstractions into concrete politically and socially transformative action. The Cartesian subject-object dichotomy springing from an "objective" understanding of reality that separates bodies from bodies and bodies from space is suddenly broken as subject-subject consciousness arises, even and especially when interacting with so-called objects. In a telling moment in the novel, Roberto is standing in front of the bathroom mirror on a journey of self-discovery and self-reflection when he suddenly remembers seeing Martin hold a Chinese vase in his hand:

> Cierro los ojos y lo veo ahí. Ahora no ES sólo el azul de siempre lo que llama mi atención, sino todos los detalles del paisaje. Los he tenido dentro, como una fotografía, y hoy los veo por primera vez . . . todo el jarrón que se puede esconder en una mano. ¡Un mandarín! ¡Una historia! ¡Una filosofía! Una atmósfera que de pronto es COMPRENSIBLE. Más de mil años en cinco dedos
> [I close my eyes and see them there. Now it IS not just the blue of everyday that catches my eye, but all the landscape's details. I have had them inside, like a photograph, and today I see them for the first time . . . the whole jar that can hide in one hand. A mandarin! A history! A philosophy! An atmosphere that suddenly is COMPREHENSIBLE. More than a thousand years in five fingers.] (Dalton 22)

The memory allows for Roberto to become one with Martin, holding the vase in his own hands and consciousness, and through that being one with Chinese philosophy and history, even though he "objectively" knows little to nothing about them. It is not precisely knowledge through reason that leads him toward unity, much less concrete rational facts that make up this image. Rather, it is this sense of embodied being-with that allows for an understanding of unity that brings him close to foreign cultures, without necessarily exoticizing or fetishizing them. This will reoccur in the novel with the images of Shiva and Parvati that Martin decorates the apartment with, and with their encounter with London itself as a globalized and global space.

This unity through shared embodiment will guide Roberto to understand his own political becoming-with alongside his fellow youth. Later in the novel, while reflecting on his life and reminiscing about his past revolutionary actions with a certain degree of fear, apprehension, and curiosity, Roberto realizes his place in history as a singular person: "pero nada conciliatorio con lo que se puede llamar ser uno. UNO. Y ahora que me doy cuenta que no lo soy, estoy detrás de todos [but nothing conciliatory with what can be called ONE.

And now I realize that I am not, I am behind everyone]" (Dalton 118). In this moment, his subjectivity erodes as a singular phenomenon and becomes one with the shared existence of his peers, a blurring of bodies that nevertheless brings more concretion to his own actions and his own understandings of them, now intimately interrelated with the lives of his peers. His body blends with the bodies of the other fighters before and around him, blurring the boundaries that define his "I"; and yet, as characteristic of a mystical experience, this moment paradoxically allows for a firmer, more defined, and more aware understanding of the "I" that is not discarded or rejected as useless in favor of a permanent dissolution. On the contrary, it is the unity of this subjective position with those around him that allows for the moment of enlightenment and reflection, as he is now relationally assembled to the cosmos itself and more concretely to the revolutionaries before and around him in a series of connections that become visible, tangible, and embodied during this alternate state.[39]

The most powerful embodied knowledge that emerges from the LSD trip, in line with the California-based sociopolitical experiments of the Electric Kool-Aid acid tests, the Merry Pranksters' gatherings, and the Grateful Dead sessions in their early careers, was the redefinition of revolution as peaceful and non-violent. During the long 1960s, the harsh consequences of armed struggle and guerrilla actions fighting against highly specialized military weapons (napalm, chemical warfare, intelligence agencies like COINTELPRO and the CIA) were motivating a resurgence of pacifist revolutionaries. The characters know this rationally, as youth who engage politically with youth across the globe, and it is their experience that embodies this knowledge. As their trip progresses, the trio finish their journey in an intercorporeal, intersubjective, and deeply positive sense of unity and peace, a plateau they have reached together. Pahnke and Richards describe the mystical experience as marked by "feelings of joy, love, blessedness and peace inherent in mystical consciousness" (180), even when the visual content itself might seem to be disturbingly violent.[40] Chapter nine, which happens eight hours into their lysergic experience, opens with a Bob Dylan quote and Martin trying to give shape to their shared experience, a symphony of many minds and voices. His narrative voice understands how "se ha logrado la intención, que era explicar el nuevo lenguaje para el 'nuevo mundo.' Hay una palabra que continúa flotando desordenada [the intention has been achieved, which was to explain the new language for the 'new world.' There is a world that keeps floating around, disordered]" (Dalton 149). The letters that float on the page, breaking the block text of the paragraph, appear jumbled and yet clearly communicate a message: E V O L V E, evolve and love.[41] A natural historic process and an emotional descriptor become assembled through a countercultural body grounded in both a scientific understanding of its own corporeal existence and interdependence in a web of life greater than itself and an emotional understanding that guides and gives shape to ethical and political relations. This feeling of love, unity, and radical positivity in the face of capitalist and colonial/state violence will only increase in the last chapter/last hour of the journey, when space and time cease to be limitations that contain bodies and minds in fixed positions. Here the typography of the text is broken into three columns, each one a stream of consciousness belonging to a specific person; now Martin climbs the Matterhorn while Roberto travels into his revolutionary memories, and Ana unites them both in, through, and with her.[42] After a few pages of individual and isolated journeying — a coming-back to their bodies by remembering their past experiences — the three columns come together into a single block once more, visually reminding the reader of the integration process integral to the mystical-psychedelic experience. In this way, they (un)learn by embodying their experience, by coming together into their bodies and ceasing to be just mind, just memory, just rational thought.

For a more complex and liberatory understanding of *LSD* and Mexican countercultural literature interventions into wider literary and cultural debates on global culture in the wake of colonialism and liberatory struggles, Pheng Cheah's notion of *worlding* is useful. Defined as a temporal process that orders the world through the imposition of a teleological time and a strict adherence to the temporal normativity emanating from the metropolitan centers, worlding brings to the forefront the ways in which the "world" in world literature is above all a (normative) temporal one.[43] As a normative force that gives rise "to the totality of meaningful relations that is the ontological condition for the production of values and norms" (Cheah 10), worlding shapes the novel from the instant the characters move through the city of London, home of the Greenwich Meridian that continues to temporally order the colonial/colonized world. The spiritual and economic ordering that shapes the lives of all (human) bodies living under coloniality is, however, abruptly interrupted by the lysergic experience; a core effect of entheogens such as lysergic acid, psylocibin, mescaline, DMT, or others is the diminishment of spatial and temporal awareness (a characteristic shared with mystical experiences across time and cultures). Typically reduced to a silly and cartoonish representation of time accelerating or slowing down while the person is "tripping," this radical disjunction in time allows for the emergence of other states of mind and other political imaginations that literally opens worlds of possibilities within the body and between the body and those around them through the experience of time.

LSD's saturation of global commodities and experiences being resignified into Western modernity during the global 1960s thus constructs alternative worlding strategies created by individuals who therapeutically and recreationally engage with psychedelics to face the multiple acts of violence, traumas, and dispossessions enacted by capitalist and colonial worlding. The novel constructs heterotemporalities, a multiplicity of timelines and temporalities within which the three characters flow into and out of, reaching back into Plato's cave while remaining in their London apartment, witnessing the end of their violent revolutionary action in fiery chaos and their own death, experiencing their birth with the awareness of their adult mind and sensorial sense-making, and more. These many temporalities understood under the concept of heterotemporality — which scholars have associated with ways of reweaving national histories (Brian L. Price, "Heterotemporal *mise-en-scene* in the films of Luis Estrada"), religious interventions in anticolonial struggles (Niels Riecken, "Heterotemporality, the Islamic tradition and the political: Laroui's concept of the antinomy of history"), philosophical and political world-building from the postcolonial world (Pheng Cheah, *What Is a World?*), and queerness and queer temporalities outside of normative times (Kathryn Bond Stockton, *Growing Sideways*) — appear in *LSD* not simply as representations of what the characters are experiencing, but as ways in which the readers are forced to travel to these times without knowing they are doing so. In other words, the different moments in the texts where heterotemporalities emerge are subtle and happen sometimes within the same sentence with no punctuation or marker for the temporal disjunction.[44] This chaotic interweaving and these immanent temporalities (may) generate in the reader a sense of untethering from their own temporality, the following of a "narrative" suddenly becoming less of a teleological path (one word after another) and more of an always already existential hyperabundance of temporality and subjectivity. This reading experience becomes embodied in the act of engaging with the book, activating a radical reader-text relation as the reader jumps time in the space of a few pages in an apparent chaos that reconstructs contemporary experiences for global youth through the psychedelic lens.

Figure 3.1a. Fragment from *Larga sinfonía en D.*
Reprinted with permission. *Source*: Margarita Dalton.
Larga sinfonía en d y había una vez. Mexico: Editorial
Diógenes, 1968

E	O	V
V	L	E

Sólo la *palabra* puede tener significado dentro de todo. ¿Cómo llegar a los costados de la música? Para hacer música hay que pintarla de verdeeeee. Para que salte. El salto dejará aun el tono y la coloración. ¿La composición? Es lo menos importante, se puede llegar a ella bailando. Dejándose caer sobre alfombras pobladas de polvo. Fumando conscientes e inconscientes la cosecha de siglos. Pero ¿uno no se deja caer en algo por nada? O ¿uno no se deja caer en nada por algo? Como diría Alice, cuando uno no sabe la respuesta, no importa en qué orden se ponga la pregunta.

Figure 3.1b. Fragment from Larga sinfonia en D.
Reprinted with permission. Source: Margarita Dalton.
Larga sinfonía en d y había una vez. Mexico: Editorial
Diógenes, 1968

¡Gracias Martin por haberme descubierto este mundo!
Caigo nuevamente   en   MY SIN.   No me
gusta tanto   como antes,   me parece
huelo mejor   sin él.   Lo conocí
por primera   vez en   diciembre
después de   navidad   pero ya no
me gusta.   Fue un   regalo pero
                LANVIN se ha vuelto viejo.
                Es un perfume viejo.
                UN PENTAGRAMA
                                hay música de clavicordio
que huele.   ALCOHOL
                MERCURIO CROMO
                ELÍXIR DE GUERLAINE
                MY SIN

                                Donde, enteras,
cuartas, blancas   y negras, compi-
    ten con el olor   a cartón y tinta de
    los dibujos hin   dúes. También con
        las telas que   nos rodean, pene-
        tradas de ambi   entes diversos,   de
        fiestas y merca   dos, de velorios esca-
            sos y parques.   Se dividen entre ellas
            y las cuartas to   man el polvo que los
        rayos del sol ha   cen flotar por la habitación. Lo
        veo en pequeñas lentejuelas de colores. Los vegeta-
        les son blancos, sobre todo las naranjas cuya piel
        hace temblar a Martin. Ahora le paso una por
        la cara y el cuello. Todo regresa. Danza para-
        dójica de olores, aire y movimiento terrestre.
—He encontrado gente que siempre habla con autoridad
sobre cosas que saben —Ana retira la naranja del cuello de
Martin y se sienta a su lado—. "… nosotros podemos identificar

In the context of unlearning that the novel requires of the reader (keep those eyes open), this particular position-taking underscores the intervention in world-building the novel enacts, particularly when read under the hetero-temporality that Cheah describes in postcolonial world literature.[45] The trio's psychedelic experiences are inserted in a history of Western psychedelic knowledge that dates back to Plato and the mysteries of Eleusis and passes through the histories of the flesh of the gods (in medieval Europe and Mesoamerican cultures). It is precisely here that countercultural literature allows for an understanding of the heterotemporal nature of Western modernity itself. The normativity imposed by the Greenwich Meridian is questioned in the activation of these alternative timelines, and the normative space of an empire's capital city is subverted. It is important to underline, however, that this heterotemporality is activated by the character's own self- reflection and is not inherent to the psychedelic experience itself; in other words, similar to what Parménides García Saldaña does in his cannabis novel *Pasto Verde*, it is not the consumption of a substance itself that matters as much as the mindset and the avenues of psychic liberation that are taken during the trip itself. Once again, the paradigmatic structure of psychedelic therapy of set and setting serves as framework to understand this nuance, for liberation is not in the substance itself as much as it is in the set within the body consuming it and in the setting in which the body moves in and around.

The novel exists in multiple temporalities and moves from ancient past to futuristic fantasies while looking around and seeing the already multilayered temporalities of colonialism in a metropolis while having one foot in the revolutionary struggles of Latin America. These complex temporal moves push the characters and the narrator to critically understand the ways in which representation must be counterculturally redefined, both politically in activism and resistance and symbolically in art and language. While approaching pop art, countercultural theorist Gila Hayim signals a core characteristic of countercultural ethics, a "merge" where "technology can itself become art; work can itself become a form of play" (121). Perhaps one of the greatest examples of this playful countercultural ethos in the world of art is Andy Warhol's *The Factory*, where work, play, and technology come together to create art. While I remain critical and aware of the ways in which this position will become commodified and absorbed into capitalist machineries of mass production, extraction, and profit, I also see in this merging a fusion of the self with the cosmos immediately surrounding the body, both the material cosmos and the social fabric that is surrounding it; in other words, the boundaries and limitations in institutions of Western art, politics, and society are blurred and anything/anyone can become a work of art, a political agent, or a social revolutionary. This merging helps to understand how the vegetables are seen by the characters in their supermarket moments, as "están presentes en texturas y formas pero nosotros los definimos. Nosotros les damos nombres [they are present in textures and shapes but we define them. We give them names]" (Dalton 36). This merging of texture, form, and sensorial stimuli with the consciousness of the eye and mind that beholds illuminates for the characters their interrelation with the world around them, empowering them as youth able to literally shape, name, and give form to the world around them; particularly understood from a political perspective, this is a liberatory and empowering move that places youth at the forefront of shaping new worlds in a revolutionary style. Their embodied experience gives them a firmer understanding of the knowledge they already know, the political potential of pop art as a tool for critique and social revolution in that it may de-alienate even through its mass circulation by placing emphasis on the process of alienation itself materialized in the alienated commodity that is art and object: "es muy fácil, por ejemplo, la CoKe se usa sin pensar, nacimos con ella. CoKe. Desde que nacimos aquí ha estado . . . si cambia o desaparece en un future, no por eso la realidad actual puede negarla. CoKe. La labor del artista es la de reflejar su época. CoKe [it's very easy, for example, CoKe is used without thinking, we were born with it. CoKe. Since we were born it has been here . . . even if it changes or disappears in a future, current reality cannot deny it. CoKe. The work of the artist is to reflect their time. CoKe]" (40). The blurring of work and play, personal and political, art and commodity, and ultimately self and other push the trio to reconsider their own revolutionary power, a counter-cultural potential of reshaping the world without burning it down with flames and bullets. Rather than focusing on *what* is being represented and rearticulated to name, identify, push back against, or celebrate, the novel pushes for a critical consideration of *how* these representations can be reshaped, resignified, and rearticulated in a liberatory manner.

As the characters experience this radically playful engagement with language and representation, they and the narrator articulate their ethics in a clear and concise way: the point is to unlearn, to recognize the possibility of shaking off cultural preconceptions that delimit, tamper with, and conceal the fullness of the experiencing of the world.[46] Language is untrustworthy insofar as naming/representing is always already a prison house, and yet language is one way to access the world outside of their bodies; in their mystical-lysergic experience, verbal communication and representational art is only one of many ways of communication, as telepathy, radical empathy, dream language, and more are used by the trio to engage with each other and the world around them, people and objects alike. Pahnke and Richards, building on what psychologist William James describes as the ineffability of mystical experiences beyond language itself, describe how a mystical experience is marked also by an inability to be properly, fully, and richly expressed in language no matter how many words are used, a certain existence that supersedes representation. In the same way, Martin remembers and plays a radio interview he gave where he talked about lysergic acid and the lysergic experience, only to realize "ahora que estoy en él, me doy cuenta de que todas esas son palabras inútiles . . . ¿cómo explicar el color azul a un ciego? [now that I am in it, I realize that all these are useless words . . . how can one explain the color blue to a blind person?]" (Dalton

122).[47] Ultimately, however, language is used to re-present the mystical-lysergic experience, and it is in these uses of re-presentation that Dalton inserts the novel in a countercultural production rather than a commodification of the hippie or acid experience; in other words, language is used as a political and subjective tool and not a means of representation, a countercultural maneuver that breaks from the cultural paradigms of art.

This rejection of language and representation in favor of embodied experiential knowledge exemplifies what Theodore Roszak described as a hallmark of counterculture: the dismissal of objective consciousness. Defined as the extreme separation of the in-here versus the out-there, objective consciousness is the offspring of Western rationalism and seeks to establish objectivity and objective language as the *only* way to access reality and exist. Roszak specifies how this extreme alienation is carried out in the modern world by technocrats in their impetus for facts and so-called objective information, and how it can be and is being battled by the counterculture through a psychological instead of an epistemological or scientific revolution (217). From another perspective, Pahnke and Richards describe this objective consciousness as the prevalence of the ego in the mode of viewing the world and specify that "only in mystical consciousness and some psychotic reaction is the subject-object dichotomy transcended and the empirical ego extinguished" (184). For the trio, the mystical-lysergic experience generates a space of reassemblage with language, one that does not reject signification or representation in favor of abstraction (visual, sonic, conceptual) but that rather depends on a critical relationship to oneself. During chapter eight covering hour six of their journey when Roberto is having epiphany upon epiphany as the substance breaks down his ego structure momentarily, the capitalized words hiding the short story can be reconstructed to read:

> algo está cambiando, estamos llegando al fin y nos encontramos, lsd, maravillosa realidad, existimos pese a todas las palabras. Habitan todos el mismo planeta y son muy parecidos biológica y químicamente. Nosotros lo podemos hacer. Si, no. Noche, día. Negro, blanco. Peón, peón. Coraje, miedo. Objetivo, negativo. Blanco, negro. Frio, caliente. Autocrítica. [something is changing, we are reaching the end and we find, lsd, wonderful reality, that we exist in spite of all the words. We all inhabit the same planet and they are very similar biologically and chemically. We can do it. Yes, no. Night, day. Black, white. Pawn, pawn. Strength, fear. Objective, negative. White, black. Cold, hot. Self-critique.] (Dalton 131–48)[48]

Existence supersedes language in the paradox of naming reality, and the binaries that Roberto passes through serve to underline the greatest binary of in-here/out-there; these are navigated not by rejecting them as much as by embracing them as a part of existence itself in a both/and move. Self-critique, already a circular and self-reflexive action, is signified here as a way of remaining in the in-between. Ultimately, Roberto is wrestling with the idea of being both oppressed and oppressor, both victim of state violence and enforcer of violence in his society. He realizes that he and his peers "somos los instrumentos de conceptos abstractos que hemos creado [we are the instruments of abstracts concepts we have created]" (135), abstract concepts that spring from brick-and-mortar institutions as well as abstract ones. This countercultural ethos guides the reader in the mystical-lysergic experience, pushing for a re-understanding of representation that breaks away from the ways in which *Onderos* and other writers in the global North were writing about and filming substances, in particular lysergic acid.

In conclusion, the novel — and the rest of Dalton's brief fictional oeuvre — constructs countercultural bodies that speak from and to an increasingly globalized youth. The trio of characters realize in their trip their ability to embody knowledge, to access knowledge from and in their bodies — in particular, political, social, and intellectual knowledge — and these experiences shape how they empower themselves, how they gain the ability to question their authorities and their leaders and, in particular, those who are "in charge" of the revolutions they are a part of. As a text that was born out of the countercultural experiences of the decade, including Dalton's participation in the literacy campaigns in Cuba and her stays in Europe during that eventful 1968, *Larga Sinfonía en D y había una vez* is a snapshot of how counterculture is (re)shaping the world around the youth. For Dalton, one of the very few women who produced culture within the *Onda* milieu, changing society is achieved by changing oneself first, embodying social transformation and, in doing so, empowering one's body and those around her; perhaps the most significant moment of this is when the trio visits the flower shop and Ana dives into a flower, able to not only communicate with it but also understand it deeply and profoundly: "viene de pronto el conocimiento y la comprensión biológica, y viene biológicamente, no por experiencia propia, sino . . . así . . . simple como el tamaño de mi naríz [suddenly comes knowledge and a biological understanding, and it comes biologically, not by self-experience but . . . thus . . . simple as the size of my nose]" (Dalton 82). The novel doesn't generate a critique of the establishment, or a critique of youth culture, or even a program for revolutionary action — even the consumption of lysergic acid is questioned as an action that *everyone* must take, and a decision left to the reader — but rather grounds countercultural revolutionary action in the bodies themselves and in their experiencing of each other and the world around them. In this way, Dalton's own biography speaks to this countercultural ethos that shaped her commitments to social transformation. After publishing the novel in 1968 and later obtaining higher education degrees, she moved to Oaxaca, one of the states with the highest Indigenous populations. There, she has worked for the last forty years, studying with and engaging in activism with the Indigenous culture and in particular Indigenous women, as well as organizing and participating in feminist organizations in the state. Countercultural being, in the corporal and not simply a philosophical-ontological or psychoanalytic sense, surpasses language itself. Words, helpful as though they might seem, appear not to be the answer. In the end, "soy y soy la conciencia en cada célula" (69), and this being is within the body as much as without, in the other bodies around her. Countercultural revolutionary bodies thus engage within their skin to reveal the nationalist and capitalistic processes of subjectification and beyond their skin to construct alternative social structures together, different ways of being and relating romantically, sexually, and, ultimately, revolutionarily.

Parménides García Saldaña's Rock Journalism: Bodily Autonomy in the Countercultural Worlds of La Juventud

I have referenced earlier the nebulous but historically useful category of *la Onda* as typically conjured to speak of three authors (José Agustín, Gustavo Sáinz, and Parménides García Saldaña) and to speak of the musical movement (*la onda chicana*) and other artistic endeavors undertaken by youth in the late 1960s. Of the three authors, Parménides García Saldaña has received much less critical attention, with a significant focus on his literary productions: the novel *Pasto verde* (1968), the short story collection *El rey criollo* (1968), and some on his long essay *En la ruta de la onda* (1972). However, as scholar Mayra Fortes has emphasized, approaching García Saldaña only through his literary ouvre without considering his journalistic and other writings runs the risk of once again discounting *Onda* writers as cultural paradigm shifters, reinstating an autonomous cultural sphere characterized by a certain degree of liberalized depoliticization. In general, *Onda* and other youth-centered authors experienced this form of delegitimization during the 1960s and 1970s on the part of the cultural and social establishment, who saw their literary experiments and irreverent social actions, as well as their foreign-influenced patterns of consumption (rock music, fashion, foreign films), as problematic denationalization (*malinchismo*). Thus, my goal in this section is first to briefly outline and approach García Saldaña's prolific journalistic writings (he was a journalist for most of his adult life) and then to understand his embodied representations of the musical and literary *onderos* movements in this particular genre as ways of documenting and participating in the dynamic world-building that youth were undertaking in the new countercultural spaces that emerged, from the geographically situated *hoyos fonkis* and major music festivals to the more symbolic relations that were being formed between and among these countercultural sociosexual dissidents. I bring forward García Saldaña as a case study to understand how these countercultural actors were constructing their positions as cultural translators and mediators, bringing together substance use, music consumption, fashion, and novel sociosexual relations into a specific body that moved in specific spaces.

This positioning became a way to participate in the world-building projects of countercultural youth and to help solidify the strategies to retake bodily autonomy from the firm grasp of nationalist ideologies in the form of the *mestizo* citizen complex that forces citizens to conform to a specific way of being tied to the reproduction of patriarchal and colonialist social relations.

In journals such as *Piedra Rodante* and *Pop* and newspapers like *Excelsior* or *Unomásuno*, García Saldaña embarks on a cultural self-positioning that speaks to a much wider conception of society than the very strict literary sphere. This position is marked by a strong self-conception as a cultural translator between the literary *Onda* (authorized by his place as a cursed poet in the likes of Rimbaud, Baudelaire, José Asunción Silva, or Porfirio Barba Jacob) and the nascent musical *onderos* who moved in the *Onda chicana* musical circuit from border cities to the metropolis. This mediating position also led him to engage with the cultural achievements of rock and roll in the United States and Europe and the significance of the emerging rock sphere in Mexico during these decades, speaking not only to the specialized audience of youth but also to the more general audiences of newspaper readers. Particularly considering his experiences studying economy at UNAM and Universidad Iberoamericana during this decade and to his subsequent politicization in various student groups, García Saldaña's mediation underscores the various ways in which youth culture was negotiating countercultural actions in the personal and individual spheres. To bring these aspects of his cultural ouvre forward, I focus on how his interventions and radical construction of a series of countercultural bodies engage in political action, personal reshaping of social and sexual relations, and a critical consumption of both substances and music. Through his own bodily reconstruction in writing, as well as those textualizations of other youthful embodiments, from jijpitecas to liberated women, García Saldaña re-presents the national and symbolic countercultural spaces as dynamic and in transformation, reuniting a legacy of revolution with the needs and demands of youth in Mexico and across the world. In this way, his journalistic work showcases an ethical and political engagement in line with the soft *contracultura* and *desbunde* in Brazil and other Latin American contexts, belying their mainstream representation as escapist and apolitical youth and demonstrating their deep political commitments and specific actions undertaken to reshape the world around them. Ultimately, these interventions trace the ways in which bodily autonomy is being constructed by youth culture, particularly in terms of the gendered and racialized constructions of *mestizo* cultural/national identities and how the (mostly Brown, mostly lower-class) mass consumers of these stages of rock culture reshape their own identities relating to and simultaneously distancing themselves from the ideologized *mestizo* body shapes.

The journalistic interventions that speak most to this endeavor revolve around the nascent musical scene of the moment, and in them García Saldaña takes on a singular position that names the various lines of flight that cross it, from dogmatic political action to literary innovation in a national and Western tradition to sexual liberation and dissident sociosexual relationships.[49] What I am describing as a critical positioning that García Saldaña undertakes is best understood in the general context of the countercultural milieu in Mexico during this period as already a mediated and refracted space. Various critics have signaled how the (counter)cultural phenomenon associated with what is now named as the wider *Onda* musical and literary spheres must be placed as a phenomenon of double reflection/refraction. In other words, Mexican countercultural youth can be more richly understood as observing and learning from American youth who in turn were gazing at and consuming the idea of Mexico as foreign, exotic, and distant, as well as literally through mushrooms and psychedelic seeds and cacti.[50] Authors such as Malcolm Lowry or the Beatniks and later streams of hippies would come down to the mountains of Central Mexico and the urban centers in search of experiences, and their writings would in turn shape the ways in which Mexicans would understand themselves.[51] This unwitting reproduction of *mestizo* and state nationalism in the guise of consuming foreignness would be constantly addressed by García Saldaña, exemplifying and calling for a critical awareness of how, in consuming these foreign ideas, Mexican youth were legitimizing the liberal society of *mestizo* sociability; ultimately, García Saldaña would trace the dissident and countercultural elements of youth culture on the ground so to speak and bring them forward. Particularly in the increasingly urbanized metropolis, this critical double reflection would motivate Mexican middle-class youth — already exposed to political movements through the marches and political demonstrations of railroad workers, health workers, and students — to come closer to their own national reality through these countercultural products, rather than accept blindly the ideological mediation of the *mestizo* ideology promoted by the state.[52] This journalistic ethics that García Saldaña explores — at times in direct opposition to more entrenched writers in the public sphere — signals to a countercultural youth audience the importance of using the consumption of music and substances and ideas ("peace and love") as subversive strategies of resistance to push back against the hegemonic subjectification of their bodies, in particular through nationalistic gender roles continuously updated in popular media to align with the globalized times;[53] in other words, not *what* to do, listen to, or consume, but *how* to listen to, *how* to consume, and *how* to relate to each other based on observations of the same circuits these new youthful behaviors are emerging from.

These countercultural ethics emerge from embodied practices, literally reshaping bodies as they contort following different rhythms, constrained, or liberated by different clothes (or a lack thereof), stimulated by different substances (from cannabis and lysergic acid to sugar in Coca-Cola and other soft drinks). While access to these substances or this fashion was marked by class differences, rock music was increasingly more accessible to all classes thanks to the mass-media industry that solidified in the 1940s and 1950s. However, the musical expressions of rock in the greater Latin American region and specifically Mexico was not without troubles. While in the 1950s rock was considered a marker of modernization, particularly in the highly sanitized *refritos* youth rock films, by the late 1960s rock was beginning to develop a firmer anti-authoritarian and revolutionary position across the continent. Increasingly, government agencies across the hemisphere saw it as a dangerous product to be allowed freely on the market, and in Mexico specifically the use of English lyrics and foreign musical styles such as blues and soul, which members of La Onda Chicana learned from and adapted, became markers of rebellion in the eyes of the state. In the cultural wedge that rock became in the 1960s, as historian Eric Zolov has described it, musicians and audiences pushed the limits that heteronormative *mestizo* nationalism was policing and enforcing on their bodies, rejecting their racialization and ethnic essentialism while celebrating and recyclizing the popular imagery of their shared nation, and especially the revolution. At the same time, rock music and its consumption reflected an ever more globalized modernity and came to characterize a middle and upper class seeking to redefine itself by global markers of consumption (Zolov, *Refried Elvis* 10). The best case in point to understand this contradictory tension is the outlaw and persecution of rock music during the regime of President Luis Echeverría (1970–1975) while Alfredo Díaz Ordaz, the son of former President Gustavo Díaz Ordaz (1964–1969) continued to play and produce music with no consequences, albeit with no commercial or cultural success, perhaps due to the massive unpopularity of his father.

In this turbulent and contradictory decade of globalization, where rock developed in both commercial industries as well as very improvised, *anthropophagic* (in the terms of Brazilian counterculture), and sometimes downright illegal venues and gatherings, Parménides García Saldaña's writings appear as cultural mediations, critically bridging different audiences and musical styles. His middle-class upbringing and his transnational/transcultural positioning allows García Saldaña to explain global counterculture as a political revolution to his youthful readers, who were initially fellow middle-class citizens and increasingly lower-class rock consumers, as can be seen in the footage and chronicles of the music festival Avándaro in 1970 where the middle-class organizers were surprised and overwhelmed by a mass of fellow *onderos* emerging from the lower classes. After writing fictional accounts in short story/novel form about the influx of rock and global counterculture in Mexico, García Saldaña focuses his texts on representations of the jipitecas and women in their bodies as they shaped Mexican countercultural spaces. Perhaps due to the circulation of his fictional texts and his overpowering physical presence, coupled with his knowledge of US/British rock, García Saldaña cultivates a persona of authority within these spaces, and he uses the journal articles to direct countercultural youth toward a critical consumption of rock, substances, and global "hippie" ideas about peace and love. Trying to speak to all these audiences, García Saldaña's writing strove to underline exactly what the political and social importance of rock is without taking an overbearing or authoritative position, mobilizing language and self-critique in order to construct a position of equal speaking to equal. In his chronicles, rock is important as a genre of cultural subversion, political resistance, and ultimately liberation through the radical bodily autonomy it necessitated in that point in time; rock is not *just* a marker of rebel youth or rebellion for the sake of rebellion, and to avoid the speedy commodification of the media industries it must be understood and used as this tool of liberation.

While I focus here on García Saldaña's rock journalism, he was by no means the only cultural mediator within the Mexican countercultural circuit. *Refritos* and homegrown rock music (albeit sung in English to avoid censorship) blasted on the airwaves, and youth-led journals such as *El Corno Emplumado* or *Revista Zona Rosa* generated a youth-centered readership educated and educating themselves in the consumption of foreign rhythms, vocabulary, fashion, and artists, even if they didn't fully read English.[54] By 1968, when the mass student mobilization that had been slowly emerging really erupted on the national stage with the summer and fall marches that took over the city, rock music was solidly nationalized. Rock bands migrated to the metropolis from various northern cities such as Durango and Tijuana, and some of them — such as *La Divisón del Norte* (a reference to Pancho Villa's army), *Los Yaki* (a reference to the Indigenous *yoreme* peoples of Sonora, critical actors in the armies of Porfirio Díaz and Álvaro Obregón), *La Revolución de Emiliano Zapata, Los Dug Dugs* (from Durango), *Peace and Love, El Ritual, Bandido*, and *Three Souls on My Mind* (later to become *El Tri*, the most famous and long-lived of all of them) — began to circulate widely and enjoy success on the airwaves and in *tocadas*. In their lyrics as well as in the spaces they played in and the sociability promoted within them, these bands used nationalist imagery associated with the revolution as a way of retaking their own bodies, shaped by the nationalist rituals of flag salutes and national anthems and military service. In this sonic space and cultural milieu, nationhood could be redefined, now liberated from the heteronormative gender roles being (en)forced on their bodies by vigilante parents, teachers, and governors; here, their sociability grounded in nuclear familial structures could be questioned, rejected, abolished, and reshaped (Zolov, *Refried Elvis* 127). By the end of the decade, these juvenile audiences were becoming interclass gatherings, social assemblages related, connected to, and distinct from the more explicitly political mobilizations, and yet similar embodiments of counterculture.

Parménides García Saldaña published regularly in the short-lived yet impactful journal *Piedra Rodante*, the unauthorized version of *Rolling Stone*, and his articles interweave cultural/musical history with direct and concrete politicization in the US and Mexico, pushing readers to actively participate in both the development of national musical spheres as well as address the national economic and political concerns that affected them all.[55] The journal was published between 1970 and 1972 and presented a mix of context translated from its US counterpart alongside its original context from Mexico. It ran in the last years of Mexico's open rock scene before President Luis Echeverría ordered a crackdown that silenced and pushed most groups underground or outside the capital, its pages including a variety of topics, from offering new records to Mexican audience, promoting fashion and alternative embodied practices (yoga, meditation, psychotherapy), presenting alternative literature, covering rock events in the country, and, most importantly, covering the violent acts against youth such as the 1971 Halconazo. Writing alongside figures like Alejandro Jodorowsky (theater/film director), Enrique Marroquín (Catholic priest/guru), Manuel Aceves (Jungian psychologist) and others, Parménides works toward inserting rock into the nation as much as the nation into rock through historical approaches, ethnographical explorations, and embodied participation.

Compared with other mass-circulated journals such as *Mexico canta* (more firmly anchored in the commercial music industry) and *POP* (which assembled rock exclusively as a popular urban middle-class genre disconnected from social problems, á la early Beatles), *Piedra Rodante* served as a meeting space between mature *onderos* who had experienced the rapid cultural adaptation of the 1960s and the rest of the more youthful population coming of age in the aftermath of Tlatelolco. The journal served as a space for critical interventions in the musical sphere, a space to critique the rock bands of the moment and celebrate their achievements. One of its most controversial issues focused exclusively on the phenomenon of drugs and substances and included interviews from state doctors next to narrations of various psychedelic experiences and therapeutic chronicles, as well as health advice (October 1971). Given its general tone, vocabulary, and, particularly, publicity advertisements, I would venture that the target audience was composed mainly of urban middle-class youth with purchasing power able to spend on vinyl records and high-end fashion; underground *tocadas* or more economically accessible venues were not promoted. The journal had a self-described print run of 50,000 copies and was distributed in Mexico City as well as northern cities such as Tijuana, Monterrey, Durango, and Ciudad Juárez; there is also some evidence of its circulation in *chicano* regions in the Southwestern US and various Latin American countries. In its moment, *Piedra Rodante* was critically placed in a moment of increasing and accelerated repression toward both rock and political activism, on the tail end of the literary success of the *Onderos* as well as the social unrest that culminated in Tlatelolco and the Jueves de Corpus.

Although Parménides would later recover and reweave his articles into a longer essay, *En la ruta de la Onda* (1972), thus aligning himself closely to an essayistic tradition focused on Mexicanness or Latin America's search for an essential identity, I want to focus on these articles as they first appeared since they are materially tied to mass-produced spheres of social engagement as opposed to elite cultural spheres and genres. In an interview with Miguel Donoso Pareja published in the *El Día* supplement "El gallo ilustrado" on November 22, 1970, García Saldaña explains his own positioning in relation to rock music and contrasts himself with the "gurúes gratuitos que creó la mass-media para ocultar la verdadera dimensión norteamericana a su más auténtica realidad, la misma que se mostró a las mayorías en el juicio a los 'ocho de Chicago' juzgados por conspiración [free gurus that mass-media has created to hide the real North American dimension from its most authentic reality, the same which showed itself to the masses in the trial of the 'Chicago eight']" (2).[56] These transnational connections that he is making explicit are also implicit in his writings, as Mayra Fortes has pointed out, serving to explain generational changes and their political weight and nuance particularly through their antiauthoritarian and irreverent behavior associated with the more radical countercultural happenings.[57] This same in-between attitude with one foot in the more radical rock moments and the other in the more politically focused youth activism will be reflected in the article in *Piedra Rodante*, focused now on contextualizing, interpreting, and politicizing the rock musical scene in Mexico.

In the journal's first issue released on May 15, 1972, Parménides publishes "La Revolución Mexicana se quita el huarache [The Mexican Revolution removes its huarache]," constructing the first of a series of articles that build a cultural history of rock in Mexico narrated from the position of and directed to an audience versed in the *ondero* slang, rock soundscapes, and the language of political resistance, as well as the visual imaginary of *mestizo* Mexico. He begins by assembling a relational narrative voice, contrasting himself with Carlos Fuentes as a naïve reader of Gustavo Sáinz's *Gazapo*, from whom he also distances himself by critiquing the novel as a "mundo vasto y cerrado [vast and closed world]." This voice builds authority by not belonging either to the intellectual cultural sphere in which Fuentes moved, nor to the *Ondero* literary milieu that was being characterized by authors such as Sáinz alongside Agustín, but rather an in-between that keeps coming back to the political commitments of counterculture. By distancing himself from Fuentes first, García Saldaña assembles a playful and irreverent voice, laughing at the growing cultural authorities who now mobilized a leftist discourse while remaining entrenched in the paradigmatic cultural institutions (Octavio Paz, Carlos Fuentes, Carlos Monsiváis, and Elena Poniatowska are examples of these cultural institutions embodied). However, by also criticizing Sáinz for his closed world, he creates distance between this narrative voice speaking to the young *onderos* and the older literary *Onda* writers, explicitly politicizing his performance by anchoring this voice in a wider national reality beyond the strictly urban, exclusively middle-class, and mostly male-centered experiences of the *Onda* writers. The article proposes a cultural history of rock in Mexico narrated from the position of and directed to an audience educated in the *ondero* slang, rock soundscape, and the vocabulary of resistance that underpins the memorialization of the revolution through nationalist discourse. He uses instead a shared national history that ties his generation, born in the economic/political stability that marked the 1940s, to the generations that fought the revolution and are defending the PRI state. By rewriting a revisionary history of postrevolutionary Mexico through the characters of Juan, Juana, and la Cucaracha — the peasant bases of the armed struggle and the urbanized masses whose labor produced later economic growth — Garcia Saldaña ties rock with a history of national citizens, pushing his readers to understand themselves as the strange and youthful subjects experiencing intense change in the incorporation of Mexico into global capitalist flows and structures.

The article retells the history of rock in Mexico from the perspective of the revolution, weaving a national history while avoiding a nationalist discourse and grammar by invoking rather the histories shared with the readers. He wonders about the current usefulness of revolutionary imagery in giving shape and body to the youthful *rockeros* of the 1960s, wondering, "¿es que la revolución bajó del caballo? Más bien: la revolución mexicana cambió el caballo por un salvaje potro mecánico [is it that the revolution got down from the horse? Or more exactly, the Mexican revolution exchanged the horse for a savage mechanical colt?]" (25). In the first part, he rewrites this history of revolution through the figures of Juan, Juana, and La Cucaracha and in doing so speaks of and to his contemporary national subjects who "fueron los hijos de los civiles iniciadores de la etapa constructiva de la rev. los hijos de aquellos que ya formaban parte de la vasta clase media acomodada [were the sons of the civil founders of the constructive stage of the rev. the sons of those who already were a part of the vast and well-off middle class]" (25). A lengthy quote from Ramón López Velarde's *Suave Patria* (1921) is recontextualized amid rock history; the youthful national poet (he died at age thirty-three) transformed into a foundational text for contemporary culture and legitimizing García Saldaña's own position as a youthful cultural producer daring to propose an-other Mexico in the cultural struggles of the 1960s. For the *ondero* writer, rock music cannot be understood without the historical backdrop of contemporary Mexico, and (especially youthful) readers must understand the young and strange national subject who experienced not only the intense economic changes as Mexico aligned and incorporated itself with global capitalist flows, but also the intense bodily experiences of being *mestizo* and being exposed to the myriads of foreign technologies and fashions — bodies who are transforming Mexico and being transformed, bodies who are consuming culture and commodities. In doing this, García Saldaña critically mobilizes the knowledge acquired in his own educational trajectory, demonstrating how to explain cultural development without appealing to essentialisms and anchored in material realities, and thus expanding and exploring the options for politicization available to youth culture. Succinctly, the article serves to ground the cultural expression of rock as alternative spheres akin to the revolutionary actions and the legacy of the nation.[58]

The article names rock as a technology that appeared in Mexico as a "consecuencia de la era tecnológica, que a través de la electrónica buscaba medios de ajuste a esa nueva realidad a partir de la bomba atómica [consequence of the technological age, which through electronics sought ways to adjust to this new reality springing from the atomic bomb]" (26). In doing so, García Saldaña situates Mexico within a global context while recognizing the specificities of the country; thus, the modes of perception of reality and art (rock music) are intrinsically tied to the material conditions that surround and shape the bodies moving within them.[59] This perspective allows for a harsher and more grounded critique of the tropical and pop music of the 1960s particularly as disconnected from their material reality, as genres that refuse to participate fully in the scientific and technical advances of the time and that chose to reproduce cultural elitism and class conflict. Rock, however, was born out of the racial tensions of the United States, and García Saldaña uses allegory to tell that tale for his Mexican readers. In the article, rock is a product of a conflicting encounter between the "Negra" music of rhythm and blues and country music, both personified in a Black, virile man who encounters a white peasant "chava" to embark on a torrid, explicitly consensual love affair. This mystical, sexual, racial, and class encounter becomes the birth of rock, narrating a concrete event that refuses to reproduce a commercial narrative of rock as simply a foreign product; rather, the allegory underlines the political force of the genre embedded already in the racialized and historicized musical forms that shape it. This allegory is another key instance of cultural mediation where García Saldaña uses his cultural capital — some class-based, some acquired during his travels to New Orleans in 1967 — to position himself as an authority in an act of mediation, sharing and speaking with his musical peers.[60] By bringing this racial conflict to the forefront, he resituates rock as a tool of class engagement and social transformation, updating the racial dynamics to a *mestizo* social order with its own national identities in struggle. Rock moves away from a simple foreign commodity to be consumed and becomes a form of juvenile rebellion *and* a birthing of other, alternative bodies — young bodies who can reshape the empty signifiers of nationalist *mestizo* (hetero)normative identities, now inserted into a historical tapestry that underscores class and racial differences and oppressions in the past and present, for a different future.[61]

By placing himself in this in-between position that rejects an either/or positioning in a generational understanding of counterculture, García Saldaña not only illustrates an-other way of being *ondero*, youthful, and rebellious, but also invites other youth to construct themselves with him. In this first article — the longest of those published by him in *Piedra Rodante* and one of the longest of the publication in general — Parménides selects key figures on multiple fronts to distinguish himself from and embody another way of being. He chooses Octavio Paz to level a critique against, an increasingly solid cultural authority in the wake of his political act of resignation from being consul after the Tlatelolco massacre. This choice is especially relevant in that Paz and other intellectuals would consistently position themselves alongside students when these groups experienced violence, and yet they would also consistently very publicly criticize their consumption habits, particularly their mass-media choices. According to García Saldaña, if tropical and pop music were wrong for not having understood the importance and relevancy of electronic and electric music when it appeared, Paz is even more mistaken for speaking of Mexican citizens as lost in a "laberinto de la soledad" where "el muchacho solo podría murmurar, gimotear, llorar su solitariedad, a veces mitigada con formulas del pasado: unas cubas, una que otra música guapachosa, una que otra cola diestra en la danza moderna [labyrinth of solitude (where) the boy could only mutter, moan, cry his solitude, sometimes relieved with formulas from the past: a couple of cubas, a few sensual songs, one or two girls versed in modern dance]" (26). The article recognizes the weight of Paz's reading on Mexico and rejects it as encapsulating youth — and in particular young men — into a subjective position of loss and meaninglessness, negating the liberating and resubjectivizing power of contemporary rhythms.

However, in making this scathing and unnamed critique of Paz, García Saldaña is also careful not to position himself as a dogmatic and uncritical defender of all musical expressions simply because they are rock. On the contrary, he ends the article with a critical reading of Mexico's hottest band of the moment, *La Revolución de Emiliano Zapata* (*LREZ*), and specifically their song "Nasty Sex," whose "sentido moralizante de la letra rechazaba la intención cínica del estilo funky (grasoso), heavy (pesado, grueso), hip (alivianado), irreverente, demoledor de los Rolling Stones [moralizing meaning of the lyrics rejected the cynical intentions of the funky (greasy), heavy (thick), hip (relaxed), irreverent, demolishing style of the Rolling Stones]" (27), which according to Parménides ends up negating the liberating potential of rock by reimposing a conservative and heteronormative moral code focused on limiting women's bodily autonomy. The song was a success and played repeatedly in radio stations in Mexico City and Guadalajara, a thing unheard of in those years for a Mexican band. However, Parménides is critical toward this song precisely for its moralizing tone, which condemns female sexuality. He contrasts the treatment of women in this song with "Aventurera" by Agustin Lara — another radio hit that became a hit film and is still being covered today — which "no creía en la redención de la cola [sexually active woman or sex worker], sino al contrario, le daba buenos consejos prácticos [did not believe in the redemption of the girl, but rather gave her good practical advice]" (27); rather than condemn the woman or seek to rescue her from a perceived moral failure through her sexual behavior, Lara engages with her sexuality as a fact of existence to be accepted and not hyperbolized.[62] In the words of Roberto Schwartz, García Saldaña is pinpointing an instance of failed transculturation — at least in liberatory terms — for *LREZ* "aún no expresan una onda personal [still don't express a personal thing]" (27) and seem to be more an idea out of place in the sphere of national rock than a liberatory intervention into the social and moral order of *mestizo* nationalism. For rock to be liberatory, it must be recontextualized into its context in such a way that speaks toward the heavily moralized sexual norms that structure the *mestizo* social order. In the end, though, this harsh critique is not a negation or a dismissal of *LREZ*, but rather a critical appreciation; Parménides closes the article with a voice that positions itself alongside a youthful radio listener tuning into rock, anxious to hear more songs like those of *LREZ* on the radio and celebrating their participation in radial waves as an opening toward more "autóctono" and Mexican rock bands.

Publishing in *Piedra Rodante* allows for Parménides to render his politicized account of rock while constructing an alternative position for a youthful public intellectual disengaging from authorized cultural circuits. His participation in this and other musical journals writing about national and economic histories contrasts with the positions and publications of other intellectuals who published mostly in journals of "high" art, such as *El Corno Emplumado* or *S.N.O.B.* — authorized in turn by their elite consumption of Far East philosophies and the Beat movements, in line with counterculture and uncritical of class oppression — as well as with his own texts published in authorized cultural spaces such as Editorial Joaquin Mortiz or newspapers such as *Excélsior*. The use of *Piedra Rodante* and other alternative platforms to publish is a countercultural strategy focused on dissolving the idea of culture as an exclusionary space by assembling critical channels where citizens come together as consumers instead of attempting to legitimize his position by appearing in more "official" channels. This critical intervention in the musical scene is also a political positioning of a particular countercultural body that seeks to motivate audiences to participate more actively and affectively in the various liberation struggles, without necessarily handing out a political program or establishing dogma, much less affiliating with a political party or group; in particular, it is a political positioning that centers female liberation as a political struggle men can and must participate in. Historian Jaime Pensado has documented the different politicization tactics used during the 1950 and 1960s, including information brigades, flash meetings, taking over buildings for short periods of time, mini-manifestations, and street-theater troupes focused on raising awareness in the public space; all of these had the objective of collectively constructing physical and conceptual spaces where bodies engaged in democratic resistance to the soft (and hard) authoritarian state (Pensado 99).[63] In these actions, women played a central role that contrasts radically with their mediatic and mediatized presence, and that ultimately runs against their representation in the visual register of the political manifestations of 1968. García Saldaña seems aware of this, and his article underlines the presence of women and their desires in countercultural spaces, explicitly demanding from his male peers a recognition and a celebration of their participation in all political and social activities, and not just the (moralized) sexual sphere.

Félix Guattari's notion of molecular revolution is useful to understand what Parménides García Saldaña is trying to get at: pushing readers to understand music not just in musical or even cultural terms, but especially in racialized terms that speak to histories and realities of oppression and liberation. For the French schizoanalyst, a molecular revolution is an alternative form of social resistance that involves an "awakening of this notion of desire, both on a microscopic level and on a social scale . . . the real social revolution involves being able to articulate oneself and to allow the process of singularization to assert itself" (*Molecular revolution* 76). Thus, the assemblage of contemporary rock with the recent histories of class struggle and internal migration, and with the specifics of street political activities, is a way in which the article pushes for a molecular revolution, a form of political participation that does not oppose itself openly to the state and its forces (and thus attracts its violence), but rather a revolution constructed in the quotidian experiences of listening to rock. It is in these experiences, spaces, and rhythms where youth can (and must) chose to reassemble their political and national subjectivities by standing against the *mestizo* subjectivity embodying traditional moral and sexual values. In its history, the article narrates a series of bodies that come together in a program of everyday life to meet countercultural goals of liberation, avoiding a depoliticized chaos of orgiastic rock consumption. The fact that this appears in *Piedra Rodante* is telling, as the journal is not exactly pushing for revolution as much as seeking to establish itself as a legitimate and authoritative voice in rock consumer culture. For García Saldaña, however, rock's singularizing potential must be processual and continuously enacted by both musicians and audience, as he demonstrates with his own embodied experiences.[64] By underscoring rock's liberatory and singularizing potential, García Saldaña follows the bands themselves in their recycling of nationalist imagery and interweaves national history with countercultural ethics, embodying a singularization that — particularly from his personal position in the "holy trinity" of the *Onda* — can be read as a call to political action through a critical consumption of rock music, aesthetics, and sexual ethics.

Mediating between nations and cultures to tease out and present the revolutionary potential of rock is Parménides's first objective, and his later articles in *Piedra Rodante* will shift attention to the internal landscape and soundscape of Mexico as it consumes and produces rock. In the journal's third number published on July 15, 1971, he continues assembling this national history of rock, focusing now on the material spaces where bodies come together to listen, trade music, and dance: the mythical *hoyos funkis*.[65] Once again, it is Parménides's embodied experiences that legitimize his critical account of these spaces, in the same way that his travels and knowledge legitimized his accounts of rock. His moving in these material spaces and the experiences he shares in them with *la chaviza* authorize his retelling and allow him to focus the attention once more on the class oppression and class liberation that is happening around him as rock is being recontextualized in the Mexican geographies. He is thus a body made in relation with the other bodies around, a countercultural body emerging from a shared social space characterized by a common consumption. Perhaps aware of his middle-class audience (at least judging by the publicity in the journal), Parménides writes of the *hoyos funkis* as spaces that proliferate in *barrios proletarios* and lower-class neighborhoods where the *chaviza* (youth) are coming together to listen to music and dance; once again, this class component brings forward the ways in which rock is revolutionary on a global scale, promoting rhythms and movements that literally shake bodies out of their nationalist and capitalist subjectifications.

He grounds this critical approach to contemporary spaces by historicizing and globalizing, connecting these *hoyos* to the *academias* of Buenos Aires where tango was born in the gathering of classes and migrant populations, as well as to the previous Mexican history of *dancings* and *tes danzantes*; and yet, he distances these contemporary *hoyos* by describing them as decidedly spaces for musical expression and engagement where youth are coming together and not spaces of sex work, social escapism, or isolation.[66] Rather, what García Saldaña wants to underline in particular for the readers who might not be from Mexico City or familiarized with these spaces is their racial composition, where "predomina el color moreno sobre el blanco [Brown skin predominates over white]" (13) in a racialized and class dynamic that does not appear in the visual or film representations of rock during this period. These spaces, echoed in the various rock scenes across Latin America, proved key to the survival and development of rock cultures anchored in the complexity of colonized populations and allowed for rock to stop being an exclusive bourgeois commodity. He is unequivocally sharp in describing the *hoyos* in their context as spaces of musical engagement and *not* spaces of sex work, social escapism, or isolation, as the mainstream media was portraying them by overemphasizing the presence of marginalized and lower-class citizens. The *hoyos funkies* were short-lived but impactful in the national/regional rock contexts, generating alternative structures of feeling grounded in the collective embodied experiences of consuming rock; this is not the individualized act of consumption undertaken by a youth who leaves his house to hit up a posh record store and comes back to his secluded bedroom, riddled with teenage angst.

In relation specifically to *En la ruta de la Onda*, Mayra Fortes has pointed out how García Saldaña destabilizes concepts of identity, nation, and revolution in his constant movements across borders.[67] In the article, he continues destabilizing these notions by grounding himself in spaces surrounded by racialized bodies, a masculine figure critical of the *mestizo* macho behavior of other men around him. Mobility and fluidity mark this positioned body, able to engage with culture surrounding him and calling his readers to join in the psychic and social task of national (re)construction without providing already-set interpretations: "por cierto que Tin Tán es un cómico del cine mexicano que necesita ser redescubierto en relación a la onda [by the way, Tin Tan is a comic of Mexican cinema that needs to be rediscovered in relation to the onda]" ("Los hoyos funkis" 13). This small gesture is immensely meaningful, already a critical appreciation of Tin Tan, who Octavio Paz and other intellectuals like him would reject as just another *pachuco*, just another consumer of foreignness who rejects their "Mexican" essence, despite his wild commercial success in the country and beyond. García Saldaña uses his own life experiences and patterns of consumption to provide another way of interpreting Tin Tan as a predecessor to the contemporary *ondero* youth. These rearticulations depend on signaling the cultural ties between nations and using them to erode the silenced class and racial differences that striate Mexican society in the illusion of equality that *mestizo* ideology promotes. *Hoyos funkis* become transnational and transcultural spaces where bodies come under a revolutionary potential, going beyond the limits of nation and consumer normativities to generate alternate modes of subjectivation that subvert both the forces of the market assembling complacent consumers *and* the state imposing *mestizo* bodies as ideal national subjects.[68] The descriptions in the article generate alternative structures of feeling grounded in the collective embodied experience of consuming rock, in contrast to a more individualized and alienated form of consumption that moves from bedroom to record store and back to a domestic space saturated with teenage angst, more characteristic of middle- to upper class consumption patterns. In the *hoyos funkis*, rock becomes more than the commercial representation in films, rehashed *refritos*, or alienated middle-/upper-class consumption.[69] Against the serialization that commercial rock promoted through market strategies focused on the making of youth complacent consumers, García Saldaña signals for his readers how, in these underground urban spaces, lower-class citizens are already generating a series of strategies to assemble alternative processes of subjective singularization, breaking out of their gendered and class-centered subjectivities in the collective embodied spaces of rock music as they listen to, dance to, and scream their feelings out with each other.

Continuing his embodied cultural mediations, Parménides uses this second article to present translations of current slang and once again uses the opportunity to underline the racial and liberatory potential of rock in building collective spaces where relational practices unite bodies: "'funky' es el lado 'hard' (macizo) 'dirty' (grosero), 'heavy' (pesado) del rock; su presencia black ['funky' is the hard, dirty, heavy side of rock; its Black presence]" (14). Critics of the *Onda* have focused on how these authors used language and vocabulary to defy the (*mestizo*) cultural hegemony imposed by institutions and canonical authors (Calderón 39). While García Saldaña does do this, he also goes beyond by using slang and underground and foreign language to explain a racialized and classed reality to himself and the youth around him, and in doing so he moves in a different direction than Agustín who uses language to construct complex literary structures, or Sáinz who uses language as humor and representation while remaining in a decidedly middle-class register. Parménides is not simply recording what youthful bodies (in the US and Mexico) are saying, but rather explaining how these words speak of and to racialized realities of liberatory actions, and he does so from a body who is consuming culture, music, and substances alongside these other youth consumers. These words matter not because they are novel or innovative, but because they are spoken by youth to describe themselves and their actions as they use rock (and other rhythms) to resist social norms. Through language, they generate collective assemblages of bodies that communicate and recognize each other as they establish and nurture communitarian bonds among themselves and with the readers García Saldaña is interpellating.

If in the first article rock is politicized through history and the racial origins of these rhythms, now García Saldaña is pushing his reader to critically examine the language they are using, in words as well as in visual symbols such as clothing, accessories, and style. Decoding this new language for the readers is important, going beyond the irreverence into the political component of this new vocabulary and how it becomes embodied manifestations of class differences already present in rock culture and spaces:

> A la calle (o la avenida) donde está el hoyo, las parejas, los maestros, las profesoras van llegándole; ellas: matas lacias acá; los ojos ónix, brillando de ganas de un buen refuego; pantos chiros que se les ven ¡cámara!, chanchísimos, ¡muy funkis! Playeras efectivas que se les ven, digo, efectivas en sus cálidos cuerpos. Digo, las hijas muy acá como buenas profesoras; otras en el rol de chavas jotpants. Y los maestros se lanzan con buenas matas algunos. Ostros con ondas de pantos y camisas acá los chiros.
> [To the street (or the avenue) where the *hoyo* is, the couples, the professors and the teachers are arriving; the girls with long sleek hair, onyx eyes glowing from the desire for a good time; sick pants that look, hold on! so great! very funky! Effective shirts that look, I mean, effective on their warm bodies. I mean, the daughters like good professors; others in their role of hotpants girls. And the guys go forward with good long hair some of them. Others with pants in style and shirts that are cool.]" ("Los hoyos funkis" 14)

The *hoyo funki* is not just a space where rock music can be listened to, it's also a place of contact between genders and classes where all social identities are being transformed; it's important to note that not all men wear long hair, and not all women wear short skirts or hot pants. Furthermore, in being named as *profesoras* and *profesores*, these youth appear as teaching the younger generations of these different ways of being; their lifestyles and their actions are legitimized by the narrative voice that underscores their interpersonal growth and development in the context of learning. Their bodies glow, sometimes due to substance use and sometimes due to sheer excitement. Rock is already a space of political resistance, and here language is mobilized by the author in the descriptions and by the youth participating in these spaces of contention and class contact. These different words not only showcase linguistic innovation, but, more importantly, are textualizations of novel social relations that are being generated by this youth culture; words give meaning and shape to bodies and the relations between them, and thus allow for the exploration, reproduction, and expansions of these different body positions and body relations. This act of languaging is embodied and political. As rhythms push bodies to move in different ways, words push bodies to relate to each other in different ways.

In the third and last article I will analyze here, published in *Piedra Rodante*'s sixth issue on October 30, 1971, García Saldaña presents a critical chronicle of the infamous Avándaro music festival, which was extensively covered from all angles in the special issue of the journal. Undoubtedly a high point in the development of rock counterculture in Mexico, this festival motivated a mix of paradoxical responses from the cultural intelligentsia of the time. Leftist writers such as Carlos Monsiváis "acknowledged the cultural legitimacy and political potential of rock, but then typically dismissed local hippies as alienated youth under the sway of imperialist propaganda" (Dunn, *Contracultura* 12). On the other hand, more apolitical and elite voices such as Salvador Elizondo would celebrate the festival and stand by youth culture.[70] The festival was held on September 11, 1971, in a private gold club in the Valle de Bravo region outside of Mexico City. Initially planned as a car race with a few select bands playing music, the organization quickly accelerated — some would way got out of hand — and the festival became a full-on musical event with many bands playing all night. According to the authorities and their estimates, around 100,000 youth gathered in the space, but unofficial records speak of 300,000 people of all classes, and especially lower and working classes that rode buses or even walked from the city. While the series of planned car races never happened due to the massive concurrence, the festival became a landmark in Mexican rock history and transformed the face of rock. The Browner folx of the *hoyos funkis* suddenly became hypervisible, and they flooded the upper-class suburban region with *jipitecas* of all sorts, liberated women, and cannabis smokers.

However, as Christopher Dunn succinctly points out, "the Avándaro Festival marked the apex of La Onda Chicana but also led to its demise and banishment from national memory as the government actively suppressed the rock counterculture" (*Contracultura* 11). In the aftermath of the concert, which itself happened amid increasing state violence (the Jueves de Corpus massacre of June 10 of that same year was the most recent major event), more repressive actions were undertaken by the federal and metropolitan armed forces. As the dust settled and the decade progressed, rock gatherings were increasingly persecuted and became a thing of the past or went deep underground, with only state-sanctioned groups literally captured by the cultural industry through contracts and agreements being allowed to play on stage or in front of cameras.[71] The festival remains in collective memory as a focal point of counterculture, an achievement of the various countercultural threads and communities coming together in a single moment in space and time. Several super 8mm cameras were able to capture the festival in all its chaotic messiness, with mud all over the place, makeshift tents, and grinning youth celebrating their existence; of these, Alfredo Gurrola's *Avandaro* (1971) remains the most accessible on YouTube and other free platforms. However, as important as this concert was for the counterculture, it also marks the moment when counterculture became solidly commodified, when *jipismo* and rock became once and for all a capitalist commodity absorbed into the media industries. In the words of Catholic priest cum countercultural guru Enrique Marroquín, "esta fue la ambivalencia del movimiento: por un lado, el rock es el himno de las reinvidicaciones de la nueva generación; por otro, es el negocio más fabuloso existente en la actualidad. El 'sistema' aprovechando a sus demoledores. Es la última e irónica verdad [this was the ambivalence of the movement: on the one hand, rock is the hymn of the vindication of the new generations; on the other, it's the most fabulous existing business currently. The 'system' taking advantage of its demolishers. This is the last and ironic truth]" (49). This commodification notwithstanding, the videos and chronicles of Avándaro (including Marroquín's own take in his book on counterculture) underscore the participation of women and lower-class *rockeros*, all coming together in a space of liberation that literally takes over the high-class suburbs for a weekend — an occupation with bodies and sounds and sociabilities that defy nationalistic normativities and that will have repercussions on the countercultural milieus for years.

Writing from a temporal, physical, and subjective proximity, García Saldana chronicles this event with two clear poles guiding his text: on the one hand, an explicit politicization of the bodies on the field that rests on their recontextualization within the historical and recent events of state and paramilitary repression, and on the other hand, a gender-critical engagement with the ways in which heteronormative masculinities and behaviors can slip by unaware. His writing does this by acknowledging, textualizing, and naming the female *jipitecas* and their autonomous desires within counterculture, not exactly speaking for or representing directly as much as making their social and political presence visible in the literary and journalistic space. By 1971, many student activists had been murdered, jailed, disappeared, or persecuted; *rockeros* were moving in times when self-identification as a rebellious youth carried with it a target for the state and its violent allies. Thus, Parménides begins the three-page article by naming the Jueves de Corpus massacre on June 10 and proceeds to narrate the concert as a distant spectator, moving throughout the chronicle from close-ups to the bodies around him and their liberatory movements to zoom-outs that place the concert in the recent history of rock concerts in the hemisphere: "en el aire de México otro happening trágico: 10 de junio . . . 10 de junio: querido diario, hoy compré mi boleto de avión para Los Ángeles [in the Mexican air, another tragic happening: june 10 . . . june 10: dear diary, today I bought my airplane ticket to Los Angeles]" ("Avándaro: amor y pasión" 35).[72] This narrative voice speaks from a contradictory body, an authoritative voice who moves in rock scenes across borders and classes and one who cannot unsee the violence of the state; a body marked by the tensions and contradictions that youth in that decade faced, with the desire and possibilities of liberation in their imaginaries alongside the very real violence of the state and its forces as they encroached on their bodies. By underlining and explicitly disclosing his contradictory counterculture of buying a plane ticket to leave Mexico on the same day violence is erupting on politicized youth, García Saldaña is pushing readers to consider how to "estar en la onda que diaramente *se puede construir* alrededor del rock [be in the groove that daily can be constructed around rock]," signaling a need to recognize the potential of rock as a tool of resistance as well the need to actively engage with it in this manner and not escape. His assemblage also underlines for the readers the ways in which the state is already viewing these youth as dangerous subjects and pushes for this youth to see itself in the same way, empowering themselves with this potential even if they think they're just listening to music.

Occupying this position of tension moving from leisure to political violence, Parménides continues the article by once again drawing on history and bringing the Mexican countercultural experiences into the greater global context. The first two pages of the three-spread article tell the stories of the 1967 Monterey Pop Festival and its impact on the development of San Francisco as a counter-cultural mecca and the Woodstock Music and Art Fair of 1969, which became a "símbolo de la cultura pop: mota, música, hacer el amor. O comer, como diría cualquier alivianado de esa onda que no habita el mundo social de los rucos . . . Woodstock pronto se volvió un estado mental necesario en todos los chavos (y chavas) que se querían alivianar de la sutil tiranía familiar [symbol of pop culture: weed, music, making love. Or eating, like anyone in the groove that doesn't live in the social world of the old folks would say. Woodstock soon became a mental state necessary in all the young men (and women) who wanted to get away from the subtle tyranny of family]" (García Saldaña 35). This rich cultural history becomes the framework to understand Avándaro and the surge of (Brown) youth that appeared on the countercultural stage in this year; rather than belonging solely to a class and racialized understanding of Mexico as a *mestizo* nation, García Saldaña pushes the readers to understand themselves explicitly in the emerging global sensibilities. This mental state that seems to shake the Mexican *onderos* is shared by youth everywhere, their existence becoming political insofar as it is descriptive of a much wider sentiment that surpasses a rebellious youth. By writing the concert in this way, Parménides constructs a narration of the event that steps outside the boundaries of a simple chronicle, as can be expected in the leading musical journal of the moment. Rather, this framing in political events and countercultural contexts in the North, especially recounted *from* a personal and embodied position familiar with both Mexico and California, rests upon a proximity to both national history and identity as well as personal experiences and not a discursive reality disconnected from the rest of social complexities. In this sense, García Saldaña is assembling and explicitly showcasing a countercultural body that brings together these paradoxes and contradictions, refusing to be contained in any subjectively normative position, whether racial or class or gendered.

Like the history of Woodstock, Avándaro was originally organized as a somewhat moderate series of car races with musical features but quickly turned into a massive event with an outpour of audience members emerging from the lower classes. When considering how it was originally a business venture, Parménides's critical approach to the festival as well as the concertgoers reveals a politics grounded in the countercultural ethics of bodily autonomy. By focusing on the erotics — the bodily sensations, including the erotics of state violence — of these countercultural spaces and their sharedness across cultures and borders, García Saldaña is constructing an understanding of counterculture always already political. It is this erotics, in the sense of a shared bodily experience characterized by music, substances, and alternative sociosexual practices, that he rests upon as he occupies this contradictory and critical position; the article oscillates between criticizing the government's violent interventions and class differences on one hand, and on the other, accepting with quiet resignation the support of the regime that allowed the concert to happen, albeit only for a single year. The article contrasts with *Piedra Rodante*'s official positioning with regard to the government, which included lauding it openly for being supportive of their rock endeavors. This apparent support, which was really a depoliticizing strategy, came from the presidency of Luis Echeverría (1970–1976), who distinguished himself with a very positive public position toward youth culture and modernization while simultaneously increasing the repressive practices of shutting down bars and *hoyos funkis* and strengthening the paramilitary groups and federal agencies that beat up *jipitecas* while carrying out the Dirty War. This placed counterintellectuals such as Parménides into a contradictory position that he navigates by remaining firmly in a class critique. The article focuses on the ways in which the shared experience of Avándaro is striated by class; he names some of the concertgoers as *fresa* (bougie/posh/stuckup), who in their consumption of rock as simply a cool commodity silence its liberating potential, and he names them with the passion of a revolutionary: "fuck, pequeños burgueses enajenados que no saben para qué demonios sirve el rock [fuck, alienated petit bourgeoises that do not know what the hell rock is for]" ("Avándaro" 36). This harsh critique of middle-class concertgoers continues by calling out their "ridiculo mundo de la gente nice [ridiculous world of nice people]," and perhaps distances some of his readers by breaking the critical and somewhat relatable narrative voice he has constructed previously in the articles. The controlled and laid-back critic, somewhat detached from the class tensions intrinsically tied to the political and social struggles of Mexico, breaks down in this instance of uncontrolled passion to reveal a body that is now explicitly aligned with and calling for more youth to understand the Brown, lower-class rockers as "parte de esa gente que habita los barrios bajos, tampoco quiere estar sola ni ser fan de Los Halcones [part of those people who live in the lower neighborhoods, they also don't want to be alone or are a fan of the Halcones]" (35). For the author, it is in this class alliance that rock's revolutionary and liberatory potential can be accessed and experienced, and this alliance must be embodied and assembled in the physical geographies of rock as much as in the popular rhythms and revolutionary aesthetics that are characterizing Mexican rock during this moment.[73]

"Avándaro: amor y pasión" becomes García Saldaña's most salient gen-der-transformative moment, when the class critique he had raised before and continuously in journaling rock suddenly becomes an intensely critical look at his peers. Whereas in his literary ventures *El rey criollo* and *Pasto verde* his characters were navigating gender relations and sociosexual relations danger-ously close to the normativities demanded by *mestizo* sociabilities, by 1971 his more embodied experiences with the emerging *funki* culture of the metrop-olis had developed into a critical lens sharp enough to observe these *mestizo* sociabilities within the counterculture itself. His subtle "es bueno ver maestra entre los profesores. Hay pocas chavas [it's good to see women among the professors. There are few girls]" ("Avándaro" 36) speaks of an awareness of the striking difference with the *hoyos funkis*, where women were a regular and important part of the social space. This gendered inequality in the mass concert is a gesture that García Saldaña offers to his (male) peers to foster inclusion and challenges their social behavior to cooperate with women in a safer space. *Maestras* and *profesores* speaks of a way of recognizing and cooperating with women on a more equal social positioning, not merely as sexual objects to be consumed in the way that pop industry was promoting the *sexiness* of rock as a commodity.

This simple change in tone and language is revelatory when placed in the context of the gender liberation that was experienced in the festival, with mixed reactions from the audience there as well as from those who read or heard about the festival through news or reports. As can be observed in various photographs or video footage of the event, nudity (both nonsexual and sexual) among men and women — typical of the gender liberation movements of hippie culture across the globe — was somewhat commonplace in the crowds. Famously, one woman got the spotlight by climbing onto a stage late at night during the con-cert and removing her clothes to dance more freely with the music in a moment that was captured by cameras and circulated (and later prosecuted by the gov-ernment) in many journals, memorialized in popular history as "la encuerada de Avándaro." In the same *Piedra Rodante*, the editorial staff published a pho-tographic series of her and other shirtless women with captions imitating audi-ence member quotes such as "'¡Qué buen patín agarró la torta esa!' '¿Estará alivianada?' '¡Mírala! Se quiere bajar el ese . . . ['What a good trip that fox caught!' 'Do you think she's down with it?' 'Look at her! She wants to take it off . . .]" or "'¿Ya viste hijo? ¡Una encuerada!' ['You see that, son? A naked girl!']" or "Coatlícue desencaneda [[Coatlicue unchained']]." Taken together, the images and the captions reveal the tension between women's liberation in the form of nonsexual nudity and patriarchal discomfort at its lack of control over the female form; namely, the representation of female nudity as sexual, objectifying, or needing to be framed by the male gaze.[74] In this sense, *Piedra Rodante*'s representation of female sexuality was similar to that of the more mainstream commercial rock films, from *5 de chocolate y 1 de fresa* (dir. Carlos Velo, 1968) to *Bikinis y rock*, which emphasized female sexuality as another commodity product of the male gaze, another object to be consumed by the male viewer.

Instead of reinstating this male gaze on women's bodies or erotic pleasure, Parménides uses the article to speak against the objectification that underpins *mestizo* sociability. The women, and all the people in the festival, experienced for a moment "la libertad de elegir su destino independientemente de los moldes rígidos que todo sistema de opresión (fragmentación) utiliza para su sostenimiento. En Avándaro el ridículo mundo de la gente nice (panties sex, brassiers no bra, kotex o támpax, vaselina sólida, champú, pelucas para secretarias) ch . . . a su madre por un ratito [the freedom to choose their destiny no matter the rigid molds that all oppressive systems (fragmentation) uses for its survival. In Avándaro, the ridiculous world of nice people (panties, sex, brassieres no bra, Kotex or Tampax, solid Vaseline, shampoo, wigs for secretaries) f**k all that for a little bit]" (García Saldaña 36).

This disengagement from the ridiculous world of "gente nice" and its gender normativities is echoed by Alfredo Gurrola's documentary *Avándaro*, where he captures a moment during the concert when a young woman seemingly fainted or was convalescent for a moment — perhaps the same encuerada, perhaps another woman — and on the audio track an off-screen voice begins to berate the mostly male audience to leave this girl alone and care for her, yelling "no sean gandallas, cuiden . . . cubran a esta muchacha, puede ser su hermana, puede ser su carnala, ella vino a pasársela bien [don't be like that, take care . . . cover that girl, she could be your sisters, she could be your friends, she came here to have a good time]." Like García Saldaña, this voice is showcasing a counterculturally radical gendered ethics of care, demanding of the male audience members to behave according to a different ethics than that of objectifying patriarchy. Historian Eric Zolov underlines the limits of female liberation in the *mestizo* machista environment that tended to surround rock culture, typical of the Mexican middle-class double standards condemning female sexuality to whoredom or virginity while celebrating male sexual prowess (*Refried Elvis* 196). In their quasi-pornographic and sexually fixated treatment of female nudity at Avándaro, *Piedra Rodante* reproduces this attitude, and yet García Saldaña is hinting at another way of being he witnesses in the festival. He signals this nudity and other quotidian acts of defiance as instances of sexual liberation that particularly emerge from female *jipitecas*; it is not casual that the ridiculous world of nice people is described with the feminine beauty and consumer products (aka tools of biopolitical control). For the readers of Parménides as a countercultural guide and mediator, and in the assemblages of bodies he is constructing in the article (from Avándaro to Monterey and Woodstock to Jueves de Corpus streets), "woman" is not an object of sexuality so much as a partner in the enjoyment of the festival *and* in political action, an equal *maestra* and *profesora* of the counterculture.

After publishing two more numbers for a total of eight during its short-lived run, *Piedra Rodante* shut down presses when the editor began to receive threats of physical violence.[75] Similar to the *hoyos funkis*, which existed outside the legalities of copyrights and permits, the *tocadas*, and other music presentations that popped up with no venues or control, *Piedra Rodante* faced the threat of the violence that was legitimized by the state's own involvement in arresting rock bands and persecuting activists. Other *jipiteca* publications such as *Yerba* and *POP* also shut down and ceased circulation, and rock bands managed to survive during this decade by singing in English to avoid censorship for their political content.[76] Parménides García Saldaña continued to write sporadically in other more mainstream publications until his death on September 18, 1982, of complications with his struggle with alcohol and other substances. His writings as a countercultural authority in the public sphere (*Piedra Rodante* referenced him as Mexico's Abbie Hoffman) passed into the background, and he achieved a cult status and a public position associated with his literary works, particularly after a series of articles published on his death memorialized his life and recontextualized his oeuvre in the tradition of a *poéte maudit*, a writer plagued by dark crows of madness. However, as I hope to have demonstrated in this section, his journalistic writings speak of radical changes in countercultural spaces and gesture toward bodily autonomy as central in the assemblage of countercultural bodies, changes that were happening beyond his immediate action and that speak to an ethics of bodies consuming counterculturally.

I close these brief notes on the short-lived history of Mexican countercultural literature by emphasizing how, in spite of the limitations of language (these texts remain untranslated) and circulation (Parménides García Saldaña's cannabis novel *Pasto verde* was only recently republished by a small press, while his journalistic work has not been fully recovered, and *Larga sinfonía en D* was just republished in 2023), the authors conceive of their work as literature speaking of and to the world, and they capture a countercultural ethos of consumption. Through the shared experiences of youth culture, rock music, psychedelic substances, global advertising, and postcolonial/revolutionary action, the authors conceive of globalized subjects existing in worldly spaces; they assemble countercultural bodies that come together to initiate processes of sociosexual liberation, construct bodily autonomy, and challenge the normativities of gender and racialization. However, the limitations of this moment in countercultural history are important. The experiences of Parménides in the rock scene and of the trio in *Larga sinfonía* remain temporally curtailed by their lack of integration into life and politics. Though they signal to the reader the need to reflect on these, the novels themselves function as snapshots: brief glimpses of the powerfully decolonial and anti-capitalist potentials of psychedelic experiences under a countercultural framework. Through them, we can glimpse countercultural modalities of consumption that some youth were enacting across Mexico, and whose actions would reverberate albeit silently for a few decades before reemerging in the punk cultures of the 1980s and 1990s, and later countercultural spaces of contemporary sexual and social dissidence.

Alongside Margarita Dalton's work, Parménides García Saldaña's journalistic writings reveal a gendered undercurrent in the Mexican countercultural movements of the 1960s. Historically appreciated as the most eccentric, problematic, and "raro" of the *Onderos*, García Saldaña's late writings showcase a series of assemblages of countercultural bodies, including his own, that defy the limits of cultural spheres and national subjectivities. These bodies and the spaces they move in signal the changes in gender liberation and sexual liberation that were already happening in the incipient LGBT and women's movements. Taken together, these two authors embody a novel kind of counterculture anchored in liberation struggles across the hemisphere and legitimize the consumption of rock music and psychedelic substances in the construction of bodily autonomy and psychic liberation, ultimately as political actions in the construction of alternative countercultural nations. Rock music, particularly live, becomes the foundation for alternative social spheres that defied the literary and culturally sanctioned spaces. Furthermore, they are writers authorized in the public sphere by their editor Emmanuel Carballo and the editorial Joaquin Mortiz, both pillars in the publishing industry of the decades. While counterculture would become a commodity in later decades (its style and rhythm products to be sold by the capitalist entertainment industries), for a moment these spaces were promises of other societies, other sociabilities, and other genders. Psychedelic experiences were mystical experiences that catalyzed bodily changes in the youth of the moment, and rock concerts were spaces of gender liberation where glimpses of other ways of being were contained in every gesture as the youth danced, sang, and shared corporeality together: bodies consuming substances and change alike.

Chapter 4

Counterculture Commodified and Sexual Liberation

Psychedelic-Assisted Psychotherapy in
Fernando del Paso's *Palinuro de México* and the
Rebellious Female Protagonists of Sergio García
Michel's Super 8 Millimeter Films

Mexico City, 1968. Somewhere near the downtown Plaza de Santo Domingo, a young couple rent a small department in the vicinity of the university's school of medicine and near the historic location of the Holy Inquisition during the colonial period. He tried to take classes at the nearby medical school the university is expanding and realized soon after his first dissection that cutting up bodies might not be for him, with the blood and bones so immediately fleshy after the extreme and violent repression that students and youth experienced in that year. So, he transitioned into working for a new advertising and publicity company that was opening an international branch in the city. Meanwhile, she takes care of their shared apartment and their myriad novel home appliances and commodity products that have begun to appear: a color TV, electric razors, electric blenders, toothpaste tubes, and new combs. They live an apparently simple and carefree life, interrupted only by the appearance of his friends (or perhaps alternate personalities) and their occasional LSD trip. During these brief moments, their small apartment suddenly becomes a space beyond their four walls, their bed and couch the geographies where they explore their individual and shared psychological and sexual histories and intervene their national subjectivities through this liberatory psychedelic journeying. In these moments, their decisions to reconfigure their national subjectivity and propose a different collective memory become enhanced, and the acid trips are revealed to be therapeutic moments for the couple to reconfigure their shared national past.

Mexico City, 1985. Four women walk along a busy avenue against traffic, arm in arm as they defy the flow of cars and stroll at their own pace in the chaotic metropolis full of sounds and smells. Around them the city bustles with economic activity, people moving to their jobs in search of economic stability and growth while huge billboards dot the skyscape above them, selling everything from lingerie to hot dogs and the latest imported automobile. Consumer capitalism is rampant, and buying is the way to prove you're unscathed in the economic turmoil that has shaken the country. On the street level, shops are bustling, and storefronts are practically overflowing with new products that just came in; the Palacio de Hierro and other large department stores have never been so successful, while the streets are crowded with people selling homemade products, juggling and singing on the street corners to make enough for a meal. The contrasts between the have and have-nots are widening every day. The city hasn't yet experienced the massive earthquake that will shock the nation and rile citizens to rise, organizing to help themselves and, in doing so, giving birth to the civil society that will shape the country in later decades. Society is still reeling from the paramilitary repression of the late 1960s and 1970s, youth culture finding ways to express itself artistically and politically in safe ways that do not hint at even a little of outright resistance to the state. Rock music has been persecuted for years now, and yet it remains alive in the underground. As they walk through the city, the four young women can hear some chords around metro stops as musicians tune their instruments and belt out their tunes with a watchful eye for any policemen coming up. The young women will continue wandering through the city as they make their way to their urban commune, a building where rebellious youth is currently squatting and keeping a low profile from the *perjudiciales*, the federal police. Their community grows and shrinks with the passing years, and it remains in all its iterations as a refuge and a place to thrive away from the limits of nation and family.

By the 1980s, the dream of a peaceful modern Mexico was more than vanishing. The violent events of Tlatelolco in 1968 and Jueves de Corpus in 1971 were only the visible points of a wave of repression that characterized the 1970s, with both urban and rural guerrillas being combated by undercover agents and paramilitary groups in what is now known as the Mexican Dirty War (Guerra Sucia), promoted under auspices of the Escuela de las Américas and the CIA. For the urban youth in particular, these events revealed an authoritarian state willing to treat its middle-class citizens with the same violence it had historically enforced on its political enemies and working-class organizers in the aftermath of the revolution. At the same time, the economic markets that had developed in the wake of the postwar economic boom and expanded with the development of advertising visual language in the 1960s reached a high point as consumer products and technologies were increasingly available; for a moment in that glorious decade, it seemed all of Mexico was prospering. Then came the state violence and the first of the oil and economic crisis of the 1970s. During the 1980s, this middle-class dream would vanish with more and deeper economic crises, the earthquakes of 1985, and the undeniable electoral corruption scandal of 1988.

While this was happening, the power of the advertising industry accelerated the development of consumer capitalism, and counterculture was not immune to its capturing potential; inevitably, the rebellious aesthetics of the 1960s counterculture with long hair, short skirts, sexual freedom, and rock music was contained and sanitized as commodities and commodified subjectivities to be circulated and consumed quietly and with no rebellion.[1] Rock music had to be transformed to continue being rebellious, and punk in particular started to develop alongside other genres as musical expressions of social discontent. Soon, however, the bodily changes that used to signify rebellion and merit persecution would be no more than selling points and products of the new *mestizo* subjectivities; electric guitars began to sound in pop songs, and Televisa was quick to produce a whole generation of pop singers that catered to adolescents and youth in a depoliticized way, the birth of boy bands like Magneto and child stars like Gloria Trevi, Pedro Fernández, or Luis Miguel. In a more global context, the film *Zabriskie Point* (dir. Michelangelo Antonioni, 1970) showcases this capturing process by focusing on how the countercultural agents and forces of sexual liberation, political activism, and communal founding would prove too weak in the face of state violence and market capturing, the film ending in an orgiastic sequence of explosions and commodities flooding the screen. In Mexico, while state agents were actively suppressing any form of political and cultural dissent, both market and state forces would ally themselves in the material institutions of the film and cultural industry, producing a flood of low-budget and narratively simple films that would sell sex and rebellious individualism while carefully policing and punishing any significant dissent.

In this early moment of neoliberal Mexico — where state violence was matched by the symbolic violence of advertising and unregulated economic development/extraction — countercultural communities as those dreamed by Parménides García Saldaña, Margarita Dalton, and other agents quickly became a faraway and unreachable fantasy. Increasingly, countercultural spaces, communes, and communal households were quickly vanishing and becoming temporary sanctuaries rather than active experiments in alternative nation-building.[2] The radical bodies of sexually liberated women (and men) were once again becoming the objects of capitalist commodification, now used not just to sell specific products through sexualization but also to police "proper" sexual behavior as it became more openly represented and talked about. The sexual liberation of the early postrevolutionary period as explored by Cube Bonifant and Nahui Olin gave way during the decade to the *cine de rumberas* of the 1940s, where women were once again owning their representation and using it to challenge sexual and gender stereotypes while having to participate nonetheless in narratives that faulted their ill fates to their sexual behavior and lack of submission to heteronormative standards of sociosexual behavior. By the 1970s, the *cine de ficheras* had appeared on scene and was the way in which the film industry continued to exploit the sexualization of women while morally condemning their behavior as well as the sexual liberation promoted by global counterculture.[3] Explicit sexual desire and its erotics became once again a central tool for the (de)subjectification of Mexican citizens, (un)training men in how to channel their desire through objectification and consumption of female bodies and (un)training women in how to properly express their desire and the consequences of carrying out this expression outside the confines of heteronormative sexuality.

During the 1970s, Mexico as a country (and Mexico City especially as the neuralgic cultural, political, and social epicenter of the ideological and material nation) experienced a tightening of the subject positions and subjectivities available for its citizens, especially for those politically oriented or socially conscious. The myriad possibilities that had been constructed and expanded upon during the long political decade of the 1960s with student activism and youth culture were suddenly curtailed, reduced to the stereotype of the radicalized (male) student or the sexually deviant and perverse young woman. This in turn generated a process of rapidly "growing up" for the youth, a sudden entry into the labor force as docile professional workers. To place an example, in José Agustín's 1969 theatrical play, *Abolición de la propiedad* (remade into a 2012 film directed by Jesus Magaña), a young couple spends the entire time on stage debating, discussing, rejecting, and embracing the heteronormative *mestizo* injunctions that are ordering their lives, from their parents' expectations to their own desires. They move in the context of an increasingly urban metropolis (the metro system was inaugurated in 1969 and rapidly expanded) functioning under capitalist economic relations, their bodies increasingly subject to what sociologist Fréderic Lordon terms the "passionate life" that "imposes itself on individuals and they are chained to it for better or worse, pretty to the fortunes of encounters that cheer or sadden them, its real causes — the key to understanding them — forever escaping their grasp" (16). And as culture shifted and adapted to the global commodities of the period, rock and countercultural expressions would be accepted as youthful adventures, behaviors, and silliness that youth were expected to grow out of to become compliant workers, citizens engaged fully in the construction of Mexico as a powerful economy and a global country. Again, Lordon (following Marx and Spinoza) signals how the process of cultural and social construction is tied to the material realm of economic relations, particularly those of labor. It is in labor that the passionate life is generated, in the specific instances of work exchange where affect pushes desires into a particular structure and direction, literally molding objects of desire into concrete consumer objects to be desired and obtained.[4] Sex and rock 'n roll (drugs would remain criminalized and demonized in popular culture, associated with lower-class violence and depravity) would be increasingly sanitized in the entertainment industry, appearing and yet remaining tied to narratives of moral punishment and depravity associated with foreignness and deviance. Countercultural bodies would engage this context by disassembling their desire from capitalist relations of consumption or affective understandings of labor, working to remain in an underground society separate from the mainstream political and material economy. They would generate textual/ literary, filmic/video, and fleetingly material communities where bodies could come together to establish other (sociosexual) relations and social structures, generating spaces where desire could run freely and allow for other structures of affect to emerge, layering their bodies with joyful but especially pleasurable affects and feelings. These spaces had to exist in the underground, though, or hidden in the folds of literary fiction and experimental film.

Continuing the cultural and social development of the 1960s, the 1970s saw an expansion of youth culture, particularly in the increasingly streamlined connections between education and work, as commodified counterculture — especially that which assembled rock music, urban fashion, and a release of late teenage angst — became of a measure of subjective development. Instead of liberating, this variation of counterculture functioned to make the youth body more flexible, allowing some engagement with global consumer goods while very clearly policing and punishing any real resistance, rebellion, or revolutionary attitudes. Flexibility to accommodate these bodies into whichever working relation was demanded at the moment, particularly professional careers, was the most important factor; this flexibility — a mark of early neoliberal socialization — was more important for middle and working classes than lower classes, who continued to consume, reappropiate, and recycle rock culture to transform it into the punk scene of the 1980s.[5] This persecution of rock culture meant that as the spaces that youth culture had developed (rock concerts, listening parties, psychedelic gatherings, et cetera) dwindled, countercultural bodies shifted their attention to the private spheres of personal bedrooms, shared apartments, households, and film festivals. Here, bodies were able to engage with themselves and each other in ways that disrupted the structuring of their desires, hidden from the watchful eye of the increasingly militarized state.

In this chapter, I focus on two specific cultural producers: the super 8mm film director Sergio García Michel and the novelist and writer Fernando del Paso —in particular, their cultural production between 1968 and 1988. Del Paso's novel *Palinuro de México* (1977) appeared ten years after his successful *José Trigo* (1966), which had already earned him the cultural capital granted by author institutions such as Juan Rulfo or Juan José Arreola; having experienced the events of the later 1960s and 1970s in Mexico City, Iowa (at the International Writers Program), and then London while working for a Guggenheim fellowship, Del Paso's second novel engages with the historical construction of postrevolutionary Mexico through a character who unfolds in a series of exhilarating and confusing episodes while consuming lysergic acid and cannabis with his girlfriend and their friends in their one-bedroom apartment. On the flip side, Sergio García Michel's fictional film production from 1968 to 1988 explores the experiences of youth — in particular young women — as they navigated the countercultural spaces available to them or that they founded. Both producers worked at some point in advertising agencies, indicative of the blurring of the lines in creativity, art, and industry, and García

Michel essentially taught himself film production in the late 1960s, choosing super 8mm as his medium of preference and helping to establish an experimental filmic sphere that flourished between 1968 and 1975. In his films and in Del Paso's novel, bodies appear as territories to be liberated, empowering themselves through radical autonomy in the form of sexual practices and substance use. They directly respond to the early yet steady neoliberalization of the Mexican cultural sphere, choosing to produce outside the institutional film venues and the Mexican literary sphere (*Palinuro* was first published in Spain and did not appear in Mexican press until 1982).

When I speak of the neoliberalization of Mexico, I think of the impact of consumer culture as it intersected with *mestizo* nationalism with the support of economic policies that opened markets and social policies, promoting a fixed and essentialist national identity. Countercultural bodies in these decades picked up on these processes that would reach a high point in the 1990s, as can be seen in the film *Sólo con tu pareja* (dir. Alfonso Cuaron, 1991) where the consumer objects of the *charro*, tequila, tacos, jalapeño peppers, and mariachis appear over and over as the synthesis of Mexican culture, now truly empty signifiers. In this early erosion of *mestizo* culture where nationalist symbols still held power, García Michel and Del Paso assemble bodies in mediums that strategically resist the process of cultural commodification itself. First, it is their choice of medium (long novel and short experimental film) and the ways they construct narratives to foreground how advertising is shaping bodies through desire and reproducing hegemonic gender norm that I highlight. Second, they produce experimental projects difficult to understand with an overwhelming flood of cultural references, demanding an audience willing to engage with the multiplicity of national, global, and countercultural references woven into the texts to decipher and enjoy them as both national and global products. Finally, these cultural products foreground the formation of communities in difference, gathering a variety of subjects into groups that resist the isolationist socialization promoted through extreme consumerism. My argument in this chapter is that these two cultural producers generate alternative countercultural embodiments anchored in the representation of sexual desire and sexual pleasure as liberatory practices. Understanding social, sexual, and erotic liberation as processes that begin in the territory of the body and flow outward into relations with objects, bodies, and ideas, this chapter focuses on the ways in which film and novel are used to counteract the commodification processes of early neoliberal culture before it was shaped by more explicit state policies. I argue that in foregrounding dissident sexual pleasure — whether it be that of female bodies or male bodies engaging in often-silenced sexual acts — these texts generate other ways of being countercultural that explicitly engage with and disconnect from the sexual normativities of colony, nation, and capital.

In the novel and films, as well as the spaces in which these films circulated, these cultural producers generate strategies to engage the *mestizo* nation on biopolitical terms by creative alternative practices of consumption, relations of urban movements, and ultimately sociofamilial structures whose materiality gives shape to their countercultural desire.[6] In their material reconfigurations of the individual, familiar, and communal relations to resist the (late) capitalist/ neoliberal act of consumption as the ultimate act of social communion, these films and this novel assemble embodied practices tied to the *mestizo* nation shared by national subjects while rejecting its normativities. My intention in this chapter is to explore these strategies as they were and are mobilized by the bodies represented to resist capture from the forces of state and market initially and to construct other ways of being sexual outside these normativities. In the films, this means exploring how female countercultural bodies literally escape from the *mestizo* nation and come together. In the novel, this means tracing the ways in which lysergic acid and cannabis are used as therapeutic tools to exorcise *mestizo* sociosexualities from their bodies while generating spaces (private *and* public) where other bodies can come together to reshape themselves, literally seeking to redefine the territories of the city.

Utopian Nations and Countercultural Heroines in Sergio García Michel's Super 8 Millimeter Cinema

A desiring machine uses guerrilla tactics
to subvert symbolic interpretation.

— Anna Powell

Introduced to the country during the 1950s, super 8mm film was initially a documentarian device, an upper- and middle-class commodity, and a marker of modernization. Arguably always a contraption of some economic privilege — as opposed to a more horizontal technology such as musical instruments — super 8mm quickly became a tool for the counterculture, a weapon of ideological resistance whose intrinsic technical limitations made it the perfect medium to avoid being captured by the growing entertainment industries. Its increasing accessibility (in buying a camera and processing the film, but also in being able to take the camera into places where the big studio cameras could not/ would not go) made it the perfect tool for capturing the changing lives of these radicalized youth; perhaps the greatest example of this is the documentary *El grito* (dir. Leobardo Arretche, 1968), telling the story of the student massacre at Tlatelolco in 1968 and including footage of youth imprisoned at Lecumberri

Prison, a feat that involved sneaking small cameras into lunchboxes. In the aftermath of Tlatelolco, Mexican filmmakers began using super 8mm in a variety of ways to explore and exploit its political, cultural, social, and artistic potentialities. Especially during the early 1970s, the emerging *superochero* cultural sphere established itself as a space where young filmmakers could come together around an extremely varied cultural production in a single medium. Using this medium, they could respond directly to the overbearing presence of the entertainment industry backed by the administration of then President Luis Echeverría (1970–1976) as well as the increasing power of the mass media and advertising agencies. As a cultural sphere in itself, the *superocheros* sought to challenge and change the forms of political engagement, learning from the anti-colonial struggles of the Global South and specifically from the Third Cinema theorization emerging from Latin America. In the specific Mexican context, the *superocheros* learned from the experimental gaze of *La formula secreta* (dir. Rubén Gámez, 1965) and their own work, such as the politically engaged documentary *El grito*. In its short but rich production period, the *superocheros* managed to release well over 200 films, including low-budget Westerns, erotic films, political communiqués, avant-garde experimentalism, political documentaries, rock documentaries, and rock operas, all while remaining in the small format.

In the context of this productive albeit small film circuit, Sergio García Michel (1945–2010) stands out as a central figure whose cultural work involved not only producing but also organizing and chronicling the diverse history of the small format; he founded several film collectives as well as the important Foro Tlalpan cultural center and taught film production in both small workshops (*talleres*) and university classrooms. His films range from short three-minute clips to long-format rock operas with plenty of documentaries in between. Together, they are a collection of adventures and countercultural enterprises that represent one of the high points of *mexperimental* cinema (Lerner and González) and that provide concise critiques of the ways in which counterculture and youth culture were being shaped as market bases phenomena, depoliticized and sanitized products to be consumed. Seeking to expand super 8mm film technology as a political tool beyond the documentary gaze narrating history, García Michel promoted contests, zines, film festivals, and collectives. Together with various other groups of *superocheros*, he published a manifesto titled "Towards the Fourth Cinema" (1972), problematizing the effectiveness of political Third Cinema that was reshaping Latin American cinema since the 1960s as dictatorships and authoritarian regimes came into power. The Mexican *superocheros*, working from a political context of superficial political stability masking the extreme political violence enforced by military, police, and paramilitary groups, wonder about the effectiveness of Third Cinema when a repressive state also works to subjectify bodies in a capitalist society through democratic institutions allied with market forces; the illusion of choice underlying both made the *superocheros* strive toward other forms of audiovisual representation.

The radical nature (in both form and content) of his films revolves around constant reiteration of anti-capitalist, anti-patriarchal, anti-nationalist, and ultimately utopic bodies and geographies; I underline these utopic characteristics to emphasize both the on-screen representations and the off-screen social gatherings where the films were screened, as well as alternative sociabilities that could have been generated among the audience as they processed their shared experiences of watching the films together. I argue that particularly his fictional films represent and reassemble another understanding of female sexuality outside the male gaze, connecting female bodies with notions of citizenship and political subjectivity by focusing on their social and political actions. This sexual liberation gives way to embodiments that enact critiques, subversions, and downright sabotage of capitalist consumption and relations of production; in this way, and especially for male citizens who participated in the super 8mm circuit as producers or viewers, García Michel's oeuvre subverts the normative structure of consumption that sexuality in the *mestizo* sociosexual habitus promotes. Thus, while remining in a cinematic milieu that rested on the male gaze, García Michel's oeuvre produces other ways of seeing women that centralize agency, autonomy and pleasure. These visual representations of liberation are furthermore anchored in recycled, resignified, and reshaped nationalist literary, visual, and audial tropes of the *mestizo* nation project, recirculated now in anti-capitalist circuits and, in doing so, generating utopic nations led by female sexual liberation. The film interventions mobilize a series of disruptive and politicized female bodies using their sexuality as tool of liberation, exploration, and society-building; in doing so, he generates what film critic Teresa Rizzo describes as molecular sexuality, explosive forces capable of destabilizing normative social and gender roles (93). As these representations of liberated female bodies circulate in (countercultural) circuits where they are screened, they generate potential affective engagements that incorporate spectators as cinematic subjects outside the heteronormative order of Mexican nationalists.

For some brief historical-technical context, super 8mm films first appeared in Mexico in the early 1960s. With a price oscillating between 1,800 and 7,000 pesos, these cameras were not exactly a cheap commodity, and yet compared with the expensive equipment required for big studio productions, they quickly changed the game of film production by allowing young filmmakers to begin experimenting without having to sign up to a major studio, thus relinquishing their creative freedom or political commitments. As historian Álvaro Vázquez Mantecón has signaled in his most important recovery of the film movement, super 8mm quickly became a ubiquitous product for the up-to-date countercultural middle-class youth of the 1960s and 1970s (15). Between 1970 and 1974, these young filmmakers produced well over 200 films and organized over 9 contests in collaboration with various institutions from the cultural center/café Las Musas to the more official Secretaría de Cultura y Deportes of the Asociación Nacional de Actores (Vázquez Mantecón 19). This hyperactive sphere was originally a response to the "stop-and-go development of the cinematic industry," which by these decades had stabilized to swing between "complete liberalism on the one hand and state monopoly on the other" (Tompkins 21). As Jesse Lerner and Rita González have documented, these spaces of exhibition and circulation became gathering spots for countercultural citizens of various ages, serving a similar function that concerts and other prohibited socialization spaces had served previously (85, 89). Self-reflecting on their own production and situation within the greater Mexican and regional film industries, the *superocheros* tended to describe themselves as consciousness actors, trying to use cinema in different ways than simply engaging with an established language of political action. Particularly for García Michel, super 8mm allowed for the production of a "cinema that raises consciousness, but does not form it" (171).[7] Given the very limited technical limitations of the film format (inability to record sound while filming, inability to mass produce copies from the reversible film with no negatives), this consciousness-raising imperative drove the directors to very creative assemblages of sound and music as forces of resistance, using them with moving images to generate spaces of projection that also served as spaces of affective resubjectification in communal relations.

To understand García Michel's feminist and liberatory interventions, I will focus now on three of his most famous and widely circulated films (still available on YouTube and other free streaming platforms, with regular contemporary viewership and engagement): *El fin* (1970), *Ah, verdá . . . ?* (1974), and *Un toke de Roc* (1988). As films that recover the countercultural spaces of rural and urban communes, rock concerts, substance use, and free sexuality, they are exemplary of how super 8mm was used as a critical representation tool that would become a "manifest form of political intervention of the image. This does not have to do with filming about, but rather with making a change of and in the image as a place of transformation of aesthetic habits" (Draper 95). In this context of transformation, the Art Centro Las Musas called for the First National Competition of Independent Cinema in 8mm in 1970, with a prize being awarded by Luis Buñuel, then a standing authority on dissident filmmaking in Mexico. A total of twenty films were submitted under the general theme of "Nuestro País/Our Country," all of them with a critical position toward the government after the events of 1968 and with a decidedly countercultural aesthetic of rock music and youth protagonists (Vázquez Mantecón 47). Sergio García Michel participated in the contest with the seven-minute short film *El Fin/The End*. In the aftermath of violence that Tlatelolco became for the youth culture, García Michel critically appraises the political and social actions available to youth, and specifically the ways in which political activism could be represented without being a reproduction of the normative and patriarchal modes of representation and without antagonizing the state in a direct way, choosing to explore the causes and social structures of the violence rather than focusing on the violence itself.

The film begins with credits written on the ruins of a building as the opening chords of the Doors' "The End" play, the camera panning to reveal a mustached man behind prison bard in the shape of Mexico, establishing the general sentiment of capture and imprisonment that troubled youth particularly in these years. The camera then cuts to a stereotypical hippie couple wandering the forest, their disappearance from society both an idealization of youthful escapism and a critique of the lack of political engagement that escapism brings with it, emphasized further with the use of the Rolling Stones' "You Can't Always Get What You Want" as a soundtrack. With this, the forest reappears as an idyllic space, and yet one that nevertheless does not protect form the far reaches of the authoritarian state. The film cuts to two young men sitting around a campfire, suddenly being chased by a *charro* on horseback and four other nationalist figures (an armed soldier, a Catholic priest, a homely housewife in a long dress, and a modern businessman in a suit and tie); they run until one of them is shot down by the soldier in a stone-ruin setting reminiscent of the Plaza de las Tres Culturas at Tlatelolco, while the other flees only to be caught later while he smokes a cannabis joint. The man who captures him is dressed in a suit and substitutes the cannabis with a bottle of Coca-Cola, capturing his body with a substance of capitalism (this is another nod to the experimental film *La formula secreta*, where one of the scenes shows a body intravenously being fed Coca-Cola). Finally, the film cuts to the last sequence, a series of kaleidoscopic images of the urban landscape that index the Coca-Cola as a hallucinatory substance, edited with a sped-up soundbite of "The End" that fades into Armando Manzanero as the camera focuses on the young man, now sitting inside the car suited up and heading to work while he adjusts the radio — a body captured by state and market, the threat of violence giving way to the threat of commodity fetishism and capitalist consumption in a world of labor and nation. The oedipal liberation that Jim Morrison seems to imbue in the lyrics of his hit song are left aside to refocus on the affective reterritorialization that the song provides as rock is being commodified as popular music, mechanically assembled now as a deterritorializing political force that could challenge subjectification, but not survive violent repression nor the onslaught of market forces.

An initial lament of the violence experienced by youth across the nation (student repressions were active in Monterrey, Sonora, Guadalajara, Puebla, and other locations), the short film understands youth outside the limited body of the (male) student and is thus embedded with a series of questions and insights that go beyond its short seven minutes. First, the film invites the viewer (and particularly the viewers of the moment) to consider what it is the end of precisely. Initially, this might have been simply the end of the dream of counterculture and youthful rebellion. And yet, as the short film recirculated in screenings and festivals in later years, ultimately appearing on YouTube and in the collected DVD of *Un toke de roc* released by UNAM in 2006, the answer to that question is expanded alongside later, more female-centric films. It signals not only the capturing power of the state and market in eliminating and capturing the bodies of the (male) rebel youth, but, most importantly, the limits of the specific countercultural assemblage of the student as a strategy for remembering.

In its first years of circulation, *El fin* sparks a critical reflection on the power of institutions (state, market, and revolutionary) to capture youth and to reinsert them into capitalist society precisely with commodities that induce some form of alternative mental-emotional state (pop music, new automobiles, Coca-Cola, sharp suits, the experience of driving through the metropolis).

The carefully constructed short film also lays the groundwork for the feminist utopian nationalism that García Michel will construct in his later films. The escapist young couple chased down by the *charro* in the forest index the impossibility of building another society without facing the nationalist forces around them; the figure on horseback smokes a cigar and sports the eponymous mustache of *macho* virility as he chases the couple down. The later murder and capture of the other young men seem to point also at the extreme vulnerability of the (male) student activists and youth, hinting already at the end of a way of ordering social transformation around male bodies. In later years, this critique of nationalism will be rewoven in the collaboration between García Michel and Botellita de Jerez with their *guacarrock* aesthetics, which will play a key role in *Un Toke de Roc*, mutating this static figure of a male *charro* into a female *charrocker*, an embodied assemblage of popular, national, and countercultural aesthetics that refuses to conform to the injunctives of the *mestizo* nation. In *El fin*, this powerful nationalist figure unfolds into specific embodiments that populate the nation as they silence and capture youth: the mother wearing a white dress and holding a baby bottle, symbolizing the purity incarnate in the suffering Mexican mother and the infantilization of youth as nonadults in spite of their immediate politicization and activism; a soldier coming out from behind the trees with a rifle in his arms, the military force of the state built upon the capturing of youth themselves, especially rural youth recruited into military forces; a priest with a long frock and collar swiftly running toward the camera, facing society head on; and a suited man, his clothes instantly marking him as a representative of "The Man." These figures appear first in an isolated manner and quickly unite to run down the hill together, signaling the coming together of these forces as they are called forth by the *charro*. In this way, the film doesn't just critique an ideological construction (in line with critical literature such as that of Juan Rulfo or Carlos Fuentes) or a familial structure (in line with the *Onda* writers), but rather focuses on unfolding a series of specific social institutions with specific embodiments that perform this subjectification: the family, religion, the militarized state, and the capitalist market. The prescience and permanence of these embodiments is not lost on me as I write these pages. Ultimately, *El fin* is making a self-critique of the escapism associated with youth culture *and* of the male-centric understanding of counterculture that does not see the bodies of women as participants in these social struggles and thus remains pretty to these subjectifying forces.

The critique of insidious patriarchy in *El fin* separates this particular film from others in its context, the awareness of how social structures are being symbolically reproduced within counterculture itself something that will guide

García Michel's oeuvre during the rest of his career. By focusing on how the young (male) *jipitecas* were (and are) being captured by different agents of state, religion, market, and military, the film underscores how what is ending could be the particular dream of a specifically masculine revolution. While the rest of the *superocheros* went on in the decade to produce larger format films (if they continued to do film), García Michel would focus on curating and nurturing spaces of exhibition as spaces of socialization, free and accessible to youth across the urban centers where festivals popped up; he thus extended a commitment of Fourth Cinema to youth culture onto a material level beyond that of visual representations (Lerner and González 85). While the forces of capital and state are difficult to escape, García Michel's film and film activism prove another understanding of youth and youth culture that is produced as much by the media industries as by the urban realities of class, education, ethnicity, and so forth. To expand on what anthropologist Roger Bartra underscores as the "political necessity of the first order" contained in the definition and defense of Mexican "national" characters, the interventions of youth culture through the lens of García Michel underscore the ethical-political potential of counterculture to disrupt state nationalism by first signaling its negative social and individual effects, and then redefining these nationalist icons through playful yet serious parody. Among the figures that García Michel will come back to resignify is the mother, from the anguished and suffering figure of *El fin* transformed into figures and actions of caretaking, nurturing, and home-building that will define later characters in his oeuvre as well as his actions of care within film exhibition spaces.

This learning from and reconfiguration of female countercultural bodies leads to the next film where a woman appears as a complex political, social, *and* sexual subject. Still participating in the *superochero* movement before they moved into larger formats or dropped the camera, García Michel released *Ah, verdá . . . .?/You thought so . . . .?* in 1974 in the III Concurso Luis Buñuel held in Zacatecas. The twenty-minute short film opens with an intertitle of a quote by countercultural hero Abbie Hoffman regarding theft and corruption, cutting to a young anarchist couple, once again the couple at the center of the founding of another society. This time, however, the couple don't escape to a remote space; rather, they fabricate home bombs they plant in national monuments and institutions throughout the city, including the offices of a major newspaper (*El Heraldo de México*, known mouthpiece of the authoritarian government), the Monumento a la Revolución, and the Palacio de Hierro. In other words, they fight back against propaganda, institutional revolution, and commodity capitalism. They continue cavorting through the city, consuming immanent popular nationalism in the form of tortas and other street foods and culminating their adventures in a sexual tryst they hold inside a plush-decorated VW bus, perhaps a reference to the aesthetics of *Barbarella* (dir. Roger Vadim, 1968) with the all-fur interior. They end up being persecuted by undercover agents, and the young man is murdered on the street; the repressive forces of the state kidnapping and murdering urban and rural guerrillas is visually represented in a moment when the government was unofficially waging a dirty war against them all over the country. Now left alone, the young woman finds refuge in the pool backyard of a rich young man who begins to sexually harass her, and the film takes a sudden feminist twist when she rejects these advances by embodying a sexual and social autonomy powerful enough to defend itself in the face of class oppression. The film ends with the young woman fabricating lysergic acid in a makeshift lab in a monastery, sowing *ololiuhqui* (morning glory seeds used by *chinanteco* and other peoples as powerful entheogenic substances) and tripping out a group of monks who then become her new society. Together, they leave their enclosed monastery, dancing across the streets to pour the LSD into the city's water reservoir tanks while the Beatles sing "Good Morning," effectively drugging Mexico City society as the camera skews and the chaotic electronic music indexes their *shared* and *communal* hallucinogenic state. A whimsical, playful, and fantastical film, *Ah, verdá . . . ?* demonstrates a commitment to radical politics in the face of violent repression and social absorption that seek to redefine militancy outside the paradigms of Third Cinema, particularly by refocusing the attention on the representations of female agency and action within counterculture and revolution.[8] In this way, the cinematic subject generated on-screen challenges the limits of heteronormative nationalism *and* revolution and provides the viewers with an affective engagement that in turn allows for the reimagination of both alternative cinema and revolutionary subjects off-screen.

I underline this firmly gendered critique of counterculture and revolution because it challenges the paradigms of the time. *Ah, verdá . . . ?* quickly becomes a film of female protagonist heroism, marking a difference with other youth films such as José Agustín's more mainstream *5 de chocolate y 1 de fresa* (dir. Carlos Velo, 1968). For García Michel, female *jipitecas* and guerilla fighters are not just sexual partners or even mischievous counterparts — they are citizens able to enact their own lines of flight and with the power to push back against heteronormativity in any guise it presents. In a central scene of the short film after the male youth is assassinated on the streets, the protagonist mourns and buries him and is then seduced (or perhaps she seduces in order to gain some protection, since the sequence is not shown) by a middle-upper class young man with a pool in his house. In a central sequence where the couple hang out by the pool, he begins to sexually advance her and she represents her nonconsent through very explicit body language (due to the technical limitations of the sound format and recording) while plotting an act of resistance; softly, she reaches to grab a nutcracker they had been using to eat walnuts by the pool and uses it against the man, specifically his genitals. In a fabulous montage, the camera suddenly zooms in on a pair of walnuts being broken apart and cuts to his grimace of pain, flashing then to her smiling as she eats the cracked nuts. The joys of fighting patriarchy. Political philosopher Slavoj Žižek defines freedom as "not a blissfully neutral state of harmony and balance, but the violent act which disturbs this balance" (186), and the violent act of castration encapsulates this freedom the protagonist is constructing: freedom from a classist and heteronormative *mestizo* order that constructs counterculture as an object to be consumed, in this case a sexually liberated woman to be taken at will. During the sequence, the couple is listening to rock music and enacting an apparent sexual "liberation," and the camera has been careful up to this moment in previous sequences to construct female pleasure as autonomous from male desire; that is, female pleasure as existing alongside the more typically represented male pleasure taking up space and traversing the territory at will. What is more, in recognizing her sexual power *but* not placing it at center stage (as the erotic films of the same super 8mm movement tended to, objectifying female bodies through a blatant and uncritical male gaze), the film constructs a nonreproductive countercultural utopia where fertility in the female body is embraced as an integral part of femininity (she plants seeds, literally) while rejected as the *only* model for womanhood (in the style of the *mestiza* mother). Together with the later acts of fabricating lysergic acid and consuming it with the monks, these moments become instances of epithumogenesis in their biochemical modification of the body itself; it is not the symbol of the acts (powerful already) as much as the *effects* of these acts on the bodies themselves, and especially the female countercultural bodies populating the screen and the nation.

For the urban youth García Michel represents here, political action is exhausted in the guerrilla tactics, from bombs to hallucinogenic drugs. Instead, political action depends on modes and topics of representation. When contextualized in the greater milieu of *sexycomedias* and other sexploitation genres that emerged in these years, the representation of female sexuality is doubly striking. Here we begin to see these countercultural heroines who resist the physical and psychic forces of patriarchy. This radically liberated body emerges as a "complex and multilayered embodied subject who has taken her distance from the institution of femininity" (Braidotti, *Metamorphoses* 12). She literally lays the groundwork for another society by liberating monks who storm society in a silly misadventure, and ultimately by planting the seeds of another possible future to be imagined and created. The utopian nation emerges from the labor of these female figures whose sexuality represented on-screen is not for the visual pleasure of the (male) viewer, distanced even from the global sexual liberation movements referenced visually in the previous scene where the guerrilla couple have sex in the plush, carpeted interior of the VW van, a nod to *Barbarella* where Jane Fonda became the sex symbol of her generation. In these playful representations, other possibilities of nation and society emerge, and this is what I found most powerful about these super 8mm media. Film critic Anna Powell speaks of altered states in film to activate imagination as a political tool, emphasizing how "the automatism of cinema deterritorializes perception. Anomalous states of consciousness can be celebrated [for] their impact on the audience who partakes of their affective contagion" (22). In this way, the sound-images of this film represent and celebrate both sexually empowered and psychically liberated countercultural embodiments without fetishizing and thus depoliticizing them; what matters is not that the protagonist is a woman who engages in sex and drugs, but that these acts are part of a wider political and countercultural community she is a part of.[9] The whimsical and humorous tone of the film indicates this possibility of counterculture not as an allegory of the nation but as an exercise in imagination of what can be. Particularly considering how for decades these films circulated in group projection spaces where bodies literally came together to watch them, this affective potential in the films is increased as this imagination and humor speaks to bodies seeking transformation. Thus, female sexuality and pleasure is made visible without becoming a tool of objectification and commodification; the sexual existence of the guerilla fighter is re-cognized, rethought in a variety of relations and positions, only to be dissolved into the forces that are signifying it, and with which she refuses to engage or directly crushes. Her revolutionary and countercultural subjectivity embodies processes of becoming that ultimately will lead to the formation of alternative communities standing for the countercultural nations that *might* be created during the Echeverría period of the 1970s.

During the rest of the decade, super 8mm was slowly put down by filmmakers as they found employment in the public or private media industries. Super 8mm became either a medium for artistic experimentation with the likes of the No Grupo collective and Silvia Gruner, or a pedagogical tool used in school projects in the CUEC and Centro de Capacitación Cinematográfica, with Luis Lupone as one of its main proponents in his classes. After traveling to Cuba in the late 1970s, Sergio García Michel focused on the promotion of super 8mm film culture in Mexico City by founding the Foro Tlalpan for production, distribution, and screening. In 1982, he released his first feature-length documentary, *Una larga experiencia*, which follows the trajectory of the rock band *El Tri*. From 1985 to 1989, he filmed and produced *Un toke de roc/A toke of roc*, a pun on the drag of a cannabis cigarette known as toke (in Mexican Spanish and in English), as well as *tocada/toquín*, the word for the impromptu or underground rock concert. It is here that the feminist utopian nationalism that García Michel had been constructing coalesces into a feature-length rock opera musicalized with the rock bands of the moment, many of them led by female musicians. In the context of the hypersexualized film industry of the late 1970s and 1990s that was the *fichera* and *sexycomedia* genres, *Un toke de roc* reworks nationalism, the rock scene of the 1980s, and countercultural politics on the ground through the affective forces of music and experimental film images, doubly resisting the commodifying aesthetics of the entertainment industry *and* the material forms and circuits that promote uncritical mass consumption.[10] Disillusioned with the transformation of drugs — and especially cannabis — into commodities of the (illegal) market, *Un toke de roc* focuses on female protagonists who engage the state and its heteronormative structuring of capitalist society through embodied and sober acts of resistance.[11] I argue that the film's engagement with nationalist (both state-sponsored and more popular) imagery through quotidian acts of urban consumption and its reassemblage of the eponymous imagery of Indigenous past (*mestizo* identity), urban statues (Mexican Revolution aesthetics), and collective *vecindario* living (Golden Age film references) become a blueprint for alternative grounded interpersonal relations; an erotic of politics that emerges from communal support and the centralization of female experiences in the urban space.

The film is a rock opera in the most classic style with a prologue and three acts, musicalized with a variety of recorded and live performances of Mexican rock bands of the moment. Rock music itself is experiencing a comeback after a decade of repression with the appearance of figures like Cecilia Toussaint, Rockdrigo González, and the *guacarrock* aesthetic of Botellita de Jerez. Musicologist Guadalupe Caro Cocotle emphasizes how the musical milieu of Botellita, which appears in several concerts, *tokines*, and communes in the film, is better understood — even with the problematic gender politics of the group — as an audiotopia, an imagined sonorous space that situates listeners in a specific time and space assembled from the pieces of the nationalist past, a capitalist present, and a utopic imagined future (153).[12] The film follows a group of young women who flee their capturing environment of family and other institutions (literally boarding schools) to form a commune with another young woman who dresses up as a nun while graffitiing the city's walls. They live briefly in an idyllic and countercultural utopia, stealing food here and there to survive and supporting street musicians. Three of them are then captured by plainclothes policemen and tortured while the last escapes to an urban rock commune that is also raided by cops. She manages to flee with the help of a superheroine who had previously appeared briefly, a masked and caped crusader whose look is coded as a gendered representation of the *guacarrock* aesthetic, the subversion of the nationalist mythos. This superheroine comes out in key moments as the savior of both male and female rebels and transforms the global aesthetic image of the superhero (tied to mass consumption and countercultural spheres through the comic form) into a female citizen powerful enough to withstand and fight back against state violence, founding a series of alternative utopias. The ending sequences of the film serve as a critical documentary of the paradigm-shifting events that shaped the 1980s: the earthquakes of 1985, the World Cup of 1968, and the ensuing protests that sparked the formation of the civil society networks that led to the contested elections of 1988 and the later reconfiguration of the political spheres in the 1990s. The film also carries out a scathing critique of the sexualization strategies that underpin the advertising industry and generate nationalist epithumogenetic processes; the representation of women and other bodies as solely sexual objects to be consumed is underlined over and over in the film. In contrast, the women protagonists of the film are assembled and represented as sociopolitical positions that gather their meaning by the relations between their bodies and the social, economic, and political institutions that surround them, distancing themselves from those of the state and allying themselves with the nascent countercultural institutions of communes and rock bands.

Whereas the utopic nationalisms of the 1970s were ephemeral imaginaries that dissipated in the moment of their screening — brief respites from waves of violence — in *Un toke de roc* García Michel presents the viewer with utopias grounded in the rock bands of the moments that are beginning to be heard in the city itself, resignifying its most iconic spaces of metro stations, public plazas, apartment buildings, 1985 earthquake spaces of solidarity, and more. The prologue of the film sets up the parameters of the affective engagement it will demand from viewers, opening onto a scene of female sacrifice in a low-budget "Aztec" setting, with her heart being cut out only to fade in montage onto the chopping board of a contemporary *taqueria*, where it will become the main ingredient of an order of tacos, the heart of the *mestizo* mythology now transformed into the meat of the everyday tacos. The soundtrack of Silvestre Revueltas continues to ring as a well-dressed woman consumes the tacos, thus anchoring this *mélange* of *mestizo* nationalism in music and visual references. This prologue thus foregrounds the processes of subjectification that happen around female bodies, particularly as they enter a workforce and literally consume the ideologies of nationalism and femininity embodied in her dress and demeanor. To counter these processes, García Michel seeks to generate another visual and musical language that will be constructed in the film, a language such as the one Fréderic Lordon calls for when critiquing neoliberal epithumogenesis, a language that can remobilize affects grounded in individual bodies as social constructs and not only rename things but, first and foremost, break down the normative orders of knowledge in doing so (64). This strong allegorical contextualization in the first minutes positions the film in relation to institutions and discourses of gender, working to align the film and its message closer with what Mexican philosopher Benjamin Arditi describes as the becoming-minoritarian that characterized "marginal" urban societies, specifically in Mexico City (20). As the protagonists disassemble themselves from their various institutions of origin, they generate processes of becoming that push back against commodification and fetishization of countercultural bodies, acts, and aesthetics.

The first act opens with a denunciation of the uncritical consumption of state nationalism mediated by capitalist economic structures, as a young male rebel steals the purse from the taco-eating woman and is pursued through the streets of downtown Mexico City by clumsy policemen. He ends up being rescued by a superheroine dressed in a red cape, eye mask, roller skates, and a shirt stamped with a cannabis leaf in the style of superhero logos. She fuses the *charro* pants with the rest of the superhero aesthetic to embody the city itself, a contradiction of modernity and tradition; this fusion will be repeated in later scenes where she poses in the style of the Diana Cazadora statue, which makes an appearance in other films such as *La diana cazadora* (dir. Tito Davison, 1956) or the more famous *Los caifanes* (dir. Juan Ibáñez, 1967). By referencing this rich visual vocabulary, the superheroine will become one more member of the collective of women who together subvert the nationalist opening of female sacrifice to establish another nation, another utopia through continuous acts of redemption. Thus, the isolated male individuals of the previous films who are easily captured and punished by the state give way to this novel idea of a communal and popular citizenship coalescing around women redeeming themselves and those who engage with their alternative societies.

Un toke de roc continues to focus on the institutions of family and school as loci of oppression and ideological subjectification through the isolation/alienation of the female body; one girl experiences typical middle-class familial conflict (tired and overworked father, stay-at-home mother, angsty teenagers) while two others are caught in a music school with a music professor who acts more like a sexual predator than a purveyor of knowledge. This overt sexualization is further condemned in the advertising industry's attempt to generate complacent consumer subjects; one sequence focuses the camera on billboards covering the urban landscape of hypersexual images of scantily clad women selling beauty and lingerie, showcasing the power of the advertising industry over the consciousnesseses of the city. This advertising fantasy is broken when the editing reveals a sexual female body who enacts her own processes of countercultural subjectification and transformation; the billboard fade transitions to a woman trying on clothes in the *Palacio de Hierro* fancy department store, proceeding to cover her body with expensive fashion and then draping a nun's outfit over it all, thus not only fighting the sexualization of her body but also ingeniously mobilizing religious morality to steal the clothes right from under the clerk's nose. She leaves the store to graffiti several subversive messages across the city as a mischievous rock version of the classic Pink Panther theme plays: "el rock ha muerto, viva el roc," "cuidado con la neurosis en el poder," and "the dream is over." After rescuing the fleeing girls from their dangerous encounters with male citizens who begin to follow them through the city, the nun introduces them to the disruptive act of vandalism as a violent act of freedom literally engraved onto the urban landscape itself.

The second act of the film shows the community these four women are forming as they push back on being absorbed into the gender, sexual, and social roles preestablished for them. This community is brief and utopic, and yet powerful, since "la comunidad no es una categoría unitaria y las diversas identidades colectivas no son entidades cerradas y autárquicas" (Arditi, *La política* 104). The four women survive by stealing fruit from mercados and collaborating with street rock performers as lookouts and coin-gatherers; they move in an informal economy that sustains their survival and even thrive, albeit momentarily; that is, until agents of the state kidnap the rock musicians and track the women down to their makeshift home only to destroy it. The women regather and construct a second commune, brief images of Tinkerbell from Disney's version of *Peter Pan* edited quickly onto the film to showcase the magical power of their home-building; this second home becomes an act of redemption that disrupts the exercise of sovereign totalitarian control that seems to cover all of Mexican society, particularly in the face of repression that doesn't seem to end. By refusing to submit to the plainclothes policemen, the gang of women redeem themselves and each other, generating stronger than ever communitarian bonds with each other and with other countercultural communes in the urban underground. Kenneth Reinhard speaks of redemption as a sort of temporal bomb, "which historical materialists can throw in the teleological historicism . . . redemption is not the final cause of history, but the interruption of the false totality of historical causality and contextualization by acts of critical creation and constellation" (20). In this way, as the four women redeem themselves multiple times, they critically assemble communes and other urban spaces that for a moment exist outside the teleological narratives of nation and even gender. Their critical creation comes from a countercultural (re)construction of home and domestic space, bringing together elements from their pasts and assembling with their presents on the street and in metro stations.

The quotidian acts of rescue, nurture, and support become the embodiment of the ethics of love that counterculture promotes, and the strong social bonds that unite these women become the visual representations of the immanence of redemption in the urban space. In the context of the 1980s, after the devastating state violence of 1968 and with the even more devastating earthquakes, this redemption is not to be taken lightly, as it provides a political structure to regenerate social bonds through affect. In the film, redemption will reappear in the later communes, the images of people helping each other out in the rubble of the 1985 earthquake, and the documentary footage of the various political marches in 1986. Taken together, these sound-images generate an affective experience that speaks much beyond the four women protagonists — a series of urban affects that are tied to the material existence of the city and that connect individual viewers to a series of shared historical events that shape collectivity. Thus, community is embodied in the four women and yet not contained in them, as an-other nation is being constructed alongside them with the other members of the communes, the citizens they encounter and engage with in their adventures, and the audiences themselves. The four women provide access; they become bridges that literally leave their middle-class and patriarchal spaces to unite with this other city right under the surface, a city of solidarity, radical family structures, and creativity. For the viewer, and particularly for the viewer of the time, this redemption is crystalized in the actions of these four women and is showcased in such a way that is easy to imitate, a micropolitics that can be taken up and spread out without the need for a dogma or an institution to obey. The religious symbolism of the hippie woman cum nun points toward this neighborly love and redemption, perhaps a wink to García Michel's previous films with monks and other religious figures now serving countercultural social formations instead of Catholic institutions. Or perhaps it is a wink to Enrique Marroquín, the counterculture's own priest, active in the scene in the later 1960s and 1970s writing about and with the youth.

These moments of redemption emerge in the face of the extreme violence unleashed by the state and its authoritarian forces. The second act ends with the capture of three women in a raid carried out by plainclothes policemen, with the last and fourth one just barely escaping. The third act opens with brief images and sequences of these tortured women, the camera focusing on their surroundings, their torturers, and the implements used instead of on their bodies and faces; in this García Michel is already critical of the ethics of representation when violence is what is being represented and the thin line between representations and objectification, something he had already demonstrated in the sexual scenes of the earlier short films. These opening sequences establish once again a visual memory of the Dirty War of the 1970s and 1980s and ground the physical effects of this violence. The psychological effects of this state violence on the rest of countercultural and Mexican societies are embodied in the fourth woman, free to wander the streets aimlessly and experience the 1985 earthquake and social devastation. Literally walking among the rubble of society, she writes on a wall, "el sueño ha terminado/the dream is over," the graffiti a reference to a Beatles lyric and a statement on the quake, and ultimately a reading of the symbolic and structural violence that is overpowering youth countercultural groups and literally ending dreams. Navigating this violence pushes the young woman to attempt suicide several times as her political, gendered, and youth subjectivity is under symbolic and physical persecution. The last attempt involves jumping from an abandoned building, and she is surprisingly rescued once again by the masked superheroine, who catches her and takes her to another underground rock commune where she regains hope and health. Although this thriving commune with children and babies is also attacked by the *perjudiciales* (a pun on the judicial, as the extremely corrupt federal police officers were named, and the word *perjudiciar*, to injure or hurt), now it is guarded by the superheroine. The policemen are easily defeated by her as she wields a bow and arrow, overpowering and following them to rescue the three captured women and reunite them with the countercultural refugees, now gathering in an underground rock concert. The film ends with the four women walking down a street, strolling against traffic as the cars and trucks swerve around them: an allegorical image of rebellion, survival, community, love, and imagination. By underscoring the agency of the four women walking hand in hand, García Michel resists the popular imagery of the metro or other phenomenon of urbanization as symbols of mass subjectivity; rather, the individual yet communal and interrelated existence of these women, including the superheroine and the communes they become a part of, are the way to understand mass culture in the processes of extreme urbanization that plagued the second half of the century and that have shaped current (countercultural) Mexican society today.

Throughout the film, the superheroine appears at key moments to embody the aesthetic and political ethos of counterculture as it evolved in these decades. She is a gendered embodiment of the *guacarrock* aesthetic, literally territorializing countercultural onto a body defined not only by its clothing and gender, but especially by her actions as she rescues, supports, protects, and dances with the countercultural rockers, always on her roller skates. Her eclectic fashion — a fusion of a cannabis-printed T-shirt, *charro* pants, roller skates, a short cape, and an eye mask in the style of the Lonesome Ranger — brings together nationalist and comic book aesthetics, the roller skates indexing a playfulness and an alternative transportation mode in the increasing urban cityscape. Moreover, she poses her body in the shape of the *Diana Cazadora* statue several times during the film, especially when using her bow and arrow. This reference, already a staple in Mexican filmic imaginary, transforms her into an embodiment of the city itself; she signals a potentiality that is activated when the youth and other countercultural rebels need her support, and yet she exists outside these specific spaces, rolling across the whole city. With the graffiti the women (and particularly the nun) write on the city's walls, these aesthetic choices construct an understanding of counterculture that exists outside the individual bodies that make it up. Thus, García Michel is presenting an allegory that speaks against a personalized understanding of rock and counterculture as a consumer-based ideology, perhaps speaking to and against films such as *De veras me atrapaste/ You really got me* (dir. Gerardo Pardo, 1985) where rock appears as a simple escapist youth fantasy, literally a ghost from the forgotten past. *Un toke de roc* rather seeks to anchor counterculture in female bodies without making them individualized and depoliticized consumers of rock, but rather parts of a greater web of counterculture that exists across the whole urban space. Together, they weave countercultural spaces wherever they move, and with the support of the superheroine, they can survive the violence of the state and walk into a different future, even if it's against traffic.

Taken together, García Michel's films intervene the iconography and soundscape of *mestizo* and state-sponsored nationalism to generate mutations in processes of becoming — utopian nationalism infused by countercultural aesthetics and politics embodied in liberated women living their sexuality. In the words of Rosi Braidotti, these super 8mm representations of mutated becomings, changes, and transformations can be viewed as "alternative representations and social locations for the kind of hybrid mix we are in the process of becoming . . . materialistic mappings of situated, embedded and embodied, positions" (*Metamorphoses* 2). In line with the cinematic style of Third Cinema in other Latin American countries, García Michel and other super 8mm directors understood the radical potentiality of super 8mm — a potentiality echoed in the digital technologies of today as they are being redefined by youth culture across the globe — as one that activates cinema as an open medium where the political message rests less on the representational level and more on the awakening/strengthening/developing together another mode of viewing level. In their manifesto, Fourth Cinema is "brief, concise and impacting; something like a *poster* or — with due allowance — it must have the force of an *advertisement*" (171). Thus, rather than creating alternative narratives of nation, already a process of subjectification within a specific cultural modality and political structure, Mexican super 8mm film and particularly García Michel and his peers sought to disrupt these nationalistic processes and leave them open.

The appropriation of the visual and aural culture of *mestizo* nationalism thus becomes a subversion by fusing it with rock and the other emerging urban cultures. In his films, García Michel increasingly mobilizes Mexican rock as the soundtrack, perhaps a simple reflection of the technical advancements in recording technology that allowed it, and nevertheless representational strategies that weave the voices of the (increasingly female) youthful counterculture into the cityscape itself. Subjected to the additional oppressive structures of patriarchy, these female protagonists lead the way toward change and revolution as they reject the stratification and static subjectification processes the nationalist state is enforcing through armed violence and that the market is promoting through uncritical consumption. By reactivating the revolutionary potential embedded in the symbolism assemblage of postrevolutionary *mestizo* nationalism, *Un toke de roc* and the previous short films empower and encourage countercultural youth to resignify their shared historical past, to reimagine Mexican society outside the gender norms of patriarchy and the economic normativities of consumer capitalism.

Furthermore, and perhaps what is most important to remember given the multiplicity of technologies increasingly available and being used by countercultural and dissident producers today, super 8mm forced these filmmakers and especially García Michel to construct networks of communities across the metropolis and the national territory. These communities came together in screenings and specific spaces to consume and celebrate these films and themselves, enacting instances of redemption, recognition of their others, and national reassembly into legitimate political subjectivities in the face of extreme violence. These creative networks managed, albeit momentarily, to break outside the centralization of culture so prevalent in Mexican arts and film especially, anticipating the video production networks of the 1990s and the virtual spaces emerging today. As Jesse Lerner and Álvaro Vázquez Mantecón have signaled, this super 8mm production is not only of historical value but especially cultural and filmic value, as their visual, ideological, and material explorations set the basis for later cinematic, video, musical, and artistic production of the century. And at the center of these explorations is a critical awareness of the ways in which patriarchy underpins nationalism and the need to resist it first and foremost to construct countercultural utopias.

Palinuro of México:
A Mexican Trip Treatment for the World

Parallel to the violent events of the 1960s, the Mexican literary sphere experienced a generational polarization that would shape literature for decades to come. It began with the explosive assessment that critic Margo Glantz would publish in 1971 under the title *Onda y escritura: jóvenes de 20 a 33*, where she categorized youth literature under these two grand poles of a narrow *"Onda"* likened with rebellious juvenile attitudes and described as egocentric and interested only in sex, drugs, and rock 'n' roll, and a more expansive and valuable "Escritura" category defined by an impetus to write literature *from* literature itself, tensioning language and seeking new forms of expression inspired in theory by the avant-garde French and English traditions.[13] This binary categorization has been questioned since then, and even the critic herself has rescinded and nuanced her comments, and yet the effects of these categorizations have never been fully erased or overcome; the *Onda* writers continue to be lumped together even though they did not write together as an aesthetic project, and the even less coalesced group of "Escritura" writers such as Fernando del Paso, Salvador Elizondo, Elena Garro, Juan García Ponce, or Julieta Campos continue to be read as a collective or a literary generation. The fundamental problem I want to underline by opening this section with this reflection is that the aesthetically complex and erudite works of these writers have been taken as the pinnacle of literary creation, thus erasing modes of reading of the other more experimental youth writers such as Margarita Dalton and categorizing them rather as simply juvenile attempts at literature. The "Escritura" writers continue to be read through a critical lens that focuses on their aesthetic components, thus silencing the political components of their texts as they engage their national, regional, and global contexts, as youth writers writing to and from youth culture. In what follows, I will read one of these writers as political writers speaking with youth through the lens of contemporary psychedelic studies.

Published first in Spain in 1977 and written between 1968 and 1974, Fernando del Paso's second novel, *Palinuro de México*, appears as a literary proposal to generate novel and different political subjectivities in contemporary Mexico, anchored in the various and diverse bodies of youth. The novel draws from English satirical tradition (Lawrence Sterne, Jonathan Swift) to narrate the adventures of Palinuro, a student of medicine, and his girlfriend and cousin, Estefanía, as they live in downtown Mexico City during the summer of 1968. Through references and reinterpretation of classic characters and canonical literary styles of Western culture (from Palinurus and Charon to James Joyce and *commedia dell'arte*) as well as a continuous intertextual dialogue with authors across the Atlantic and Mexican national history, the novel is an extension of countercultural literature emerging onto the world literature stage. Using aesthetics as a way to bypass cultural censorship (the novel was initially published in Spain and was only republished in Mexico after garnering success), *Palinuro de México* mobilizes a strategic performance (in the sense of posing and performing) of a series of "canonical discursive formation in ways that parody their cultural authority and that ultimately rely on elements of the archive preserved on the fringes and interstices of Western culture" (Sánchez-Prado, "Dying Mirrors" 146). As these references are woven into the text, the two main characters unfold onto various subjectivie personalities; during the chapters, they consume LSD and cannabis in various key narrative moments. Their mental, geographic, and political explorations while coexisting with these substances become central moments in the reimagination of themselves and their nation, and by extension their greater Western and global cultural developments. For this reason, I propose a reading of the novel that centralizes the psychedelic experience and will read these through the lens of contemporary psychedelic therapy.

Today, psychedelic-assisted therapy (PAP) typically consists of three specific moments. First, a series of sessions where client and therapist meet, learn about the client's past, and establish trust; this moment involved no psychedelics. Second, a session that typically lasts between four and eight hours, during which the client has consumed a high dose of a psychedelic; this takes places in a safe and controlled environment (usually a hospital room furnished into a relaxing lounge area) using eyeshades to block out visual stimuli and headphones with a carefully curated playlist intended to complement and heighten the arc of the psychedelic experience. Third, typically a day or several days afterward, client and therapist meet for a series of integration sessions where they "make sense" of the experiences; research has emphasized this as *the* key essential component of PAP, as it allows for the neurological changes to be incorporated through psychological, philosophical, emotional, and social understandings of an extremely embodied experience. Contemporary therapy models vary to a degree, and institutional practitioners are still developing models in conversation with more underground therapists who have been using psychedelics for decades, but the basic structure presented here remains unquestioned as a solid approach for therapeutic uses.

The novel is divided into twenty-five chapters, with roughly half of them focused on the adventures of Palinuro and Estefanía in their tiny apartment on the Plaza de Santo Domingo, the central plaza closest to UNAM's School of Medicine, and the other half focused on the adventures of Palinuro with his two closest friends, Fabricio and Molkas, who may be secondary characters, unfoldings of his own personality, or "simply" a series of repeating hallucinations along with the rest of the colorful characters they encounter together. In their tiny apartment, Palinuro and Estefanía drop acid, arrange and rearrange their room, explore tantric and other forms of sexual expressions, work as an advertising agent (Palinuro) and a nurse (Estefanía), write a novel together, paint (on canvas, their bodies, and their room), and in general embark on a series of linguistic and psychedelic "trips" where the limits between wordplay, reality, imagination, and hallucination blur constantly. It's important to underline that while the mention of psychedelics such as LSD or cannabis is extremely brief (twice in passing in the whole 700-plus pages), the experiences narrated unfold like a series of psychedelic sessions, and as such I will treat them accordingly. With his friends, Palinuro wanders the city streets and specifically the areas associated with medical studies; this marks not simply a biographical fact of del Paso's brief attempt to study medicine, but it also signals the direct engagement of the novel with the science and institutions of medicine as biopolitical machineries of categorization, diagnoses, medicalization, pathologization, and ultimately control over (human) bodies. Their wanderings take them to the various landmarks of medical history in the country from the colonial period and the institutions of the Holy Inquisition, as well as the early medical schools of New Spain, the landmarks of national history with statues and plaques and cemeteries, and the landmarks of student activism during that decade. All these wanderings are narrated out in a parodic style that constantly blurs the line between their existence as autonomous individuals or schizophrenic personalities. This parodic undertone also unfolds into a variety of specific literary styles (structurally similar to James Joyce's experiments in *Ulysses*), serving also to comment on a specific youth phenomenon of the decade: the consumption of LSD; creative employment in the advertising, media, and similar industries; historical narrative of the revolution particularly as textualized in nationalist ideology, and *commedia dell'arte* to represent the violent and senseless murders of students in street manifestations and gatherings. The novel also includes several chapters where the family history of Palinuro and Estefanía is explored in detail, relating the lives of their uncles, parents, grandparents, great-grandparents, and, most of all, their cousin Walter. This family history places the protagonists firmly within the folds of a national history of revolution, independence, and imperial colony, as well as firmly within a greater global context with narratives of migrations and participation in the World Wars.

Following the recent developments of psychotherapy-assisted psychedelics (PAP), I propose a reading of *Palinuro de México* as a countercultural reenactment of a series of psychedelic sessions set up under a therapeutic framework, a trip treatment focused on the tensions between nation-world that emerge in a global capitalist system as Mexico entered into the neoliberal age, as well as the inner workings of capitalist subjectivation increasingly imposed on global subjects to become compliant consumers. The novel is enriched by Del Paso's experiences in Mexico City, Iowa City (participating in the acclaimed Iowa Writer's Workshop), and then London; it is informed by a real and material cosmopolitanism anchored in youthful bodies that reenact countercultural performances rooted in the contemporary urban experiences of postwar industrial and technological development. Considering its time of publication in the mid-1970s, *Palinuro* also speaks once more to the countercultural potential of world transformation through personal revolution while avoiding alienation and individualism; as in *Larga sinfonía en D*, here the focus of political action is circumscribed to youth and their bodies first and foremost, provoking social change while avoiding the establishment of new authoritarian regimes as well as inviting state repression.[14] Thus, I argue that *Palinuro de México* is crossed through with a series of countercultural axis, among them the emphasis of individual over institutional revolution, centering the body as the first territory for social, national, cultural, and psychic liberation and change. While the 1960s had seen language as the promise of change with an infusion of vocabulary and syntaxis from the margins, by the 1970s with the power of capitalist commodification in full display, language appears in *Palinuro* as a tool of biopolitical and social control, demanding from the readers a revolutionary attitude that leaves no word unturned. In this line, I argue also that the presence of LSD and other substances, rather than speak of generational experiences, serve as catalysts for resistance and revolution in their biochemical changes, and most importantly are to be read under the therapeutic guidelines established in the 1950s and continued in current psychedelic therapy. Ultimately, I argue that this youthful couple become representative of a global generation and assemble a series of bodies that far surpass their nationalist subjectivities, bodies that resist the depoliticized commodification of counterculture by reenacting the same strategies (sexual liberation, substance use, student activism) while decoupling them from the *jipiteca* and *ondero* spheres. In the same way, the PAP model of reading *Palinuro* allows for a more complex understanding of the ways in which counterculture (in Mexico and the rest of the colonial world) is engaging with the histories of violence in the wake of colony, capital, and nation; taken together, the experiences in the novel work to name, identify, face, and ultimately integrate these violent experiences without rejecting, denying, repressing, or abstracting them, from the sexual violence of colony, to the bureaucratic violence of medicine, to the state violence of Tlatelolco.

Particularly when read alongside current (and very exciting) research on the neuroscience and psychotherapeutic uses of psychedelic substances in carefully structured and cared-for therapeutic sessions, *Palinuro* offers a series of "sessions" that cover a Mexico literary and cultural past re-created in and through the characters from their singularized and singular positions as already globalized countercultural citizens. In the novel, the adventures of Palinuro and Estefanía on the streets of Mexico City contextualize their psychotherapeutic disentanglements as they navigate neoliberal Mexico. For example, the chapters that explore advertising and other imaginary islands anchor an engagement with the epithumogenetic factories of neoliberal capitalism, the morgue of the hospital anchors the medical institutions of modernity and their dehumanizing and alienating forces, and the catacombs under the national cemeteries become the repositories of the literal and figurative bones of the nation. Ultimately and in the literary chaos that is the novel where the line between realism and literary imaginations are blurred over and over, the couple's small room in the Plaza de Santo Domingo functions in much the same way that the highly controlled and "safe" space of a therapy room functions in contemporary psychotherapy; by making explicit a mindset of subjective expansions and liberation in a setting of care, domesticity, and family (with the futurity contained in these ideological spaces), the novel reveals and dwells on the patterns of individual and collective self-destructive behavior that our current capitalist, colonial, heteronormative, and anthropocentric world system imposes on the temporal and spatial fabrics of the world. Furthermore, and perhaps most importantly, in recreating these sessions — without centralizing the substance itself and thus fetishizing and participating in the commodification of psychedelia — the novel develops the crucial element of integration. In doing so, the characters integrate their psychedelic experiences into their subjectivities and incorporate the politically and socially disruptive experiences of the global counterculture, as well as the violent responses from the state and capitalist consumer culture. In this way, *Palinuro de México* uses counterculture to imagine and generate other ways of being in the world — and other ways of being worlds — that are increasingly becoming socially, ethically, and aesthetically relevant.

I want to take a moment to contextualize this particular use of lysergic acid as a literary device and an ethical tool in the service of countercultural bodies. In *Larga sinfonía en D*, Dalton explores lysergic acid as a component of youth counterculture, one more (mystical) experience in a series of experiences that give shape to youth bodies in Mexico and across the world as they/we unlearn norms of patriarchy, capitalism, and colonialism. In the current psychedelic renaissance that is uniting therapists, researchers, medical experts, and traditional healers from across a variety of cultures, there is still a twist of the screw, a re-turn on the spiral to understand how the use of psychedelics — particularly but not only in a therapeutic setting — can be a tool for psychic, emotional, social, and political liberation and healing. To understand how del Paso takes this twist and does so by downplaying the appearance of substances while foregrounding their psychic, emotional, psychological, social, and political effects, it is helpful to take a moment to understand what current neuroscientific, medical, and therapeutic research is revealing about psychedelic substances.

The first step on this understanding is what is now being called the default mode network (DMN), a network that was only just recently mapped by neuroscientists and that is being revealed to be a central component of our construction of subjectivity. First described by neurologist Marcus Raichle in 2001, the DMN functions as a central network that organizes the specialized systems within our nervous systems and especially activates them to establish specific connections between regions of the brain. It has been described as a "network of brain structures that light up with activity when there are not demands on our attention and we have no mental task to perform" (Pollan 302). In other words, it is a brain network that serves to "make sense" of our experience of the world when the nervous system is not focused on a specific task, processing sensorial stimuli, and creating connections between memory, emotion, and other parts of the brain. By working at a distance from the direct sensory processing of the outside world through sensorial stimuli, as well as from the concrete task-based operations (particularly when it is a new task being carried out), the DMN becomes the network that generates the formation of a sense of individual self/ego able to conceive itself through time and space, touching and connecting the different aspects of what it means *to be*. What is more, this is a network that develops as the body grows into adulthood, and it is a network that becomes solidified then. While it can be modified later in life, it also provides stability by predicting situations and providing quick processing for responses to outside stimuli so a body can react quicker, easier, and with less danger to the circumstances around it. What is more important in this is that this network learns as we experience similar or the same situations repeatedly; thus, it is a neurological model that helps us understand the formation of social structures within our bodies.

The DMN becomes solidified in our neural networks in the passage from childhood to adulthood. This explains how children experience the world in a vastly different way than adults, processing sensorial stimuli in much richer tones that do not quickly "interpret" something and give it meaning to survive, and experiencing emotional situations without attaching a specific emotion to a social hierarchy or structure that dictates how one "should" feel or affectively respond to the situation. Currently, research is showing how the DMN is especially activated during specific higher-level metacognitive processes "such as self-reflection, mental time travel, mental constructions (such as the self or ego), moral reasoning, and 'theory of mind' — the ability to attribute mental states to others, as when we try to imagine 'what it is like' to be someone else" (Pollan 302). These cognitive functions are especially important in more complex and highly organized societies where, to navigate structures of oppression, the individual must consider how to respond, what the other person might be thinking, how they might react, et cetera. This becomes particularly important when we consider specific bodies that experience oppression, whether it be racial, gender, ethnic, linguistic, class, or otherwise. I bring this forward to nuance neuroscience's understanding of this neural network in a greater social and cultural context. The DMN, then, is the part of the brain that "grows" and keeps us alive by learning social norms and habits that better allow for survival in the immediate environment. It is also the part of the brain that controls the processing of information we are constantly receiving from the various sensorial stimuli; as we experience touch, taste, sight, sound, and smell in a specific way, we learn to associate it with specific memories or situations of safety/danger, and we cease to process the stimuli fully (the simple experiment of eating with eyes closed will reveal how this network functions to diminish sensorial stimuli processing). By regulating these stimuli, the DMN also activates the capacity for "predictive interpretation," the ability to take as few stimuli as possible and make a series of inferences and logical predictions based on previous experiences (Pollan 308). With this understanding of neural networks, science is finally giving a framework to understand how a "world" is created not only in literary or cultural terms, but ultimately in the shared social contexts that literally shape our brains and minds; in other words, the world that is inside our brains and that we all share. A common metaphor that is used by neuroscientists and popular science reporters currently is to think of the brain as a hill covered with snow and the DMN as the series of tracks that are made as we slide down the hill on sleds, getting progressively deeper and harder to leave as we continue to slide down. Another metaphor is the DMN as a system of highways that connect an urban area, where there are streets that also connect places but that are avoided as we race down the highway (or get stuck in its traffic).

The reason I bring the DMN as the first step in understanding the liberatory potential of psychedelics, especially in a therapeutic modality (as Palinuro and Estefanía use them to exorcize their nationalist subjectivities while remaining in the center of Mexico itself), is because one of the main effects of psychedelics on the human brain is the temporary diminution of this network. This does not mean that sensorial processing or cognitive functions are impaired, but rather that different parts of the nervous system that are used to communicate in a specific way are now free to interact in other ways; for example, emotional processing and memory, or sensorial stimuli processing and emotion, to name a few. This temporary (it lasts only as long as the psychedelic substance lasts and then the DMN turns back on, albeit with the new connections made during the psychedelic state as well) diminution explains what mystics, neuroscientists, medical experts, and religious scholars — as well as experienced psychonauts — have all referred to as "ego dissolution" or "ego death" (Pollan 304). This is the sense of a narrative "I" that is suspended for a time being. However, and as Palinuro will explore as he unfolds into various Palinuros throughout the novel, while the notion and experience of an ego/self may dissolve in the psychedelic state as boundaries between subject/object are blurred, consciousness remains. Stimuli is processed, information is received, cognitive functions are operative, and memory is activated. Ultimately, consciousness remains, and it is this fact that illustrates neatly and succinctly how consciousness lies less within the individual and more within the relations between a body and the surrounding world it inhabits, whether this is a social world or a more "natural" environment. Counterculture, operating at odds with the liberal notion of solitary individual, understands this profoundly.

Neuroscience is still understanding how this brain network interfaces with our conception of self, ego, and consciousness, since it is not active in childhood and yet children experience the world through an "I" as much as adults. For the purposes of a more decolonial and countercultural understanding of *Palinuro de México*, I want to underline the anti-capitalist, anti-patriarchal, feminist, and deeply decolonial implications of understanding consciousness in this redefinition through interrelational embodiments that run deep and provide explicit and embodied counterpoints to the various modes of symbolic and psychological violence mobilized by normative world constructions (epistemologies, temporalities, racial hierarchies) and nation-states. Furthermore, the DMN's dual operations of repression (controlling access to specific memories or emotions in various parts of the brain, in relation but not exclusively to trauma and violence) and filtering (reducing the flow of sensory information to the nervous system as a whole) again can have deep political implications, particularly when we consider how a contemporary globalized citizen is shaped not so much by an evolutionary need to survive in the "wild" or harsh environmental conditions as much as by an individual's position in a society ordered by hierarchical structures of oppression, be they racial, class, gendered, ethnic, linguistic, or other. As such, the temporary diminution of the DMN brings forward the opportunity for radical empathy for others and for oneself in the process of liberation, and a radical empathy that structures the direct access to past and current sensory information. In the context of the extreme violence of the 1960s and 1970s that Mexican youth and youth across the globe experienced as they sought to create other worlds, this radical empathy toward the outside and the inside cannot be understated. Thus, the characters in *Palinuro de México* (and other psychedelic-structured texts) interact with themselves, each other, and their environments in ways that radically challenge the dominating economic and political orders precisely by using literary devices and techniques that re-create these psychedelic moments for the readers rather than re-present them. In this way, while the mention of substance is sparse (a few times in the novel with over 700 pages), the re-creation of these effects run deep and generate in the reader a similar destabilizing of self and subjectivity in the aesthetic experience itself.

In a therapeutic context — as opposed to the more (re)creational ones observed in previous novels, with their own particular and high value — this effect of the temporary diminution of the DMN and the increase in other neural networks becomes functionalized through the careful control of the external stimuli. This is the main difference between a (re)creational and therapeutic use, with the support of the therapist and space-holder of the session who will be aware of while not controlling the space in a laboratory-style sense. The basic structure being used today in therapeutic contexts builds on the therapy work of the 1950s and 1960s when LSD and psylocibin were used (extremely successfully) in novel treatments across the world to treat alcohol and other addictions, depression, and other psychic disturbances. Fundamentally, this means a careful and critical attention to the tenets of *set* (the mindset with which a substance is consumed, both on the part of the person consuming and the person caretaking) and the *setting* (the physical environment where the substance is consumed and where the person consuming it will be during the effects). Canonically, researchers like Timothy Leary in his early years at Harvard, Bill Richards, Walter Pahnke, Roland Griffiths, Richard Alpert, Stanislav Grof, and others were part of the early wave of research and therapy that solidified this approach, silenced during the decades of the War on Drugs initiated by Richard Nixon in 1971 with the Controlled Substances Act.

Today, psychedelic-assisted psychotherapy (PAP) consists of three moments.[15] First is a series of sessions with the therapist who will support the client, carried out without the use of substances and where the therapist learns about the client's past, and the client establishes trust with the therapist. These moments appear in *Palinuro* in the opening chapters and in the many sections of the book dedicated to learning about Palinuro and Estefanía's family background and their global genealogy: a setting of the stage and a development of the characters' familial history. While these sections can be taken to construct historical and regional context, they also become a way (for the reader *and* narrative voice) to understand Palinuro and Estefanía in their own personal and familiar history of colonial, capitalist, national, gendered, racial, and class trauma. After these initial series of meetings with the therapist, the second moment is a session generally between for and eight hours where the client consumes a high dose of the psychedelic substance in a safe and controlled environment. This typically means a hospital or private room furnished to resemble a relaxed lounge area with a couch or bed, pillows and blankets, bookcase or furniture with art or other decorative objects, soft lighting, and access to a private bathroom. Here, the client typically lays on the couch/bed and wears eyeshades and headphones with a carefully curated playlist designed to complement the arc of the psychedelic experience.[16] These moments are specifically and precisely found in the novel during the chapters that focus on the experiences of Palinuro and Estefanía within their small apartment, physically isolated from the stimuli of the external world while they engage with the worlds within. Here they lay on the bed, eat at the table, paint, and talk; here they also travel through their imaginations and visions. Third and most importantly, the therapy models end with a series of integration sessions where the client and therapist "make sense" of the experiences had; this moment is crucial in creating a supportive context to understand the psychedelic experience and is regarded by therapists and researchers as *the* essential component of PAP, the distinctive feature that makes the therapeutic modality therapeutic. In the chaotic and nonlinear structure of the novel, this integration appears in the final chapters that focus on and focalize the psychedelic experiences in the context of state violence lived in Mexico during the later 1960s (Tlatelolco and other student massacres specifically) and place the characters and their alter egos in the context of global political and social struggle. Throughout the rest of the novel, there are fragments interspersed that become moments of self-reflection where Palinuro, Estefania, and their cousin Walter self-reflect on their experiences and integrate their psychedelic knowledge into their existence as subjects of global capitalism living in the histories of colonialism and as citizens of Mexico.

Although similar to the effects reported in (re)creative contexts and/or with lower doses, the concrete and very specific effects of these forms of therapeutic uses of psychedelics are profoundly revealing and highlight the political potentiality of *Palinuro of Mexico*, particularly in the world system we inhabit — and that inhabits us. In this way, Palinuro and Estefanía allow for an access to the ways in which psychedelics can be used as countercultural tools, catalyzers of radical psychological and social change in their disruption of normative temporalities, subjectivities, and sociabilities far beyond their effects as "altering" reality. To name a few of these effects and how they transform both the characters and our own countercultural reading of the text, I will start with how the barriers between self/other and subject/object are lowered, diminished, or dissolved. While there has been philosophical, cultural, and medical research on this phenomenon, much of it has worked within the normative and hegemonic (uncritical) constructions of self and subject as constructs of Western modernity. However, the decolonial, anti-capitalist, and feminist implications of this lowering of barriers and dissolution of self run deep in the text, marking a shared preoccupation of/from youth culture in the moment, and speaking to youth cultures in the here and now. From this perspective, Palinuro's and Estefanía's relationships as central protagonists in the text mark a radical disjuncture from the normativities of nation and capital; that is, they establish a series of reciprocal relations between themselves, and then between the two of them and everyone else, but especially objects, things, and words that populate their world. Thus, the relationships of these two characters embody and exemplify alternatives in romantic/domestic relationship structures informed and shaped by their shared psychedelic experiences, and the relationships both and each have with the objects and people surrounding them embody and exemplify alternative sociabilities. In chapters such as "The Death of Our Mirror," they interact with objects in humorous and at times scatological style, and while these parodic chapters have been taken to represent their silliness and love for each other, I believe they serve as a marker of how they (and del Paso is tracing his own youth experiences as well as those of his generation) are resignifying their relations to the world, where consumer products (from hygiene products to clothing and typewriters and decorations and more) are not just simply products but become subjects in and of themselves in a recognition of the complex economic and social networks that must exist for these products to arrive in their apartment. This anti-consumerist position is highly relational and speaks to a world-building project based on subject-subject relationality, even when and particularly when engaging with nonhuman others.[17]

Second, PAP functionalizes (or pays close attention to how the mind is functionalizing) the specific psychedelic effect of changes in thought patterns and brain functions, through the visualization of thoughts and abstractions that characterize the trip; in other words, what is commonly named as "hallucination." While these substances have been named psychedelics, hallucinogens, mind-altering, and entheogens, each with their own specific categorical implications, I want to underline here how PAP is working with the ability of these substances to give shape and form to the internalized thought structures generated in response to the experiences of oppression we navigate in a colonial and capitalist world.[18] Thus, during the novel, Palinuro (and Estefanía and the readers in accompaniment) literally "sees" the history of Mexico as a particular development of Western culture. For example, streets are populated by national/fatherland "heroes" they are named after, and statues come alive as Palinuro exorcizes their internalized violence, genealogically related to his Abuelo Francisco who fought in the revolution. This same effect reappears in the Imaginary Islands and other imaginary spaces that Palinuro and Estefanía explore, and I underline their appearance in relation to the histories of violence that underpin the nationalist construction of nation. I find these instances especially powerful as they allow Palinuro to experience and del Paso to explore how to move away from these nationalist images while remaining firmly in the terrain of nation and Mexican reality; that is, to utilize countercultural aesthetics in a way that mobilizes an ethics of relating to a concrete and grounded time and space, and not an escapism. In this way, one of the key moments of hallucination is the voyage the trio of Palinuro, Molkas, and Fabricio make to the national cemetery and end up substituting the masculinist national bones with the iliac crest of a new motherland, a new nation grounded now in the bones and labor of the many women who have shaped it and not on the blood and violence of "national heroes." As Palinuro is sent down to the catacombs, he finds the rib of Adam (a parody of femininity defined only in relation to man), the femur of Emperador Cuauhtemoc (a parody of nativist and Indigenist nationalism), the skull of Benito Juárez (the parody of reform), the iliac crest of the Father of the Motherland Miguel Hidalgo (a double parody of independence and the pseudofascist idea of mother/fatherland), and then the bones of Zapata, Villa, Miramón, Mama Clementina, Hernán Cortez, Corregidor de Querétaro, and Abuelo Francisco; in short, the bones of the nation and its heroes. Ultimately, though, these bones give way to a full skeleton made up of bones of different people at different ages in their life, colored in a hot Mexican pink shade (del Paso 483–85). This episode, brief and parodic as it seems with a colorful imagination of national and personal history, serves as an example of how the visual and auditory images produced by Palinuro's minds are less hallucinations in the strict definition of the word and more representations of internalized histories being rejected, reshaped, and redefined under the effect of the psychedelic substance. The countercultural nation is now made up of the many bones of all its nameless citizens, colorfully pink and collective.

Third, the novel includes momentary ruptures of the mental patterns generated by surviving, living, and at time thriving in a capitalist society built on the histories of violent colonialism and state violence. In a central chapter titled "Palinuro's Travels among the Advertising Agencies and Other Imaginary Islands," Palinuro escapes the subjectivation imposed by consumer capitalism through a Swiftean parody of the advertising machinery and its power to shape inner and outer worlds, generating a multidimensional subjectivity that can speak to the complex oppressions of coloniality, nation, and capital (Sánchez Prado, "Dying Mirrors" 154). In his journey in these islands, which culminates in him vomiting the consumer products (gin, evaporated milk, Campbell soups) all over the advertising executives in a boardroom, Palinuro and Estefanía rupture the violent objectivation, sexualization, and capturing of pleasure that underpin capitalist (visual) economies particularly in the representation of female sexualities and bodies.[19] This parodic, humorous, and extremely visual/visceral narrative spills over into the chapter where Palinuro and Estefanía explore their sexuality in all manner of forms, from Indian-inspired tantric sexuality to playing with food, role-playing, and more. Thus, the novel ruptures the processes of capitalist and patriarchal subjectivation by exploiting-exploding the structure of the voyeuristic faze of pornographic discourse, centralizing female pleasure *without* fetishizing or objectifying bodies.

Taken together, the act of reading the lengthy novelization of these alternative sociopolitical relations the couple work toward building with their friends and objects push toward an aesthetic experience where, even if momentarily and caught in the rapture of reading, the reader can disrupt their relation to the normative world around them. In doing so, the normative relations that are mediated by capitalism and nation (relations of consumption, objectification, subjectification into specific and well-contained political positions) are disrupted, and their multiplicity and multilayered subjectivities are laid bare and potentially even generated; no longer are the individuals fixed in time and space to each other in gender or social relations, to objects in relations of consumption, to temporalities in relations of being in time, and ultimately to existence in ontological terms. The multitudes that inhabit Palinuro and Estefania, and Palinuro himself, and by extension the readers, are not meant to be a fully formed political subjectivity as much as a confusion of histories, temporalities, and possibilities, since "multitude . . . is not a full subject, an absolute presence, which it is sufficient to evoke in the imaginary dimension of ontology in order to win at the roulette table against power; it is a weaving, an articulation of times that cannot be reduced to an essential contemporaneity and that constitutes the ineluctable horizon of all political action" (Morfino 15).[20] Thus, the power of imagination and play springs forward from a psychedelic-mystical-countercultural experience, a being-with Palinuro that activates not only the histories of Mexico but also the Western world and that spills onto a generation of youth who are finding their world absolutely commodified, objectified, and traded in the global market in processes that have only accelerated since the 1970s. From a positionality that self-reflects on the uses of psychedelics as both tools of liberation and presciently as tools of oppression — as can be observed in the increasingly widespread opioid crisis in the US and globally, and the spread of fentanyl as well as the myriad of prescription drugs that are ravaging youth in the guise of pharmaceutic therapy — *Palinuro* works to politicize and motivate the reader to politicize their understanding of counterculture *and also* to counterculturalize (through the parodic references to high/low culture) politics, making fun of the state as it massacres and making fun of capital as it commodifies.

This project of liberation of desire revolves around the central idea that "desire is never of *me* and yet always *mine*" (Lordon 92). Thus, the recognition of the myriad commodity objects, historical events and subjects, national histories, and experiences that shape Palinuro and Estefania (and their sexual and social desires) is meant to liberate their desire in the process of (un)tying from the world around them. From their room in the Plaza de Santo Domingo, where multiple temporalities and spatialities of Western culture coexist in a specific time/place — objects from remote antiquity to the ultramodern pop art and the latest technology — the novel unfolds as a series of psychotherapeutic sessions where the traumatic moments of national history from the sexual violence of its founding to the recent bloodshed of students are integrated into a contemporary Mexican's subject position and body, now as a global citizen with a common history. As the primordial couple that gives shape to the new Mexico emerging in the Global Sixties, Palinuro and Estefanía's genealogy anchor them in the revolution as the ideology and landscape to be engaged with and challenged, specifically grounded in the Abuelo Francisco, who sired his whole family by intermarrying to produce Estefanía, a "grandfather's aunt, great-grandmother's half-sister, mother's great-granddaughter, great-granddaughter's daughters and also half-sister to her great aunt" (del Paso 429). The revolution as ideological discourse that silences and is used to legitimize the histories of state violence that came in its aftermath is used to contextualize the silenced histories of violence that the World Wars and Vietnam are carrying out in the rest of the world, and the violence that underpins the global order of capital and nation.

Alongside this more explicit violence of the state, the implicit violence of biopolitics is named and faced in the chapter "The Last of the Imaginary Islands: This House of the Sick." Here, Palinuro passes through the various schools and histories of medicine, guided by a Virgil-like character who caters to his every bodily whim while relishing the prospect of opening him up on the dissection table. One of the longest and most poetic of the twenty-five chapters, it complements the other Imaginary Islands of advertising where the language of sales was capturing minds and shaping desires, now the language of medicine capturing bodies and thus equating medical institution and discourses as another form of biopolitical control on par with the subconsciously manipulative discourse of advertising. This journey culminates in the Pavilion of the Sane, immense as a city and where hundreds of people wander waiting to be admitted into the hospital, not knowing they are already within. This striking image brings home the way in which biopower is operating in contemporary nation-states (and now necropower, where most subjects are navigating death by hands of the state in some form or another). In this making explicit of violence, del Paso emphasizes how for the state subjects (and particularly those under racial, class, gender, and ethnic oppression) are no more than bodies on which to practice autopsies as the ultimate categorizations of life.

I have not spoken yet of the cultural genealogy of Palinuro as a mythical character from the annals of Western culture, and now that the violence of state and capital are being brought forward it is helpful to understand how this history ties into and is related to a psychotherapeutic reading of the novel. In Virgil's *Aenid*, Palinurus is the hapless but masterful helmsman and navigator who leads Aeneas's ships from the ruins of Troy to the glorious founding of Rome. However, he is also the single scapegoat who pays for their safe passage with his life when the gods put him to sleep at the helm and he falls overboard. The character will resurface over the centuries in the Anglo lettered tradition as the sacrificial scapegoat and the wayward wanderer who lacks control of his life and is punished for it, either by gods or fate. In contemporary times,

Cyril Connolly rebirths the character in his *Unquiet Grave* (1944, first published under the pseudonym Palinurus) to become the embodiment of those who consciously decide to opt out of their specific social positionings; he anticipates the conscientious objecter of the 1960s and the myriad of youth who globally dropped out of war and continue to do so.[21] While Connolly's text is mentioned once in the course of the novel, the priority is not to draw these historical references explicitly (as Joyce does in *Ulysses* with the explicit mention of the Cyclops and Circe) but rather to situate this character in and of Mexico, and thus render a character and a nation that become a postcolonial member of Western culture while simultaneously founding an-Other nation in his fate as outcast of Rome/Mexico post-1968. This character who is denied civilization becomes the focal point to understand a generation and a youth culture that is alive and navigating their material rejection/persecution and their symbolic capturing by the market. Palinurus becomes Palinuro to reimagine and reactivate the possibilities of alternative sociabilities not necessarily embodied by him and yet signaled in his life and relations; the redefinition and rearticulation of consensual sexual pleasure outside the paradigms of pornography and objectification; the political and therapeutic uses of psychedelic substances; and ultimately the escape from revolutionary *mestizo* identity to reweave alternative historicities and temporalities. The historical failure of Palinurus is mirrored in the real material failure of countercultural youth to remake the work, and then is again positively reactivated in the relations he, Estefanía, and their friends and family and objects embody, relations that continue to exist even after Palinuro is murdered on the staircase. Palinuro has been interpreted as a "gathering of subjectivities that unfolds in both a persona and collective unconsciousness" that responds to the complex and multiple realities of the Global Sixties (Sánchez-Prado, "Dying Mirrors" 149). I agree with this assessment and I believe that understanding this gathering as a multitude anchored in the character of failure/surrender that mythical Palinurus embodies allows us to better understand the way these bodies are being mobilized in time/space to re-create a set/setting, a temporal-spatial-ideological landscape in which the Western-national-colonial psyches can be confronted within a psychotherapeutic ethics of redemption and refoundation, an alternative weaving of temporalities-spatialities that "constitute the ineluctable horizon of all political action" (Morfino 15).

Placed in this sociohistorical and cultural context, the brief mention of substances helps place the novel in and of the world; they function less as generational markers and more as contextual clues to understand Palinuro and Estefanía as radical world-builders unlearning and learning other ways of being. The ideological limit that has been pointed out by many critics in the texts' utopian promise can — particularly under a PAP lens — be reinterpreted as an expression of the ineffability and paradoxicality that characterize the mystical/psychedelic experience (Sánchez-Prado 156). That is, the limits of the utopic imagination within the text can be understood as manifesting within the framework of psychedelic experiences, and thus their effects can be understood

beyond the temporal limits of these experiences and hint at how these characters, and in turn the youth they are representing, can and maybe are reshaping
their bodies and relations outside the normativities of nation and capital. Rather
than being limits to the imagination, they signal the intrinsic nature of the trip
treatment unable to be articulated in language (ineffable), unable to be com-
municated via words (untranslatable), and unable to be represented in visual,
poetic, linguistic, or any kind of representational structure (immanent and not
transcendental). Thus, it is in the wildly imaginative moments of the text when
the subjective-political ethos of the text appears as the central tenets of counterculture; it is not about creating another commune or escaping into a world, but
rather it is about transforming the quotidian world around them into a countercultural paradise grounded in critical consumption practices that are continually
updated. And it is during these wildly imaginative moments when things appear
out of their order that the mystical experience of psychedelics is politicized. An
example of these moments is during the subjective displacements that occur
between Palinuro and the Palinuros (over forty-five of them throughout the
text), between the I and the multiple I's that appear in the narrative voice. What
is politicized in the psychedelic experience is the liberation of desire, the poetic
use of language and imagination as decolonial acts, the relational construction
of subjectivity that becomes an ontology of relation, and ultimately the fragility
of the lineal-teleological temporality that underpins world and nation, and specifically *mestizo* Mexico as a modern project.

The liberation of desire coalesces in the engagement with the machinery
of publicity in the Advertising Agencies and Other Imaginary Islands, where
Palinuro reassembles his global subjectivity onto the networks of global desire
production. Publicity here appears as the capitalist machinery that not only
shapes specific desires, but also captures desire even as it is springing from
the margins of counterculture. In this way, publicity appears to establish itself
as the historical antecedent of what is now being described as the tyranny of
commons that neoliberalism (economically rooted in the liberalizations of the
1970s that began in Mexico and Chile) establishes toward a global governmentality (Emmelhainz 19). Against this capitalist individualism constantly generating production/consumption desire — both the pleasure of consuming and the
erotic pleasure of creating — *Palinuro* mobilizes the psychedelic experience
to literally see, feel, hear, and sense the publicity barons in their economically
systemic role. In this adventure, it ultimately becomes a matter of facing the
"danger of depalinurizing (what would most depalinurize Palinuro would be
a good depalinurizer)" and thus subvert the perfect flexibility of the neoliberal
subject from within (del Paso 191). This willful destabilizing of the self is carried out in a liberatory way, a path that leads to an unbecoming subject, and a
path that rests on exploiting the same mechanism of capturing and fetishism
that capitalism depends on. Palinuro liberates desire by rupturing this commodity fetishism, allowing for a radical discontinuity grounded in the explicit
revealing of the absurd by "declaring that he did not buy all these products to

do all these things but that he did all these things in order to buy all these products" (del Paso 214). The Swiftean voyage through these Advertising islands is revealed then to be an important moment of the psychedelic sessions, particularly with their effect of visualizing the most abstract thoughts and psychological structures. In doing so, the characters and readers thus understand the affective manipulation carried out by advertising and mediatization in general, and what is more, they mobilize together a most powerful and politically effective tool of liberation: laughter.

Building on this laughter and humorous recognition of the power and limitations of psychic manipulation that consumer capitalism and neoliberalism will promote, *Palinuro of Mexico* emphasizes the decolonial potential of language in its poetic function under a countercultural ethos of radical disruption and change. In the chapter "The Death of Our Mirror," the couple solve their problems with "intellijence" (a witty wordplay and a reference to Juan Ramón Jímenez and his take on the Saussurean distance between signified and signifier), attempting to find the true name of things. Though this silly wordplay appears to only lead them to the profound unhappiness of a prelinguistic existence condemned to an absolute silence when facing the absolute chaos of signified-signifier and the total lack of meaning, it is ultimately this voyage into language that liberates the decolonial potential of speech. In this murky chaos of words and meaning, things (and words) cease to be simply objects/merchandise/commodities to be traded, used, bought, and sold. For the pair, their quotidian objects, and the words they use every way to relate to each other, become rather points in a wide and complex web of being, subjects with which to enter into reciprocal relations of meaning; they give meaning to the object/words as much as the object/words give meaning to them. Following the PAP protocols, integrating these visual experiences the couple share in their apartment with their things and words become acts of countercultural knowledge construction emerging from embodied knowledges, pushing the couple to develop deeply relational subjectivities. The reflection the characters experience in the first-person narration, and the subsequent act of reading these reflections, become moments of psycho-subjective integration *for* the reader. Emerging from their immanent existence (the humans and the objects and even language itself), this ontology of relation radically subverts the capitalist ethos that underpins hegemonic constructions of nation and world. Limited by the subject-object/consumer-product relation, capitalist logic is discarded in favor of a countercultural ethos rooted in psychedelic imagination and carrying profound decolonial implications that engage with the *mestizo* state's idea of nation. Because if the objects in the room (and come with me for a moment to imagine as well so-called natural resources, animals bred as food sources, objectified and otherized bodies made vulnerable converted into labor, et cetera) are the real source of subjectivity in the relations that are established between the individual body and the "outside" world — relations that not only signify but ultimately sustain and nourish existence itself on all levels — then the exploitation of these objects and bodies as consumer products is ultimately unthinkable, radically unimaginable within the countercultural ethos.

It is from these immanent and ontological relationalities that the transcendence of space/time (another point in the categorization of mystical experiences and healing modalities of psychedelics) is to be understood as political. The paradoxical being/nonbeing that Palinuro embodies becomes a way to understand Palinuro neither as a hero, nor an antihero, but something closer to a group-subject who contains and is contained by multitudes; in specific relation to his generation's political and social experiences, this group-being that PAP brings forward as one of the effects of the substance is powerful and meaningful in a moment when consumer capitalism and neoliberal policies are shaping the nation in much more alienated and authoritative ways than ever. The momentary collapses of lineal temporalities that occupy the text force Palinuro (and his reader) to inhabit, for example, the revolutionary history of Abuelo Francisco *alongside* the state violence unleashed in 1968 against student groups. These collapses generate a series of subjective unfoldings that move Palinuro away from being a psychoanalytic hero in the style of Joseph Campbell, and rather place him in the lineage of Connolly (writing in the wake of World War II and the psychic devastation that extreme violence meant for Europe) for whom Palinuros is a group-man who takes the "leap from the poorly organized wolf-pack and the sheep-flock into an insect society, a community in which the individual is not merely a gregarious unit, but a cell in the body itself. Community and individual are, in fact, indistinguishable" (27). In the novel, Palinuro unfolds into his friends Molkas and Fabricio — who may or may not be embodiments of his gall bladder and his liver — as well as his cousin Walter when he dons his quilted vest, and his many other selves; he (and Estefanía with him) is a subject who can be singular and multiple simultaneously, and this paradoxicality matters. This group subject "that respects the heterogeneity of its component parts and does not try to subsume them under an illusion of unity . . . one that multiplies rather than subtracts potential to abolish the very fact of domination" (Massumi 440). This paradoxical coexistence of a multiplicity of subjects in the same body (Palinuro) and various bodies into the same space (Palinuro and his friends in the bars, Palinuro and Estefanía and their friends in the apartment) and of various spaces in the same place (the apartment containing the whole world) thus generate a transcendence of space/time that nevertheless remains explicitly tied to the history and geography of Mexico. However, this countercultural nation is now untethered from a teleological and progressive understanding of (human, social, literary) development, and it contains subjects who can reimagine their past, present, and futures in relation to each other, and not simply the market or the nation.

Though he will die — murdered by state violence due to his political activism on the staircase of his downtown apartment building in the key chapter "Palinuro on the Stairs," written in *commedia dell'arte* style — *Palinuro of Mexico* resists the teleological base of modernity that would transform Palinuro (and by extension other students) into martyrs and heroes.[22] Rather, the novel works to give up the liberal myth of literature as a space of democracy or social (re)construction, a fictional scape where the imagination can give sense to the world. Instead, this particular chapter where Palinuro dies and the next and last chapter, "All the Roses, All the Animals, All the Squares, All the Planets, All the Characters of the Earth," work to "affirm a subjectivity that ultimately undermines ALL power . . . open up a more political (and more ethical) discourse: one that performs, in all its fluidity, the spirit of the fallen subjects that never gave in to institutional politics" (Sánchez-Prado, "Dying Mirrors" 158). This ethical-political discourse seeks to embody, incarnate, and literally flesh out the countercultural politics through the quotidian, rather than memorialize. Of all the mental effects psychedelics have on the DMN — particularly when considered in a therapeutic context — this radical destabilizing of a lineal temporality is the most politically provocative, since it situates the subject/character in a temporary "outside" modernity and capitalism. Capital and nation's power to remove temporal barriers in the processes of constant symbolic and material circulation, to control and appropriate time in a continuous reproduction of the extraction-commodification-consumption process is disrupted with the aid of a substance and a setting for its therapeutic/recreational use. The pluralization of temporalities that become multiple and postcolonial and that reject both the normative national and global world order to establish connections with other temporalities emerging in other global countercultural contexts across the globe becomes the path to escape and (re)build. The *mestizo* national order depends on a teleological ordering of historical events in a lineal progression from lost Indigenous pasts (a blatant lie in the face of current Indigenous nations still demanding recognition from the state) to modern development under the watchful and caring eye of a benevolent state that guards and protects. Under this fiction lie histories of violence that continue to shape bodies, especially through the generational trauma and structural systems of oppression that update to the vocabulary of the times. The final chapters of state/national violence and psychic reconstruction bring together the threads of time, family, and future possibilities in order to disrupt these teleological and subjectifiying processes, generating in Palinuro, Estefanía, their fellow characters, and potentially their readers a series of nonteleological ways of temporalizing and historicizing their experiences without memorializing. Together, they/we build worlds that explicitly rest on a bed of plural temporalities that *will not submit* to the order of nation or capital, worlds where bodies embark on liberatory processes that begin in bodies experiencing (sexual) pleasure or ingesting substances with a set and setting that promote liberation instead of consumption.

As part of the global countercultural generation growing up in a world where commodity capitalism is expanding, developing and becoming "natural" economic order, Palinuro and Estefanía disrupt these subjectification processes of market *and* these teleological processes of (national) identity that underpin contemporary subjectivities. Their extremely explicit sexual (mis)adventures

— which have been read by many critics as quasi-pornographic in spite of their radical erotic nature centering on Estefanía's pleasure equal to and at times more symbolically important than Palinuro's — serve to underscore the radical liberation of desire the novel is constructing. Desire is identified as the force underpinning both the capturing of countercultural life in the form of substances, fashion, language, cultural production, and identity formation, as well as the force that underpins the possibilities of liberation for these countercultural bodies. Under the aegis of PAP, these projects of liberation do not lead to any specific utopia or promised land, but rather push multiple bodies to resignify their lives and become aware of the possibilities before them, and the ones that cannot yet be understood but are contained in the myriad of objects (from typewriters to mirrors to lingerie) and subjects (from themselves to the students and other youth around them, as well as their older generations) and the relations they can establish with them; relations of pleasure, reciprocity, and re-cognition, both in terms of recognizing something previously known and in perceiving again as if for the first time.

One last example I want to bring forward from these liberatory moments is Palinuro and his friends' masturbatory practices, which serve to exemplify nonnormative sexualities that defy the *mestizo* normativity particularly in the vigilance on sexual expression that the *macho* body enforces. In the chapter "In the Name of Science," Palinuro, Fabricio, and particularly Molkas digress on their predilection for masturbation. This exploration and textualization of masturbatory practices, coupled with the homosocial and homoerotic setting of the scene where three students gather to discuss medicine, eat oranges, and narrate their personal masturbatory practices are written in a parody of medical discourse. The weaving of medical histories becomes an act of simultaneous re-cognition particularly of some cultural authority, while firmly remaining a ridiculous delegitimizing of philosophers from Pythagoras to Hippocrates to Kant, each of whom had some theory or another, which Molkas takes the time to disprove from his own empiric observations (111–18). By placing these three youthful and virile-enough male bodies in an explicitly sexual and homoerotic space that fluctuates between embodied pleasure and scientific detachment, del Paso disassembles *mestizo* heterosexuality from these novel sociosexual subjectivities, allowing for a more liberated expression of desire that explicitly *refuses* to submit to being captured; this sentiment is perfectly summed up in the ironic statement made by Molkas when his friends attempt to diagnose his sexual predilection through psychoanalytic speak.[23] He interrupts by exclaiming, "bullshit . . . I masturbate in the name of science" (111). Pleasure is liberated not only from the strict relationalities of heteronormativity, but most importantly also from the diagnostic/pathologization that ultimately leads to bodily capturing (in criminal or medical establishments). This fluid and liberation expression of desire — happening in the time/space of psychedelic unfoldings — will reappear in the chapter when Palinuro, Molkas, Walter, and others speak of their real and potential masturbatory practices carried out subversively in the spaces around them:

> Palinuro when he was eight years old. Molkas when he's eighty. Cousin Walter, in the bath. Palinuro, with his eyes. Molkas, with a smile. Palinuro with a banana skin. Gagarin in space. Milkas with the same banana skin. Palinuro thinking of Raquel Welch. Molkas, thinking of Vesuvius . . . Palinuro with shaving cream. Molkas with McCormick mayonnaise. Karl Marx in the British Museum. Cousin Walter also in the British Museum, thinking of Karl Marx. Palinuro in slow motion. Molkas on the wheel of fortune. Palinuro in a lift. Walter in the Paris metro. Molkas with Colgate toothpaste. Palinuro with Estefanía . . . Palinuro in the Statue of Independence. Count von Zeppelin in his dirigible balloon. Molkas with his father's gloves. Palinuro with Mamma Clementina's hand-cream. Adam in Paradise. (del Paso 118)

These places and times resituate their and other bodies and reassemble them alongside heroic bodies of Western and national culture, anchored in the unnamed and often ridiculed practice of masturbation as erotic pleasure. The psychedelic language (which reappears in other episodes such as their diving into the catacombs of the nation, Charon's cave of bones) is nuanced with an erotics that refuses to become fully pornographic by using humor and physical sensations as a way to liberate these male bodies from their *mestizo* norms on their sociosexual behavior. At the same time, they are not alone in these liberatory practices, joined now by a constellation of (counter)cultural figures from astronauts to economists to heroes. Their sexual and erotic bodies also come together with consumer products like shaving cream, mayonnaise, toothpaste, and more, again subverting and refunctionalizing these products now relationally assembled with pleasure and desire.

By way of concluding this psychedelic-informed approach to *Palinuro de México* and the other (counter)cultural producers in this and previous chapters, I want to underscore the third and most important stage of psychedelic-assisted psychotherapy: integration. *Palinuro* is a novel that del Paso inserts in a tradition of counterculture and resistance in the contexts of Mexico post-1968, with references to other texts that engaged with the medicalization and diagnosis of bodies as strategies of bodily and subjective capturing, such as Salvador Elizondo's groundbreaking experimental novel, *Farabeuf* (1965). As opposed to Dr. Farabeuf, however, whom Elizondo uses to showcase how medical discourse intervenes and cuts open the bodies it comes across, Palinuro ends up rejecting medicine's (and discourse's) power on the body by choosing parody, carnivalization, and play as a strategy for liberation (Gutiérrez Cham 84). Furthermore, del Paso uses psychedelic (and other) substances as tools to catalyze and understand psychosocial liberation, narrativizing their consumption in a manner detached from their *ondero*, *jipiteca*, and even global hippie and

countercultural spheres. In doing so, he literarily constructs a series of countercultural acts that can powerfully resist the commodification of the youthful stereotypes of worldly and globalized youth (such as that embodied by Walter) as
well as the increasing commodification of the act of consumption of substances
as an act of teenage angst in the process of growing up to become a proper
mestizo worker-consumer.[24]

In this sense, *Palinuro* builds on the liberatory potential of dissident sexual
practices and politically inclined substance use to fully resist and push back on
the dogmatic principle of dominant reality that will increasingly shape society
in later neoliberal decades. Félix Guattari describes how this "reality" "is con-
veyed by a dominant semiology. Therefore, one should not go from a principled
opposition between pleasure and reality, between a principle of desire and a
principle of reality, but rather from a *principle of reality* and a *principle of licit
pleasure*" (*Chaosophy* 236).[25] Palinuro and his companions thus push back on
these licit pleasures, whether they be sexual, erotic, substance-informed, or in
general the pleasure of social mischief in the style of *Los caifanes* (dir. Juan
Ibañez 1968). In terms of the novel, the assemblages of the playful adventures
of these characters with the historicized versions of Mexican history postrevo-
lution *and* with an Anglo anti-institutional tradition of writing (from Jonathan
Swift to James Joyce and Cyril Connolly) become instances of liberation that
refuse to be easily commodified by the cultural sphere/market of the 1970s.
The novel, which would go on to garner national and international prizes in
later years, would for decades be understood as an elite aesthetic project whose
politics are set in the background, and yet a countercultural reading can bring
forward how the novel is working to subvert and generate alternative political
subjectivities, or at least catalyze a process in the reader. In general, the novel
functions as an integration of the violent experiences of the 1960s in Mexico
into the collective psyche, from the development of a consumer-capitalist market to the instances of state violence, both processes that continue to shape
Mexican society to this day.

In its historical moment, counterculture emerged as a gathering of experiences where psychedelic substances played a central role as youth culture
sought to differentiate itself from previous generations and to learn other ways
of being with each other. Before the emergence of these groups, psychedelic
research had explored the possibilities and promises of substances, beginning
to reestablish a historic relationship between humans and plants/fungi that had
been silenced during the centuries of colonialism. Today, more than half a century later, research on these substances is rescuing and developing the therapeutic potential behind them (in the Western establishments at least, because
Indigenous and traditional cultures have kept these lineages alive for millennia). The insights these countercultural literary and film interventions provide
toward a more global understanding of body, gender, and polis (in relation to
nation but not exclusively contained within it) are many, from the redefinition of
self/subject without falling back on Indigenous models (a path that too quickly

leads to exoticization, especially in the cultural products emerging from and circulating in global markets), to the increasingly pressing need to recognize the multiple temporalities we inhabit in order to imagine an outside not only to the economic crisis looming ahead but to the environmental crisis we are experiencing already. This radical redefinition of self/subject from a relational and reciprocal lens emerges first from a radical acceptance of the realities of nationalism and consumer capitalism solidifying around both García Michel and del Paso as they observe their national and foreign contexts, and then from a radical detachment from the subjectifying processes these ideologies construct. As the female characters of García Michel and the literary archetypes of del Paso propose, national and global histories must be *re-created* and, in their reordering as part of a Western history (the history of capital and nation), offer readers and viewers other ways of being individually in community, alternate forms to the alienating logics and structures of colony and capital. Countercultural literature and film push us to think of our embodied existences, not only to make visible the legacy of colony and capital on our mind and bodies, but moreover to use our (psychedelic) experiences to generate embodied knowledges, to reshape our bodies and minds to become territories where many worlds abound.

Coda

The Familiar Magicians of Alejandro Jodorowsky; Or, How to Mobilize Affectual Assemblages against the Neoliberalization of Subjectivity

Quiero decir, quiero ver lo que está detrás de la seguridad,
de ese esquema mental, de ese esquema físico,
de lo que nos han hecho ver como realidad.
¿Qué pasa con eso? ¿Cómo lo rompemos?
¿Cómo sacamos este rompecabezas y le quitamos las piezas
y formamos otra cosa con él?
[I want to say, I want to see what is behind all that security,
that mental scheme, that physical scheme,
of what has been shown to us as reality.
What happens with that? How do we break it?
How do we take out this puzzle and take a few pieces out
and build something else with it?]

— Margarita Dalton, interview, July 2014

I began this project almost a decade ago, well before the current psychedelic renaissance became public and just as we started noticing the current rise of right-wing and fascist politics across the globe. As I look back now, I see greater similarities between our global times today and the changes (social, economic, political, and more) that Mexico was experiencing in the 1920s. Once more, we are facing the emergence of fascism across the globe in a variety of styles and uniforms as our Western/liberal political systems enter crisis mode and shock doctrine is normalized. Now we are also faced with the even deeper environmental crises that are bringing major climate and environmental changes. During the writing of this book, I learned about relationality and reciprocity in the construction of being-in-the-world, about acceptance of things and desire for change as political forces of transformation, about pleasure as power, and about community as resistance. I have tried (and hopefully been somewhat successful, and that's up to you, reader) to tell a story of counterculture as one that begins long before the 1960s and hasn't ended yet, a story where bodies shape themselves in relation to the economic and political structures that capitalism and nationalism enforce. This has been a story where bodies become the central territories from which sexual and erotic desires emerge, territories that defy the boundaries of the skin as they come together with other bodies in moments of mutual, consensual, enthusiastic, and celebratory moments of pleasure in and for itself. In the moment of here and now, explicit female sexual desire and pleasure, as well as explicit male homosexual and particularly anal desire and pleasure, do not seem like sexual representations that are *that* dissident (or are they?). And yet, in their particular contexts of production, Cube Bonifant and Nahui Olin, Salvador Novo, and Abigael Bohórquez remain voices that dare to speak their desire and pleasure in ways that challenge the norms of what can be experienced, let alone acknowledged, and much less celebrated in the public sphere. In the same way, Parménides García Saldaña, Margarita Dalton, Sergio García Michel, and Fernando del Paso celebrate the radical changes that youth culture generated in the 1960s in México and the world, challenging the norms of Western modernity imposed on an ideal of body and daring to intervene the territory of the body through music, dance, and movement as well as substance and consumption to highlight many forms of pleasure and bodily autonomy.

While the critical frameworks and political-ethical scopes of this project have greatly expanded since I first began thinking about these cultural producers and their work, fascinated by the explicit representations of pleasure, the daring use of the body in autonomy, and the continuous engagement with consumer culture, the core questions remain the same for me. Is it possible to imagine another way of being historically and culturally Mexican (or any national identity or culture for that matter) while also rejecting the heteronormative and violently capitalist constraints of the hegemonic models of subjectivation? How can an ethical approximation to counterculture (hippies, *jipitecas*, substance use, electronic music, radical sexuality, pleasure, alternative domestic and social relations, and bodily autonomy, to name a few of its historical and current manifestations) resist fetishizing the behavior while learning from and with it? Futhermore, how can these instances of liberation from hegemonic processes of socialization be understood as historically situated and connected, their contingencies allowing for the formation of a singularization that nevertheless does not alienate their bodies from their material and ideological surroundings? And ultimately, what does it mean to be countercultural especially now in the face of environmental crisis, political radicalization and polarization, economic imbalances and crisis, and social unrest?

By way of ending this weaving of counterculture across bodies in time and space, I want to close with a brief reading and reflection on Alejandro Jodorowsky's film *Santa Sangre* (1989) as a way of reiterating the liberatory potential of countercultural bodies through a more globalized understanding of their development, circulation, and embodiments. I speak of *Santa Sangre* and Jodorowsky here not necessarily as an exemplary figure of Mexican counterculture, but as one more iteration of a whole ethics and politics of counterculture, a particular embodiment that speaks to the liberatory potential accessible to (most, if not all) bodies living in the times of nation and capital. As has been demonstrated in the book so far, what makes these countercultural bodies powerful and liberatory is their quotidian engagement with their/our own bodies as autonomous zones, territories striated by ideology that can nevertheless be liberated through sexuality, substances, and rhythms. I have told a story that began in the 1920s and ends in the 1980s, and yet it has only become more relevant, particularly as Mexico and the rest of the capitalist globe entered the neoliberal stages of hypercommodification of experiences and subjectivities, let alone the floods of consumer goods. The liberatory potentialities of countercultural bodies resonate (in the sonic, physical, emotional, and political meaning of the word) more than ever, as opportunities of disruption, flight, escape, transformation, and ultimately liberation.

Perhaps the single cultural producer in this project that is widely known outside of Mexico, Jodorowsky serves as a prime example of the ways in which counterculture emerged midcentury and has evolved through the decades as an ethics, an aesthetics, and a politics that centers embodied liberation. In the context of Mexican cinema in the late 1980s, the Chilean-born former student of mime legend Marcel Marceau reemerges in Mexico as the prodigal son of counterculture returning to make one last epic super-production in the by now fully modernized metropolis and country. After studying in Paris, Jodorowsky moved to Mexico in the 1960s and gained (and built) a notoriety hard to escape from as a radical figure, the urban legends around his eccentric film strategies only surmounted by the hard facts. He set up *panic* theater troupes inspired by Antonin Artaud, wrote in avant-garde and experimental journals and magazines, brushed up against syndicates and unions in his film endeavors with his wild demands and filming strategies, and dared to consume psychedelic substances openly and publicly without fear of the social consequences. He released *El Topo* in 1970 with moderate reception in Mexico but with amazing reviews and reception after being screened in the midnight movie circuit in the United States, which ended up getting him the attention of figures such as John Lennon, who produced his third film, *Holy Mountain* (1973), a landmark for countercultural groups across the globe to this day. With this release, Jodorowsky jumped onto the global cultural circuit as a cult figure whose status only grew with his much-anticipated and never-produced adaptation of *Dune* and his later comics from the 1980s onward, especially those in collaboration with the artist Moebius.[1] Putting this (valuable and historic) canonical and cult-centered reading of Jodorowsky aside, I want to approach *Santa Sangre* by taking into account its specifically Mexican countercultural cinematic strategies that center community and relationality, from a strong dependency on a variety of professional and nonprofessional actors and film workers to a strong anti-institutional stance toward film in general.[2]

In the context of countercultural bodies and liberatory praxis, *Santa Sangre* is a film that exemplifies the socially therapeutic ethos of Jodorowsky (and other countercultural producers focused on transformation of their bodies and those around them) focalized now on the male *mestizo* body and the various subjectivation processes these embodiments go through in contemporary Mexican society. Particularly when understood under a contemporary queer theory lens that destabilizes notions of author and subject, the film can be seen as an assemblage of characters that embody queer and dissident subjectivities as they liberate themselves from the social structures around them. I argue that this affectual composition is less the result of a singular artistic genius (who nevertheless greatly impacts the shaping of the story and message) and more a result of the intense collaboration that results from the network of actors, sound and image technicians, choreographers, painters, singers, costume designers, and much more to collectively produce this film (and others) that affectively engages the viewer on multiple levels beyond the merely visual or purely aural. Thus, the collective labor behind the production of the film (and the production of subjectivity, as it emerges from the folds of family and nation) produces an interweaving of signification that rests upon music, images, popular national symbols, and genre conventions. Through these sounds and images, *Santa Sangre* generates in the viewer small ruptures with heteronormative subjectifying processes, most particularly in fleeting scenes where violence is used to break a taboo or to hyperbolize/explode an emotion or affect.[3] In this way, Jodorowsky uses his life stories to tell the story of *mestizo* masculinities as they are projected onto bodies, and thus uses film to expand (political and social) imagination by presenting alternatives to the psychic devastation left in the wake of social structures anchored in the generation and exploitation of the Other.[4] It is this characteristic of anchoring masculinity in specific national territories, soundscapes, and imagery that transforms the film into a tool to resist commodification (which will nevertheless paradoxically promote it through the cult readings of Jodorowsky himself) as well as identify and reject death-driven hegemonic heteromasculinity in the guise of national stereotypes.

In combining ambient sounds, imagery, urban legends, popular music, and cultural imagery of postrevolutionary *and* early neoliberal Mexico inflected through a kitsch aesthetic, *Santa Sangre* becomes a deeply political narrative of gendered citizenship working against the grain of capitalist and nationalist subjectification machines. Influenced by David Cronenberg and other horror grand masters such as Clive Barker and John Carpenter, Jodorowsky uses the aesthetic of horror (a distinct move from his other films) to address specific social structures grounded in sexualized affects, emotions turned into sexual desire through a specific structuring of body and mind that national capitalism depends on. Rosi Braidotti notes, when speaking specifically of *Videodrome* (1983) and its storyline of literally transforming a body that consumes snuff films, that "sexuality is the dominant discourse of power in the West" (*Nomadic Bodies* 127). In the same way, by weaving a horror film where the protagonist's murderous desires are inflected by his exposure to violent heteronormative sexuality in the nuclear family *and* also exploring an ethical engagement with the Other where mutual pleasure allows for the subjective and political redemption of the killer, Jodorowsky's film resignifies sexuality as a discourse of power and resistance that can be mobilized through communal cooperation. Once again, it is the relation between bodies, and between bodies and objects of consumption (music, film, art), and between bodies and technologies that gives rise to these potential moments of liberation.

Santa Sangre tells the story of Fénix, played by sons Axel and Adan Jodorowsky in adult and child roles. Fénix is the child of a circus-owner father Orgo, played by Guy Stockwell, and a very religious-oriented mother played by Blanca Guerra. The couple violently end their lives in a double-murder suicide, leaving the child to grow up as a serial killer haunted and pushed to kill by the memory of his mother; he is finally liberated by his childhood friend Alma (soul) and the memory of his circus friends from childhood. The plot is loosely based on the account of Mexico City serial killer Gregorio "Goyo" Cárdenas, who in the 1940s committed a series of violent kidnappings and murders and was deemed criminally insane after being caught. He became a folklore legend in the metropolis and an inspiration for pulp fictions for decades, as well as underground pornographic films such as *Bigamia Legal* (c. 1940).[5] As opposed to his earlier films focused on the individual psychological development isolated from social contexts (*El Topo* takes place in isolated deserts, *Holy Mountain* moves from private rooms to faraway mountains), *Santa Sangre* re-creates classical family drama narratives to explode them from within in a countercultural fashion while deeply attaching itself to Mexico City, centering bodies in the horror-genre conventions to construct and present alternative embodied social assemblages as options to the self-destruction of violent heteronormative relationships in a highly contextualized geopolitical space.[6] What is more, by anchoring the plot in the loose account of Gregorio Cárdenas, *Santa Sangre* exploits popular subconscious (in a very countercultural fashion) and explores psychosis and violence as direct products of specifically gendered *mestizo* nationalism and not simply secondary effects of vague heteronormative masculinities.

Beyond the material collaboration of an Italo-Mexican production team that already speaks of a global countercultural milieu, *Santa Sangre* mobilizes specific audiovisual strategies to ground itself in contemporary Mexican society and its gender normativities.[7] A core characteristic of Jodorowsky's use of film — similar to the editing techniques of García Michel and other *superocheros* — is his foregrounding and making explicit the artificiality of cinema; his early films depended on additional sound recording to perfectly control songs, incidental sounds, and dialogue while making their constructed nature obvious and "unrealistic."[8] Throughout *Santa Sangre*, background characters speak Mexican slang and other phrases in Mexican Spanish while the protagonists are dubbed into neutral Spanish or English for global distribution; this sonic construction thus signals the material reality where the film is taking place, no matter if the main characters speak in Spanish, English, Italian, or other languages, depending on where it was screened and distributed. Sonically, the film depends on and constructs a national community made up of *mestizo* citizens. Alongside these incidental dialogues and speech recordings, the film uses music to build a sonic nationscape; most of the incidental music is Mexican popular music ranging from boleros to rancheras, thus generating an audiotopia directly anchored in Mexican popular imagery, what is heard and felt on the street and in the shared public life.[9] These songs include instantly recognizable rhythms and lyrics such as Tomás Pérez's "Cucurrucucú Paloma" or Agustín Lara's "Mujer," which signal Jodorowsky's use of popular culture and art not as an exotic identity-construction marker, but rather as one more expression of a collective subjectifying process, highlighting the presence of shared social structures that affectively compose the *mestizo* national experiences.

Besides these aural techniques, the film also uses visual cues to signal the specificity of its geopolitical location: the opening sequence shows an adult Fénix contained in a mental institution before his release into the world, zooming in to his chest where he carries a tattoo of a bird. The camera then suddenly cuts to a bird embarking on a flight, playing on the symbol of soul/anima as a winged being, *and* also taking the perspective of an animal that can fly over the plaza where the circus is setting up and the nation is being symbolically built, thus effectively zooming out from a singular citizen to a greater Mexican urban context that contains him. This sequence as well as the motif of the flying bird, which will reappear with his friend Alma who engages Fénix in acts of individual and collective redemption, illuminates one of the central strategies that Jodorowsky is using to erode the *mestizo* normative embodiments and that Bohórquez had already used in his theatrical work: the generation of humanimal intersubjectivities. By jumping from human to bird to human and back, placing the camera within the intersubjective perspective of the bird-man, the viewer is continuously anchored in a viewing position that refuses to remain exclusively human and that refuses to simply read Fénix as another manifestation of a mythological creature.[10] More than a symbol, Fénix becomes an embodied intersubjective being, a becoming-bird and becoming-human that is both the actual bird flying over the city and the bird literally engraved onto his chest, as well as the chest that bears it.

Jodorowky's deconstruction and subsequent rejection of heteronormative family structures echo in the contemporary calls to abolish (nuclear) families and construct instead networks of care and support that rest upon decolonial affect-building relationalities. Beyond simply naming and signaling *machista* behavior as ultimately (and colonially) violent — which he had already carried out in his previous films — *Santa Sangre* works to place the hegemonic male body in direct relation to a series of other bodies.[11] Fénix appears in the film as the (post)national *mestizo* male — in his family heritage as the racially mixed son of a blonde immigrant and a Brown mother, and in his *macho*-style sexual education — that initially moves within a social space populated by Othered bodies and then chooses to reestablish relations with them after being severed by the forces of state and (mental) institution. From his deaf-mute lifelong love, Alma, to his childhood best friend, Aladino, and the rest of the circus cast and later spiritual entities, Fénix works to establish subjectivity-building relations with other bodies that begin to erode the foundations of an isolated *mestizo* masculinity. The film tackles heteronormativity head-on through the figures of Fénix's parents, who are constructed in their interaction as the new *mestizo* complex of sexuality and desire as a zero-sum theater of conquest, dominance, and subjugation. The central pillar in this complex is the hypermacho male body in the figure of the father, Orgo, whose name indexed orgasm, organic, and ogre simultaneously. Appearing first as the *gringo* who fled the US after murdering a woman, Orgo wears a stylized cowboy outfit that places him in direct lineage with the hyperviolent masculinities of *El Topo* while also indexing the penetration of US products in the consumer culture of late capitalism in the figure of the Western cowboy as the epitome of masculinity. However, more than flesh, the symbol that brings power to this body is the phallus, visually represented in the extremely stereotypical object of the knife as the tool of male dominance. Orgo's central circus performance involves a knife-throwing act with a painted lady (famously tattooed by Sergio Arau, frontman of Botellita de Jerez and prominent member of the *guacarrock* movement celebrated by Sergio García Michel in *Un Toke de Roc*); this hypercharged performance will give way to the mother's suspicion of sexual trysts and subsequent murder-suicide. Going further in this gendered critique, the self-aware film (another mark of countercultural ethos) takes this symbol of patriarchal power and does another proverbial turn of the screw by commenting on the power and use of the male gaze as a tool of objectification, extraction, and domination. Throughout the film, Orgo uses the knife to hypnotize his wife and lover and gain control over their bodies; ultimately, however, it is his gaze focusing on sexualizing the female body that subjugates them to his will, and the camera proves this by occupying both his point of view (POV) and that of the women while he is physically lowering them to an inferior position as they kneel looking up at the camera.

Countercultural bodies are thus constructed by how they look at the world and how they mobilize the gaze, not just by what they look like. In contrast to the heteronormative gaze of Orgo and the women he surrounds himself with, Fénix uses his eyes to ethically engage with Alma and his circus friends on another level. Several scenes throughout the film emphasize characters looking into each other's eyes on an equal plane, despite their height differences at times. This bonding on an equal visual plan signals as well their equal political and social standing, especially when Alma places within Fénix's chest the seed of flight after his very traumatic and forced tattooing when Orgo uses his knife to paint the bird onto his chest; the first violence experienced by male-identified bodies under patriarchy is by hands of patriarchal men themselves. These many scenes of equal gazing into each other's bodies visually assembles an anticommunity, a gathering of bodies in becoming that "requires not face-to-face contention for dominance as much as a continual, often covert negotiation (not denial) of difference" (McGuirk 298). Like the anticommunities of women (and men) riding vehicles that Bonifant is textualizing, or those generated among homosexual men in hidden urban spaces that Novo chronicles, or those generated by the human-animal-mineral-vegetable assemblages that populate Bohórquez's desert, these anticommunities come together through and because of difference. Theorized by anthropologist Irving Goh while developing the deleuzo-guattarian notion of war machine, the anticommunity emerges as a response to the identitarian notions of community grounded in principles of similarity, exclusion, and tolerance. In contrast, the anticommunity is built by bringing together "other experimental people, those who have left behind the striated spaces of State-communities. They do not bind nor delimit themselves with a defined territorial organization" (223). In *Santa Sangre*, this countercultural anticommunity emerges out of the striated and alienated communities of nation and capital, already a part of contemporary Mexican society; they do not exist outside the ideological and material boundaries of the nation, and in their coming together, they form assemblages whose existence is an always already manifestation of alternative subjectivities. In coming together, particularly through the nexus point that Fénix as protagonist/focal point provides through his body, these secondary characters generate with the protagonist an-other way of being both man and Mexican that can exist outside of the injunctive of violence and conquest.

On the other side of this heteronormative complex, Blanca Guerra portrays Concha, the mother cum leader of a popular religious sect centered around the child Saint Lucía, a girl raped and murdered by two men who ripped her arms off.[12] Her blood has the power to wash believers and especially young women from guilt and sin, particularly those associated with instances of sexual violence. Concha is thus a complicated character that signals feminine complicity in patriarchal structures of violence while also decrying the violence that is directed at female bodies; in a very powerful sequence laden with critiques of urban development at the cost of destroying popular/shamanistic religions, Concha appears as a deconstruction of *mestizo* femininity. Placed in the historical context of Mexico City post-1985 during reconstruction, this sequence of Concha and her church instantly assembles the film as a popular collective inhabiting urban space, perhaps even illegally. After receiving the visit from the bishop, who comes to save the church from being torn and yet ultimately abandons them upon learning of the Saint's sexual innuendo behind the power of her blood, Concha tells the story of the girl through a series of passion-like vignettes that decorate the makeshift church. Again, this anticommunity, now revolving around a religious figure with miraculous power, is represented through camera techniques that emphasize relationality. As Concha tells the story, the camera suddenly places itself *within* the paintings looking out, placing the viewer not only within the moment of sexual violence in extreme proximity but also within the emotional subjectivity of Concha and her fellow believers.

Painted in the style of Frida Kahlo, these vignettes serve to contextualize femininity specifically within a concrete Mexican *mestiza* imaginary assembled in the wake of state nationalism through the absorption of an authorized female cultural producer, particularly in the late 1980s as Frida was picking up steam in the global art spheres. Art historians such as María Cecilia Rosales have signaled how this absorption might be attributed in part to Frida's position within the gendered nationalisms that *mestizaje* produces, pointing at Frida's relation to Diego Rivera coupled with her self-construction in several paintings as a failed yet potential mother generating the idea of a docile mother to the ideological nation. In this way, the figure of Frida and her construction in the circulation of images that are taken to be representative of an essential interior (and not exactly representation of female autonomy, as was later recontextualized in the 2002 film *Frida* by Julie Taylor), an essentialized national femininity tied to motherhood and procreation, containing the danger that a sexualized and sexual female body exercising autonomy and pleasure might pose for the gendered nation.[13] However, Frida is nevertheless a radical queer figure, particularly in her historical relations with other women such as Chavela Vargas, Tina Modotti, or María Izquierdo, as well as in her participation with artist organizations and workers organization and unions. Thus, this queering potential of the female body that many critics have signaled in her more cyborgian and surrealist paintings — particularly in the post-1980s global recognition of her work, during which Jodorowsky was filming — is suddenly made visible in the film through a scene where Concha decides to sacrifice herself in order to save the Church, freeing her body momentarily from the institutional violence of patriarchy through this act of female-centric martyrdom. However, she is held back from fulfilling this promise of escape by the power of futurity embodied in the figure of the child, a product of her very real reproductive function and her symbolic position within the nation. Right before she is run over by a bulldozer, Fénix runs up to embrace her and arguably rescues her from martyrdom while simultaneously placing her squarely back in the heteronormative family structure. Futurity, which queer theory has explored as both the promise of liberation in the uncertainty of utopia (Muñoz) and the trap of heteronormativity in the strict defining of (re)production (Edelman), appears here as both, as this specific child contains the liberation that will transform him while also condemning the woman to her maternal role, and ultimately placing her back on the path that will lead to the sexual violence of Orgo, who will end up murdering her in the same manner as her saint.

Countercultural bodies emerge from a process of subjectification and capture, and liberation and transformation. They/we both contain the histories of violence that nation and capital have enforced on populations and bodies for centuries, through family and society, and become countercultural in their/our choices and consumption as they/we enact paths of liberation. Thus, Fénix is the body that metaphorically represents these models of masculinity and *mestizo* male identities that emerge from both concrete histories and geographies of nation in downtown Mexico City and from the histories of market and consumption embodied in Orgo. Fénix is subjectivized into a *mestizo* male identity by his parents and their histories to the point of having its symbols literally engraved upon his body. As mentioned earlier, this powerfully productive human-animal subjectivity will emerge from the bird on his chest, and yet initially this image is a symbol of violence and domination, an engraving of nationalism and patriarchal ritual. Upon the death of the circus elephant — which in turn is an image for his lost "innocence" after witnessing the primal scene of his parents fucking — Orgo takes Fénix and straps him to a chair, tattooing upon his chest an American Eagle–like bird that he himself carries and that will make Fénix a man. This scene illustrates the literal perforation and engraving of the body by heteronormative structures of subjectivity formation, now in the form of a phallic knife. Jodorowsky takes care to signal the deeply confusing and affective layers of these moments of subjectification, making explicit the troubling aspect of homosocial affective relations when reproducing heteronormative behavior. During the tattooing scene, Orgo handles the knife with extreme care and caresses Fénix's skin with endearing touches while an emotional guitar solo plays in the background. The erotic and hyperemotional moment is charged with meaning and symbolism, and violence. This affective composition lays bare and contrasts with the heroic father-son relationship of *El Topo*, revealing the violence inherent in heteropatriarchy and making the viewer uncomfortable and more sensitive to the ways in which affect is mobilized by structures of dominations, as the camera and sound editing make visible the ways in which Orgo is emotionally manipulating young Fénix. Ultimately, this contrast allows for a deeper and more enriching understanding of the other more positive and communal aspects of affective subjective formation with the other nonfamilial characters, providing an affective structure for Fénix (and viewers) to understand and build upon, generating alternative ways of being and feeling.

The nuclear family is central in *Santa Sangre* not just as a pathological diagnosis of Fénix's murderous behavior later in his life (in the more typical Hitchcockian structure), but rather as embodiments of *mestizo* nationalism to be acknowledged in their power and violence under the guise of care and community. *Santa Sangre* uses this familial background, which climaxes in its story arc with the traumatic double murder he witnesses when Concha throws sulfuric acid on Orgo's genitals upon catching him with the Painted Lady; this seed of violence will shape Fénix and his murder spree later in life, reenacting both his mother and father in various moments of violence. However, along this (re)production of violence, another countercultural narrative continually accompanies Fénix (and, by extension, *mestizo* citizens), embodied in the nonverbal (nonsymbolic) engagement with Alma and the other circus members who keep coming together to form the anticommunity that will hold Fénix and allow an escape from himself. As a killer, Fénix will embody both *mestizo* masculinity and femininity in his violent behavior, dressing like his father to hypnotize and murder his victims with knife-throwing acts as well as sometimes being the arms of his dead mother, a hallucination that curtains his sexual desire when it arises and impedes his potential sexual union with other queer bodies as a liberating act.[14] This heteronormative force is so powerful once engraved onto his psyche and body that Fénix is unable to break free even with the ultimate queer body of La Santa, a trans* luchador inspired by the popular figure of El Santo; when they meet on a dark night, Fénix almost breaks out of his subjective trappings only to fall back into them, and La Santa meets their death on his sword. Only in the final sequences is Fénix able to successfully break free from his familial traps, and only through an act of redemption that involves the recognition — once again — of Alma as his neighbor and of Others in a real and ethical sense as the circus member and urban dwellers materialize around him..[15] Though Alma will not unite with him sexually or romantically — or at least that is unknown, since Fénix will turn himself in and be committed — this recognition will bring forward a series of hallucinations that mark Fénix's subjective liberation in the form of a clown that celebrates and dances with him. Thus, Alma becomes soul, becomes Fénix himself now fully integrated in a Jungian sense.

In this way, *Santa Sangre* constructs a narrative arc that explores how a (male) *mestizo* body is captured into normative gender and social structures, and how counterculturally he enacts processes of liberation together with an anticommunity of others. Fénix thus breaks off from being simply a narration of the story of Gregorio Cárdenas the serial killer to become an embodied archetype of Mexican heteronormativity, now psychomagically reassembled through music, genre conventions, gory images, and spatial placements in Mexico City, transformed into a countercultural body liberated from destructive sexual behaviors rooted in colonial and patriarchal violence. Furthermore, this process is initiated and held by a group, a collective who also liberates themselves in the moment of liberating Fénix; it is Alma who engages with his gaze on an equal plan throughout the film, and the rest of the circus crew who support him even when that means being committed to the authorities. Paradoxically, liberation from the psychic structures of patriarchy and *mestizo* nationalism does not leave the citizen disconnected from legal or social authorities, but rather allows for an arc of social and cultural redemption.

Thus, despite his important contributions to global counterculture as an extraterritorial cultural producer in film, comic, theater, tarot, and other marginal art forms, when read from a national-centric position, Jodorowsky's *Santa Sangre* appears as a countercultural healing device directed at violent heteronormative patterns and their reproduction in *mestizo* Mexico. Counterculture here appears not simply in the material formation of the art object, or in the visual style of representations, but in the ethical-political drive of the art object itself, the intentionality of disrupting psychological expectations and paradigms to generate moments of liberation in the viewer: psychomagic, as Jodorowsky himself has named it. By recasting a real family into roles that replay the familial and social drama in a hyperbolic and surrealist setting, *Santa Sangre* generates queer anticommunities that come together through difference expressed in non-normative bodies, disabled bodies, and egalitarian nonreproductive romantic relationship structures. Following a more Jungian than Freudian understanding of psychological development, *Santa Sangre* counterculturally enacts a production network that brings together global figures in the production team, as well as resisting easy commodification through its explicit goriness and horror aesthetic that, particularly in the context of Mexican cinematic tastes, makes it hard to sell on the mass market. The use of a popular urban legend as framework as well as the audiotopia of nation generates, then, an arc of national redemption, and in particular an arc that recognizes the colonial legacy while grounding itself in the development of postrevolutionary Mexico. Thus, the film provides a blueprint for familial affective recomposition and Jungian integration of anima (soul) in a most classical act of psychomagic. By engaging with global cultural flows of cinema and recontextualizing Mexico City itself as a national subject also subjected to the capitalist process of subject formation that produces psychosis and neurotic violence, Jodorowsky counterculturally constructs a series of national bodies who *can* liberate themselves and who *are* resisting gender violence and its reproduction.

As I hope to have demonstrated, countercultural producers emerge in relationality to both capital and nation, working within the modern industries of journalism, media, entertainment, and cinema and remaining attached to ideas and structures of nation as they weave culture in their art forms. However, their work — even and especially when circulating within the authorized networks of journalism, literature, and cinema — tends to refuse commodification and rather generates strategies of subversion, dissidence, and sometimes outright liberation that has the potential to radically disturb national subjects in their bodies, exploring the limits of gender, sexual, and national identity. With the epochal changes of the 1990s — from the signing of NAFTA (North American Free Trade Agreement) to the reappearance of Indigenous political mobilization in the EZLN (Ejercito Zapatista de Liberación Nacional), the economic crisis and peso devaluation, as well as the systemic changes in policy and media/communication industries that neoliberalism brought — Mexican cultural dynamics shifted profoundly, and the representation of countercultural bodies as positions of alternative constructions of nation slowly became resignified as commodities to be traded on a more global cultural market; the film *Esto no es Berlín* (dir. Hari Sama, 2019), which tells the story of a 1986 Mexico City nightlight scene through the lens of a sexually questioning teenager is an example of how counterculture can become social capital to be traded today, in its representation as well as its circulation in the cultural fields of contemporary independent and festival films.

The undoing of culture that Gila Hayim traced as the core mark of counterculture, akin to the undoing of fixed gender positions that Braidotti calls for, become the platform upon which the countercultural bodies of the men and women in the texts studied here enact their liberation. By resisting the reproductive/heteronormative as well as any binary understanding of sexuality in fixed active-passive identities, these characters become queer and queer the space around them. The youth culture of later decades builds on this by mobilizing bodily autonomy further, and their pleasures expand their erotic engagement with the city and the nation as they become a political tool whose significance relies on being mapped onto the urban spaces, pleasures that flood bodies and disrupt processes of hegemonic socialization embedded into the city itself through stone and ritual. More importantly, these countercultural bodies are textualized and represented without becoming another paragon of *mexicanidad*; their presence and interventions on the nationscape emerge from the material conditions of the country and, at the same time, do not seek to replace hegemonic models of national identity, but rather erode and expand them from within. In the same way, these countercultural bodies engage the forces of market subjectification, recognizing the power of advertising and other epithumogenetic machinery while exploring strategies of resistance and, more importantly, liberation. The point ultimately is not to reject consumption nor nation as group identity but rather to generate conscious and critical consumption, to consume the object and substance alone and reject the ideological relations that seek to be imposed with it.

Ultimately, this rich history of sexual bodies constructing their subjectivities around acts of pleasure and not identities, of humanimal intersubjectivities that unite bodies and reject anthropocentric citizenship as the sole model to engage with plants, animals, and fungi beyond relations of exploitative extraction, of countercultural bodies consuming entheogenic substances and listening to rock and other strange rhythms, provides a key to understand Mexico outside the paradigms and histories of nation. Together, these bodies weave a national tapestry grounded in the revolutionary imagery and yet reject the heteronormative violence that capital and nation normalize through institutional relations. As they/we drive through the city, engage pleasure in our bodies without a reproductive goal or a sense of shame or guilt, and enact bodily autonomy to relate with objects, substances, and ideas without the limits of what should be, these countercultural citizens have constructed Mexico and continue to do so.

Notes

Introduction

1. I use this term following Anibal Quijano, Mabel Moraña, Bolivar Echeverría, Silvia Federici, and many others who have discussed the origins and structure of the world system that modernity has established as it brings together the geographies of the planet into an economic, social, and political system with roots in the European expansion through colonialism of the Americas and the global South. I emphasize that what we refer to as coloniality — the ordering of society through racialization and sexualization of populations — is the other side of modernity inasmuch as one cannot have existed without the other. I call attention to this dynamic not to signal the hopelessly complex systems of oppressions in place, but to gesture toward an urgent need to orient our critical attention to those bodies who have been silenced, particularly as producers of other knowledges and sociabilities.

2. The colonial encounters in the Americas replaced ontological and economic systems of reciprocal relationality with the binaries constructed in the early centuries of modernity (man-woman, whiteness-otherness, owner-owned, landlord-tenant). However, as many contemporary philosophers and activists are noting, this is not a process of the past but a continuous imposing that happens every day, lest we remember "que somos seres reproductivos, que producimos subjetividad, que una subjetividad equilibrada se produce bajo la necesariedad de la mutual dependencia y que ese equilibrio es entre ser mismidad y nostredad [we are reproductive beings, that we produce subjectivity and that this balance is between being sameness and togetherness]" (Wayar 17).

3. Building on Wendy Brown, Franco Berardi, and Michel Foucault, Mexican writer Irmgard Emmelhainz notes that it is paramount to understand neoliberalism well beyond the strict economic policies implemented to see "neoliberalismo como una racionalidad política y de gobierno, y como una racionalidad normativa que implica que el poder gobierna a partir de un régimen de verdad que se convierte en sentido común . . . la forma de nuestra existencia, cómo nos comportamos y cómo nos relacionamos con los demás y con nosotros mismos [neoliberalism as a political and governance rationality, and as a normative rationality that implies that power governs through a regime of truth that becomes common sense . . . the way in which our existence, how we behave and how we relate with others and with ourselves]" (Emmelhainz 19).

4. The Fourth Transformation is self-described as national project uniting popular leadership and social union against neoliberalism by changing the paradigms of development. It involves a radical transformation of the state focused on establishing peace in the wake of decades of cartel-related violence, eliminating corruption, recovering sovereignty, and recentralizing PEMEX (Petroleums of México) and CFE (Federal Commission of Electricity) as strategic state enterprises that for decades served as the catalyzers of national development. Discursively, it constructs itself as the continuation of the independence and the reform promulgated by Benito Juárez, a post-neoliberal modernity from below prioritizing the poor and socially inclusive.

5. Other examples of this mestizo nationalism in less-state-controlled spaces are Grupo Lala's recent limited edition *Sabores de México* (*Flavors of Mexico*), where the milk products have flavors such as Tuna Guanábana, Elote Miel, and Sueño del Ángel. Another is La Costeña, a canned-vegetables business that was already parodied for its nationalist tendencies in Algonso Cuarón's film *Sólo con tu pareja* (1991), and which also recently released massive Día de los Muertos campaigns in México City. Many thanks to Irmgard Emmelhainz for bringing these and other marketing examples to the forefront.

6. "Modern nationality, whatever it may be, including that of states with non-white (or 'tropical') populations, requires 'whiteness' from its members . . . being authentically modern came to include among its essential conditions belonging in some way or to some extent to the white race, and consequently also to relegating, as a matter of principle, all singular or collective individuals that were 'of color' or simply foreign or 'non-Western,' to the abstract field of pre-, anti-, or non-modern (or non-human)." (Echeverría, *Modernity and whiteness*, 41).

7. I highlight Christopher Dunn's work on Tropicalia and other Brazilian countercultures, particularly *Contracultura: Alternative Arts and Social Transformation in Authoritarian Brazil*, and Susana Draper's recently published *1968 Mexico: Constellations of Freedom and Democracy*, as examples of intersectional approaches considering race, gender, and class vis-à-vis counterculture.

8. In his 1968 study of the countercultures of Europe and the United States during the moment of their explosion, Theodore Roszak emphasizes the impossibility of delimiting them and defines them by their varied resistances to the normative societal structures they existed with, naming this the technocracy. As such, the countercultural "exploration of the non-intellective powers assumes its greatest importance, not when the project becomes a free-for-all of pixilated dynamism, but when it becomes a critique of the scientific world view upon which the technocracy builds its citadel and in the shadow of which too many of the brightest splendors of our experience lie hidden" (83).

9. Frédéric Lordon describes how capitalism (and particularly what is defined as its neoliberal modality) extends objective, tangible, and material structures into subjective, psychological, and affective structures within the individual through a process he terms *epithumogenesis*. Understanding the processes of consumption in this light, I appreciate how "desire is never *of* me and yet always *mine*, in other words, it never originates exclusively within desiring individuals but is nevertheless absolutely theirs — the 'I am the one desiring' is incontestable. In the case of joyful affects this ambivalence of desire is therefore even more doomed to the disavowal that throws the 'not of me' into oblivion, keeping only the 'mine'" (92).

10. That is, "a way of rejecting all those modes of preestablished encoding, all those modes of manipulation and remote control, rejecting them in order to construct modes of sensibility, modes of relation with the other, modes of production, modes of creativity that produce a singular subjectivity. An existential singularization that coincides with a desire, a taste for living, a will to construct the world in which we find ourselves, and the establishment of devices to change types of society and types of values that are not ours" (Guattari and Rolnik, *Molecular Revolution* 23).

11. "No interesaría en la experiencia travesti QUÉ soy y cerrarlo en algún momento; más bien que voy siendo hoy la mejor versión de mí . . . en una mesa micro o macro política dejamos en claro: no es tan necesario afirmar si soy travesti, transgénero, transexual o género no binario; sí interesa qué NO SOY: no soy fundamentalista religioso/a, genocida, ladrón/a, asesina/o, violento/a, torturador/a, cruel, terrorista, etc. Por ende, con esa nostredad que me conoce y conozco en las posiciones más oscuras y las más frágiles, sabemos qué se puede esperar de cada quien en el grupo. El No nos define tanto o más que el SÍ [It would not be important in the transvestite/trans* experience WHAT I am and close that off at any moment; rather, that I am becoming today the best version of myself . . . on a micro or macropolitical round table let's leave it clear and simple: it is not necessary to affirm if I am transvetite, transgender, transexual or nonbinary gender; it is important to note what I AM NOT: I am not a religious fundamentalist, genocidal, thief, murderer, violent, torturer, cruel, terrorist, etc. Thus, with this togetherness that knows me and that I know in the darkest and most fragile positions, we know what can be expected of each person in the group. The No defines us as much or more than the YES]" (Wayar 24–25).

12. I am deeply indebted to Khonsu X for this understanding of bodies of culture.

13. In *The Road to Eleusis*, chemist Albert Hoffman join arms with mycologist R. Gordon Wasson and classicist Carl Ruck to describe the central role ergot (a fungi containing precursors to LSD) and other psychedelic substances played in the Eleusinian Mysteries, which were key in the religious, cultural, and social life of the ancient Mediterranean basin for over

two millennia before their closure by the Christian Roman Emperors of the fourth century CE.

14. Journalist Michael Pollan's recent *How to Change Your Mind: What the New Science of Psychedelic Research Teaches Us about Consciousness, Dying, Addiction, Depression and Transcendence* (2018) provides a thorough overview of some of the findings of these scientific and therapeutic researchers over the twentieth century. Treatments of depression, anxiety, addiction, and other ailments with psychedelic-assisted-psychotherapy (PAP) have proven to be extremely successful in the various trials already published and underway.

15. Norman Zinberg coined the term "alternate states" in 1973 as a critique of the widely accepted "altered states of consciousness." He proposes a change of terms, "which makes it clear that different states of consciousness prevail at different times for different reasons and that no one state is considered standard. *Alternate states of consciousness* is a plural, all-inclusive term, unlike *usual state consciousness*, which is merely one specific state of ASC" (1). Even though with the passing of time his definition may seem also a stretch, as critics have pointed out, I want to underline the gesture of inclusivity as a serious and legitimate approach to a phenomenon that cannot be deemed as simply an "altered" way of things. See also Peter Furst, "'High States' in Culture-Historical Perspective" (1977); John Mann, *Turn On and Tune In* (2009); R. E. L. Masters and Jean Houston, *The Varieties of Psychedelic Experiences* (1966); Walter N. Pahnke and William A. Richards, "Implications of LSD and Experimental Mysticism" (1966); and Ronald Siegel, *Intoxication: The Universal Drive for Mind-Altering States* (2005).

16. For more details, see Eduardo Ekman Schenberg, "Psychedelic-Assisted Psychotherapy: A Paradigm Shift in Psychiatric Research and Development" (2018).

17. Ilona Katzew, *La pintura de castas. Representaciones raciales en el México del siglo XVIII* (2004), and Magaly Carrera, *Imagining Identity in New Spain: Race, Lineage, and the Colonial Body in Portraiture and Casta Paintings* (2003), are two excellent studies of the cultural history and political importance of casta paintings as representations of a political system. Ana Martinez, *Performance in the Zócalo: Constructing History, Race, and Identity in Mexico's Central Square from the Colonial Era to the Present* (2020), provides an analysis of how the casta system was embedded also in the architecture and urban planning of the colonial metropolis of Mexico City, structuring society well beyond the visual representations of paintings.

18. "For the Americas, both North and South, the Mexican Revolution was the greatest demographic catastrophe of the twentieth century. From a millennial perspective, the human cost of the Mexican Revolution was

exceeded only by the devastation of Christian conquest, colonization, and accompanying epidemics, nearly four centuries earlier" (McCaa 397).

19. As Joshua Lund has pointed out, "ultimately, the mestizo would come to symbolize the resolution of the central political problem of the time, the negotiation of sovereignty and hegemony, the formation of a state that would not only represent but also somehow reflect its nation" (xvii).

20. I use the masculine pronoun for the mestizo because heteropatriarchal normativity is one of the key characteristics of this particular body; time and again, the miscegenation that produces this body, whether in popular or intellectual histories, places the Indigenous body as Woman and the (white) colonizer as Man. For this reason, I believe it is ethically important to underline the gender normativity that the mestizo project (and other nationalist-colonialist projects) impose upon their citizens, especially when disguised.

21. Vasconcelos's text is a complex utopic essay that intervenes in the philosophical-ontological conception of progress with a strong Bergsonian background that must be understood in the anticolonialist politics behind the text, activated time and again by liberation movements across the continent, including the Plan Aztlán and certain roots of Chicano movement (Sánchez Prado, "El mestizaje en el corazón de la utopía"). However, I highlight Vasconcelos's text along with his work as the secretary of education to underline the institutional workings of both forms of intellectual labor, their circulation in the cultural and symbolic spheres, and, above all, the structuring they perform for the empty signifier of *mestizaje* to become the master signifier that will order the nation as a material and ideological entity. Vasconcelos's text remains, despite its racist shortcomings, a keystone in the liberatory philosophies Latin America offers to a global community.

22. I suggest Ruben Gallo's *Mexican Modernity: The Avant-Garde and the Technological Revolution* as an excellent introduction into the culturally rich dynamics of early postrevolutionary Mexico.

23. Ageeth Sluis defines the *camposcape* as "a distinctive form of orientalist that equated exotic landscapes of the countryside with indígenas, the past, and national identity. Because of the campo's perceived ties to an eternal and unchanging nature, camposcape represented a constellation of spatial imaginaries imbued with pastoral qualities rendered as timeless, static in geographic, physical and human features" (*Deco Body, Deco City* 18).

24. Increasingly, we see in the nations of the world that the "Estado es el garante de la acumulación de capital, mientras que los procesos políticos lidian con temas ajenos al capitalismo, por ejemplo, las guerras culturales [the state is the guarantor of capital accumulation, while the political processes deal with topics foreign to capital, such as cultural wars]" (Emmelhainz 16).

25. For a visual history of the central role women played in the national growth during these decades, I recommend Julia Tuñon's *Mujeres: entre la imagen y la acción*. (2015).

26. In this manner, Lone Bertelsen and Andrew Murphie speak of affective events that break the orders previously established by refrains: "affective events begin in a *powerful indetermination*, one 'on the horizon.' The force of this indetermination — a chaos that soon beings to press upon a context — calls for refrains to fold the chaos into the beginnings of a structure, to bring a little order" (139).

27. Museo Nacional de Arte (MUNAL), "Exposición Nahui Olin. La mirada infinita" curated by Tomás Zurián, (Junio-Septiembre, 2018).

28. She appears in Rivera's murals *La Creación*, where she is Erato the muse of erotic poetry; *Día de Muertos*, where her characteristic green eyes identify her; *Historia del teatro en México*, where she blends in with the *burguesía porfirista*; and the murals in the stairs of the National Palace. Edward Weston also photographed her on various occasions.

29. Jasbir Puar's deep approach of the bodies of queer and Sikh migrants in the contemporary United States mirrors my own definition and comprehension of countercultural bodies seen as "terrorists" to the nation, unable to be comprehended in their extreme differences while simultaneously inhabiting the most intimate folds of the nation. It is important to underline that they are *seen* as such, and do not construct themselves as such.

30. "To see queerness as a horizon is to perceive it as a modality of ecstatic time in which the temporal stranglehold that I describe as straight time is interrupted or stepped out of. Ecstatic time is signaled at the moment one feels ecstasy, announced perhaps in a scream or a grunt of pleasure, and more importantly during moments of contemplation when one looks back at a scene from one's past, present, or future" (Muñoz 32).

31. Pedro Angel Palou describes this way of conceptualizing politics as "an erotics of politics. The politics of bodies become the only way to be freed from the national trauma of foreign violation. The substitute father or the soldier that claim the bodies of women just as he claims the vanquished territory" (87).

32. This may be due to a political choice or an effect of the marginalization from intellectual circles that Bohórquez experienced because of his openly held socialist position, as well as his open sexual desire in the face of mestizo silencing.

33. For a deeper explanation of some of the current protocols, see Alexander B. Belser, Gabriel Agin-Liebes, et al., "Patient Experiences of Psilocybin-Assisted Psychotherapy: An Interpretative Phenomenological Analysis" (2017).

34. For a more thorough approach to sports in the construction of modern Mexico City, see *Asamblea de Ciudades. Años 20s/50s Ciudad de México* (1992).

35. Criticism has rightfully noted "la decidida e iconoclasta intención de Agustín de destruir lo establecido como 'normal' por las clases medias mexicanas [the decidedly iconoclastic intention of Agustín to destroy the established as 'normal' by the Mexican middle classes]," an attitude that can be extended to a collection of writers beginning to write in the 1960s (Pelayo 70).

36. As with the case of *pelonas* in the 1920s, these subjectification processes were not always carried in ideological terms. Young men and women in the 1960s who performed and presented a countercultural attitude were often met with physical violence in the form of street beatings, getting ganged up on and having their long hair cut short, and being kidnapped for the thrill of it. Aggressors were often plain-clothes or off-duty policemen, but not exclusively, as the public in general were incentivized through advertising and articles in major newspapers to beware of this foreign influence emasculating the young men of the nation.

37. In this way, "what characterizes the new social movements is not only a resistance against this general process serializing subjectivity, but also an attempt to produce original, singular modes of subjectivation, processes of subjective singularization" (Guattari & Rolnik 61).

Chapter 1

1. Written by Jose Moriche and recorded in 1927, the song weaves a foxtrot with popular national rhythms such as *corrido, huapangos*, and *adelitas*. It can be heard at https://www.youtube.com/watch?v=B_gYlu9kkR4.

2. In Mexican Spanish, "vacilar" is colloquially used to tease, trick, or pull someone's leg. As a noun, it refers to the act of collectively teasing.

3. I reference here the famous debate provoked by Jimenez Rueda's article, which lasted well over a year, with authors and cultural figures lamenting a lack of virile and masculine literature able to face the nation-building times they were experiencing. Pedro Ángel Palou explains how this debate began on December 1924 with the publication of the article "El afeminamiento de la literatura mexicana" by Julio Jiménez Rueda, where he states that literature is being feminized by a lack of male value, while implicitly blaming processes of consumption and mass culture as the realm of feminine values overtaking the male public sphere. Francisco Monterde answered with the article "Existe una literatura mexicana viril" in January 1925, which placed *Los de abajo* by Mariano Azuela in the cultural milieu and kickstarted the canonization process for this novel, promoting more authors to engage and categorize culture through the lens of male values and heteronormative masculinity.

4. The judges of the contest were Jorge Enciso (nativist artist and painter), Manuel Gamio (anthropologist), Rafael Pérez Taylor (organizer), and

Carlos Ortega and Aurelio González Carrasco (dance and theater producers). The contest was widely publicized in the newspaper and consisted of a beauty pageant that ended up focusing on "gatitas," Indigenous domestic workers, to crown a beauty queen, Maria Bibiana Uribe, who lived in Xochimilico but was dressed up with makeup and decoration to present the "authentic" Indigenous woman, the origin of the nation. In the end, this contest was key in extending the "nationalist project into the realm of aesthetics and the policing of the female indigenous body, which would continue to shape narrations of ethnicity, class, and collective identity" (López, *Ethnicizing the nation* 53). The global continuation of this colonial dynamic can be seen in Yalitza Aparicio's mediatic interventions in the wake of the success of Alfonso Cuaron's *Roma* (2018) and the multiple racist attacks she faced from Mexicans disclaiming her existence as both Indigenous *and* modern.

5.   "The identification between nationality and cultural modernity was strongly fortified in the aftermath of the 1910–20 Revolution, when the state intervened actively to shape a lay, modern citizenry out of Mexico's agrarian classes. This process was to be achieved through education and economic redistribution, through 'land and books,' as one agrarista from Michoacán put it. The result of this would be, according to president Lázaro Cárdenas's well-known formulation, not to Indianize Mexico, but to transform Indians into Mexicans" (Lomnitz, "Fissures in Contemporary Nationalism" 59).

6.   As John Mraz has signaled, this cultural dynamic where the *charro* becomes synonymous with the nation is complex and happens on several levels. A rich example is Emiliano Zapata's astute use of Hugo Brehme, another foreign photographer, to capture a picture of him dressed in a charro outfit with the sash and sword of the state governor of Morelos, as a portrayal that would legitimize his armed peasant movement as a political movement worthy of Madero's and the population's support. Equaling the famous picture to Korda's picture of Che Guevara, Mraz underlines how "the fact that a foreigner could get close to the fearsome warrior reinforces the idea of Zapata's concern for constructing his own image; he may have felt that an outsider would be more neutral, and the image would thus reach eyes outside the country, for he had little trust in the Mexican media (and rightly so, considering the uses made of this picture)" (68).

7.   In analyzing the key role *Santa* plays, in Gamboa's novel but also in the several film adaptations of the period, Palou speaks of this gendering of the *mestizo* body in the most lucid and eloquent way: "mestizaje depended on the erasure of the racial and ethnic characteristics of all Mexican women reducing them to their reproductive function. This discourse brutally inscribed itself on that which was invisible, the violated bodies of Mexican women as the use of racial essentialism made the mestizo politically invisible. To put it more bluntly, the primary operation of mestizaje

as a project consisted in making the woman invisible except for her function in the social construct (read: reproductive and sexual). As such, Santa finds herself lost (perdida) twice, first from her family and then her social role, since she does not have children" (*Mestizo Failures* 71).

8. The foregrounding of the "failed" public health institutions that need to be rebuilt in Cuaron's *Roma* is one prime cultural example. For a deeper understanding of how the ideological co-optation of these revolutionary figures (some of which were in direct opposition to the military who ended up in power) legitimized the PRI as the exclusive/exclusionary part of Mexico, see Mraz's *Looking for Mexico*, particularly chapters 1 and 2.

9. In a commendable study with a rich archive of photographic and film references due to their access to the Cineteca before 1982 (the year it burned down), O'Malley states what may seem an obvious component of *mestizo* masculinity but oftentimes is not underlined in such political terms: "the glorification of machismo is an especially effective deterrent to political consciousness because it functions as a safety valve, giving politically innocuous (though personally destructive) expression to what are, in the final analysis, political discontented caused by domestic and international socioeconomic inequities. *The legitimation of machismo leaves intact the system that engineers the need for its compensatory mechanisms and even protects that system by co-opting the revolutionary potential of hostility toward the 'father' and the dominant order*" (145; emphasis mine).

10. "Bourgeois views, including those of city administrators, held that women who sold goods and services, whether domestic or sexual constituted 'public' and hence sexualized women" (Sluis, "Projecting Pornography" 477).

11. Cultural appearances of this class-defined abusive structure include José Emilio Pacheco's *Las batallas en el desierto* (1981) or the now-viral classic "maldita lisiada" scene in the telenovela *María la del Barrio*, where employer Soraya Montenegro (Itati Cantoral) physically abuses her employee and beats her, refusing to humanize her by calling her "la gata esa."

12. In this sense, Sluis remarks on how the Deco bodies, potentially subversive if left to their own devices and expressing their sexuality in a fluid and unchecked manner, "expressed a mestizo modernity that celebrated cosmopolitanism while staying in the bounds of revolutionary nationalism, thus offering a way to neutralize the tension between indigenismo and mestizaje" (*Deco Bodies* 299).

13. One can see how the "inner state" of these men enforcing patriarchal violence upon short-haired (thus dangerous) women mimicked the formation of a "mestizo nationalism [that] thus implicitly supported the creation of a protectionist and modernizing state. It was to be a modernizing state because the mestizo, like his European father, had a propensity for action, for history. It was protectionist because the mestizo sought to protect

his maternal legacy from exploitation by Europeans, who felt no loyalty whatsoever to the land or to the Indian" (Lomnitz, *Deep Mexico* 54).

14. The neurological implications of this conception of the body as directly responding to the environment with that response being refracted by previous engagement with the same or other environments are many. For a deeper consideration of the relationships between coloniality, particularly in its most violent manifestations of murder, sexual abuse, slavery, and genocide, and the body as a kind of neurological mirror/historical repository of events, I highly recommend the reader explore Resmaa Menakem's work, particularly *My Grandmother's Hands* (2017).

15. Emphasis mine.

16. While there are multiple recordings of the song accessible today, and there were probably many performances that differed each time, for the remainder of the analysis I will be referring to the lyrics registered by E. Guerrero in the loose-leaf flyer accessed at the Archivo General de la Nación in summer of 2014.

17. I highlight the problematic nature of the concept of victimhood and the insidious ways in which it removes agency, particularly when used as a metaphor.

18. The fact that the song is most attributed to a tenor and songwriter who traveled from Spain to Mexico City, Los Angeles, Cuba, Colombia, New York, Chicago, and other major urban cultural centers in the Americas highlights this ability to "know" these bodies being shaped by the same fashion at the same time, but in different national locations.

19. The two main novels I am referencing are Arqueles Vela's *La señorita Etcétera* (1922) and *El café de nadie* (1926).

20. In this sense, Carlos Monsiváis underlines how with these new female stars of *carpas*, *tandas*, revue theaters, and more "aparece una mujer diferente, ya no la Madre, ni la Virgen, ni la Prostituta, sino la mujer inaccesible para quienes carecen de poder y dinero, a quien le encomiendan interpretar a la mujer accesible deslumbrante [there appears a different woman, no more Mother nor Virgen, nor Whore, but a woman inaccessible to those who lack power and money, to whom it is entrusted to interpret the dazzling accessible woman]" (*Celia Montalván* 66).

21. "The pelona and the India Bonita were two representations of femininity that worked together rather than in opposition, precisely because they 'condensed not only modernity and tradition, but also the Vasconcelian dream of the Cosmic Race and the perfect conjunction between the New Woman and the good mother'" (Gabara 181).

22. For a deeper study of consumption as a double-edged tool of market and state subjectivation and simultaneously a liberatory action springing from feminist agency, I highly recommend Joanne Hershfield's *Imagining la Chica Moderna. Women, Nation and Visual Culture in Mexico, 1917–1936.*

23. As Mexican philosopher Benjamin Arditi describes it, "la identidad no es una propiedad intrínseca sino el resultado de la relación del uno con el otro y, por ello, es el efecto de vínculos de todo tipo, culturales, políticos, religiosos, comerciales, étcetera, que cambian con el tiempo [identity is not an intrinsic property but the result of the relation of the one with the other, and thus it is the effect of links of all kinds, cultural, political, religious, comercial, et cetera, that change over time]" (30).

24. In this way, *vacilópolis* can be understood alongside *estridentópolis*, the response from the experimental avant-garde of the Estridentistas.

25. "The novel of the revolution, which was to become the major literary genre in Mexico by the thirties, grew in part out of a reactionary sentiment, a desire to re-masculinize Mexican literature, a wish to put an end to the numerous discourses that had erupted during the *porfiriato* that had questioned aspects of Mexican masculinity previously taken for granted" (McKee Irwin, *Mexican Masculinities* 131).

26. In this sense, I refer the reader to Vinodh Venkatesh's *The Body as Capital: Masculinites* for an understanding of the market of masculinities in a neoliberal Latin American context, where cultural production responds to the changes in economic and social relations created by neoliberal reforms.

27. That is, "the savage force of heterosexual desire is contained by the civilizing structure of marriage, which is supported, precariously, by the illusion of heterosexual romance" (McKee Irwin, *Mexican Masculinities* 7).

28. I define heteronormative in the case of Mexico as the particular mode of patriarchal values that naturalizes gender roles into the binary male-female; aligns biological sex, sexuality, gender identity, and gender roles with this binary; and silences homosexual and other dissident identities while promoting "deviant" sexual acts so long as they are carried out by compliant docile female bodies and patriarchal male bodies that reject any alternative subjecthood in their embodiments.

29. Apen Ruiz Martínez. "La India Bonita. National Beauty in Revolutionary Mexico," 287.

30. Rick López, *Crafting Mexico. Intellectuals, Artisans and the State after the Revolution*, 35.

31. The camposcape is that "visual vocabulary of an anachronistic and often feminized and racialized countryside tied to ideas of national 'authenticity'" (Sluis, "Projecting Pornography" 473).

32. For a visual and musical approach to Vacilópolis as a place of moral relaxation and social creativity, see Alfonso Morales's *El país de las tandas. Teatro de revista 1900–1940*.

33. I use the term heteronormative reproductivity in the Mexican context to signal the sexual foundation at the base of the cultural construction that is normative/institutional Mexico within coloniality. Throughout this history, male bodies are constructed as penetrators of territories/bodies and inseminators of genetics and civilization/knowledge, whereas

female bodies are territories/bodies to be taken and used to gestate the next generation to be educated, whether in their bodies or in the domestic enclosures of the household/school. Hernán Cortés and Malintzin are the foundational couple with Doña Marina and Juan de Jaramillo as the less violent iteration, and examples abound in literary pieces and films like Ignacio Altamirano's *El Zarco* (1901), Emilio "El Indio" Fernández's *Flor Silvestre* (1943), and Alfonso Cuarón's *Roma* (2018).

34. Emphasis mine.

35. Described as a model of editorial innovation, *El Universal Ilustrado* became a place where writers during the 1920s shaped their craft, practiced their posed public performance, and worked for a living. The short novels published in its pages tended to portray, in a very self-aware manner, "la representación del *reporter* como escritor esforzado, actor literario, héroe joven y sin recursos que sobrevive a la adversa brega del periodismo cotidiano [the representation of the reporter as diligent writer, literary actor, young hero with no resources that survives the unfavorable struggle of quotidian journalism]" (Hadatty Mora 183).

36. I use "pose" here in the greater sense of Silvia Molloy, as a strategy of self-construction, self-projection, and political-social intervention in the public sphere, constantly changing as global markets expand and gender roles are challenged. To pose is to know oneself to be seen, to mobilize one's body as symbol and stage, to perform (consciously or not, willingly or not) in order to maintain or subvert the social theater ordering our surroundings.

37. In her selection and introduction to Bonifant's texts, Mahieux signals how mass culture became synonymous in Mexico due in part to the high percentage of female workers with new consumer power: "el concepto de literatura 'afeminada' designaría en este caso una literatura contaminada por una cultura de masas que, dada la creciente presencia de mujeres como consumidoras culturales, se codifica como 'femenina' [the concept of 'effeminate' literature would in this case designate a literature contaminated by a mass culture that due to the growing presence of women as cultural consumers codifies itself as 'feminine']" (*Una pequeña marquesa* 30).

38. Emphasis mine.

39. The automobile was and is "the vehicle of choice to map women's physical and social mobility onto an increasingly sexualized urban landscape" (*Deco bodies* 167).

40. As a historical aside, the use of automobile technology to represent transgressive sexuality is something that gathers force in the 1950s, with the rebels without a cause who use their automobiles as extensions of their sociosexual selves. This can be seen also in the mystical car-chase film *Vanishing Point* (dir. Richard C. Sarafian, 1971), written by Cuban Guillermo Cabrera-Infante under the pseudonym Guillermo Cain, and

reaches a point of outright intercorporeal transgression and dissent in J. G. Ballard's novel *Crash* (1975) and its film adaptation *Crash* (dir. David Cronenberg, 1996). Rosi Braidotti, whose ideas underlie this chapter, develops the structures and implications of this intercorporeal and machinic (sexual) drive.

41. I point to the infamous *último vagón* (last car) of the Mexico City metro subway lines as another instance of urban transportation technology intersecting with dissident sexual behavior. Particularly in the major metro lines, the last car is known as a cruising spot for men; while authorities know this happens and it has made its way into urban slang, men still cruise other men for sexual trysts in these liminal and technological urban spaces.

42. Baptized as María del Carmen Mondragón Valseca, Nahui Olin grew up in Tacubaya. Due to her father's military profession, her family relocated to France between 1897 and 1905, after which she came back to Mexico City and met painter Manuel Rodríguez Lozano, whom she later married and lived with from 1913 to 1921. The family was exiled in Spain during the revolution due to their close ties to the Porfirian and later Huerta regimes. Lozano and Olin's ill-fated union fell apart when Olin came to terms with Lozano's homosexual desires and her own desires, both unable to coexist within the structures of normative sexualities, even within the freedom of aristocratic eccentricities.

43. While the philosophical implications of *nahui olin* are deep and have been enriched by Chicano/Xicanx intellectual and activists as pedagogical frameworks, I want to mark a distance from this history and rather place the artist's chosen name in the greater context of *mestizo* nationalism that generously appropriates culture as another manifestation of coloniality.

44. See Jorge Vázquez Piñon's *Accidentalidad y mecanicidad: dinámica existencial del Dr Atl. Carmen Mondragón Valseca. Nahui Olin: aproximación a un misterio* for an example of this approach. The historian carries out a psychoanalytic-historical biography that approaches her only in relation to Dr Atl as means to enter the psyche of the woman through the autobiographical novel *Gentes profanas en el convent* by Dr Atl and the love letters he published therein.

45. In 1923, "Llega Siqueiros corriendo a la preparatoria, tras él entran los preparatorianos con piedras y palos que lo amenazan y atacan su pintura. Ella [Nahui Olin] saca su pistola, lanza disparos al aire, se presenta [Ignacio] Asúnsolo [sculptor in charge of the guard brigade], al frente de los sesenta canteros que defendían los patios y fachadas de la SEP, inicia la balacera que agota los tiros de sus tres cananas, lanza mueras con su brigada a los estudiantes reacios a la belleza, así, a punta de bala se defiende de los enemigos. Terminada la refriega, ella acuerda con Jean [Charlot] la fecha para que le dibuje de cuerpo entero [Siquieros arrives running to the preparatory and behind him enter

students with sticks and stones who threaten him and attack his painting. She (Nahui Olin) takes out her pistol, shoots into the air, then (Ignacio) Asúnsolo steps forward in front of the sixty stones that defended the patios and façade of the SEP and the shootout begins in earnest until the bullets of her three bullet belts run out, she screams bloody murder with the brigade to the students who disliked beauty so that, at the point of bullet she defends herself from the enemies. The scuffle over, she accords with Jean (Charlot) the date for her bull body drawing]" (Sánchez Reyes, *Totalmente desnuda* 144).

46. She appears in Rivera's murals *La creación*, where she is Erato, the muse of erotic poetry; *Día de Muertos*, where her characteristic green eyes identify her among the skeletons; and *Historia del teatro en México*, where she blends in with the *burguesía porfirista*; as well as the murals in the stairs of the National Palace. Edward Weston also photographed her on various occasions.

47. In this regard, Anne Rubinstein criticizes Olin's lack of an explicitly feminist set of politics, for "her art made no feminist statements — she celebrated traditional gender roles rather than critiquing them — unless her viewers read into her rebellious depictions of her own sensuality a specifically political viewpoint" ("Nahui Olin. The General's Daughter Disrobes" 162). Complimenting and complicating this approach, I signal in her texts a set of politics that strongly brush against the patriarchy of *mestizo* nationalism through implicit and explicit actions.

48. This gesture appears once again in the brief interaction between Hollywood and Nahui Olin in 1927, where she visited Metro-Goldwyn-Mayer studios along with Antonio Garduño. She quit the production of the film she was starring in when she became aware of the overt sexualization of her body by the industry and the camera, going back to Mexico to continue her work with Garduño during the 1920s.

49. The recent exposition at the Museo Nacional de Arte (2018) and its journalistic covering underscore precisely this intervention in the public sphere from a dissident gender perspective, constructing Nahui Olin's career as a gender rebel who proposes other ways of being both Mexican and a woman.

50. For example, "hay en sus páginas todo el misterio desconcertante y enloquecedor que brilla en el fondo abismático de las esmeraldas fatales de sus ojos. Misterios que no es simplemente un misterio exterior de colorido, sino el reflejo alucinante del cerebro vibratorio, exquisito y enigmático de Carmen Mondragón [there is in her pages all the disconcerting and maddening mystery that shines in the abysmatic bottom of the fatal emeralds of her eyes. Mysteries that are not simply the exterior mystery of the colorful, but the hallucinating reflection of the vibratory, exquisite and enigmatic brain of Carmen Mondragón]" (Emilio Pisón. "Galería Femenina. Carmen Mondragón." La Prensa, San

Sebastián, España, April 14, 1922); "el reino de Nahui Olin no es de este mundo. Su turbulencia frenética, su manera de ver las almas y las cosas con esas pupilas verdes que le ha dado el misterio, ayudarían a encontrar una fácil solución al conflicto espiritual que ella trata de revelarnos. Una prosodia rara, una movilidad tremenda en el estilo y la no disimulada incertidumbre de haber transmitido su llama interna a la palabra mísera, caracterizan las palabras de este libro [the kingdom of Nahui Olin is not of this world. Her frenetic turbulence, her manner of seeing souls and things with those green pupils that have given her the mystery would help to find an easy solution to the spiritual conflict that she tries to reveal to us. A rare prosody, a tremendous mobility in the style and the not concealed uncertainty of having transmitted her internal flame to the miserable word characterize the words of this book]" (Luis G Nuila. "*Óptica cerebral (poemas dinámicos)* de Nahui Olin (Carmen Mondragón)" El Universal Ilustrado, 728. México, August 24, 1922, 9); and "he aquí un caso único de mujer . . . sin duda, la prosa es incorrecta, poca cuidada, nerviosísima; pero de una feminidad evidente que contrasta con lo profundo de los temas. Y la ideas de Nahui Olin son resultado de una observación directa y sencilla, ajena a la torcedura de una previa ilustración teológica. *Óptica cerebral* es un libro puro donde no cayó la semilla de otros libros; su virginidad tiene el mismo dulce encanto que en las mujeres y en las selvas [there is here a unique case of a woman . . . no doubt, the prose is incorrect, untaken care of, nervous to the extreme; but of an evident femininity that contrasts with the depth of the topics. And the ideas of Nahui Olin are the result of direct and simple observations, foreign to the twisting of a previous theological illustration. Cerebral Optics is a pure book where the seeds of other books did not fall; its virginity has the same sweet charm that lies in women and in jungles]" (José Gorostiza. "*Óptica cerebral. Poemas dinámicos* de Nahui Olin. México: Ediciones México Moderno, 1922." México Moderno, 1, no. 2, México: September 1, 1922, p. 126); emphasis mine.

51. Arqueles Vela (1899–1977) was a Guatemalan-born writer, journalist, and academic residing in Mexico who became a key figure in the Estridentista movement alongside Manuel Maples Arce and German List Azurbide. His short novels *La señorita Etcétera* (1922) and *El café de nadie* (1926) became important texts in the avant-garde and literary spheres, providing a differently gendered and urban alternative to the norms *novela de la revolución*.

52. Emphasis here and following are mine.

53. While I do not seek to equate terrorist assemblages with countercultural bodies, Jasbir Puar's approach of queer and Sikh migrants in the contemporary United States allows for another comprehension of countercultural bodies as "terrorists" to the nation, unable to be comprehended in their

extreme differences while simultaneously inhabiting its most intimate folds.

54. Araceli Barbosa describes Nahui Olin's creative enterprises as rupturing and transgressive: "el discurso visual en la obra de Nahui Olin propone una nueva forma de representación de la identidad femenina desde su propia alteridad subjetiva. Transgrede los códigos de representación hegemónicos al mostrar a la autora como sujetos activos de sus propios deseos eróticos y experiencias de vida. Con ello la artista realiza un acto de libertad inaudito en el discurso visual femenino de la época. Más allá, propicia el discurso erótico de la representación del deseo femenino en el arte y sienta un precedente histórico en la plástica de mujeres en México [the visual discourse in the oeuvre of Nahui Olin proposes a new form of representation of the feminine identity from its own subjective alterity. It transgresses the codes of hegemonic representation by showing the author as active subjects of her own erotic desires and life experiences. With this, the artist carries out an act of liberty unheard of in the feminine visual discourse of the time. Beyond that, it propitiates an erotic discourse of the representation of feminine desire in art and sets a historic precedent in the plastic arts of women in Mexico]" (194).

55. As Claudio Lomnitz has written, the nation is "a community that is conceived of as deep comradeship among full citizens, each of whom is a potential broker between the national state and weak, embryonic, or part citizens whom he or she can construe as dependents" (*Deep Mexico* 13).

Chapter 2

1. For a rich history of this particular sexual activity, the reader may consult Alex Espinoza's *Cruising, An Intimate History of a Radical Pastime.* For a specifically Mexican example, I recommend Kevin Chrisman *Meet Me at Sanborns: Labor, Leisure, Gender and Sexuality in Twentieth-Century Mexico.*

2. This fictional account is based on Guillermo Nuñez Noriega's *Just Between Us: An Ethnography of Male Identity and Intimacy in Rural Communities of Northern Mexico*, a landmark ethnography that traces the sexual practices outside of the social norms in rural spaces. For further historical reference, I recommend Zeb Tortorici's work in colonial archives, and Oliver Rendón's documentary films.

3. I follow Vinodh Venkatesh and his work on neoliberal masculinities in Latin America, particularly his monograph *The Body as Capital: Masculinities in Contemporary Latin American Fiction* (2015), where he underscores how "we must conceive of the masculine not as a solidified, unchanging, and eternal subject position, but as a fluid, sociohistorically specific, and interrelational identity that is plural in nature yet often seen

as singular in practice" (3). Keeping these hegemonic practices in mind, I want to bring forward bodies performing dissident sexuality as countercultural, their acts encoded by symbolic structures that are unable to contain their creative force vis-à-vis the nation (and normative gender).

4. The scandal of the 41 happened on November 17, 1901, when police officers were tipped off to and thus raided a private dance party attended only by men, where half the attendees were dressed and performing as women. It was rumored that Ignacio (Nacho) de la Torre, Porfirio Diaz's son-in-law, was among them, but he was not among the detainees sent to prison camps in Yucatán. The scandal gathered much attention from the press, especially from José Guadalupe Posada who made an engraving with corridos, and Eduardo Castrejón who wrote a novel about them sensationalizing and providing a clear moral judgment for any men thinking of straying from the straight path of heteronormativity. To this day, 41 remains a number synonymous with homosexual acts of behavior in popular and homophobic Mexican culture.

5. The focus on anal pleasure follows Spanish sociologist Javier Saez, who in turn recovers Guy Hocquenghem's work on homosexual desire from the 1970s. Thinking outside of identitarian categories whose roots lead to criminological and biopolitical institutions of the nineteenth century, anal pleasure shows how "el culo cumple un papel primordial en la construcción contemporánea de la sexualidad en la medida que está cargado de fuertes valoraciones sobre lo que es ser hombre y lo que es ser mujer, sobre lo que es un cuerpo valorado y un cuerpo abyecto, un cuerpo marica y un cuerpo hetero, sobre la definición de lo masculino y lo femenino . . . el culo es fundamental en la constitución del actual sistema de sexo-género, y es quien organiza y define las diferentes sexualidades" [the ass fulfills a primordial role in the contemporary construction of sexuality in the sense that it is loaded with strong valorizations about what it means to be a man and what it means to be a woman, what it means to be a valued body and an abject body, a faggot body and a hetero body, about the definition of the masculine and the feminine . . . the ass is fundamental in the constitution of the present system of sex-gender and it is the ass that organizes and defines different sexualities] (Saez 172–73).

6. The active-passive Mediterranean dichotomy refers to a conceptualization of homosexuality grounded in the valorization of the penetrative partner as non-homosexual and masculine and the penetrated partner as the one who embodies homosexuality and loses masculinity. Historically influenced by Catholic morality that condemns the penetrated sodomite while allowing the penetrator to be pardoned or not categorized as sodomite, this conceptualization has been applied to understand Hispanic sexuality since the conquest of the Americas. I refer the reader to Richard Trexler's *Sex and Conquest: Gendered Violence, Political Order and the European Conquest of the Americas* for a historical overview of this scheme, and

Matthew Gutman's *The Meanings of Macho: Being a Man in Mexico City* for an anthropological application of it. Octavio Paz in his grounding essay *Labyrinth of Solitude*, working on theorizing Mexican sexuality grounded in the violent encounter between Cortez and the Malinche, expounds on sexual acts (and especially popular Mexican sexuality) as inherently violent, where the "Chingada" is the position occupied by both female and male bodies that are broken, torn, violently penetrated, and ultimately raped, with absolutely no consideration or mention of pleasure. While the historical understanding of these two historical figures is complex and nuanced by the dynamics of power and abuse, and yet a narrative in which Malintzin/Malinche's voice is notoriously absent, I believe using this relationship to analyze and categorize all subsequent Mexican sexualities in a psychoanalytic manner is highly problematic, and yet remains commonplace in popular and intellectual descriptions of Mexican sexualities, at least until recently.

7. I would like to differentiate my position from previous scholarly work on Salvador Novo and other homosexual Contemporáneos, which tends to focus on sexual identities and the intellectual genealogies of homosexual identities through the (neo)baroque heritage of Góngora and the Generación del '27. While remaining acutely aware of the high-art intellectual circles that Novo constructed and moved in, along with Xavier Villaurrutia and other poets, I would rather like to push back on the association of homosexuality with elite artistic cultural spheres in order to highlight the historical continuity of same-sex desire, following Luis Felipe Fabre's approach in *Escribir con caca* (2017) (*Writing with Caca*, 2021), where he traces the political, social, and cultural weight of bodily pleasure in Novo's writings, anchored in the most embodied of all substances that is shit.

8. In addressing his gendered positionality vis-à-vis his writings, Guy Hocquenhem was explicit: "Yes, I can only think of homosexual as male. Yes, I refuse to speak of feminine homosexuality that I do not understand and of which I can only produce a fatally masculine theory. And all queers can say the same" (*Screwball Asses* 66). I follow this lead, not to delimit the potentialities of my queer interventions, but to recognize the limitations and hope to bridge them through dialogue and attentive listening.

9. See particularly the works of Zeb Tortorici, José Piedra's "Nationalizing Sissies" essay, and Pete Sigal's writings on colonial sexuality.

10. Robert Buffington's writings on homophobia and the working class in Mexico City from 1900 to 1910 in the wake of the scandal of the 41 provides a stark example of precisely this phenomenon, where the public press mobilizes the public category of the homosexual (named as *invertido* or *desviado*) to slander and generate class conflict. By constantly defining the citizen (whether that citizen was Porfirio Díaz or Francisco Madero or a representative of a "popular" working class) always in direct

opposition to the homosexual, the press generated (and continues to generate) a need for the homosexual body to exist as a public category, an "empty" signifier that serves to define the other empty signifier of the acceptable and proper citizen (the body that penetrates, as Octavio Paz will summarize). The complex web of meanings assigned to the homosexual body as a marginal sexuality thus resides more in class conflict, political struggles over power, and territorial control than in the homosexual acts per se; let us not forget that the scandal of the 41 was not precisely a scandal over sodomy (no sexuality itself was charged) but a scandal over a cross-dressing soirée, and most importantly a cross-dressing spectacle involving important political and business figures of the time.

11. As Brian Gollnick has signaled, "normative subjectivities require the construction of deviance" (245), where deviance becomes important insofar as it provides the structural boundaries and limits for normative subjectivities. In this case, *mestizo* citizens are ideologically constructed as male and heterosexual, their gender performance mattering much more than their sexual activity, forcing them to remain *macho* to avoid the effeminacy that threatens the body of the nation and opens the door to political delegitimization.

12. I highly recommend the work of Pablo Piccato for a critical approach to the role of criminology in the construction of nation across Latin America during the nineteenth and twentieth centuries.

13. In this sense, Robert McKee Irwin documents how the "conflation of effeminacy and male homosexuality has dominated Mexican views of homosexuality since the turn of the century when Mexican discourse on male transvestism and homosexual desire was raucously inaugurated with the scandal of the famous 41 transvestite ball" ("La pedo embotellado" 128).

14. That is, we must "reflect, on the one hand, on how homophobia was a major force in the construction of homosexual identities in Mexico and, on the other, examine its historical transformations and articulations from the early 1900s to the late 1970s" (McManus 236). As we approach literature and culture, "instead of being 'liberated' from its concrete conditions of production (and consumption) — in other words, erased from everyday life — gay literature must be located in shifting and frequently controversial dialogue with the dominant culture" (Schaefer 16).

15. I particularly direct the reader to the work of Robert Buffington, especially his writings on working-class masculinity and homophobia. By demonstrating how homophobia was mobilized in the Porfirian press as a strategy to manipulate male bonds across class lines through visual cues in political satire, Buffington provides a distinction between bourgeois and lower-class understandings of homophobia and homosexuals acts and how it has been used to construct social alliances across class divisions (195, 212).

16. In these lectures, "Martínez chose homosexuality as his topic and he argued extensively that, although homosexuals were not criminals per se, homosexuality should be seen as a constitutive index of the tendency to engage in criminal behavior. Martínez also emphasized that homosexuality was an illness caused by hormonal alterations and, therefore, was not punishable in itself even if it certainly was a social problem" (McManus 249).

17. In this sense, Carlo Coccioli's novel *Fabrizzio Lupo* (1953) deals with the Catholic moral prohibition of homosexual acts that underpins the criminological and medical rejections of homosexual bodies, translating morality into criminological biopolitical categorizations and hormonal imbalances instead of moral faults. In the end, the homosexual character engages with God and rejects an exclusionary morality, defending his existence as valid on all fronts. In the same way, Luis Zapata's novel *El vampiro de la colonia Roma* (1979), where the protagonist narrates his life to a recording journalist, constantly engages with the textual authority of the interviewer and the psychologist he sees, constructing his sexual identity in relation to these two sources of biopolitical discourse (the public eye and the medical gaze). See also Héctor Domínguez Ruvalcaba's work on *Modernity and the Nation in Mexican Representations of Masculinity* (2007), where he stresses how "the masculine is known by what it rejects" (3); namely, the 41, effeminate intellectuals and self- or socially identified homosexuals.

18. "Under the guise of perpetual drift and sway, it is a strange machine that nonetheless displays strong analogies with capitalism accumulation, in that it continuously projects into the past, due to its mechanism of collection and seriality, just as it projects into the future due to its forward-looking mechanism through which the conqueror thinks of his next conquest immediately upon completing the first . . . constructed like capitalism against death, the cruising machine carries death within it just like capitalism, for instead of being madly in love with what is present, it desires what is absent, it always desires the next object, it constructs itself on the establishment and secret assumption of lack, according to the absolute criteria of consumption" (Hocquenghem, *Screwball Asses* 73, 75).

19. Emphasis is mine.

20. "The most vigorous weapon against the couple is the immanent desire to desire. It must, of course, extend way beyond those structures known or unknown to sexual desire, and it must also have curbed the desire to be desired, which supposes that we start by desiring ourselves well. The desire to desire and to be desired, that's love, finally wrenched from the fetor of bourgeois humanism as well as from the childishness of mystical liturgies . . . the desire that says Why not? rather than No. The desire that shoots its refuses one by one. The phoenix of desire, snatched away from avarice and usury, finally engaged in polymorphous expenditure, in seepage, in prodigality, in dilapidation" (Hocquenghem, *Screwball Asses* 81).

21. One of his biographers, Sergio González Rodríguez says, "el descu-
    brimiento de su identidad homosexual, en Novo se entrelaza con el
    paisaje urbano, el de los primeros brillos modernos y sus símbolos:
    los escaparates, los autos, el vértigo de las actividad en la calle, los
    anuncios, la multitud [in Novo, the discovery of his homosexual iden-
    tity is entwined with the urban landscape, with the first modern glimmers
    and their symbols: the shining storefronts, the automobiles, the vertigo of
    street activities, the billboards, the crowds]" (74).
22. As Carlos Monsiváis states, "much of Novo's work and behavior revolved
    around his sexual transgression: the poems of a desolated outcast . . . the
    cultivation of a provocative dandyism, the exaltation of the pose in the
    very niche of an identity never to be forsaken. Without beating around the
    bush, in Novo homosexuality is the primordial impulse, stimulant, and
    sign of his identity" ("The Sidelong World" 4).
23. Emphasis is mine.
24. It is important to note here that *Pillar of Salt*, even if it was not published
    until 1998, did circulate in oral form from at least 1945 until Novo's death
    in 1974. Carlos Monsiváis and others recall social gatherings where Novo
    would read excerpts from this text to his guests, charging the words with
    a tonality that can only be reimagined. The parodic nature of certain pas-
    sages, such as the critical use of "normal" in the one quoted above, cannot
    be understated; on the one hand, it mobilizes self-deprecating humor as
    a strategy of survival, while on the other, it astutely names the (hetero)
    normative structures that deny his full existence.
25. "The body is involuntarily marked, but it is also incised through 'vol-
    untary' procedures, lifestyles, habits and behaviors. Makeup, stilettos,
    bras, hair sprays, clothing, underclothing mark women's bodies, whether
    black or white, in ways in which hair styles, professional training, per-
    sonal grooming, gait, posture, body-building, and sports may mark men's.
    *There is nothing natural or ahistorical about these modes of corporeal
    inscription*" (Grosz, *Volatile Bodies* 142). Emphasis is mine.
26. During his very brief study at the Escuela Modelo para Niñas (Model
    School for Girls) in Torreón due to the closing of the boys' school in the
    midst of the revolutionary violence, Novo "found it odd that they didn't
    assign me embroidery tasks, which I was certain I could accomplish, and
    I asked the girls to let me help them. A few were beginning to talk of
    sweethearts. They shared their secrets. . . . The contradictions in the rules
    that restricted the boys to the small patio during recess, separated from the
    girls, whereas in class we were all together, underscored in my eyes the
    injustice of a sexual discrimination that was as irritating as it was incom-
    prehensible" (*Pillar of Salt* 65).
27. The Escuela Normal Superior de Mexico was established in 1881 by Justo
    Sierra as an institution dedicated to the formation of professors for the
    nation. By the revolutionary decade, the school was in crisis due to a

lack of government support, but with the support of intellectuals such as Alfonso Reyes, Justo Sierra, Pedro Enriquez Ureña, Antonio Caso, and others, the school survived and continued to train professors. During the years of Novo's attendance at the Preparatoria Nacional, the faculty was composed of "activist *normalistas*, who awarded themselves the Preparatoria classes previously taught by the Scientists" (Novo, *Pillar* 89). This new generation of teachers bridged the gaps between Porfirian, revolutionary, and postrevolutionary constructions of (urban) masculinities, investing themselves in the education of urban men who would begin to hold offices during the 1920s and 1930s. I bring this forward to contextualize the men in cultural power at the time, and the various masculinities in conflict and negotiation on the stage of postrevolutionary México.

28. In other words, "freedom to shop is thus not synonymous with consumption. It is more specifically a means of imaging different forms of masculine identity. This discovery of new possible identities most defined Novo's excitement at walking the streets" (Gollnick 242).

29. While still at the Model School for Girls in Torren, Novo "imagined a boy who would come down the street in order to see me embroidering, who would smile, giving me a sign of love" (*Pillar* 65). Later, his reading of *The Physiology of Marriage* allowed him a deeper understanding of his teen desire in the context of (hetero)normative sexual initiations, "the characteristics of virginity and the stages of deflowering" (77). While this intellectual understanding of sexuality was developing, Novo's erotic engagements provided a parallel education on sexual, erotic, and romantic desire.

30. Emphasis is mine.

31. Emphasis is mine.

32. For a troubling of these rural masculinities particularly inflected by class positionality and with an inclusion of lower-class male sexualities, I highly recommend Guillermo Nuñez-Noriega's work, in particular *Just Between Us: An Ethnography of Male Identity and Intimacy in Rural Communities of Northern Mexico*.

33. Domestic workers' quarters are typically placed on the rooftops of houses in Mexico City, an architectural trend that can be observed in detail in Alfonso Cuaron's *Roma* (2018), set in 1970s Mexico.

34. This olfactory sensuality and eroticism will characterize Novo's desire as he recounts his experiences with Arturito, the chauffeur of one of the first passenger buses in the central Colonia Roma: "I began to fall in love with [Arturito], which had me waiting long hours on the corner of Tacuba and Brasil for the return of his vehicle, so I could take a seat next to him and breathe, with a delight both retrospective and promising, the emanations of gasoline from his body" (*Pillar* 115).

35. Contrary to scenes of interclass domination or exploitation, Novo talks about how "drivers were my passionate predilection: truck drivers, whom

I approached to start a conversation that ended with a date for that very night; or the chauffeurs of hired cars in which they would drive to us some appropriately dark or shady spot. One of these drivers on Calle San Juan de Letrán, famous among the 'crazy girls' for his sexaggeration, took me to the house on -4 Calle Pescaditos- on one Fidencio, who rented, for two pesos, his room with the wide brass bed" (Novo, *Pillar of Salt* 137). While the power dynamics of an educated middle-class man working closely with governments approaching a bus driver must not be underscored, I also want to call to attention the treatment of the 41 in 1901 and the cruel history of homophobic violence in Mexico: from families in conversion therapies still active, to the murders and sexual assaults that happen and continue with state impunity, to the economic violence of being unhired due to certain behavior or gender expression, such as the case of magistrate Ociel Baena. While Novo talks and writes about his sexual trysts very openly, this was more a weapon of self-defense than evidence of changing attitudes or upper-class privilege; the way in which the Contemporáneos were publicly spoken about and literarily attacked in the cultural sphere due to their sexual choices or their social behavior evidence the structural homophobia upon which the Mexican postrevolutionary state and society is constructed. Novo's class privilege, in economic as well as educational terms, does evidence a very cosmopolitan habitus characteristic of global capital, and yet his memoirs and experiences allow for a glimpse into the worlds of other sexualities, some of which are also being shaped by global capitalism and technology in very different ways.

36. Salvador Oropesa studies this queer encounter in *The Contemporáneos Group: Rewriting Mexico in the Thirties and Forties*, focusing on the construction of a homosexual identity through the connection with Lorca and a mutual baroque conceptualization of their homosubjectivities.

37. Humberto Guerra explores the question of the closet following Eve Kosofsky Sedgwick's work, reading Novo as unable to name homosexual identities as such and thus reinforcing the closet: "en este sentido, el texto de Salvador Novo refrenda este postulado, pues sus páginas se impregnan de esa imposibilidad al momento de nombrar la experiencia homosexual, ya que no puede hacerlo de otra forma que no sea binariamente, inscribiendo la tradicional dicotomía masculino-femenino. El homosexual es, entonces, un no-hombre, una aspiración a lo femenino que busca ser sujetado por un hombre verdadero. Este último es objeto de deseo y repudio de manera simultánea [in this sense, Salvador Novo's text endorses this hypothesis, since its pages are impregnated with this possibility in the moment of naming the homosexual experience, since it cannot name in a nonbinary way, inscribing the traditional masculine-feminine dichotomy. The homosexual is then a non-man, an aspiration to the feminine that seeks to be held down by a real

man. This last one is the object of desire and rejection simultaneously]" (1151).

38. This gay ghetto in Mexico City appears similar to the other middle-/upper-class ghettos that appear in other repressive and oppressive societies in the West (New York City, Paris, Madrid), which seem to be organized according to specific rules such as: "fleeing the norm means giving up happiness and an amorous life; 'bitching (the exchange of mutual insults) is the incessant reminder of the measure of scorn from those outside [the ghetto]; 'verbal transvestism' is obligatory because the closest identity for the 'weirdos' is feminine, and the result of contagion; relationship among gays do not work (' . . . for in his judgement, one *sullied himself*, by sleeping with those of one's own sex'); an exclusive relationship is clearly inferior to promiscuity" ("The Sidelong World" 44).

39. Lower- and working-class homosexual men have historically been the prime target of homophobic, heteronormative, and patriarchal violence. In Mexico, the prisons of Belem and Lecumberri contained prisoners, the San Marcos Fair was a space of exoticization and ridicule, and the figures of the berdache and the muxe were constantly used to contain deviant sexuality to a racialized and classed Other; Monsiváis speaks about how "'effeminates' of the lower classes — simply because of their appearance — were subjected to serial humiliations, stripped of all recognizable humanity, and only then allowed to survive" ("The Sidelong World" 17). For a visual archive of these homosexual detentions, I recommend the reader consult the online archive at the Fototeca of the Instituto Nacional de Antropología e Historia.

40. For "la *Estatua de sal* no es solo una biografía, es el retrato apasionado de una ciudad que palpita de una manera desconocida, desde el sitio mismo de lo reprimido. El amor que no puede decir su nombre tiene una serie de representantes con nombre y apellido, ilustre, aristocrático. Es una sociedad que ha cambiado de nombre a favor de sobrenombres en muchas ocasiones infamantes y que responde a otras coordenadas dictadas por la lógica del ghetto [*Pillar of salt* is not just a biography, it is the passionate portrayal of a city that beats in an unknown way, from the very site of the most repressed. The love that cannot speak its name has a series of representatives with name and last name, illustrious and aristocratic. It is a society that has changed name to favor nicknames in many cases badmouthing and which respond to other coordinates dictated by the logic of the ghetto]" (Marquet 58). In this sense, while the ghetto described by Monsiváis and Marquet must be read with caution as a textualization of an exclusionary community built around normative rules on the masculine body with a strong class component structured around consumption of lower and working classes, it nevertheless becomes a space where countercultural sexualities and countercultural acts may emerge.

41. Previously in the narrative, Novo made clear this understanding of homosexuality as a dangerous identity to embody or perform, as it placed him in the position of being a victim of heteronormative violence. While living with his extended family and sharing a room with his young uncle Guillermo, Novo saw him arrive beat up one evening and upon inquiring was told he (Guillermo) had found out his lifelong friend Carlos turned out to be a "puto" (either someone who hired the services of a female sex worker, or a man who engages other men in sexual acts). Then, "listening to Guillermo condemn Carlos, I felt myself turn red; that such contempt, that the violent rupture of long-standing friendship stemmed justifiably from the same sinister crime of which I knew I was the defenseless criminal; and that life held for me the same fate — of being the abject, sudden and irremediable outcast — when each one of those normal, well-balanced beings who had girlfriends and caressed whores found out that I, on the other hand, breathed life into an anguished, unquenchable thirst for the kiss of a cinematic hero" (*Pillar of Salt* 94).

42. Buffington rescues Roumagnac's writings and observations on homosexual behavior among the lower-class inmates of Belem prison and draws out the implications of his association between criminality as a series of acts and homosexuality as an identity. Later criminologists such as Alfonso Millán, Susana Solano, and Raúl González Enriquez would take this line of thought further, medicalizing the homosexual as deviant, corrupted beyond hope or redemption, and inherently criminal (123–24). The key point here is the circulation of a discourse with institutional definitions of homosexuality; beyond it being a moral or literary problem, as can be seen in the virility debates, this criminalization rooted in homophobia was producing bodies to be punished, naming homosexual acts, and generating identities in the process.

43. The mediatized nation "se trata de una concepción que el gobierno y sus simpatizantes capitalizan en provecho propio: se extraen de 'lo popular' expresiones supuestamente auténticas, claramente neutralizadas por la mediatización. El objetivo final es crear la Alta Cultura nacional [is about the idea that government and its sympathizers capitalize on self-benefit: they extract themselves from the more supposedly authentic 'popular' expressions, clearly neutralized by mediatizations. The final objective is to create a national High Culture]" (Díaz Arciniega 106).

44. María "spent the morning leaning over the washboard, rubbing almost to shreds our cloth handkerchiefs, from which, years later, with the benediction of Kleenex, we would finally be free. At night, she would carry halfway down the stairs a small mattress, on which she would doze, ready to open the door each time a lodger, at unexpected hours, started up the stairs accompanied by a quick shadow" (Novo, *Pillar of Salt* 150).

45. In her study of Salvador Novo as a queer icon, Rosa María Acero describes these studios as "sustitutos de sus hogares y representan un esfuerzo

por vivir su vida, dentro de la mayor normalidad posible. También pueden ser interpretados como una inversión de lo que la sociedad consideraba como un 'hogar normal.' Los momentos que pasaba en estos espacios privados eran de liberación y gratísimos para Novo [substitutes for their home, they represent an effort to live their life within the most normalcy possible. They can also be interpreted as an inversion of what society considers a 'normal home.' The moments that passed in these private spaces were moments of liberation and very dear to Novo]" (Acero 190).

46. "No hablemos del baño por salud. No hay, para mí, cosa más repugnante de saludar que los atletas profesionales y vegetarianos que no usan sino agua fría en chorros imprudentes, a las cinco de la mañana, y luego corren — ¿o corren antes? — antes de echar fuera la lengua, para conservarse como anuncios del Hierro Nuxado [We don't speak of the bathroom due to health. For me, there is nothing more repugnant than greeting the vegetarian professional athletes who only use cold water in imprudent jets at five in the morning and then run — or do they run before — before sticking their tongue out due to health, all to keep themselves like advertisements for Hierro Nuxado]" (Novo, "Motivos del baño" 131).

47. The version of the journal used for this analysis is a microfilm copy housed in the New York Public Library. Given the age and state of the microfilm, as well as its popular nature, pages numbers are not always visible or printed. For citing purposes, I will refer to the publication number and date.

48. Ruben Gallo paints a vivid image of these citizens in his study of Novo's engagement with Freud in Mexico: "in the 1920s most drivers were working-men, young enough to learn the complicated workings of automotive machinery, strong enough to crank the engine, lift the hood, and change a tire when the need arose, and presentable enough to look good in a freshly pressed uniform" (Gallo, *Freud's Mexico* 31).

49. "Desde el primer número, el periódico define su posición política, que consiste en disuadir a los choferes de la idea de organizarse sindicalmente. Estas páginas analizan las tácticas por medio de las cuales *El Chafirete* ofrece a sus lectores un ideal opuesto: una masculinidad definida por su individualismo, autonomía y libertad sexual, valores que la alejan de los ideales de solidaridad gremial más afines al sindicalismo. En cambio, la libertad sexual del chofer se propone como un atractivo que, como se verá, sirve para reinterpretar la diferencia de clases en una forma conveniente para los intereses declarados por el periódico [Since the first number, the journal defined its political position that consisted of dissuading drivers from the idea of unionizing. These pages analyze the tactics through which El Chafirete offered their readers an ideal opposite: a masculinity defined by individualism, autonomy and

sexual freedom, values that led it away from the ideal of union solidarity more in line with syndicalism. In turn, the sexual freedom of the driver was proposed as an attractive quality that, as can be seen, serves to reinterpret class difference in a convenient way for the declared interest of the journal]" (González Mateos 103).

50. "Apparently, the director and other collaborators of the journal [*El Chafirete*] had more of a taste for the newsboys who sold it or for the young fare collectors on the buses while Novo went after the most solidly built of the drivers themselves" (McKee Irwin, "La Pedo" 126).

51. "El ano es una gran metáfora del control de los sistemas sociales. Podemos definir un sistema como una estructura topológica (lo espacial) con un dispositivo termodinámico (la energía que circula por ese espacio). Lo político es una regulación de esos espacios y de esos flujos de energía. Todo sistema social es un sistema abierto, necesita de intercambios de energía, información, población, fuerza, materia. Intentad cerrar una ciudad y moriría. Intentad cerrar el culo de una persona y moriría [The anus is a great metaphor of control of social systems. We can define the system as a topological structure (the spatial) with a thermodynamic mechanism (the energy that flows through this space). The political is a regulation of these spaces and these energy flows. Every social system is an open system, it needs an exchange of energy, information, population, force, matter. Try to close a city and it will die. Try to close a person's anus and they will die]" (Saez and Carrascosa 70).

52. Adriana González Mateos describes these masculinities "cuyos rasgos se afinan número tras número: los choferes son conquistadores e irresistibles para las mujeres ("chica a quien él le tira el ojo, la convierte en su 'Pato,'" El Chafirete, número 1), pero al mismo tiempo responsables de sus hijos ("tiene necesidad de comer y vestir a sus hijos, y por tanto se busca la vida en el volante" El Chafirete, número 2). Uno de los rasgos más importantes de esta masculinidad es el hecho de que el chofer no obedece a nadie, y si bien trabaja duro y gana dinero, en ningún momento deja de divertirse; su trabajo lo convierte en "el rey del volante" (El Chafirete, número 28) [whose features become finer with each journal issue: the drivers are conquered and irresistible for women (girls to whom the driver launches an eye, he makes into his 'Duck'" El Chafirete, number 1), but at the same time responsible for his children ("he needs to feed and dress his children, and thus seeks a living behind the wheel" (El Chafirete, number 2). One of the most important features of this masculinity is the fact that the driver does not obey anyone, and while he works hard and earns money he does not stop having fun at any moment; his work makes him into the "king of the wheel" (El Chafirete, number 28)]." (Gónzales Mateos, 8).

53. For a visual essay on the last metro car and homosexual cruising in Mexico City, I recommend David Graham's *The Last Car: Cruising in Mexico City* (2017).

54. This aesthetic is echoed globally in the early paintings of the homoerotic artist Tom of Finland (Touko Valio Laaksonen, 1920–1991), whose drawings of military men, mechanics, bikers, cowboys, and other male bodies associated with labor and national service have had a global impact on the visual representation of male homosexuality.

55. The song can be accessed via YouTube in multiple recordings and was greatly popularized by Pedro Infante after his 1943 recording. I want to stress the heteronormative (and quasiracist) nature of the song, describing a man who seeks to consume a female body by whatever means possible, because he wants to. The *Chafirete* version, by placing two bodies in this act, subverts these *mestizo* notions of homosexuality and places full agency in the body consuming the male phallus.

56. In the words of Brian Gollnick, "the impact of Novo's sexuality, like that of his writing, derives not from his marginality, but from its unsettling closeness to the center of things. That is to say, from its suggestion that what has been repressed may be ubiquitous" (246).

57. Carlos Monsiváis describes Novo's most important contribution as his right to exist: "Novo writes to be read one day, and to be read, in the moment of writing, by himself. For this reason, *Pillar of Salt* is no mere provocation; first and foremost it is the exercise of rights denied" ("The Sidelong World" 45). For his part, Antonio Marquet elaborates on the provocative use of scandal as a strategy to name the unnamable, by describing forbidden details that are to be silenced (50, 52).

58. For a visual representation of this economic process and its complexities and inequalities, I point the reader to films such as *Los olvidados* (dir. Luis Buñuel, 1950), the *Nosotros los pobres* trilogy (dir. Ismael Rodríguez, 1948, 1953), or *El bombero atómico* (dir. Miguel M. Delgado, 1950).

59. "Al contrario de muchísimos poetas de los que hasta entonces escribían, Bohórquez nunca oculta o traviste al receptor o inspirador de sus versos: el hombre, el amado, la belleza del cuerpo masculino [As opposed to many poets who wrote at that time, Bohórquez never hid or cross-dressed the receiver or muse of his verses: the man, the lover, the beauty of the male body]" (Tellez-Pon 112).

60. Andrew Gordus focuses on Bohórquez's poetry and his engagement with political activism during the 1960s where "interwoven within these experiences is the influence of his sexuality. For Bohórquez his sexuality reinforces his sense of exile. To live one's homosexuality openly means risking exile from family and friends. To conceal one's homosexuality means exiling part of oneself to a dark corner" (143). While I agree this may be an appropriate reading of the social treatment the poet received during his cultural career, particularly in Mexico City and in relation to the cultural

institutions of the time, I believe this approach runs the risk of depoliticizing and negating the productive thrust of his theatrical and more socially
engaged latter-day writings such as *Poesida* (1991).

61. "La propuesta propiamente barroca consiste en re-vitalizar los cánones
clásicos . . . mediante un proceso ambivalente en que el despertar la
vitalidad cristalizada en ellos llega a confundirse con el *otorgarles* una
vida nueva [The properly baroque proposal consists of revitalizing classical cannons . . . through an ambivalent process in which the awakening of
a vitality crystallized in them gets to confuse itself with the giving of new
life]" (Echeverría, *La modernidad de lo barroco* 93).

62. In this way, I position my reading of the neobaroque differently than other
critics such as Salvador Oropesa, who characterizes Novo as an "escritor neobarroco, es decir, cuando imita modos literarios del barroco no
solo está imitando ciertos formalismos, sino que apela a un lector culto
que sepa leer poesía barroca, es decir, alguien que busca los significa-
dos ocultos y sepa encontrar las trampas y los acertijos literarios que
se encuentran en el texto barroco [a neobaroque writer, that is, when
he imitates literary modes of the baroque he is not only imitating certain
formalisms, but he is also appealing to a learned reader who knows how to
read baroque poetry, that is, someone who looks for the hidden meanings
and knows how to find the literary traps and riddles hidden in the baroque
text]" ("La representación del yo" 44). While the knowledge of certain
specific erudite references does allow for a more complex reading of the
neobaroque texts, I argue that their political impulse lies more in their
inclusion of popular references and vocabularies, generating assemblages
that break down cultural hierarchies and subvert and complicate representations and definitions of *mestizo* bodies, particularly those that appear in
popular film and media.

63. As poet and critic Sergio Tellez-Pon summarizes, Bohórquez is a "gran
lector de los clásicos, en la parte última de su obra escribe muchos
poemas intercalando versos en español antiguo, en nahuatl y en inglés,
además de los muchos neologismos que persisten a lo largo de prác-
ticamente toda su poesía. La virtuosa utilización que Bohórquez hace
del lenguaje lo convierte en un poeta portentoso al que, sin duda, hay
que volver la mirada [great reader of the classics, in the last part of his
work he writes many poems interweaving verses in old Spanish, Nahuatl
and English, as well as the many neologisms that persist throughout practically all his poetry. The virtuous use that Bohorquez makes of language
transforms him into a powerful poet to which no doubt we must look
toward" (113).

64. I want to signal in particular Bohórquez's poetry collections *Acta de confirmación* (1966) and *Canción de amor y muerte por Rubén Jaramillo y
otros poemas civiles* (1967) as two books that stand out as involved political poetry, where he directly engages with political history and figures

such as Rubén Jaramillo, a murdered activist who fought for land reform, or Silvestre Revueltas, brother of José Revueltas and composer of Marxist tendencies. In *Acta de confirmación*, whose title plays on the Catholic ritual of confirmation typically practiced in adolescence in Mexico when the individual becomes a social subject, he published his most political engaged poem, "Patria, es decir."

65. Pedro Ángel Palou describes this way of conceptualizing politics as an "erotics of politics. The politics of bodies become the only way to be freed from the national trauma of foreign violation. The substitute father or the soldier that claim the bodies of women just as he claims the vanquished territory" (87).

66. The astrological references that abound in the play are in line with the rich queer countercultural bodies of dissident culture where magic, herbal remedies, and other nonnormative cultural and epistemological practices are strategies for survival as well as depositories of cultural knowledge. Aldebarán is a reference to the star, a cultural symbol of torch-bearing and illumination, and a visual contrast with the equine references of Sagittarius, the astrological sign associated with Chiron. Golondrina may be a reference to the mythological importance of the swallow as an image of eternal and cyclical rebirth and resurrection; in the Mediterranean cultural mythos, Isis is the mother goddess who mourns the death of Osiris and transforms into a swallow, while in ecological systems swallows are migratory birds that return to certain areas after leaving for a period, thus literally "resurrecting" after an absence. I signal these references to underline a rich mythical underpinning that is both in line with a Mexican theatrical sphere with the likes of Emilio Carballido or Alfonso Reyes, and with a queer history of astrology and alternative cultural practices.

67. "Igual que en una madeja de interminables nudos ciegos, en el teatro de este autor la familia aparece como la más ridícula caricatura del poder que se organiza para la continuidad interminable de la tiranía doméstica [Just as a skein of unending blind knots, in this author's theater the family appears as the most ridiculed caricature of power that organizes itself for the unending continuity of domestic tyranny]" (Salcedo "La obra dramática de Abigael Bohórquez." Estudio preliminar 14).

68. "They have sought to punish the homosexual, the transvestite and to a lesser extent other sexual deviants both as a means of reinforcing the distinctive identity of a group by emphasizing its boundaries and as a means of maintaining the boundaries between the different layers of military or religious hierarchy" (Davies 1033).

69. The image of the horse as a stand-in for staged (homo)sexual desire has concrete references in the theater of Federico García Lorca, another famous homosexual playwright who suffered at the hands of institutional homophobic violence. Lorca tends to use horses to represent sexual desire, and in particular dissident female and homosexual desire, in ways

that bypass socially normative expressions of this sexual desire. This can be seen in the stallion in *La casa de Bernarda Alba*, which may represent the powerful sexual urges that motivate Adela to escape in sexual trysts with Pepe, as well as in the avant-garde play *El público* (1930). Critic Rafael Martínez Nadal has signaled how "one could say that these horses, in the form of a charade, enunciate the core of the drama we are about to see: the power of hidden desires, the normality in abnormal relations, the apparently strange correlations, the inter-communication between different levels and spheres" (212). In the experimental play, four horses (men in costume) appear on stage and engage the director, making explicit their previous sexual relations and ongoing desire with the man allegedly in control of the theatrical space. In the end, the public takes over the representation when the director goes too far in letting his desires run free, queering the classical Romeo and Juliet death scene by making Juliet an obvious man in drag. Lorca's use of the equine symbol to make visible the latent violence of normative societies quietly directed against homosexual and dissident citizens anticipates Bohórquez's play and creates a wider context for us to understand the historical presence of alternative sexualities.

70. That is, the *mestizo* camposcape is "a distinctive form of orientalism that equated exotic landscapes of the countryside with indígenas, the past, and national identity. Because of the campo's perceived ties to an eternal and unchanging nature, camposcape represented a constellation of spatial imaginaries imbued with pastoral qualities rendered as timeless, static in geographic, physical and human features" (Sluis, *Deco Bodies* 18).

71. For instance, Andrew Gordus has read the appearance of the desert as a "need to return to the land, to find the origins of their existence and identity is a response to internal exile. In some sense each author feels isolated and/or excluded from the world and society he or she inhabits. They are culturally and spatially excluded within Mexico because of their distance from the national center, Mexico City. To participate in the national culture, though, means risking separation or alienation from their regional roots. . . . The vast desert of Sonora metaphorically comes to represent the isolation and abandonment they feel" (142).

72. Another example of this charging of the local space (the desert) with Indigenous and autochthonous culture (typically the Other side of *mestizo* nationalism) without Othering them appears in the already mentioned *Abigaeles*. *Poeniñimos*, published by the government of the state of Sonora through the Instituto Sonorense de Cultura in 1990 after it won the Concurso del Libro Sonorense. In the first and third sections of the book, Bohórquez writes a series of small poems dedicated to children, the *poeniñimos*; between them, he inserts an *Intermedio sobre Jesus Niño en Sonora*. In this longer poem, he describes the sacred family of Mary, Joseph, and Jesus in exclusively regional terminology, recycling a series

of figures and dis-Othering them, erasing the distance in their differences and anchoring them in an extremely localized regional space and time. The erotic nature of the relationship between Mary and Joseph is underscored with a retelling of a verse from *Madrugada* when their bodies are described as "bebiéndose, enlazados // fueron entre la vid y el trigo y la Solana // a procurarse un beso // de pinole" [and María and José, drinking each other and entwined // went between the grapevine and the wheat and the solarium // to give each other a kiss . . . of pinole]" (30). Upon Jesus's birth, the family is visited by the three wise men, now reappearing as three Indigenous elders from what is now known as the region of Sonora: Comcáac (Seri), Yoéme (Yaqui), and Tohono O'odham (Papago). Each of these elders bless the baby Jesus with a gift from their culture and lands (32). In this way, Bohórquez generates a regional desert space where cultures come together, fuse, support each other, and gift each other; rather than a process of *mestizaje* that erases the past, Bohórquez's desert reconnects the local and contingent material space (the heat of the desert, the food, the trees, the bodies) with a national religiosity to (re) generate alternative temporalities and nationalities.

73.   Anticommunity is defined by Irving Goh in dialogue with Deleuze and Guattari's multiple works as an answer to the problems of arboreal social organizations. Building on the nomad machine and smooth spaces, Goh proposes "this *other* social relation, this new communitarian assemblage, may be 'nonorganic' perhaps because it will be an inhuman community, inhuman because freed from the anxieties of subjectivity, representational drive, and consciousness of the metaphysical human Being — Being that thinks limitedly and inclusively only in the image of itself, and Being that only looks towards a One of totality of community or a community of a quantitatively accumulative One" ("The question of community in Deleuze and Guattari (I): Anti-Community" 226).

74.   That is, because "of the active historical suppression of information related to the topic of homosexuality, it has become in many cases both necessary and efficacious to search in the shadows for the 'semantic figures' which relate to the *lived experiences* of those whom today we might call queer" (Benshoff 23). Emphasis is mine.

75.   In this sense, "straight time tells us that there is no future but the here and now of our everyday life. The only futurity promised is that of reproductive majoritarian heterosexuality, the spectacle of the state refurbishing its ranks through over and subsidized acts of reproduction" (Muñoz, *Cruising Utopia* 22).

76.   This ethical difference is slight and serves to underline the boundaries of heteropatriarchal society that captures heterosexual desire into strict social structures that are carefully watched and policed by the institutions of marriage, courtship, and monogamy. Ultimately, all characters stage a complex society that becomes recognizable, as Sagitario speaks in his

last monologue: "lo sabemos todos. Lo hemos leído. Nos cuentan. Esto sucede. Sucedió. Sucederá. Podría sucedernos. Nuestros hogares son historias. Nuestros países son historias más. En nuestra fauna criolla conocimos, conocemos y conoceremos saurios gigantescos, simios equilibristas que han sufrido muchas veces metamorfosis extraordi-narias y se convierten rápidamente de demagogos en magnates, que tienen el signo de cierta aristocracia o cierta parlería y parecen mov-idos por una fuerza desolada, no por eso menos implacable. Esta es, pues, una historia de historias . . . Pero, si nuestra pobre historia, fuera la de usted, señor . . . .Usted, ¿qué haría? [we all know it. We have all read it. It is told to us. This happens. It happened. It will happen. It could happen to us. Our homes are histories. Our countries are more histories. In our creole fauna we knew, we know and we will know giant saurus, balancing simians that have suffered extraordinary metamorphosis many times and that quickly transform from demagogues to tycoons, who have the sign of a certain aristocracy or talkative gesture and seem to be moved by a desolating force, but by no means less implacable. This is, then, a story of stories . . . but, if our poor story was that of yours, sir . . . you, what would you do?]" (Bohórquez 42).

77. In this sense, Sagitario embodies a revolutionary ethos of justice and lib-erty, words he repeats along with Golondrina several times. Thus, as Palou observes in *Los Olvidados* (dir. Luis Buñuel, 1950), "the mestizo revolu-tionary project intended to establish social justice had failed. It could not be realized because rather than liberated, the mestizo was installed as an indentured servant to capitalism. This project was mediated by the bio-political power, the life and death of the state itself. The mestizo's new 'freedom,' then, was the possibility of surviving as an invisible being. He or she was free to join the labor force and to accept property or goods from the state" (*Mestizo Failures* 99).

78. Emphasis is mine.

Chapter 3

1. In this way, I follow Christopher Dunn in his approach to Brazilian counter-cultural movements, who stresses on the one hand how "the counterculture was a product of Madison Avenue innovations in the realm of advertise-ment that promoted niche-product consumption as a way of expressing individualism, nonconformity, and social distinction" (*Contracultura* 7) while refocusing our attention on the specific actions the youth were tak-ing in their immediate contexts and on the effects of these intentions and actions on their bodies as liberatory practices.

2. As Christopher Dunn has established in the Brazilian countercultural context of the 1960s and 1970s, commodification of counterculture is a

complex and sometimes contradictory experience, depending on the specific national context where it happens; "the fact that contestation found expressions through consumption, especially in an advanced consumer society such as the United States, hardly comes as a surprise. If commodification relativized or undermined some of the more radical claims of the counterculture, it also ensured that it would have an extended reach . . . while it is important to recognize the limitations of counterculture, it is also essential to *understand its significance in motivating young people* in many different national contexts to reconceive politics in both personal and public spheres during the Cold War period" (*Contracultura* 8). Emphasis is mine.

3. Films such as *Los tres huástecos* (dir. Ismael Rodríguez, 1948), *Enamorada* (dir. Emilio Fernández, 1946), or *Flor silvestre* (dir. Emilio Fernández, 1943) solidify the imagery of the revolutionary hero and the peasant armies behind them, while leaving the actual social changes (or lack thereof) on the sidelines in favor of (re)presenting war, violence, and won battles.

4. The modern UNAM had existed as such since 1910 in various locations in downtown Mexico City and began to be moved to its current location in Ciudad Universitaria in southern Mexico City after 1943, with various historical buildings such as the Biblioteca Central and the Estadio Olímpico going up during the 1950s. It was a modernization of the Real y Pontificia Universidad de México, a viceroyalty institution established in 1553 that lasted until 1865, to be refounded in 1910 by Justo Sierra. The Instituto Politécnico was founded in 1936 in the socialist years of President Lázaro Cárdenas and has grown to be the second most important educational institution in Mexico. For the specific history of student mobilization and activism in the 1950s and 1960s, see Jaime Pensado *Rebel México: Student Unrest and the Authoritarian Political Culture During the Long Sixties* (Stanford: Stanford University Press, 2013).

5. *Formando el cuerpo de una nación. El deporte en el México posrevolucionario.* Comps. Montserrat Sánchez Soler and Dafne Cruz Porcini (México: Conaculta: 2012).

6. Diana Sorensen explores the reception of the oeuvre of Herbert Marcuse as a key factor in the changing mindscape of the decade. Compounded with the effects of the Cuban Revolution and the surge of anti-capitalist ideologies such as the theology of liberation, Marcuse's *Eros and Civilization* (1955) and *One-Dimensional Man* (1964) — translated into Spanish by Mexican writer Juan García Ponce — quickly caught on with "more receptive audiences in the sixties, when the horizon of expectation was receptive to the kind of critical thinking that combined Marxism, psychonalaysis, and traces of surrealism to proclaim the need for new social, political and cultural forms to be built on the ashes of the old one. Marcuse's work called for a total transformation in which the utopian

character was psychic, political and cultural" (Sorensen 4). Marcuse's call for a *great refusal* would reverberate with the youth of these decades, reappearing in later global countercultural high moments.

7.   Two important texts serve to understand these changes on a quotidian level, especially for the middle-class experience during these and later decades: first, José Emilio Pacheco *Las batallas en el desierto* (1981), where the author describes what it felt like to be a child in Mexico City in the midcentury, and especially the contradictory experiences of higher education where conservative ideology was as strong as leftist sentiments; second, Octavio Paz's *Laberinto de la soledad* (1950), and especially the chapter "El pachuco y otros extremos," which used the figure of this transborder citizen to critique Mexican society as a whole and serves as an example of the insidiousness of heteronormative and colonial ideologies in the guise of liberal leftist thought.

8.   As Price states, "not only were they [rock films] instrumental in modernizing Mexican cinema, they were wildly popular. They drew large crowds and created audiences, taught adolescents new dance steps, and exposed viewers to modern sights and sounds that connected with the broader youth culture of the day" (56).

9.   Roberto Avant-Mier signals how "the Mexican government in the 1950s and 60s saw rock 'n' roll music as a way to inculcate youth with Mexican nationalism. Artists were encouraged to sing in Spanish, to sing 'safe' love songs and to serve a nationalist hegemony. Consequently, forms of social protest included singing in English, singing political songs, or both" (13).

10.   It must be underlined that the tag "Onda generation" had circulated informally in the latter part of the 1960s and was solidified by the publishing of the anthology *Onda y escritura* (Margo Glantz, 1971); the authors themselves did not identify as a movement nor did they publish/write as such. However, there are certain thematic lines that characterize their texts in the milieu of writing of those times, particularly a search for a youthful identity; a use of linguistic neologisms that mixed English, French, Spanish, and popular slang; a redefinition of gender politics (that sometimes ended in reinforcing patriarchal control over women's bodies); and a musical taste where rock and blues were the paradigmatic poles.

11.   Christopher Dunn documents how the Brazilian counterculture was a series of responses to similar conditions, where both countries experienced "authoritarian modernization, which emphasized capital accumulation, infrastructural and technological development, expansion of communication networks, investment in higher education, and growth of consumer markets, *while suppressing political dissent, curtailing labor demands, and establishing and enforcing a regime of heavy-handed security*" (*Contracultura* 32). Emphasis is mine. This same process can be seen playing out in different contexts, including in the United States with the COINTELPRO (Counter Intelligence Program, 1956–1971).

12. I point the reader to the documentary *El grito* (dir. Leobardo López Arretche, 1970) as an archive of student activism and state violence, and to Susana Draper's *1968 Mexico: Constellations of Freedom and Democracy* as a recent text that covers a deeper history of feminist struggles in the period.

13. Specifically in the Mexico City context, I refer to Carlos Monsováis's appraisal of the Avándaro concert in 1971 and his take on the counterculture in general included in his essay "La naturaleza de la onda" published in the book *Amor perdido* (1971). Here, the renowned essayist (at this moment a burgeoning critic but not yet with the cultural capital he would have in later decades) understands this globalized youth culture from a "colonialismo mental" perspective, where youth are merely imitating foreign trends and consuming goods in an uncritical way, leading into escapism and depoliticization. This same (self)critique can be observed in the short films of Sergio García Michel and José Agustín analyzed in later chapters, and I underscore how Monsiváis is not particularly alone in speaking this critique and how he chooses to go a step further to condemn the youth for their actions. A voice that counters Monsiváis is surprisingly that of the elitist and hyperintellectual writer Salvador Elizondo, who published "Física y metafísica de la Onda" in his book *Contextos* (1973), where he describes the consumption of hallucinogens as mystical tools to be used against corrupted institutions that are failing society, such as the Catholic Church and the family.

14. A core tenet of countercultural movements throughout the globe, but especially in the Americas, was personal transformation where through various strategies, groups "typically assign primacy to 'consciousness-raising,' a process of mind-expanding self-critique that embraces new ideas and perspectives. For some people, this process was aided by the consumption of mind-altering drugs, especially marihuana and hallucinogens such as LSD and psylocibin mushrooms. For others, countercultural consciousness-raising involved a radical critique of 'the West' — understood in terms of European and Christian civilization — and the embrace of Asian, African and Native American cultures and religions" (Dunn *Contracultura* 5).

15. As a historical footnote, recent archeological findings are proving that the rite of the mysteries of Eleusis, which were a staple of Mediterranean culture for at least 2,000 years before 0 BCE, and the rise of the Christian Church included ritualized ceremonies where ergot fungi was consumed in bread and wine format. Ergot fungi contains LSA, one of the precursors of LSD and a substance responsible for hallucinations and other psychedelic effects. Alternative evidence suggests the use of mushrooms in the preparation of the concoctions that were ritually consumed in the mysteries. Whatever the case, there is currently strong evidence that points to the ritualized consumption of psychedelic substances at the core of Western

culture as we know in the Greek and Roman worlds, with Plato, Sophocles, Pericles, Marcus Aurelius, Cato, and the rest of the ancient Greek and Roman philosophers, statesmen, and thinkers as regular attendees of these rituals, alongside the cultural and political elite. For more information on this, see Albert Hoffman's *The Road to Eleusis*, coauthored by Carl A.P. Ruck and R. Gordon Wasson.

16. Walter Benjamin, *On Hashish*.

17. The day April 19, 1943, continues to be celebrated as Bicycle Day, a psychedelic holiday worldwide.

18. Walter Pahnke, "The Contribution of the Psychology of Religion to the Therapeutic Use of the Psychedelic Substances," in *The Use of LSD in Psychotherapy and Alcoholism*, ed. H. A. Abramson (Indianapolis: Bobbs-Merril, 1967), 629–52.

19. Critic Rachel Adams calls attention to the lineage of Beatnik and other countercultural travelers (Kerouac, Ken Kesey and Tom Wolfe, Oscar Zeta Acosta) as they voyage to Mexico and brings them together despite their generational, racial, and class differences in that "what these authors share is that they return to the US having learned a great deal about their own commitments and remarkably little about Mexico itself. Each is countercultural in that protest against the constraints of national culture leads him to travel outward in search of alternatives" (71).

20. In this, Dalton is directly influenced by Julio Cortázar's *Rayuela* (1963), which sought to resignify the relations of interpretation between text, reader, and author.

21. In the lineage of (masculine-centered) psychedelic literature, we find authors such as Charles Baudelaire, Samuel L. Coleridge, Antonin Artaud, Aldous Huxley, Ken Kesey, Parménides García Saldaña, José Agustín, Hunter S. Thompson, or Tao Lin. I bring these forward not to reject their contributions to psychedelic and world literature in the name of gender, but rather to highlight the particularity of Dalton's ouvre and the greater canon in which her novel coexists, as well as its particularities in terms of gendered representations of psychedelic experiences. It goes without saying that the hormonal experiences of LSD or another psychedelic are wildly different across bodies as we seek (and fail wonderfully) to classify ourselves according to gendered identities defined by modern institutions.

22. See Figure 3 for other visual examples of typographic imagination and playfulness in *Larga sinfonía en d.*

23. Pollan, *How to Change Your Mind*, 322–23.

24. Prohibited by laws and stigmatized by the medical and scientific establishment, psychedelic research lay dormant for thirty years before the recent explosion in global research over the 2010s. Psilocybin and LSD are currently promising substances in the treatment of addiction, depression, and terminal-diagnosis anxiety. This section offers a more thorough overview of these findings, but suffice it to say here, one of the most

promising is the mapping of the networks that make up the human brain. One of these, the default mode network, has been defined as the "network of brain structures that light up with activity when there is no demand on our attention and we have no mental task to perform" (Pollan 302). Described originally by Marcus Raichle in 2011, the DMN exists among the complex series of specialized networks and systems that make up our brain as *the* network that in some way conducts orders, establishes hierarchies in the connections between regions of the brain, and "learns" from past experiences. It solidifies in the neural networks in the passage from childhood to adulthood, thus allowing for a more complex understanding of the social learning that informs and shapes the production of identity. Psychedelics tend to temporarily diminish the activity on this particular neural network, allowing for the brain to access neural connections (and make new ones) between regions of the brain, such as emotion, memory, and sensory processing. Neuroscientists are still exploring the implications and workings of this network, and results so far are pointing toward its deep relationship in building the psychological construct of Self and the political construct of Subject.

25. In an interview, Dalton specified how this narrative structure was inspired in part by Julio Cortázar's *Rayuela* (1963), which demonstrates an engagement with a wider hemispheric literary sphere.

26. Critic Timothy Robbins explores how José Agustín's cultural references in *La Tumba* serve to construct Gabriel Guía as a highly intellectual youth with plenty of cultural capital to share, where rock culture is embraced to resist parental authority with little to no attention paid to the lyrics themselves (16, 19). I agree with this reading, and I add that this particular aesthetic characteristic of capitalist-like accumulation of (counter)cultural capital is what makes these male authors so powerful in the literary sphere, whereas Dalton's and García Saldaña's more anti-accumulative and playfully creative uses of countercultural references and capital construct narratives that do not establish these authors as authorities with capital but as shifting creators in flux.

27. In line with other countercultural theorists of the time, Berke also pointed out how, in accordance with the individual over social change, the revolution must be carried out inside the individuals themselves as much as outside in society: "it is at this level that the revolution really takes place, for if people cannot find some way collectively to destroy — destructure this system of operations inside themselves — then the overthrow of the state degenerates into a simple power struggle between X and Y with the nature of society remaining the same. And it is at this level that what is happening now is qualitatively different than previous attempts at revolution" (34).

28. In this sense, the work of Herbert Marcuse, especially *The One-Dimensional Man*, is extremely important to mark the historical context.

Theorized in the cradle of US counterculture that was California, the work of Marcuse explores answers to the impasse that critical theory of the Frankfurt School came up against as they navigated philosophical and political thought in the wake of fascism and nuclear destruction. His reception in Mexico, alongside that of Marshal McLuchan's *The Medium Is the Message*, triggered a wave of countercultural thought that in rock music, comic zines, and other alternative artistic formats sought to break with the social and cultural establishment and simultaneously create a new and different society (Margarita Dalton in discussion with the author, July 2012).

29. "Representational space is constructed by signification. Unlike conceptualization, which works through thematic construction, that is, the shaping and construction of physical reality by ideas, signification changes the *meaning* of psychical reality to prepare for the changing of reality itself . . . representational space influences the spatial practices of individual subjects when they become aware that they do not merely inhabit social space as passive subjects but can actively participate in making it" (Cheah 85).

30. After saying how lysergic acid can disrupt capitalist relations, "yo no se lo daría a los obreros, se lo daría a ellos y al patrón a la vez, simplemente los haría darse cuenta de su relación estúpida y del absurdo juego que los mantiene en tal situación [I wouldn't give it to the workers, I would give it to them and the boss at the same time, I would simply make them become aware of their stupid relationship and the silly game that keeps them in that situation]" (Dalton 26), Martin then realizes that this simple act would be a violent foundational event in curtailing individual freedom and distances himself from that line of thought, suddenly aware of the patriarchal injunction to establish his will over those of others.

31. "Whatever their objective or subjective effects, it is hardly for the purpose of enculturation that LSD or DMT is employed in our society, at least in the sense in which the traditional Indian learns to see himself as a functioning member of his society. And yet, objectively, the chemistry of these modern drugs differs little from that of substances long employed in the 'primitive' world; moreover, as noted earlier, as science has recently discovered, the botanical psychochemical used for millenia in ecstatic-religious and therapeutic rites and their laboratory equivalents are structurally very similar to compounds that occur naturally in the mammalian brain" (Furst 87).

32. Critic Hugo Viera points out how "after Roberto's drug experience, during which he literally steps outside of himself, the young narrator will not return to a place in mainstream society but will seek refuge in the mountains, in the margins, reproducing the gestures of Fidel Castro and Che Guevara in the Sierra Maestra, as he attempts to de-stabilize the state through armed conflict" (153).

33. In José Agustín's *La tumba*, the protagonist, Gabriel Guía, commits suicide at the end of the novel. In *Gazapo*, the male adolescents witness acts of violence and do nothing, leaving their middle-class identities to dissolve into the anonymous mass of the city at the end of the novel. Even in *Pasto Verde*, Parménides García Saldaña's main character and alter ego drives around the city with ever-increasing speed while shrouded in green smoke, looking for and never finding his idealized sexually liberated woman until he fades away into the ocean of global rock references he has placed around him.

34. Although now being critically approached as the embodiment of extractivism and colonial approaches to traditional uses, R. Gordon Wasson and his wife, Valentina Pavlovna, were important figures in the popularization of the uses of mushrooms and other substances in ancient ritual as well as in contemporary groups. Throughout their life's work, the couple collected convincing evidence that three major ancient cultures (Hindu, Greek, and Mesoamerican) used a variety of substances to achieve alternate states and communed with the divine, hence the name *entheogen* or calling forth the divine within. However, while there is historical evidence of their cultural presence (soma in the Rig-Veda, kykeon in the Eleusinian Mysteries, various mushrooms, seeds and cacti in American cultures), there is no recording of the specific effects as these ceremonies were highly ritualized and typically reserved for the political and social elites or used as healing practices with carefully guarded secrets. In what is now being described as the "psychedelic renaissance," the studies of the 1960s are being recovered and greatly expanded upon by current researchers in a variety of fields and disciplines, finally providing other ways of understanding psychedelics outside the limited paradigms of recreation.

35. "Flesh of the gods" is a term that anthropologist Peter Furst recovered in his understandings of the uses of entheogens by Mesoamerican cultures. Dalton's use of the term here, decades before anthropology came upon this, underscores the research that went into creating the novel, from personal experiences as well as many visits to libraries in México and Europe.

36. Huxley had published *Doors of Perception* a few years earlier in 1954, where he focuses on his own experiences.

37. When the three characters enter a flower shop at some point in their journey, Martin suddenly and literally sees Roberto in a new light: "nunca antes me di cuenta de su parecido con San Juan de la Cruz [never before had I realized his resemblance to Saint John of the Cross]" (Dalton 79), a renowned Spanish mystic from the Iberian Golden Age.

38. In the words of the German philosopher, "nothing distinguished the ancient from the modern man so much as the former's absorption in a cosmic experience scarcely known to later periods. Its waning is marked by the flowering of astronomy at the beginning of the modern age. Kepler,

Copernicus and Tycho Brahe were certainly not driven by scientific impulses alone. All the same, the exclusive emphasis on an optical connection to the universe, to which astronomy very quickly led, contained a portent of what was to come. The ancients' intercourse with the cosmos had been different: the ecstatic trance [*Rausch*]. *For it is in this experience alone that we assure ourselves of what is nearest to us and what is remotest from us, and never of one without the other*" (Benjamin 129). Emphasis is mine.

39. In the same way, Martin achieves this kernel of enlightenment of and through his own existence, "darme cuenta que yo, Martin Carven, soy la esencia de todos los hombres y Ana de todas las mujeres me aturde y llena de entusiasmo. Nosotros, gusanos del universo, somos la esencia del mismo. Yo, conciencia de la relatividad, arqueología de un organismo, pero sobre todo síntesis [becoming aware that I, Martin Carven, am the essence of all the men, and that Ana of all the women, that shocks me and leaves me full of enthusiasm. We, worms of the universe, are the essence of the same. I, awareness of relativity, archeology of an organism but above all, synthesis]" (Dalton 92).

40. This paradox of the mystical experience is explored deeply in Alejandro Jodorowksy's early filmic career, and most particularly in *Holy Mountain* (1973), which follows a series of initiates on their way to meet a guru-like figure and go through a series of mystical experiences in the process.

41. See figure 3.1.

42. Dalton will further explore this "transcendence" of space and time in the children's book *Marichuloca* (1981), which tells the story of a little girl that befriends Espacio and Tiempo and travels the planets and cosmos. I mark "transcendence" here as a questionable yet useful way of naming a process of shedding of concepts, a transgression of the epistemological limits of a linear conception of space/time and a conception of the subject as discreetly separate from existence, and a way of subverting the thought processes that sustain these epistemological cages.

43. According to Pheng Cheah, worlding "refers to how a world is held together and given unity by the force of time. In giving rise to existence, temporization worlds a world . . . worlding is not a cartographical process that epistemologically constructs the world by means of discursive representations but a process of temporalization. Cartography reduces the world to a spatial object. In contradistinction, worlding is a force that subtends and exceeds all human calculations that reduce the world as a temporal structure to the sum of objects in space" (8).

44. Another way of visualizing the multiple temporalities that coexist in counterculture in general and in *LSD* in particular is as a culmination and rupture of modernity through the notion of plural temporalities, contained in the necessary contingency of durations between things and ideas; that is, "time, not understood according to its traditional image of a circle or a

line, but as a plurality of durations, *a complex and articulated intertwining*. Its structure *is* the non-contemporaneous, understood not in the sense of survival of archaic forms in a contemporaneity which is given as a term of comparison, but rather as the radical impossibility of any absolute contemporaneity, as the impossibility on the ontological level of positing one rhythm as an absolute measure for others" (Morfino 14, emphasis mine).

45. According to Cheah, heterotemporality "suggests that non-Western temporalities coexist with the time of modern progress and are important resources for resisting and subverting Western teleological time and the bases of alternative modernities in capitalist globalization" (12).

46. This ethics as a way of engaging with the phenomenological paradox of existence (I cannot see what I do not know) is succinctly summarized by Martin: "existe la posibilidad de desaprender. Imagínate que desde que haces has estado encerrada en una casa sin puertas. Tu conocimiento del universo se reduce a eso. Lo que entra en la casa es parte del cosmos, lo otro no. Has creado una organización alrededor y la sostienes a rajatabla. Puedes imaginar o sospechar, quizá, que fuera de esas cuatro paredes hay algo más. Pero nunca ha pasado por tu cabeza la posibilidad de tirar una pared. Una mañana despiertas y encuentras que hay una puerta. ¿Con qué te encuentras? Con un mundo que no estaba dentro de tu organización, pero que no la excluye. Te das cuenta de lo absurdo de tus paredes, porque no las necesitas. Te parece que lo pasado ha sido un sueño. Despiertas. Pero para despertar, tienes que estas realmente despierto, quiero decir *con los ojos abiertos*. Porque, ¿de qué te servirá abrir la puerta y cerrar los ojos [The possibility of unlearning exists. Imagine that ever since you were born you've been locked in a house with no doors. Your knowledge of the universe has been reduced to that. What enters in your house is part of the cosmos, the rest isn't. You have created an organization around yourself, and you defend and maintain it to the T. You can imagine, or maybe even suspect, that outside those four walls there may be something else. But the possibility of throwing down a wall has never crossed your mind. One morning you wake up and you find there is a door. Not only that, you come close and open it. What do you find? With a world that wasn't in your organization, but that doesn't exclude it. You realize the absurdity of the walls, because you don't need them. It seems the past has been just a dream. You wake up. But in order to wake up, you have to be really awake, I mean, you have to have your eyes wide open. Because, what good is it to open a door and close your eyes?]" (Dalton 108). Emphasis is mine.

47. "El inventarles nombres es caer en el error de interpretación. Error de todos los que han querido traspasar la cortina. No, no los llamaré de ninguna forma, están ahí, simples. Hay que descubrirlos uno mismo [Inventing a name for them is falling into the trap of interpretation. The mistake of everyone who has wants to go beyond the curtain. No, I will

call them in any way, they are there, simple. One has to discover them oneself]" (Dalton 164).

48. These are the capitalized letters sprinkled out through a series of pages, here recovered and strung together to form a coherent paragraph. The words re-create epiphanic thoughts now restructured into coherent reflections.

49. As José Agustín puts it, "así como Ken Kesey inventó a los hippies pero nunca los narró literariamente, Parménides convivió con los chavos de 'La Onda,' pero no escribió sobre ellos. Lo hizo, rabiosamente crítico, de la clase media, y su propuesta maciza está en su personaje, Epicuro Aristipo Quevedo Galdós del Valle Inclán, que en realidad es un beat más anarco [just as Ken Kesey invented hippies but never wrote about them literarily, so Parménides hung out with the youth from 'la Onda' but he didn't write about them. He did write, with critical rage, of the middle class, and his heavy proposal is in his character Epicuro Aristipo Quevedo Galdós del Valle Inclán, who really is a more anarco-beat]" (Agustín, "La onda" 14). Even though Agustín is referring mostly to *Pasto verde* and in doing so repeats the gesture of lowering the validity of García Saldaña's more public writings in nonliterary spheres, it is important to note that in the novel as much as the journal articles, Parménides is mobilizing a language of the youth to write *for* these "chavos de Onda" instead of narrating their scene for a more "cultured" or elite reader audience, in the style of José Agustín's *La tumba* or the short story "¿Cuál es la onda?"

50. The history of Maria Sabina in Cuautla and the impact of mushrooms and psylocibin in the greater global counterculture cannot be understated, from the Beatles to the Rolling Stones and more.

51. "In emulating the hippies, Mexican jijpitecas thus reappropriated a counter-cultural discourse grounded in their own indigenous roots yet dressed up as avant-garde. What is double ironic, moreover, is that the Mexican state facilitated this process by promoting an image of the nation abounding in indigenous cultures" (Zolov, "Discovering a Land 'Mysterious and Obvious'" 257).

52. In this direction, critic Rachel Adams signals the heritage of the Beatniks in Mexico as voyagers who, more than learn something about the places they visit, learn something about their own culture and themselves in an-other space, "what these authors share is that they return to the US having learned a great deal about their own commitments and remarkably little about Mexico itself. Each is countercultural in that protest against the constraints of national culture leads him to travel outward in search of alternatives" (71). In the same way, the Onderos that appropriate Anglo counterculture (and reappropriated the exotic representations of Mexico) through these travelers did not learn about the foreign cultures they read about as much as about themselves; "the Onderos are savvy readers who appropriate the innovative aspects of the North American counterculture,

while replacing its portraits of Mexico with their own vivid representations" (80).

53. The film *Los caifanes* (dir. Juan Ibáñez, 1967) serves as an example of this continuous updating of gender roles in global capitalist times.

54. Critic Alan Davison underscores how the impactful editorial adventure that was *El Corno Emplumado* came together around an idea of youthful revolution and cultural cooperation, publishing beatnik and other Anglo poetry in a bilingual format. Their name and logo came from the nahuatl ideogram for literature/verbal communication, and the "revolution they proposed was spiritual and would take issue not with governmental institutions, but with the onslaught of technocracy . . . the 'New Man' was the person who could come to a greater awareness of self and other by means of a spiritual transformation effected from within. If people are a chaos within, proponents believed, their external world will be a chaos as well" (5).

55. I emphasize this political positioning of Parménides García Saldaña in the publication because the general editorial line of *Piedra Rodante* was more focused on promoting music and fashion as commodity products in vogue, understating the rebellious and dangerous elements of rock culture. This differentiation is important to consider in a publication context that included other countercultural journals such as *Yerba*, which circulated hemispherically and touched on more radical issues of women's liberation, substance use, and commune-building.

56. The Chicago Eight refers to the infamous court cases of Abbie Hoffman, Jerry Rubin, David Dellinger, Tom Hayden, Rennie Davis, John Froines, Lee Weiner, and Bobby Seale, arrested in Chicago during the National Democratic Convention of 1968. Their court cases moved into the national spotlight and made these eight men figures and symbols of state repression as well as examples of the political strength of countercultural movements of all kinds, from the flower-power hippies to the Black Panthers and every other group in between. In the end, these eight men were tried and sentenced with fines and a five-year sentence for inciting civil unrest, and their case was evidence to the youth across the world of the civilized violence that the state would mobilize against them.

57. That is, Parménides's position is "articulada en un estilo desmitificador, cuestiona desde una posición transnacional la operatividad política del discurso revolucionario, tanto en su acepción nacional como internacional [articulated in a demystifying style, he questions from a transnational position the political effectiveness of a revolutionary discourse, in its national as well as international acceptance]" (Fortes 138). I cannot emphasize enough the importance of Fortes's work, one of the critics who is opening space in the recovery of Parménides García Saldaña, especially in relation to the essay and other critical genres.

58. In contrast to this political position, the journal *Mexico Canta*, which circulated in the 1960s, constructed "almost an exaggerated effort by writers to present an image of rocanrol as nonthreatening, healthy environment. In an article on the twist, for instance, one writer noted that while prohibited in certain places around the world, 'every generation has its own craziness'" (Zolov, *Refried* 79–80).

59. "¿Por qué? La respuesta tal vez está en otra interrogante: ¿qué podía hacer un muchacho que no entendía su relación con los avances científicos y técnicos hasta su tiempo? Avances que iban abriendo una percepción contraria a la que el ser humano trataba de aferrarse [Why? The answer is maybe in another question: what can a boy who doesn't understand his relations with the scientific and technical advances of the time really do? These advances were opening up a perspective counter to the one that human beings tried to grab onto]" (García Saldaña, "La revolución mexicana" 26).

60. Christopher Dunn signals how in the Brazilian context, writers who would address rock music through a historical lens were "important for informing rock enthusiasts in Brazil about the African-American origins of rock (a fact that was obscured throughout Latin America), its global circulation as youth music, its complex association with consumer society, and its relation to countercultural movements" (*Contracultura* 32).

61. In this sense, García Saldaña is aware of the generational differences in Mexico and seeks to politicize rock as a musical expression; "la realidad social y económica de aquellos años hizo necesario reformular la cuestión acerca de la relación entre el individuo y la sociedad, lo cual llevaba al rechazo de la sociedad de consumo, la enajenación y el desamor, e implicaba el retorno a modelos de vida juzgados más humanos . . . la juventud mexicana por primera vez se atrevió al autoanálisis, a la búsqueda de una identidad propia y a la definición del papel personal dentro de la sociedad [the social and economic reality of those years made it necessary to reformulate the question around the relation between individual and society, which led to the rejection of a consumer society, alienation and lack of love, and implied a return to life models judged to be more human . . . for the first time Mexican youth dared to self-reflect and self-analyze, to go into the search for a self-identity and to define the personal role within society]" (Gunia, "¿Qué onda bróder?" 22).

62. The history of this particular song and the longer history of the representation of female sex work in the context of building a nation goes back to the novel *Santa* (1901) by Federico Gamboa, along with its multiple film adaptations, and also includes films such as *La mujer del puerto* (dir. Arcady Boytler, 1934) and the wild success of *cabaretera* films in the 1940s and *fichera* films in the 1970s.

63. Expanding on what Elena Poniatowska also documents in *La noche de Tlatelolco*, Pensado traces the students' movements from the 1950s

onward and criticizes the official discourse that *only* focuses on 1968, ignoring the events and actions that led up to it: "this is the period when a new culture of student politics emerged, where students are first identified as 'subversive threat' to the nation by the governing elite and the Right-leaning print media, and where a new culture exploiting student-centered violence has its origins. While the official history states that student democratic activism began during the 1968 movements, in actuality a discourse on democracy — specifically calling, in this case, for greater participation in the management of schools and student organizations — had begun to form, however vaguely articulated, more than a decade earlier" (84).

64. In this sense, the "idea of revolution is identified with the idea of process. Producing something that doesn't exist, producing a singularity in the very existence of things, thoughts, and sensibilities. *It's a process that brings about mutations in the unconscious social field, at a level beyond discourse.* We could call it a process of existential singularization. The question is how to ensure that the singular processes — which almost swerve into the incommunicable — are maintained by articulating them in a work, a text, a way of living with oneself or with other, or the invention of areas of life and freedom to create" (Guattari and Rolnik 259). Emphasis is mine.

65. During the 1950s until 1963 when increased police interventions massively closed them down, there existed the *café cantantes* that, "while they varied in size and category, ranging from fancier nightspots such as the Chamonix, which served upper-class youth in Polanco, to danker holes such as the Sótano (Basement), which catered more to the middle classes, all featured live music (frequently by the same bands) playing songs from the hit charts. These were not clubs in the traditional sense: no alcohol was served, and generally they were not for dancing" (Zolov, *Refried Elvis* 88). They were replaced later in the decade by an increase in American-style restaurants with jukeboxes and occasional live music catering to the middle classes, and by *hoyos funkis* catering to the lower classes, where, "en colonias medioproletarias-medioclasemedia, mientras adolescentes y jóvenes en el lado sur se habitúan al aire acondicionado de los restoranes 'estilo americano,' en los hoyos funkis empieza el reventón: en improvisados salones de baile -por ejemplo, en el local de una ex-carbonería, en una bodega- gira la música y la gente baila. Baila música del rocanrol [in semi-working-class, semi-middle-class neighborhoods, while adolescents and youths on the south side get used to the air conditioning of the 'American style' restaurants, in the *hoyos funkis* the party really starts: in improvised dance halls — for example, in the location of an old charcoal place, in a warehouse — the music spins and the people dance. They dance rock and roll music]" (García Saldaña, "Los hoyos funkis" 12).

66. "Desde sus inicios el tango, en Argentina, tuvo sus hoyos funkies. Nada más que allá se les decía 'academias' . . . [en México] . . . en los cincuenta, cuando el rock aún no mostraba su lado funki, proliferaron los 'tes danzantes' organizados por el alumnado de escuelas oficiales y particulares; sobre todo, de secundaria y de preparatoria [Since its beginnings, tango in Argentina had its own *hoyos funkies*. They just called them 'academias' over there . . . in the fifties, when rock hadn't yet shown its funky side, the 'dancing tease' proliferated, organized by the young students of official and private schools; especially from secondary and high schools]" (García Saldaña, "Los hoyos funki" 12).

67. That is, he "replantea el significado de revolución a partir de la exploración de la transformación ideológica del rock y el hipismo, manifestaciones contraculturales que, irónicamente, están estrechamente vinculadas al discurso oficial revolucionario. Este ejercicio intelectual supone una transgresión a la noción tradicional de frontera puesto que Parménides se ve obligado a realizar un movimiento constante entre Estados Unidos y México para abordar el cambio en la acepción de la idea de revolución [raises again the meaning of revolution from the exploration of an ideological transformation of rock and hippie culture, countercultural manifestations that ironically are closely linked to the official revolutionary discourse. This intellectual exercise supposes a transgression of the traditional notion of border, since Parménides is forced to make a constant coming and going between the United States and Mexico in order to properly approach the change in accepting of an idea of revolution]" (Fortes 157).

68. In this way, "what characterizes the new social movements is not only a resistance against this general process serializing subjectivity, but also an attempt to produce original, singular modes of subjectivation, processes of subjective singularization" (Guattari and Rolnik 61).

69. The parallels and connections between the *hoyos funkis* and the later punk culture of Mexico City during the late 1980s and 1990s are striking and must not be forgotten, and they are too rich to explore properly in this study. I hint at this geneaology for now.

70. "A mí no me parece que haya nada de malo en eso. No creo que en el festival de Avándaro se hayan producido o pudieran haberse producido desmanes o aún crímenes como los que más o menos por las mismas fechas se han cometido en algunas cárceles . . . antes bien habría que preguntarse si esos encuentros no responden a motivaciones más profundas, a causas que ponen en entredicho la estabilidad y el prestigio de muchas instituciones falsamente prestigiadas por las religiones institucionales y por las instituciones sociales que faltas de otra posibilidad pretenden perseguir legamente una fiesta que no sólo aquí, sino en todas partes del mundo tiene las de ganar . . . el festival fue todo un éxito y no hubo nada que lamentar [I don't think there is anything

wrong with this. I don't think that in the festival in Avándaro there was or could have been misgrievings or even crimes, at least as can be compared to those that happened in some prisons during the same period . . . even more, one would do well to wonder if these gatherings do not correspond to much deeper motivations, to causes that question the stability and prestige of many institutions falsely celebrated by institutional religions and by social institutions that lacking any other possibility pretend to legally persecute a party that not only here, but everywhere in the world has all the chances of winning . . . the festival was a total success and there is nothing to lament]" (Elizondo 55–56).

71. I reference the aforementioned song "Abuso de autoridad" by *El tri*, which states how "ya sólo podrá tocar, el hijo de Díaz Ordaz [now only the son of Diaz Ordaz will be able to play]" in a reference to the sanctioned rock of Alfredo Díaz Ordaz. For an audiovisual example of this capturing, I point toward the film *Bikinis y rock* (dir. Alfrezo Salazar, 1972), itself a remake of *A ritmo de twist* (dir. Benito Alazraki, 1962), which cannibalizes rock and promotes a youthful playfulness that is decidedly depoliticized.

72. June 10, 1971, was the day of the infamous Jueves de Corpus, also known as the Massacre of Corpus Christi or El Halconazo. A peaceful student gathering marching in solidarity with students from Monterrey was violently repressed by the paramilitary group Los Halcones, which some say was also responsible for the events of October 2, 1968. The number of deaths is estimated to be around 120 people, and the federal and local governments have completely denied their participation in the event, with no one claiming responsibility for the deaths and no sentences being carried out. For a cultural representation of this event and the psychological and political impact it had in successfully silencing the political radicalness of peaceful countercultural demonstrations, I recommend the film *El bulto* (dir. Gabriel Retes, 1991), whose director was a strong collaborator in the super 8mm countercultural sphere during these decades. For a more artistic rendition of this event, I point toward *Roma* (dir. Alfonso Cuarón, 2018), where the event appears in the narrative film and the ways in which lower-class citizens are captured by the state through development programs to enforce violence are critically explored.

73. "At Avándaro, the increasingly diverse class makeup of La Onda showed its forces. Above all, it was the striking presence of so many lower-class youth, the nacos, as they were derogatorily called by the middle and upper classes, sharing a common space and a musical culture with other youth that caught the attention of many writers . . . it was via the middle classes especially that foreign rock was sustained throughout the 1970s as 'high' popular culture. For barrio youth, meanwhile, rock had worked its way into an integral aspect of everyday life, where live performance offered

the possibility of self-representation in a society which mocked and marginalized them" (Zolov, *Refried* 204).

74. In the issue of January 1972, *Piedra Rodante*'s last number focusing on "Las chavas y el catre" included several articles about sexuality and interviews with liberated women, including an interview with the "encuerada de Avándaro," who supposedly showed up to the journal offices one evening asking for payment since they had published many images of her. The probably fictional interview reveals a liberated female voice who speaks of how she took off her clothes in order to be more free and to "alivianar" or relax the young men around her who were staring at her, and an (male?) interviewer fixated on learning her sexual and substance use history; again, the framing of the voice (fictional or not) captured the feminine body into specific forms of consumable and objectified femininity.

75. "While called to the attention of the ineffectual Qualifying Commission of Magazines and Illustrated Publications (the government censorship bureau for printed matter) in a letter by a member of Congress, the magazine nonetheless met a quicker fate than what would have been the arduous process of bringing the publisher to court under the rules of the commission: facing threats of physical harm, the editor simply ceased publications "(Zolov, *Refried* 222).

76. One of the best examples of political rock was *Los Locos*'s song "Viva Zapata": "I'm gonna talk to you about Zapata // he fought for the land // he was Zapata // He died a long time ago // but he's still on the road // follow his teaching // follow Zapata // I'm digging the earth // until I'm exhausted // when seeds are growing up // it makes me feel fine // I fight the way he did // and that is how I feel // viva Zapata // viva Zapata." I recommend the reader listen to the song on YouTube.

Chapter 4

1. In English-speaking contexts, Joseph Heath and Andrew Potter's *Nation of Rebels: Why Counterculture Became Consumer Culture* traces how market structures were too powerful in their capturing of desire and exploited the countercultures' emphasis on agency and individualism to depoliticize cultural production and turn a profit by selling culture. On the other hand, Thomas Frank's *The Conquest of Cool* zooms out to signal the centrality of Madison Avenue and their advertising agencies in absorbing and commodifying counterculture, specifically by noting how the already sanitized manifestations (those conforming to and reproducing paradigms of racialization, gender normativity, sexual normativity, ethnic superiority, and national elitism) became the measuring stick by which agencies would value counterculture. In this way, counterculture was paradoxically

preserved by the forces of the market and simultaneously split into a multiplicity of depoliticized and disconnected marginal spheres whose political potentiality was reduced to their field of distribution, but whose potential symbolic capital was increased in their rarity. As the decades progressed and countercultural aesthetics were developed across the globe, this double process would solidify the feedback loop wherein the more marginal, antiestablishment, and obscure a specific countercultural figure or product could be, the more value it accumulated — so long as it was able to be transformed into a commodity to be traded in the economic and symbolic markets; thence the centrality of some underground art as experience that must not be recorded or captured in any. The evolution of the graffiti artist Bansky and their products, and their commodification by the art industry and the pop entertainment media, is a good example of this phenomenon.

2. As José Agustín documents, "las comunas jipitecas funcionaron accidentalmente durante algunos años, y en los años setenta se volvieron urbanas, pues los integrantes renunciaron a la idea de los pequeños núcleos humanos que se autoabastecen en la medida de los posible y crean sus propias reglas de comportamiento. Entre las más notorias se hallaba la de los chavos adinerados que se conoció como Hotel Gurdieff; la de El Vergel, en el valle de Oaxaca, capitaneada por Margarita Dalton, hermana de Roque Dalton y autora de la novela *Larga Sinfonía en D*, en cuyas siglas también se lee LSD [the hippie communes functioned in accidental ways for some years, and in the seventies they became urban since the members gave up on the idea of small human nuclei that were as self-sufficient as possible and created their own rules of behavior. Among the most notorious was the wealthy kids' one known as Hotel Gurdieff; the El Vergel one, in the Oaxaca valley, captained by Margarita Dalton, sister of Roque Dalton and author of Long Symphony in D, whose acronym also reads LSD]" (*La contracultura*, 81).

3. A great example of this double standard is the film *Tintorera* (dir. René Cardona Jr, 1977), which punishes sexually liberated women and men (both foreign and international) by having them and/or their lovers eaten by a murderous shark.

4. That is, "an affection, something that happens; an affect, which is the effect, sad or joyful, of that affection; the feeling that follows of wanting to do something, to possess, to run away, to destroy, to pursue, or whatever it may be" (Lordon 15).

5. "Perfect flexibility — the unilateral affirmation of a desire that engages knowing that it can disengage, that invests with the guarantee of being able to disengage, that invests with the guarantee of being able to disinvest, and that hires in the knowledge that I can fire (*at whim*) — is the fantasy of an individualism pushed to its ultimate consequences, the imaginative flight of a whole era" (Lordon 44).

6. "Capitalism must therefore be grasped not only in its structures but also as a certain *regime of desire*; for the pleasure of a Foucaldian derivation, we could call it an *epithumé*. To speak of *epithumé* is another way of recalling that objective structures, as Bourdieu already noted, but also Marx, extend necessarily into subjective structures, and that in addition to being external, social things, they must also exist as inscriptions inside individual psyche. In other terms, social structures find expressions as configurations of desires and affects, and thus have their own specific imaginary" (Lordon 49).

7. Thus, in the manifesto titled "Towards a Fourth Cinema," a nod and problematization of the effectiveness of Third Cinema in the context of a repressive state working in tandem with a capitalist economic/social order, García Michel would underline how "8mm cinema can contribute greatly towards the collective escape from alienation and the formation of an active critical consciousness. 8mm cinema is called upon to be an antidote to the alienating media, giving back to the individual his/her function as subject, making him/her a direct participant in the work of cinema, since in traditional media and education the individual is a mere object" (169). The similarities between this discourse and Paulo Freire's *Pedagogy of the Oppressed,* as well as Augusto Boal's Theatre of the Oppressed projects, are striking and cannot be understated.

8. In this way, the film dialogues with Sara Gómez's *De cierta manera* (1974), which also recontextualizes the Cuban revolution through the actions and eyes of various women participating in the rebuilding of society.

9. I use the term sound-image to describe the assemblages between image and sounds that appear in cinema, and in particular in super 8mm where the soundtrack is highly edited to communicate in a film with no set recording. Sound-images also point at the ways in which sounds generate images as they are heard and interpreted, both imaginary representations within the imagination as well as reconstructions of the loci from where these sounds emerge.

10. Two films, *Bikinis y rock* (dir. Alfredo Salazar, 1972) and *De veras me atrapaste* (dir. Gerardo Pardo, 1985), are examples of this commodified and depoliticized representation of rock culture.

11. This move away from representing the consumption of substances is on par with what Christopher Dunn has signaled for the Brazilian context, where "the use of drugs for both recreational and 'mind-expanding' pursuits lost some of its hopeful innocence with the rise of violence associated with heavily armed narco-trafficking gangs and the state-sponsored militarization of efforts to control the production, sale and export of drugs" (*Contracultura* 202).

12. Caro Cocotle uses *audiotopia,* coined by Josh Kun, to describe the specific countercultural musical and aesthetic spaces that Botellita de Jerez construct in their various albums, videos, and concerts spaces. She rightly

locates the tension in their aesthetic (and ethical) project by focusing on the colonial metaphor the band depends on, at times reproducing some gender normativities while simultaneously seeking gender liberation particularly for themselves and their male listeners. Their song *Alármala de tos*, which plays with the scandalous crime journal *Alarma* and its uncritical reproduction of gender violence inflicted on female bodies, is a succinct example of this tension that Caro Cocotle traces in their musical oeuvre.

13. The "Onda" was defined by the "imperialismo del yo" and a "dinamismo de la acción y el lenguaje creado por el propio adolescente para apartarse de los demás, de los adultos y del mundo que él cree establecido, nos llevan a su mundo en el momento en que se encuentra sumergido en esa visión que lo desdibuja al tiempo que presente estampar su efigie [imperialism of the I . . . a dynamism in action and language created by the own adolescent to separate themself from the rest, from the adults and the world that he thought was established, they take us into his world in the moment in which he finds himself submerged in this vision that undraws him at the same time that he stamps his effigy]" (Glantz 32). The Escritura group, on the other hand, saw the "novela como experimentación del lenguaje [que] se efectúa en un territorio distinto al de la poesía y plantea una estética novelística que se erige en el cuerpo mismo de lo narrado, o en la materia narrativa misma, en la 'escritura' [novel as experimentation with langauge that effectuated itself in a territory different than poetry and set down a novelistic aesthetic that erected itself in the body of the text itself, or in the narrative matter itself, in the 'writing']" (33).

14. In this sense, countercultural critic Joseph Berke signals how countercultural movements seek to define changes on the personal level foremost, since "it is at this level that the revolution really takes place, for if people cannot find some way collectively to destroy — destructure this system of operations inside themselves — then the overthrow of the state degenerates into a simple power struggle between X and Y with the nature of society remaining the same. And it is at this level that what is now happening is qualitatively different from previous attempts at revolution" (34).

15. For decades, psychedelic therapy was carried out underground by rogue therapists and practitioners. Today, with the renaissance in the medical establishment of various countries (US, Canada, England, France, Spain, Portugal, and others), there are some variations in how specifically the therapy is structured, with some general and structural similarities. For a more thorough explanation of a specific protocol currently being used today, I recommend Belser et al.'s "Patient Experiences of Psylocibin-Assisted Psychotherapy."

16. Bill Richards — a central player in the therapies of the 1960s who worked with Walter Pahnke and many others — developed a playlist based on

symphonic, jazz, and popular music of the 1960s designed to re-create and catalyze a mystical journey. This playlist can be accessed on Spotify and other streaming platforms.

17. In this sense, Palinuro describes Estefanía as a sexual and social subject to build relationships with (and not a sexual object to consume), "a being in whom it was possible to see yourself as a whole, as cousin and friend, as admirer and lover, and rekindle yourself daily from a flame of omen" (60). Or Palinuro and Estefanía that realize the objects around them are subjects of their own reality (very object-oriented-ontologically) and are relating to them through the power of love as a relational force: "If anything filled our room with meaning, it was this: our love for each other since childhood . . . until at last the things got fed up (with their being used as objects) and decided to impose on us their will to live . . . [until] . . . we accepted the objects we owned, being a part of our lives, were themselves alive and . . . we decided to learn to live with them . . . we also decided, after reading a pamphlet on Shintoism, never again to allow our intelligence to be jinxed by language" (del Paso 124–29).

18. "Psychedelic" was coined by Humphrey Osmond around 1957 and is derived from the Greek words "psyche" meaning "soul" and "delein' meaning "to manifest," with the implications of soul/mind manifesting. "Hallucinogen" is derived from the world "hallucination," which in turn is derived from the Latin "hallucinatus" meaning to wander in the mind; thus, a hallucinogen is a substance that promotes the wandering of the mind. "Mind-altering" was a term used previously and currently being questioned, as researched since the 1970s have questioned the paradigm of a "normative" mental state from which there are alterations. "Entheogen" is used to mean "that which produced the divine within" from the Greek roots "entheo" meaning divine and "genésthai" meaning to generate; this term was coined in 1979 by ethnobotanist and mythology/religious scholars including Carl A.P. Ruck, Richard Evans Schultes, Jonathan Ott, and R. Gordon Wasson. As can be seen, all of these terms carry with them a specific cultural weight and underpin a whole epistemology that reveal the relations being generated between human and substance. Indigenous and traditional epistemologies that understand these plants, fungi, and substances as fellow beings are not being considered for the purposes of this research to avoid any essentialization, and I signal their existence as a way to keep in mind other ways of relation to these substances that have been used by (and arguably have used) humans for millennia.

19. "And while the executives went *Smash, Screech, Clap, Smiff, Slurp, Knock, Crack, Pum, Tap, Woo, Ehem, Erp, Cough* and *Achoo!*, Palinuro's vomit went *Splash, Gurgle, Gulp, Slurp* and *Splat!* As there, in the middle of the Enchanted Agency conference room, he spewed up all the *Oso Negro* gin that he had drunk and vomited the *Carnation* milk that Mamma Clementina had given him as a child and threw up the *Campbell's* soups

that Estefanía had heated for him and vomited vomigurgle and vomigulp and vomislurp and vomisplash" (del Paso 221).

20. Emphasis is mine.

21. "As a myth, however, and particularly as a myth with a valuable psychological interpretation, Palinurus clearly stands for a certain will-to-failure or repugnance-to-success, a desire to give up at the last moment, an urge towards loneliness, isolation and obscurity. Palinurus, in spite of his great ability and his conspicuous public position, deserted his post in the moment of victory and opted for the unknown shore" (Connolly 56).

22. Robin Fiddian develops this martyr reading in their article, "*Palinuro de México*: entre la protesta y el mito." Similarly, Carmen Álvarez Lobato reads "Palinuro en la escalera" as the triumph of Palinuro over national hisory, where "a pesar de la furia del estado, permanece despierto, construye la memoria histórica y hace un llamado a que México despierte . . . héroe y nación reconstruyen su identidad y se salvan [in spite of the state's fury, he remained awake, he builds a historical memory and he makes a call for Mexico to awaken . . . nation and hero rebuild their identity and save each other]" (133).

23. This homosocial bonding underpinning nation has been signaled by Robert Mckee Irwin, since "Mexico is protagonized by young men, and national unity is allegorized by male homosocial bonding" (xiii) and can be seen in *Madrugada del centuaro* in the characters of Aldebarán and his fellow rural workers, as well as in the many images of tevolutionary culture, and in films that center the nation, from *Enamorada* (dir. Emilio "El Indio" Fernández, 1946) to *Y tu mamá también* (dir. Alfonso Cuarón, 1999).

24. This capturing of substance use as a stage in the development of proper political and social subjectivities will be echoed and reiterated in later decades; for example, the substance use of "liberal" US presidents such as Barack Obama or Bill Clinton in their college years will be understood as a stage in their development and not a moment of radical detachment from the normative political structuring of their bodies.

25. Emphasis is mine.

Coda

1. Authors who have written on Jodorowsky as a cult figure include Ben Cobb, Justin Guida, Frances Morgan, and Robert Neustadt. While I agree that the artist's legacy in the global context of cult and marginal art circuits is valuable, I also believe that using this lens exclusively can silence the artist's engagement with issues of nationalism, capitalism, and consumerism, particularly when his psychomagic or therapeutic approaches are foregrounded with little historical anchoring or context. As case in

point, I signal the appearance of Ciudad Satélite in *Holy Mountain*, which typically becomes aestheticized and detached from the urban development critique the film is making in foregrounding the colorful towers. Similar issues happen with *Santa Sangre*, whose strongly contextualized space becomes reduced to a horror-movie setting when viewed exclusively through the cult legacy of the author; or *Dance of Reality* (2012), whose Chilean history and commentary on (neo)fascism becomes erased when viewed exclusively as a cult object or an autobiographical film.

2.   As case in point and keeping in mind the many gendered critiques Jodorowsky has received over the years, I signal his first film, *Fando y Lis* (1967), where the director famously hired trans* people to represent themselves on screen. This film was so provocative in its raw style that it is rumored to have pushed canonical director Emilio "El Indio" Fernández to draw his gun and shoot at Jodorowsky during the screening of the film in the 1967 Acapulco *Arieles* awards.

3.   A more contemporary example of this ethical drive in film as a tool to intervene subjectivities is the work of Nicolas Winding Ren, particularly *Drive* (2011) and *Only God Forgives* (2013), both of which affectually engage the viewer in a deconstruction of heteromasculinity through the popular figure of the Hollywood actor Ryan Gosling, whose latest appearance in *Barbie* (dir. Greta Gerwig, 2023) continues down a similar path of subverting contemporary heteronormative masculinity.

4.   Critics have signalled how Jodorowsky thus continues the surrealist ethos of Luis Buñuel by seeking to "expandir al máximo la imaginación en el campo del cine, sin importarle violar el tabú sexual, el social, o el religioso; más bien, se diría lo contrario: se complace en hacerlo [expand to the maximum the imagination in the field of cinema, without caring about violating a sexual taboo, a social taboo or a religious taboo; one could say the opposite, actually: he takes joy in doing so]" (Moldes 13).

5.   Between August and September 1942, Gregorio Cárdenas murdered an unknown number of women until he turned himself in and was committed and jailed until 1976, when President Luis Echeverría pardoned him in the last year of his punishment. Cárdenas was a journalist and writer who defended himself during his tenure in person and claimed total amnesia after the murderous incidents.

6.   Diego Moldes comments on how "el simbolismo -para algunos, criticismo- de su cine no es un ejercicio pasivo del espectador sino que requiere de una toma de conciencia, incluso inconsciente, valga el oximorón, en la que la interpretación de los símbolos presentes en sus películas provoca una reacción (de atracción o rechazo, poco importa eso) que desemboca en una trasformación del estado cognitivo, es decir, que opera a un nivel interior y, en cierta forma, espiritual [the symbolism — for some, criticism — of his films is not a passive exercise on the part of the spectator, but one that requires taking some awareness,

even unconscious awareness if you'll pardon the oxymoron, in which the interpretation of symbols present in his films provokes a reaction (of attraction or rejection, little does that matter) that leads to a transformation of a cognitive state, that is, that operates on an interior level, and in a certain way, a spiritual level]" (38).

7. The film was coproduced by Italian Produzioni Intersound and Mexican Productora Fílmica Real, with the participation of Claudio Argento (brother of acclaimed horror director Dario Argento) and René Cardona Jr. (producer of the *El Santo* films), as well as *Tintorera* (1977) and other horror and *sexycomedia* hits.

8. The legendary zoom-out of *Holy Mountain*'s ending where the camera suddenly reveals the whole set is the most striking example of this strategy used by Jodorowsky in his films.

9. The artists sampled include Dámaso Pérez Prado ("Caballo Negro," "Lupita," "Mambo"), Tomás Méndez ("Cucurrucucu Paloma"), Enrique Mora ("Alejandra"), Luiz Martínes Serrano ("Dónde Estás Corazón"), Alfonso Esparza Otero ("Déjame llorar"), Genaro Codina ("Marcha Zacateca"), Consuelo Velázquez ("Bésame Mucho"), Esperón y Cortázar ("No Volveré"), and Alonso Jiménez ("De Este Lado de Acá"). As Diego Moldes notes, Jodorowsky collected these songs literally from the street, "seleccionó todos los cortes, a través de antiguos discos de vinilo que fue encontrando por las calles mexicanas y en mercados callejeros hasta encontrar lo que más se adecuaba a sus sentimientos respecto de la evolución psicológica de Fénix" (371).

10. Moldes signals how this placing of the camera's gaze onto the animals on-screen is a typical Jodorowsky strategy, which ends up constructing humanimal intersubjectivities projected on-screen and composed in the viewers as they engage with the film itself. In the elephant-themed film *Tusk* (1980), "con frecuencia la cámara se sitúa a la altura de la visión de un elefante, o mejor aún, la de un hombre subido a lomos de un elefante, a unos tres metros del suelo, dando la sensación de que todas las acciones humanas están expuestas y captadas desde la visión de un elefante o de un hombre que percibe al mundo desde la altura de un elefante [frequently the camera is situated at the height of an elephant's vision, or better yet of a man sitting on top of an elephant, some ten feet from the group, giving the feeling that all the human actions are exposed and captured from the viewpoint of an elephant or a man that perceives the world from the height of an elephant]" (325).

11. In previous films, Jodorowsky uses Othered bodies through the communities of disabled persons and individuals whose bodies go against the hegemonic construction of "human" to signal the limits of society and highlight the margins, as these are bodies outrightly excluded and cast out from the folds of the nation. While the circus is also a liminal space that contains difference while bringing it into the space, I highlight how the

circus performers move into the city and navigate it as part of their life, thus blurring the lines of exclusion while making their ideological force visible.

12. Like Orgo, Concha is a wordplay on femininity. In colloquial jargon, *concha* refers to female genitalia, thus working to construct the character and her body as exclusively tied to her reproductive sexuality and not pleasure, agency, or autonomy.

13. That is, "la obra de Kahlo no representa ningún peligro ni desestabiliza los cimientos culturales, ya que estas representaciones sobrevaluan la maternidad y evidencian su calvario como mujer infértil, lo que comprueba con las imágenes recurrentes de lágrimas. . . . Kahlo se convierte en un ícono nacional porque su martirio como mujer infértil la redime y la glorifica. Al suprimir el deseo femenino de la representación pictórica y autorrepresentarse como la mexicanidad encarnada en busca perenne de un hijo, Kahlo se posiciona en el centro mismo del discurso oficial que busca apadrinar al nuevo mexicano emergente de la revolución [the work of Kahlo does not represent a threat nor destabilizes the cultural foundations, since these representations overvalue maternity and give evidence of her torment as an infertile woman, which is proven with the recurring images of tears. . . . Kahlo becomes a national icon because her martyrdom as an infertile woman redeems and glorifies her. By suppressing the feminine desire for pictorial representations and self-representations as embodied Mexicanness in perennial search of a child, Kahlo positions herself in the very center of an official discourse that seeks to godfather the new Mexican emerging from the revolution]" (Rosales 3).

14. In this, Jodorowsky plays on Hitchcock's classic *Psycho* (1960), especially in the strong maternal figure who, once murdered, becomes an alternate personality within the mind of the son.

15. That is, "the nearness of the neighbor materializes the immanence of redemption, releasing the here and now from the fetters of teleology in the infinitesimal calculus of proximity" (Reinhard 21).

Works Cited

Acero, Rosa María. *Novo ante Novo. Un novísimo personaje homosexual.* [*Novo before Novo. A hypernovel homosexual character*]. Madrid, Editorial Pliegos, 2003.

Adams, Rachel. "Hipsters and Jipitecas: Literary Counterculture on Both Sides of the Border." *American Literary History*, vol. 16, no. 1, 2004, 58–84.

Adéle Greeley, Robin. "Muralism and the State in Post-Revolution Mexico, 1920–1970." *Mexican Muralism. A Critical History*, edited by Alejandro Anreus, Leonard Folgarait, and Robin Adéle Greeley, U of California P, 2012.

Aguirre Darancou, Iván Eusebio. "Parménides García Saldaña en la escritura pública del rock [*Parménides García Saldaña in rock's public writings*]." *Romance Notes*, vol. 56, no. 1, 2016, 107–17.

Agustin, José. *La contracultura en México* [*Counterculture in Mexico*]. México, DeBolsillo, 2004.

———. "La onda que nunca existió [*The onda that never existed*]." *Revista de Crítica Literaria Latinoamericana*, vol. 30, no. 59, 2004, 9–17.

Álvarez Lobato, Carmen. "Identidad y ambivalencia : una lectura de *Palinuro de México* desde el grotesco[*Identity and ambivalence: a reading of Palinuro of Mexico from the grotesque*]." *Nueva Revista de Filología Hispánica*, vol. 56, no. 1, 2008, 123–13.

Arditi, Benjamín. *La política en los bordes del liberalismo. Diferencia, populismo, revolución, emancipación* [*Politica on the borders of liberalism. Difference, populism, revolution, emancipation*]. Barcelona, Gedisa, 2011.

Arditi, Benjamín, and Gianni Vattimo. *El reverso de la diferencia: identidad y política* [*The reverse of difference: identity and politics*]. Caracas, Venezuela, Nueva Sociedad, 2000.

Asamblea de ciudades. Años 20s/50s ciudad de México [*Assembyl of cities: Mexico City in the 20s/50s*]. México, Instituto Nacional de Bellas Artes, 1992.

Avant-Mier, Roberto. *Rock The Nation. Latin/o Identities and the Latin Rock Diaspora*. Continuum, 2010.

Barbosa S., Araceli. "Nahui Olin: el deseo desnudo ["Nahui Olin: nude desire]." *Placeres en imagen. Fotografía y cine eróticos. 1900–1960* [*Pleasures of the image: Erotic photography and cinema*], edited by Angel Miquel, México, Ediciones Sin Nombre, 2009, 193–204.

Bartra, Roger. *The Cage of Melancholy: Identity and Metamorphosis in the Mexican Character*. Rutgers UP, 1992.

Bell, David, and Jon Binnie. *The Sexual Citizen. Queer Politics and Beyond.* Cambridge, Polity, 2000.

Belser, Alexander B., Gabriel Agin-Liebes, et al. "Patient Experiences of Psilocybin-Assisted Psychotherapy: An Interpretative Phenomenological Analysis." *Journal of Humanistic Psychology*, vol. 57, no. 4, 2017, 354–88.

Benjamin, Walter. *On Hashish.* Translated by Howard Eiland, Harvard UP, 2006.

Benshoff, Harry M. *Monsters in the Closet. Homosexuality and Horror Film.* Manchester: Manchester UP, 1997.

Berke, Joseph. "The Creation of an Alternative Society." *Counterculture*, edited by Joseph Berke, London, Peter Owen Limited, 1969, 12–35.

Bertelsen, Lone and Andrew Murphie. "An Ethics of Everyday Infinities and Powers." *The Affect Theory Reader*, edited by Melissa Greg and Gregory J. Seigworth, Durham, Duke UP, 2010, 138–60.

Bohórquez, Abigael. *Abigaeles. Poeñínimos [Abigaeles. Tinypoems].* Hermosillo, Sonora, Instituto Sonorense de Cultura, 1990.

———. *Digo lo que amo [I say what I love].* México, Federación Editorial Mexicana, 1976.

———. *Heredad. Antología Provisional [Heredad. Provisional anthology].* México, Federación Editorial Mexicana, 1981.

———. *Primera reunión de teatro breve [First reunion of short theatre].* Toluca, México, Universidad Autónoma del Estado de México, 1992.

Bonifant, Cube. "El amor en automóvil ["Love in automobile"]." *El Universal Ilustrado.* 18 Nov 1926, p.35. Rpt in *Una pequeña marquesa de Sade. Crónicas selectas (1921-1948). Cube Bonifant [A small marquess de Sade. Selected chronicles (1921-1938) Cube Bonifant].* México: CONACULTA/UNAM/Equilibrista, 2009. 337–40.

———. "Cabellos largos e ideas cortas ["Long hair and short ideas"]." *El Universal Ilustrado.* 8 Dec 1921, p. 24. Rpt in *Una pequeña marquesa de Sade. Crónicas selectas (1921–-1948). Cube Bonifant [A small marquess de Sade. Selected chronicles (1921–1938) Cube Bonifant].* México, CONACULTA/UNAM/Equilibrista, 2009, 97–100.

———. "Psicologías en la alfombra ["Psychologies on the carpet"]." *El Universal Ilustrado.* 13 Oct 1921, p. 18. Rpt in *Una pequeña marquesa de Sade. Crónicas selectas (1921–1948). Cube Bonifant. [A small marquess de Sade. Selected chronicles (1921–1938) Cube Bonifant].* México, CONACULTA/UNAM/Equilibrista, 2009, 81–85.

Braidotti, Rosi. "Animals, Anomalies and Organic Others." *PMLA*, vol. 124, no. 2, 2009, 526–32.

———. *Metamorphoses. Towards a Materialist Theory of Becoming.* Cambridge, Polity, 2002.

———. *Nomadic Subjects. Embodiment and Sexual Difference in Contemporary Feminist Theory*. 2nd ed., Columbia UP, 2011.

Buffington, Robert. "Homophobia and the Mexican Working Class, 1900–1910." *The Famous 41. Sexuality and Social Control in Mexico. 1901*, edited by Robert Mckee Irwin, Michelle Rocío Nasser, and Edward J. McCaughan, Palgrave-Macmillan, 2003, 193–225.

Bustamante Bermúdez, Gerardo. "Introducción." *Dramaturgia reunida de Abigael Bohórquez*. ["Introduction." *Gathered theatre works of Abigael Bohórquez*]. México, Universidad Autónoma de la Ciudad de México, 2014, 1–32.

———. "Juan Bañuelos y Abigael Bohórquez: la poesía como resistencia y representación social ["Juan Bañuelos and Abigael Bohorquez: poetry as resistance and social representation]." *Acta Poética*, vol. 37, no. 2, 2016, 87–115.

Carhart-Harris, Robin. "The Entropic Brain. Revisited." *Neuropharmacology*, vol. 142, 2018, 167–78.

Caro Cocotle, Guadalupe. "¿Complejos o acomplejados?: del *Guacarrock de la Malinche* a *Alármala de Tos*, Botellita de Jerez y la metáfora de lo colonial. ["Complex or full of complexes? from *Guacarrock of the Malinche* to *Alármala de Tos,* Botellita de Jerez and the metaphors of the colonial]." *Arizona Journal of Hispanic Cultural Studies*, vol. 16, 2012, 149–60.

Carrera, Magaly. *Imagining Identity in New Spain: Race, Lineage, and the Colonial Body in Portraiture and Casta Paintings*. U of Texas P, 2003.

El Chafirete. México DF. March–October 1923.

Cheah, Pheng. *What Is a World? On Postcolonial Literature as World Literature*. Duke UP, 2016.

Chrisman, Kevin. *Meet Me at Sanborms: Labor, Leisure, Gender and Sexuality in Twentieth Century Mexico*. Diss., York University, 2018.

Cobb, Ben. *Anarchy and Alchemy: The Films of Alejandro Jodorowsky*. London, Creation, 2007.

Connolly, Cyril. *The Unquiet Grave*. Persea Books, 1999.

Dalton, Margarita. *Larga sinfonía en D y había una vez. . . . [Long sympony in D and once upon a time]*. México, Editorial Diógenes, 1968.

Davies, Christie. "Sexual Taboos and Social Boundaries." *American Journal of Sociology*, vol. 87, no. 5, 1982, 1032–063.

Davison, Alan R. *El Corno Emplumado / The Plumed Horn: A Voice of the Sixties*. Toledo, Textos toledanos, 1994.

del Paso, Fernando. *Palinuro of México*. Translated by Elisabeth Plaister, Normal, IL: Dalkey Archive Press, 1996.

Díaz Arciniega, Victor. *Querella por la cultura 'revolucionaria' (1925)* [*Quarrel for 'revolutionary' culture*]. México, Fondo de Cultura Económica, 1989.

Diprose, Rosalind. "The Hand That Writes Community in Blood." *Cultural Studies Review*, vol. 9, no. 1, 2001, 35–50.

Domínguez Ruvalcaba, Héctor. Mod*ernity and the Nation in Mexican Representations of Masculinity*. Palgrave-Macmillan, 2007.

Donoso Pareja, Miguel. "El gallo ilustrado [The illustrated rooster]." *El Día*, November 22, 1970.

Draper, Susana. *1968 Mexico: Constellation of Freedom and Democracy.* Duke UP, 2018.

Dunn, Christopher. *Brutality Garden: Tropicalia and the Emergence of Brazilian Counterculture*. U of North Carolina P, 2001.

———. *Contracultura. Alternative Arts and Social Transformation in Authoritarian Brazil*. U of North Carolina P, 2016.

Echeverría, Bolivar. *La modernidad de lo barroco* [*The modernity of the baroque*]. México, Editorial Era, 1998.

———. *Modernity and Whiteness.* Translated by Rodrigo Ferreira, Polity, 2019.

Ekman Schenberg, Eduardo. "Psychedelic-Assisted Psychotherapy: A Paradigm Shift in Psychiatric Research and Development." *Frontiers in Pharmacology*, vol. 9, no. 733, 2018.

Elizondo, Salvador. "Física y metafísica de la Onda." *Contextos*. ["Physics and metaphysics of the Onda." *Contexts*]. Edited by Salvador Elizondo, México, Fondo de Cultura Mexicana, Letras Mexicanas, 1973.

Emmelhainz, Irmgard. *La tiranía del sentido común. La reconversión neoliberal de México* [*The tyranny of common sense. The neoliberal reconversion of Mexico*]. México, Paradiso Editores, 2016.

Espinoza, Alex. *Cruising. An Intimate History of a Radical Pastime.* Los Angeles: The Unnamed Press, 2019.

Fabre, Luis Felipe. *Writing with Caca.* Translated by JD Pluecker, Green Lantern Press, 2021.

Feu López, María Montserrat. "The U.S. Hispanic Flapper: Pelonas and Flapperismo in U.S. Spanish-Language Newspapers, 1920–1929." *Studies in American Humor*, vol. 1, no. 2, 2015, 192–217.

Fiddian, Robin. "A Case of Literary Infection: *Palinuro de México* and *Ulysses*." *Comparative Literary Studies*, vol. 19, no. 2, 1982, 220–35.

———. *The Novels of Fernando del Paso.* Florida UP, 2000.

———. "*Palinuro de México:* Entre la protesta y el mito [Palinuro of Mexico: Between protest and myth]." *Literatura mexicana hoy: del 68 al ocaso de la Revolución* [Mexican literature today: from 68 to the twilight of the

Revolution], edited by Karl Kohut, Frankfurt am Main, Verveurt, 1991, 214–22.

Figueroa, Iván. Antípodas: *Dos antípodas fundacionales en la poética de Abigael Bohórquez* [*Two foundational antipodes in the poetics of Abigael Bohórquez*]. Hermosillo, México, Instituto Sonorense de Cultura, 2013.

Flores, Tatiana. "Strategic Modernists: Women Artists in Post-Revolutionary Mexico." *Woman's Art Journal*, vol. 29, no. 2, 2008, 12–22.

Fortes, Mayra. "Too Much Confusion Here: Juventud, nación y revolución en *En la ruta de la Onda* de Parménides García Saldaña ["Too much confusion here: Youth, nation and revolutions in *On the route of the Onda* by Parménides García Saldaña"]." *Ensayando el ensayo: Artilugios del género en la literatura mexicana contemporánea* [*Essaying the essay: gender/genre devices in contemporary mexican literatura*], edited by Mayra Fortes González and Ana Sabau Fernández, Puebla, México, El Colegio de Puebla; México, D.F., Ediciones y Gráficos Eón, 2012, 137–60.

Franco, Jean. *Plotting Women. Gender and Representation in Mexico*. Columbia UP, 1989.

Furst, Peter. "'High States' in Culture-Historical Perspective." *Alternate States of Consciousness*, edited by Norman Zinberg, The Free Press, 1977, 53–58.

Gabara, Esther. *Errant Modernism: The Ethos of Photography in Mexico and Brazil*. Duke UP, 2008.

Gallo, Rubén. *Freud's Mexico. Into the Wilds of Psychoanalysis*. MIT Press, 2010.

———. *Mexican Modernity: The Avant-Garde and the Technological Revolution*. MIT Press, 2005.

García Michel, Sergio. "Toward a Fourth Cinema." *Wide Angle*, vol. 21, no. 3, 1999, 70–175.

García Saldaña, Parménides. "Avándaro: amor y pasión ["Avándaro: love and passion"]." *Piedra Rodante* [*Rolling Stone*], 30 October 1971, 34–36.

———. "Los hoyos fonkis. ["Funky holes"]" *Piedra Rodante* [*Rolling Stone*], 15 July 1971, 12–14.

———. "La revolución mexicana se quita el huarache. ["Mexican revolution takes off its sandals]" *Piedra Rodante* [*Rolling Stone*], 15 May 1971, 25–27.

Glantz, Margo. "Estudio Preliminar [Preliminary study]." *Onda y escritura en México: Jóvenes de 20 a 33* [*Onda and writing in Mexico: youth from 30 to 33*], edited by Margo Glantz, México, DF, Siglo XXI, 1971, 5–42.

Graham, David. *The Last Car: Cruising in Mexico City*. Germany: Kehrer Verlag, 2017.

Goh, Irving. "The Question of Community in Deleuze and Guattaru (I): Anti-community." *Symploke*, vol. 14, no. 1/2, 2006, 216–31.

———. "The Question of Community in Deleuze and Guattaru (II): After Friendship." *Symploke*, vol. 15, no. 1/2, 2007, 218–43.

Gollnick, Brian. "Silent Idylls, Double Lives. Sex and the City in Salvador Novo's La estatua de sal." *Mexican Studies*, vol. 21, no. 1, 2005, 231–50.

González Mateos, Adriana. "El fifí y su chofer: Control social, homosexualidad y clase en un periódico del México postrevolucionario [The fifi and his driver: Social control, homosexuality and class in a postrevolutionary Mexico journal]." *Signos Literarios* [*Literary signs*], vol 2, 2005, 103–25.

González Rodríguez, Sergio. "Usos amorosos del joven Novo: el secreto y el estudio [Amorous uses of young Novo: secret and study]." *Cuidado con el corazón: los usos amorosos en el México moderno* [*Careful with the heart: uses of the amorous in modern Mexico*]. México, INAH, 1995, 65–80.

Gordus, Andrew. "Silence and Celebration: Queer Markings in the Poetry of Abigael Bohórquez." *Mexican Studies*, vol. 15, no. 1, 1999, 131–50.

Gorostiza, José. "Óptica cerebral. Poemas dinámicos de Nahui Olin. México: Ediciones México Moderno, 1922. [Cerebal optics: dynamic poems from Nahui Olin. Mexico: Modern Mexico editions, 1922]." *México Moderno* [*Modern Mexico*]. México. 1 Sept 1922, p. 126. Rpt in *Nahui Olin: Sin principio ni fin: vida, obra y varia invención* [*Nahui Olin: without beginning nor end: life, ouvre and various inventions*], edited by Patricia Rosas Lopátegui, Monterrey, Universidad Autónoma de Nuevo León, 2011, 270.

Grosz, Elizabeth. *Space, Time and Perversion*. Routledge, 1995.

———. *Volatile Bodies. Toward a Corporeal Feminism*. Indiana UP, 1994.

Guattari, Félix. *Chaosophy*. Edited by Sylvere Lotringer. Translated by David L. Sweet, Jarred Becker, and Taylor Adkins, Los Angeles, Semiotext(e), 2009.

———. "To Have Done Away with the Massacre of the Body." *Chaosophy*. Translated by David L. Sweet, Jarred Becker, and Taylor Adkins, Los Angeles, Semiotext(e), 2007, 207–14.

Guattari, Félix, and Suely Rolnik. *Molecular Revolution in Brazil*. Translated by Karel Clapshow and Brian Holmes, Los Angeles, Semiotext(e), 2008.

Guerra, Humberto. "La dicotomía estructuradora en Salvador Novo: Afeminamiento y virilidad [The stucturing dichotomy in Salvador Novo: Effeminacy and virility]." *Revista Iberoamericana*, vol. 74, no. 225, 2008, 1149–159.

Guida, Justin. "Producing and Explaining Charisma: A Case Study of the Films of Alejandro Jodorowsky." *Journal of the American Academy of Religion Journal of the American Academy of Religion*, vol. 83, no. 2, 2015, 537–53.

Gunia, Inke. ¿ *"Cuál es la onda"?* [*What's the Onda?*] Frankfurt, Verveurt, 2009.

——. "Qué onda broder? Las condiciones de formación y el desenvolvimiento de una literatura de la contracultura juvenil en el México de los años sesenta y setenta [What's uo, brother. The conditions of formation and developing of a juvenile countercultural literatura in Mexico from the sixties and seventies]." *Revista de Crítica Literaria Latinoamericana*, vol. 30, no. 59, 2004, 19–31.

Gutmann, Matthew C. *The Meanings of Macho: Being a Man in Mexico City*. U of California P, 1996.

Hadatty Mora, Yanna. "*El Universal Ilustrado* en los años 20: el posicionamiento en el campo cultural [*The Universal Ilustrado in the twenties: positioning in a cultural field*]." *Laboratorios de los nuevo: revistas literarias y culturales de México, España y el Río de la Plata en la década de los 1920* [*Laboratory of the new: literary and cultural jornals of Mexico, Spain and Río de la Plata in the decade of the 1920s*], edited by Rose Corral, Anthony Stanton, and James Valender, México, Colegio de México, 2018, 173–89.

Hayim, Gila J. "The Sense Experience in the Legacy of Counterculture." *Counterculture and Social Transformation*, edited by Seymour Leventman, Springfield, Illinois, Charles C. Thomas, 1982, 101–24.

Heath, Joseph, and Andrew Potter. *Nation of Rebels: Why Counterculture Became Consumer Culture*. Harper-Collins, 2014.

Hershfield, Joanne. *Imagining la Chica Moderna: Women, Nation, and Visual Culture in Mexico, 1917–1936*. London, Duke UP, 2008.

Highmore, Ben. "Bitter after Taste: Affect, Food and Social Aesthetics." *The Affect Theory Reader*, edited by M. Gregg and G. Seigworth, Duke UP, 2010, 118–37.

Hocquenhem, Guy, and Félix Guattari. *Recherches. Trois Milliards de Pervers: Grand Encyclopédie des Homosexualités* [*Searches: Three Millions Perverts and Perversities: Great Encyclopedia of Homosexualities*]. Paris, 1973.

Hocquenhem, Guy. *The Screwball Asses*. Translated by Noura Wedell, Los Angeles, Semiotext(e), 2009.

Hoffman, Albert, R. Gordon Wasson, and Carl A.P. Ruck. *The Road to Eleusis. Unveiling the Secret of the Mysteries*. North Atlantic Books, 2008.

Janzen, Rebecca. The *National Body in Mexican Literature. Collective Challenged to Biopolitical Control*. Palgrave-MacMillan, 2015.

Karageorgou-Bastea, Christina. "Abigael Bohórquez o la voz sobre la Frontera [Abigael Bohorques or the voice on the Border]." *Romance Quarterly*, vol. 53, no. 2, 2006, 144–60.

Katzew, Ilona. *La pintura de castas. Representaciones raciales en el México del siglo XVIII* [*Caste paintings: Racial representations in Mexico of the eighteenth century*]. México, Turner-CONACULTA, 2004.

Kaup, Monika. *Neobaroque in the Americas. Alternative Modernities in Literature, Visual Art, and Film*. U of Virginia P, 2012.

Laris, Ismael. *Abigael Bohórquez. La creación como catarsis* [*Abigael Bohorquez: Creation as catharsis*]. México, Tierra Adentro, 2012.

Limon, José. "'Carne, carnales,' and the Carnavelesque: Bahktinian 'Batos,' Disorder and Narrative Discourses." *American Ethnologist*, vol. 16, no. 3, 1989, 471–86.

Lomnitz, Claudio. "Bordering on Anthropology. The Dialectics of a National Tradition in Mexico." *Revue de synthése*, vol. 4, no. 4, 2000, 345–80.

———. *Deep Mexico, Silent Mexico*. U of Minnesota P, 2001.

———. "Fissures in Contemporary Mexican Nationalism." *Public Culture*, vol. 9, 1996, 55–68.

Long, Mary K. "Consumer Society and National Identity in the Work of Salvador Novo and Guadalupe Loaeza" *Chasqui*, vol. 30, no. 2, 2001, 116–216.

———. "Writing the City: The Chronicles of Salvador Novo." *The Contemporary Mexican Chronicle. Theoretical Perspective on the Liminal Genre*, edited by Ignacio Corona and Beth E. Jörgensen, State of New York Press, 2002, 181–200.

López, Rick. *Crafting Mexico. Intellectuals, Artisans and the State after the Revolution*. Duke UP, 2010.

———. *Ethinicizing the Nation: The India Bonita Contest of 1921*. Duke UP, 2020.

———. "The India Bonita Contest of 1921 and the Ethnicization of Mexican National Culture." *Hispanic American Historical Review*, vol. 82, no. 2, 2002, 291–328.

Lordon, Frederic. *Willing Slaves of Capital: Spinoza and Marx on Desire*. London, Verso, 2014.

Lund, Joshua. *The Mestizo State: Reading Race in Modern Mexico*. Minneapolis: U of Minnesota P, 2012.

Macías-González, Víctor. "Bathhouses and Male Homosexuality in Porfirian Mexico." *Masculinity and Sexuality in Modern Mexico*, edited by Víctor Macías-González and Anne Rubinstein, U of New Mexico P, 2012, 25–52.

Mahieux, Viviane. The Chronicler as Streetwalker: Salvador Novo and the Performance of Genre." *Hispanic Review*, vol. 76, no. 2, 2008, 155–77.

———. *Una pequeña marquesa de Sade. Crónicas selectas (1921–1948) Cube Bonifant* [*A small marquesse de Sade. Selected chronicles (1921–1948) Cube Bonifant*]. México, CONACULTA/UNAM/Equilibrista, 2009.

———. *Urban Chroniclers in Modern Latin America*. U of Texas P, 2011.

Mann, John. *Turn On and Tune In*. London, RSC Publishing, 2009.

Manriquez Duran, Miguel. *Abigael Bohórquez: pasión, cicatriz y relámpago* [Abigael Bohórquez: pasión, scar and lightning]. Hermosillo, México, Editora La Voz de Sonora, 1999.

Marquet, Antonio. "Castrejón, Cóccioli y Novo: La novela gay en la primera mitad del siglo XX [Castrejon, Coccioli and Novo: The gay novel in the first half of the twentieth century]." *Literatura Mexicana*, vol. 17, no. 2, 2006, 47–72.

Martinez, Ana. *Performance in the Zócalo: Constructing History, Race, and Identity in Mexico's Central Square from the Colonial Era to the Present*. U of Michigan P, 2020.

Martínez Nadal, Rafael. *Federico García Lorca and the Public: A Study of an Unfinished Play and of Love and Death in Lorca's Work*. Schocken Books, 1974.

Massumi, Brian. "Deleuze and Guattari's Theory of the Group Subject, through a Reading of Corneille's *Le Cid*." *Discours Social: The International Working Papers Series in Comparative Literature*, vol. 4, 1998, 423–40.

Masters, R. E. L., and Jean Houston. *The Varieties of Psychedelic Experience*. New York: Holt, Rinehart, and Winston, 1966.

McCaa, Robert. "Missing Millions: The Demographic Costs of the Mexican Revolution." *Mexican Studies/Estudios Mexicanos*, vol 19, no. 2, 2003, 367–400.

Mraz, John. *Looking for Mexico: Modern Visual Culture and National Identity*. Duke UP, 2009.

Menakem, Reesma. *My Grandmother's Hands: Racialized Trauma and the Pathway to Mending Our Hearts and Bodies*. Las Vegas, Central Recovery Press, 2017.

McGuirk, Carol. "Science Fiction's Renegade Becomings." *Science Fiction Studies*, vol. 35, no. 2, 2008, 281–307.

McKee Irwin, Robert. *Mexican Masculinities*. U of Minnesota P, 2003.

———. "La Pedo Embotellado: Sexual Roles and Play in Salvador Novo's *La Estatua de Sal*." *Studies in the Literary Imagination*, vol. 33, no. 1, 2000, 125–32.

McKee Irwin, Robert, Michelle Roció Nasser, and Edward J McCaughan. "Sexuality and Social Control in Mexico, 1901." *The Famous 41: Sexuality and Social Control in Mexico, 1901*, edited by Robert Mckee Irwin, Michelle Rocío Nasser, and Edward J. McCaughan. Palgrave-Macmillan, 2003, 1–18.

McManus, Siobhan Guerrero. "Homosexuality, Homophobia, and Biomedical sciences in Twentieth Century Mexico." *Sexuality and Culture*, vol. 18, 2014, 235–56.

Metzner, Ralph. "Psychedelic, Psychoactive, and Addictive Drugs and States of Consciousness." *Mind-Altering Drugs, The Science of Subjective Experience*, edited by Mitch Earleywine, Oxford UP, 2005, 25–48.

Meza Marroquín, Mariano. "Nahui Olin y la síntesis del cosmos [Nahui Olin and the synthesis of the cosmos]." *Nahui Olin. La mirada infinita [Nahui Olin. The infinite gaze]*. México, Secretaría de Cultura, Instituto Nacional de Bellas Artes, Patronato del Museo Nacional de Arte A.C., 2018.

Moldes, Diego. *Alejandro Jodorowsky*. Madrid, Cátedra, 2012.

Morales, Alfonso. *El País de las tandas. Teatro de revista 1900–1940 [The country of circus. Revue theatre 1900–1940]*. México, Museo Nacional de Culturas Populares/SEP, 1984.

Morfino, Vittorio. *Plural Temporality: Transindividuality and the Aleatory Between Spinoza and Althusser*. Haymarket Books, 2014.

Monsiváis, Carlos. *Celia Montalván (te brindas, voluptuosa e impudente) [Celia Montalván. (you give yourself, voluptious and impudent]*. México, SEP/Martín Casillas Editores, 1982.

———. *Maravillas que son, sombras que fueron. La fotografía en México [Wonders that are, shadows that were]*. México, Ediciones Era/CONACULTA, 2012.

———. "La naturaleza de la onda [*The nature of the onda*]." *Amor perdido [Love lost]*. México, Ediciones Era, 1973.

———. "The Sidelong World. Where Confession and Proclamation are Compounded." *The Pillar of Salt*, by Salvador Novo, translated by Marguerite Feitlowitz, U of Texas P, 2014, 2–45.

Moraña, Mabel. "Baroque/Neobaroque/Ultrabaroque: Disruptive Readings of Modernity." *Hispanic Baroques: Reading Cultures in Context*, edited by Nicolas Spadaccini and Luis Martin-Estudillo, Vanderbilt UP, 2005, 240–81.

Morgan, Frances. "The Dance of Unreality." *Sight and Sound*, vol. 25, no. 3, 2015, 56–57.

Muñoz, José Esteban. *Cruising Utopia. The Then and There of Queer Futurity*. New York UP, 2009.

————. "Ephemera as Evidence. Introductory Notes to Queer Acts." *Women and Performance: A Journal of Feminist Theory*, vol. 8, no. 2, 1996, 5–12.

Novo, Salvador. *Continente Vacío* [*Empty continent*]. Madrid, Espasa-Calpe, 1935.

————. "Motivos del baño [*Reasons of the bathroom*]." *Mapa Callejero. Crónicas sobre lo gay desde América Latina* [*Street map. Chronicles of gay life from Latin America*], edited by José Quiroga, Buenos Aires, Eterna Cadencia, 2010, 129–32.

————. "Nuevos conceptos sobre el ultrapelonismo [New concepts on ultra-short hair]." *El Universal Ilustrado*, 8 Oct 1925, 34–35.

————. *The Pillar of Salt*. Translated by Marguerite Feitlowitz, U of Texas P, 2014.

Neustadt, Robert. "Alejandro Jodorowsky: Reiterating Chaos, Rattling the Cage of Representation." *Chasqui*, vol. 26, no. 1, 1997, 56–74.

Nuñez Noriega, Guillermo. *Just Between Us. An Ethnography of Male Identity and Intimacy in Rural Communities of Northern Mexico*. U of Arizona P, 2014.

Nuila, Luis G. "Óptica cerebral (poemas dinámicos) de Nahui Olin (Carmen Mondragón) [Cerebral optics (dynamic poems) by Nahui Olin (Carmen Mondragón)]." *El Universal Ilustrado*. 24 Aug 1922. Rpt in. *Nahui Olin: Sin principio ni fin: vida, obra y varia invención* [*Nahui Olin: without beginning nor end: life, ouvre and various inventions*], edited by Patricia Rosas Lopátegui, Monterrey, Universidad Autónoma de Nuevo León, 2011, 270.

O'Malley, Ilene V. *The Myth of the Revolution. Hero Cults and the Institutionalization of the Mexican State. 1920–1940*. Greenwood Pess, 1986.

Olin, Nahui. "Nahui Olin." Self-published. Rpt in *Nahui Olin: Sin principio ni fin: vida, obra y varia invención* [*Nahui Olin: without beginning nor end: life, ouvre and various inventions*], edited by Patricia Rosas Lopátegui, Monterrey, Universidad Autónoma de Nuevo León, 2011, 181–84.

————. *Óptica cerebral. Poemas dinámicos* [*Cerebral optics. Dynamic poems*]. México, Ediciones Moderno, 1922.

Oropesa, Salvador A. *The Contemporáneos Group. Rewriting Mexico in the Thirties and Forties*. U of Texas P, 2003.

————. "La representación del yo y del tú en la poesía satírica de Salvador Novo: la influencia del albur [The representation of the I and you in the satirical poetry of Salvador Novo: the influence of double entendres]." *Chasqui*, vol. 24, no. 1, 1995, 38–52.

———. "Salvador Novo. The American Friend, the American Critic." *Mexico Reading the United States*, edited by Linda Egan and Mary K Long, Vanderbilt UP, 2009, 57–77.

Pahnke, Walter. "The Contribution of the Psychology of Religion to the Therapeutic Use of the Psychedelic Substances." *The Use of LSD in Psychotherapy and Alcoholism*, edited by H. A. Abramson, Indianapolis, Bobbs-Merril, 1967, 629–52.

Pahnke, Walter N., and William A. Richards. "Implications of LSD and Experimental Mysticism." *Journal of Religion and Health*, vol. 5, no. 3, 1966, 175–208.

Palou, Pedro Angel. *La casa del silencio: aproximación en tres tiempos a Contemporáneos* [*The house of silence: approximations to the Contemporáneos in three moments*]. Zamora, Michoacán, El Colegio de Michoacán, 1997.

———. *Mestizo Failures. Race, Film and Literarure in Twentieth Century Mexico*. Translated by Sara Potter, Boston, Art Life Lab, 2015.

Pelayo, Ruben. "Treinta años de erotismo en la novelística de José Agustin [Thirty years of eroticism in the novels of José Agustín]." *Texto Crítico*, vol. 18, 1998, 69–81.

Pensado, Jaime. *Rebel Mexico: Student Unrest and Authoritarian Political Culture During the Long Sixties*. Stanford UP, 2013.

Piedra, José. "Nationalizing Sissies." *¿Entiendes? Queer Readings, Hispanic Writings*, edited by Emilie L. Bergmann and Paul Julian Smith, Duke UP, 1995, 370–410.

Pisón, Emilio. "Galería Femenina. Carmen Mondragón." *La Prensa*. San Sebastian, España, 14 Apr 1922. Rpt in. *Nahui Olin: Sin principio ni fin: vida, obra y varia invención [Nahui Olin: without beginning nor end: life, ouvre and various inventions]*, edited Patricia Rosas Lopátegui, Monterrey, Universidad Autónoma de Nuevo León, 2011, 270.

Pollan, Michael. *How to Change Your Mind. What the New Science of Psychedelics Teaches Us about Consciousness, Dying, Addiction, Depression and Transcendence*. Penguin, 2018.

Poniatowska, Elena. *Las siete cabritas* [*The seven little goats*]. México, Era, 2000.

Powell, Anna. *Deleuze, Altered States and Film*. Edinburgh, Edinburgh UP, 2007.

Price, Brian L. "I Know It's Only Rock and Rock, but I Like It." *The Lost Cinema of Mexico: From Lucha Libre to Cine Familiar and Other Churros*, edited by Brian L. Price and Olivia Cosentino, Florida UP, 2022, 34–62.

Puar, Jasbir K. *Terrorist Assemblages: Homonationalism in Queer Times*. Duke UP, 2007.

Raichle, Marcus. "The Brain's Default Mode Network." *Annual Review of Neurosciences*, vol. 38, 2015, 433–48.

Rashkin, Elissa. *The Stridentist Movement in Mexico. The Avant-Garde and Cultural Change in the 1920s.* Lexington Books, 2009.

Reinhard, Kenneth. "Toward a Political Theology of the Neighbor." *The Neighbor Three Inquiries in Political Theology*, edited by Kenneth Reinhard, Eric L. Satner, and Slaj Zizek, U of Chicago P, 2005, 11–77.

Robbins, Timothy. "From the Mexican Onda to McOndo: The Shifting Ideology of Mass Culture." *New Trends in Contemporary Latin American Narrative*, edited by Timothy Robbins and José Eduardo González, Palgrave-Mcmillan, 2014, 15–38.

Rosales, María Cecilia. *Cyborgs, ángeles y quimeras: La representación del cuerpo femenino en la plástica mexicana* [*Cyborgs, angels and chimeras: the representation of the female body in Mexican visual arts*]. Diss., Arizona State U, 2000.

Rosas Lopátegui, Patricia. *Nahui Olin: Sin principio ni fin: vida, obra y varia invención* [*Nahui Olin: without beginning nor end: life, ouvre and various inventions*]. Monterrey, Universidad Autónoma de Nuevo León, 2011.

Roszak, Theodore. *The Making of a Counter Culture.* U of California P, 1995.

Rubinstein, Anne. *Bad Language, Naked Ladies, and Other Threats to the Nation: A Political History of Comic Books in Mexico.* Durham: Duke University Press, 1998.

———. "Nahui Olin. The General's Daughter Disrobes." *The Human Tradition in México*, edited by Jeffrey M Pilcher, Wilmington, Scholarly Resources, 2003.

———. "The War on 'Las Pelonas': Modern Women and Their Enemies, Mexico City, 1924" in *Sex in Revolution: Gender, Politics and Power in Modern Mexico*, edited by Jocelyn Olcott, Mary Kay Vaughn, and Gabriela Cano, London, Duke UP, 2006, 57.

Ruiz, Apen. "La India Bonita. National Beauty in Revolutionary Mexico." *Cultural Dynamics.* 14.3 (2002): 283-301.

Saez, Javier, and Sejo Carrascosa. *Por el culo. Políticas anales* [*Up the ass. Anal politics*]. Madrid: Editorial EGALES, 2011.

Salcedo, Hugo. "Claves para la ubicación del drama bohorqueano: Pasiones, picardías, crímenes y otras provocaciones [Keys to locate the bohorquean drama: passion, mischief, crimes and other provocations]." in *Las fronteras del texto. Un acercamiento de análisis cultural y lingüístico* [*The borders of the text. A cultural and linguistic analysis approach*]. La Zonámbula—UABC, México, 2013, 100–120.

———. "La obra dramática de Abigael Bohórquez. Estudio preliminar [The dramatic ouvre of Abigael Bohórquez. Preliminary study]" in Abigael Bohórquez. *Noroestrada.* Tijuana, México: Caen Editores, 2002. 11-38

Sánchez-Prado, Ignacio. "Dying Mirrors, Medieval Moralistas and Tristram Shandies: The Literary Traditions of Fernando del Paso's *Palinuro of Mexico*" *Comparative Literature*, vol. 60, no. 2, 2008, 142–63.

———. *Naciones intelectuales. Las fundaciones de la modernidad literaria mexicana (1917-1959)* [*Intellectual nations. The foundations of Mexican literary modernity (1917-1959)*]. Purdue UP, 2009.

———. "El mestizaje en el corazón de la utopía: la raza cósmica entre Aztlán y América Latina [Mestizaje in the heart of utopia: the cosmic race between Aztlán and Latin America]." *Revista Canadiense de Estudios Hispánicos*, vol. 33, no. 2, 2009, 381–404.

Sánchez Reyes, Felipe. *Totalmente desnuda: vida de Nahui Olin* [*Totally nude: the life of Nahui Olin*]. México: Instituto Veracruzano de la Cultura, 2013.

Sánchez Soler, Montserrat, and Dafne Cruz Porcini, comps. *Formando el cuerpo de una nación. El deporte en el México posrevolucionario* [*Shaping the body of the nation. Sports in postrevolutionary Mexico*]. México: CONACULTA, 2012.

Schaefer, Claudia. *Danger Zones. Homosexuality, National Identity, and Mexican Culture.* Tucson: U of Arizona P, 1996.

Sefamí, Jacobo. "Neobarrocos y neomodernistas en la poesía latinoamericana [Neobaroque and neomodernists poets in Latinamerican poetry]." *Actas del XIII Congreso de la Asociación Internacional de Hispanistas.* Coords. Florencio Sevilla Arroyo and Carlos Alvar Ezquerra. 3. (2000, 420–27.

Siegel, Ronald. *Intoxication: The Universal Drive for Mind-Altering States.* Rosemont, Vermont, Park Street Press, 2005.

Sluis, Ageeth. *Deco Body, Deco City. Female Spectacle & Modernity in Mexico City, 1900–1939.* U of Nebraska P, 2016.

———. "Projecting Pornography and Mapping Modernity in Mexico City." *Journal of Urban History*, vol. 38, no. 3, 2012, 467–87.

Sorensen, Diana. *A Turbulent Decade Remembered.* Stanford UP, 2007.

Tellez-Pon, Sergio. "La fuerza oculta del otro amor. La poesía homoerótica [The hidden forcé of the the other love. Homoerotic poetry]" in *México se escribe con J* [*Mexico is spelled with a J*], edited by Michael Schuessler and Miguel Capistrán, México, Editorial Planeta/Temas de Hoy, 2010, 101–17.

Trexler, Richard C. *Sex and Conquest: Gendered Violence, Political Order, and the European Conquest of the Americas.* Cornell UP, 1995.

Tuñon, Julia. *Mujeres: Entre la imagen y la acción* [*Women: between image and action*]. México, Debate/CONACULTA, 2015.

"Ultrapelonicemos la vida [Let's ultra-short hair life]." *El Universal Ilustrado.* 8 Oct 1925, 37.

Uresti, Silvestre. *Conciencia de una letra. Poesía en Sonora a fin de siglo* [*Conscience of a letter. Sonoran poetry at the turn of the century*]. Hermosillo, Instituto Sonorense de Cultura, 1999.

Valencia, Sayak. *Gore Capitalism.* Translated by John Pluecker, Los Angeles, Semiotexte, 2018.

Vázquez Mantecón, Álvaro. *El cine super 8 en Mexico: 1970–1989* [*Super 8 film in Mexico: 1970–1989*], México, UNAM/Filmoteca, 2012.

Vázquez Piñon, Jorge. *Accidentalidad y mecanicidad: dinámica existencial del Dr Atl: Carmen Mondragón Valseca. Nahui Olin: Aproximación a un misterio* [*Accident and mechanics: the existencial dynamics of Dr Atl: Carmen Mondragón Valseca. Nahui Olin: Approximations to a mystery*]. Morelia, México, Universidad Michoacana de San Nicolas de Hidalgo, 2007.

Vaughn, Mary Kay. "Introduction. Pancho Villa, the Daughters of Mary and the Modern Woman: Gender in the Long Mexican Revolution." *Sex in Revolution: Gender, Politics and Power in Modern Mexico,* edited by Jocelyn Olcott, Mary Kay Vaughn, and Gabriela Cano, London, Duke UP, 2006, 21–34.

Venkatesh, Vinodh. *The Body as Capital: Masculinties in Contemporary Latin American Fiction.* U of Arizona P, 2015.

"Victor matrix BVE-38154. ¡Ya no lloverá, pelonas! [It will not rain pelonas anymore!] / José Moriche." *Discography of American Historical Recordings.* UC Santa Barbara Library, 2021. Accessed 30 April 2021, https://adp.library.ucsb.edu/index.php/matrix/detail/800012412/BVE-38154-Ya_no_llover_pelonas.

Viera, Hugo. "Intoxicated Writing: Onda Writers and the Drug Experience in 1960s Mexico." *Studies in Latin American Popular Culture,* vol. 33, 2015, 146–63.

Wayar, Marlene. *Teoria travesti. Una teoría lo suficientemente buena* [*Travesti theory. A good enough theory*]. Buenos Aires, Editorial Muchas Nueces, 2018.

Weiss, Gail. *Body Images: Embodiment as Intercorporality.* London, Routledge, 1999.

Winfield, Fernando N. "The Avant-Garde in the Architecture and Visual Arts of Post-Revolutionary Mexico" *Architecture, Media, Politics, Society,* vol. 1, no. 3, 2012, 1–18.

Žižek, Slavoj. "Neighbors and Others Monsters: A Plea for Ethical Violence." *The Neighbor. Three Inquiries in Political Theology,* edited by Kenneth Reinhard, Eric L. Satner, and Slavoj Žižek, U of Chicago P, 2005, 134–90.

Zolov, Eric. "Discovering a Land 'Mysterious and Obvious': The Renarrativizing of Postrevolutionary Mexico." *Fragments of a Golden Age: The Politics and Culture of Mexico since 1940*, edited by Gilbert Joseph, Anne Rubenstein, and Eric Zolov, Duke UP, 2001, 234–72.

———. *Refried Elvis: Rise of the Mexican Counterculture*. U of California P, 1999.

Index

Page references in *italics* indicate illustrations.